GLOBAL ENERGY GOVERNANCE

GLOBAL ENERGY GOVERNANCE

The New Rules of the Game

ANDREAS GOLDTHAU

JAN MARTIN WITTE

editors

GLOBAL PUBLIC POLICY INSTITUTE
Berlin

BROOKINGS INSTITUTION PRESS
Washington, D.C.

Copyright © 2010
GLOBAL PUBLIC POLICY INSTITUTE, BERLIN

Library of Congress Cataloging-in-Publication data
Global energy governance : the new rules of the game / Andreas Goldthau and
  Jan Martin Witte, editors.
    p.   cm.
Includes index.
ISBN 978-0-8157-0343-3 (soft cover : alk. paper)
  1. Power resources—Forecasting. 2. Energy policy. 3. International organization.
4. Globalization. I. Goldthau, Andreas. II. Witte, Jan Martin.
  HD9502.A2G544 2010
  333.79—dc22   2009042016

9 8 7 6 5 4 3 2 1

Printed on acid-free paper

Typeset in Adobe Garamond
Composition by Circle Graphics
Columbia, Maryland

Printed by R. R. Donnelley
Harrisonburg, Virginia

Contents

Foreword   ix
Wolfgang Reinicke

1   *The Role of Rules and Institutions in Global Energy:*   1
    An Introduction
    Andreas Goldthau and Jan Martin Witte

PART ONE
Global Energy and Trade and Investment

2   *Energy Diplomacy in Trade and Investment*   25
    of Oil and Gas
    Andreas Goldthau

3   *Managing the Patchwork of Agreements*   49
    in Trade and Investment
    Yulia Selivanova

4   *Development of the Emerging Biofuels Market*   73
    Simonetta Zarrilli

5   *Trade and Investment in Global Energy:*   99
    A Policy Perspective
    Ralf Dickel

PART TWO
Global Energy and Financial Markets

6   *State-Backed Financing in Oil and Gas Projects*   107
    Amy Myers Jaffe and Ronald Soligo

7   *How Do Emerging Carbon Markets Influence*   133
    Energy Sector Investments?
    William Blyth

8   *Financing the Future: Investments in Alternative*   161
    Sources of Energy
    Hillard Huntington and Christine Jojarth

9   *A New Green Deal and the Future of Global Energy:*   183
    A Policy Perspective
    Joseph A. Stanislaw

PART THREE
Short-Term Supply Management and
Long-Term Energy Cooperation

10 *Consumer Country Energy Cooperation:*   195
    The International Energy Agency and
    the Global Energy Order
    Wilfrid L. Kohl

11 *The Evolving Role of LNG in the Gas Market*   221
    Dick de Jong, Coby van der Linde, and Tom Smeenk

12 *The International Energy Forum and*   247
    the Mitigation of Oil Market Risks
    Enno Harks

13   *The Future of Producer-Consumer Cooperation:*   269
     A Policy Perspective
     Albert Bressand

PART FOUR
Emerging Issues and Outlook

14   *The Good/Bad Nexus in Global Energy Governance*   287
     Thorsten Benner and Ricardo Soares de Oliveira
     with Frederic Kalinke

15   *Building Global Rules for Sovereign Wealth Funds*   315
     Jamie Manzer and Jan Martin Witte

16   *Global Energy Governance: The Way Forward*   341
     Andreas Goldthau, Wade Hoxtell, and Jan Martin Witte

Contributors   357

Index   359

Foreword

In his contribution to this volume, Joe Stanislaw writes about the "monumental, multigenerational global challenge" that we are confronted with in the energy domain today. He is not exaggerating. Dwindling low-cost hydrocarbon reserves, the rise of new consumers such as China and India, and of course the specter of climate change dictate a fundamental reordering of existing energy systems. That reordering will be neither easy nor cheap. Whether we will succeed in tackling the resulting challenges depends on our ingenuity and particularly on the availability of sufficient political will to make change happen.

Traditionally, discussions on energy security have focused primarily on the supply side of the energy equation. With the onset of the Industrial Revolution and the rising prominence, especially of oil, in fueling economies as well as modern warfare, access to oil has emerged as a key strategic foreign policy goal of nations around the world and thus the object of high-stakes geopolitical competition. To this day academic and policy discussions on energy security tend to remain stuck in this geopolitical paradigm.

This paradigm, however, is not useful in analyzing contemporary global energy challenges or, for that matter, the development of policy solutions. For one thing, the focus on state-to-state competition suggests that global energy politics is a zero-sum game. That however is utterly misleading. In addition, and even more

ix

important, the geopolitical lens ignores the fact that markets and nonstate actors (in particular international energy companies, financial institutions, and others) play a key role in determining outcomes in global energy. Thus it is important to understand how energy markets, which are increasingly global in nature, are structured and how they must change in the years ahead to adapt to the new realities of the twenty-first century.

Building on a governance approach, this book offers an innovative and complementary perspective in analyzing global energy politics. It is based on the premise that the analysis of the historical and present roles of energy producers and consumers, as well as the detailed study of rules and institutional mechanisms, is crucial to give shape to a global energy governance system that not only incorporates the above-mentioned challenges but also maximizes the strengths of interconnecting institutions working to manage them. By focusing on competition and collaboration and the role of markets and rules in mediating positive-sum outcomes on international energy markets, the contributions to this book seek to provide clear-cut policy recommendations toward the reform of the nascent global energy governance architecture.

The book is the result of a two-year research project undertaken by the Global Public Policy Institute's Energy Program. The Global Public Policy Institute (GPPi) acknowledges the financial support that has been provided for this research program by the Dräger Foundation, E.ON Ruhrgas AG, the European Commission, the German Marshall Fund of the United States, and Vattenfall Europe AG.

GPPi would like to thank the Steering Committee, which has guided the work of the institute on energy issues. This committee consisted of Reinhold Buttgereit (Vattenfall Europe AG), Ralf Dickel (Energy Charter Secretariat), Thomas Geisel (E.ON Ruhrgas AG), Randy Gossen (World Petroleum Council), Dagmar Graczyk (International Energy Agency), Mehmet Gürcan Daimagüler (Yale University), Enno Harks (Deutsche BP AG), Alan Hegburg (U.S. Department of Energy), Achim von Heynitz (FAO/IFAD), Rolf Hempelmann (German Parliament), Jörg Himmelreich (German Marshall Fund of the United States), Jing Huang (Brookings Institution), Julia Nanay (PFC Energy), Joachim Pfeiffer (German Parliament), Paul Saunders (Nixon Center), and Charlotte Streck (ClimateFocus BV).

A number of individuals have been instrumental in developing this volume. In particular, the editors would like to thank Thierry Bros (Société Générale), Bill Farmer (Uganda Carbon Bureau), Sanam Salem Haghighi (Econgas), Astrid Harnisch (German Federal Ministry for Environment, Nature Conservation, and Nuclear Safety), Peter Hartley (Rice University), Stuart Hensel (GPPi),

Llewelyn Hughes (Harvard University), Jan Kalicki (Chevron), Willy Olsen (Statoil), and Nicolas Veron (Bruegel Institute) for providing feedback on various drafts of the chapters in this volume. Also, the editors appreciate comments from the anonymous reviewer commissioned by Brookings and from our internal anonymous reviewers. Finally, the editors would also like to recognize the ideas and constructive feedback provided by not only the participants in GPPi's Transatlantic Energy Security Dialogues held in 2008 and 2009 but also workshop participants at the La Follette School of Public Affairs and Nelson Institute for Environmental Studies, University of Wisconsin, the annual convention of the International Studies Association, and several other conferences in Europe and the United States.

Finally, the GPPi Energy Program team, and particularly Wade Hoxtell and Jamie Manzer, provided invaluable support during the entire process of producing this volume. Additional research and editing assistance was provided by Joyce Yao and Naomi Woods. Last but not least the Brookings Institution Press deserves credit for a highly professional and smooth editing and production process for this book.

WOLFGANG REINICKE
Global Public Policy Institute

1

The Role of Rules and Institutions in Global Energy: An Introduction

Andreas Goldthau and Jan Martin Witte

C urrent public policy debates on energy security are characterized by a sharp focus on questions regarding access to resources and associated geopolitical and geoeconomic challenges. China's new "scramble for Africa" has already become the stuff of legend; access to the gas resources of the Caspian Sea region is the subject of extensive geopolitical scheming; and the race for the presumed resource wealth of the Arctic has begun in earnest.

This focus on the geopolitics of energy is rooted in the deep fears of consumers about security of supply, leading them to put strong pressure on policymakers to come up with effective fixes. In the United States, where during 2008 gas prices that briefly reached US$4 a gallon created a jittery political climate, energy independence emerged as a top issue in the recent election campaigns and will continue to play a prominent role on the agenda of President Obama's administration. In Europe, where consumers are more accustomed to consistently high energy prices, the debate has long been less shrill. However, high imports of Russian natural gas, combined with dwindling resources at home, have created a volatile political environment and have fueled fears of an energy weapon, with Russians and Europeans trading not just gas but also, increasingly, accusations. Russia's violent forays into Georgia in 2008 and the unresolved Russian-Ukrainian energy disputes have further heightened tensions over crucial

Eurasian transit routes. The more recent slackening in oil prices, and the global financial crisis, may take energy issues off the top of the political agenda for a time but will certainly not do so for long.

Oil and gas have always been politically charged commodities, as they have been (and will continue to be for decades to come) the primary sources of global energy supply. Oil is forecast to remain the single largest element in the primary fuel mix, supplying an estimated 30 percent of global energy until at least 2030. Gas, which accounted for 21 percent of energy on the world market in 2006, will increase its share to an estimated 22 percent by 2030. The world's total primary consumption is expected to increase by 45 percent during that same period.[1] Thus for consumers reliable access to oil and gas at a reasonable cost will continue to be of prime strategic value and consequently subject to significant government intervention. For producers, oil and gas are often dominant sources of state revenues and thus key growth engines for their economies.

However, this lopsided attention to the geopolitical dimension of energy security is based on the myopic and erroneous presumption that global energy politics is necessarily a zero-sum game, in which one country's energy security is another's lack thereof. This preoccupation deflects attention from some key issues that policymakers need to consider in their attempts to establish effective global energy governance: first, the central role played by increasingly international (in the case of oil, thoroughly global) energy markets in balancing demand and supply; second, and even more important, the significance of the rules of the game—national as well as international—that structure these markets. These rules of the game— that is to say, the institutional architecture that underpins global energy—govern central aspects of financing, trading, and hedging oil and gas ventures via financial markets, investment treaties, and trade agreements. These rules also address short-term supply risks in the event of market failure or disruption.

Rather than focusing exclusively on the supply side and thus the geopolitical dimension of energy security, it is imperative for researchers and policymakers to broaden their perspective and assess whether and to what extent the existing institutional architecture of global energy needs to be reformed in response to three major trends: first, rapidly changing framework conditions, driven above all by the rise of new consumers such as China and India; second, the growing relevance of state players in oil and gas markets; and third, emerging regional and global climate mitigation regimes.

1. International Energy Agency (2008), p. 78.

This book makes a first attempt to apply such a broader perspective by identifying and analyzing the important role that rules and institutions play in determining outcomes in international oil and gas markets, by examining how current trends are affecting the existing rules of the game, and by highlighting the consequences for public policy.

Why Markets and Rules Matter in International Oil and Gas

Current public policy debates on energy are shaped primarily by geopolitical and mercantilist frameworks. Typically, international energy policy is portrayed as being fashioned by states that compete for resources and are thus locked into a competitive struggle with zero-sum outcomes. This state-centered perspective not only neglects the fact that market forces matter in international oil and gas, it also ignores the fact that during the past three decades market forces have assumed a position of prime importance in determining outcomes in global energy, driven by reforms that were in many cases demanded by producers and consumers alike.

Already in Place: A Liquid and Competitive Global Market for Oil

Since the late 1970s international oil markets have been fundamentally transformed. One important consequence of these transformations is the existence of a liquid, competitive, and truly global market for oil. Before the first oil shock in 1973 international oil markets were dominated by the internal trading schemes of the major Western oil companies that had concessions in oil-exporting countries. Alongside these arrangements, though less prominently, ran state-to-state deals between consumer and producer nations. As a result, most of the globally traded oil was bound up in long-term bilateral contracts, resulting in low liquidity in international markets. These bilateral contracts were drawn up in an era during which supply cutoffs were simply not expected and rarely materialized (the few exceptions included the closing of the Suez Canal in 1956 and the embargo on Iranian oil exports in 1967 after the nationalization of the Anglo-Iranian Oil Company by the shah).

The oil shocks of the 1970s fundamentally changed the rules of the game in international oil. Consumers found themselves facing tremendous difficulty in replacing oil supplies lost as a result of the 1973 embargo and the political turmoil in the Persian Gulf region at the end of the decade. In the immediate aftermath of the 1973 crisis (compounded by the removal of U.S. import quotas by the Nixon administration), finding alternative sources proved complicated and costly. While oil market conditions eased significantly in the late 1970s, consumers had, for the first time in history, seen the effective application of the oil weapon by producer nations.[2] This perceived vulnerability also triggered the sense that a forum for consumers was needed for effective information sharing and emergency coordination in response to supply shocks.[3]

Thus in the aftermath of the oil shocks, consumer nations of the Organization for Economic Cooperation and Development (OECD) created emergency sharing mechanisms and combined forces in the International Energy Agency (IEA). At the same time, oil exporters' efforts to nationalize domestic production not only deprived Western Big Oil of concessions and hence access to reserves, it also broke up the vertical integration of the industry and, as a consequence, deprived the newly created national oil companies (NOCs) of refining and retail outlets in importing markets. This process had dramatic results, significantly increasing the fungibility of crude oil and thus helping to create a virtual global pool of oil that made price formation more transparent and predictable. In fact it marked the starting point of large-scale liberalization of the global oil market. This push toward liberalization was at least tolerated by some of the producer countries (most notably Saudi Arabia), which hoped to attain a higher degree of control over government budgets that were highly sensitive to fluctuating oil prices. While admittedly driven by market forces rather than government design, this process also resulted in the creation of spot oil markets in New York and London and of oil futures contracts (paper oil), thereby crafting a new oil world no longer depending on bilateral long-term contracts.[4] In turn, the liberalization of international oil generated major efficiencies, facilitated the development of new supplies, and fostered price competition.[5]

The liberalization of international oil markets proved spectacularly effective. Today the bulk of oil is traded on exchanges or at least under relatively short-term contracts whose prices are linked to prices on the commodity exchanges. In that it has become "visible." A certain amount of oil produced remains bound in long-

2. As it turned out, however, the years following the 1973 embargo saw an easing of oil market conditions, primarily as a result of the global economic downturn, which depressed demand for oil. In addition, the price hike initiated by OPEC also triggered powerful conservation and technology-switching efforts in consumer countries, which progressively reduced the energy intensity of consuming economies.

3. See also Maugeri and Lyons (2006), p. 116.

4. See, for example, Biolsi (1995).

5. Price competition is primarily a result of the fact that, in a liberalized market, new oil producers find it easier to sell through spot markets because long-term contracts are often out of reach in the absence of a significant, long-term production record.

term contracts and bilateral deals. Yet even if it is assumed that only 50 percent of all globally produced oil is subject to market mechanisms, that amounts to more than 40 million barrels a day being currently traded under open-market schemes.[6] Thus there exists a liquid, global market at volumes that exceed the markets of almost all other commodities—in terms of physically traded volumes as well as derivatives.

The existence of a global and liquid market for oil has several important consequences. First, it makes effective oil embargoes literally impossible. Therefore talk about the oil weapon, which has recently come back into fashion, simply does not make sense. Once oil is sold on the global market, no producer can control where and to whom it goes.[7] Also the extensive strategic reserves developed by most consuming nations in recent decades effectively reduce the potency of potential disruptions. Second, given the competitive forces to which the global oil market is subject, price stability through national or even international policy intervention is an unattainable goal. A case in point is OPEC's repeated failure in its attempt to steer global production and, with it, prices. That does not mean that betting on price levels may not force oil prices up or down in the short term. It does mean that the global price for oil is first and foremost a function of market forces and cannot be artificially lowered or increased by policy design in the long term. In fact, attempts to manipulate price levels or otherwise influence the global oil market will prove inefficient and, as demonstrated on occasion, even counterproductive.

In the Making: A Global Market for Gas

To date, primarily as a result of transport based on pipelines, natural gas has remained mostly a regionally traded commodity. Major markets are by and large geographically restricted to Eurasia, North America, and the Asia-Pacific region. As a consequence, markets for gas have been slower to liberalize, with the bulk of supply contracts remaining long term in nature. While major consumer markets, in particular the United States, have liberalized, much gas trading, notably in Eurasia, remains tied to long-term bilateral deals characterized by destination clauses and prices indexed to a gas substitute, most commonly oil.

---

6. Moreover, excluding volumes from trading does not necessarily mean they cost less; that will depend first and foremost on the contract in question.

7. It is important to note that some OPEC producers tend to sell oil under contracts entailing destination clauses that limit further resale by the buyer. Hence the most successful spot markets are located in the United States and Europe.

However, recent years have begun to see a global market for gas in the making, driven primarily by the expanding role of liquefied natural gas (LNG). Falling indigenous supplies of natural gas, combined with rising demand, falling costs, and enhanced technologies for the liquefaction of gas, are turning LNG into an increasingly attractive, indeed necessary, alternative source of energy, particularly in Europe.[8] True, the recent economic slowdown has yet again turned the European market into a buyers' market, while recent discoveries of unconventional gas have helped to slow down the need for increased LNG imports into the United States. Yet the widely expected gas glut in Europe may turn out to be rather short-lived once the economy picks up again—and particularly if the EU is to comply with its ambitious climate goals. In the liberalized U.S. market, depending on evolving cost structures, LNG may still play an important role in gas-to-gas competition.

For consumers, LNG both helps diversify sources of supply (thereby fostering energy security) and contributes to price competition in gas markets (since price arbitrage is possible across different, previously disconnected regions). On the basis of recent trends the IEA projects that by 2010 up to 20 percent of demand for gas in the OECD countries will be met by LNG. In fact it is believed that LNG will account for 80 percent of the increase in interregional trade up to 2030.[9]

Clearly, a truly global market for gas does not currently exist and will take time to develop fully. In addition, as is argued in further detail in this book, a global gas market will not have the same characteristics as the global market for oil. Cost structures in the two industries are fundamentally different; the costs of liquefaction, transport, and regasification will remain significant, despite technological advances; and in contrast to oil, gas deteriorates over time, rendering storage difficult. In consequence, even an internationalized market for gas is likely to remain dominated by long-term contracts. Yet the natural gas business is in flux and is likely to further integrate in the years to come. In this context, the rise of LNG may fuel the development of spot markets for gas (already operating, albeit on a fairly small scale) and thus provide an additional buffer for consumers, who may be confronted with unexpected supply disruptions triggered by political or other events.

No Markets without Institutions: The Rules of the Game

Thus despite all the talk about access and the often-invoked specter of supply disruptions, it is important to recognize that both oil and gas are commodities that

8. See also Yergin (2004).
9. International Energy Agency (2008), p. 119.

are already (in the case of oil) or increasingly (in the case of gas) traded on a global scale. Market forces of demand and supply, mediated by the price mechanism, are key factors in determining levels of investment in, as well as the production and consumption of, oil and gas.

But it is equally important to recognize that these markets, like any others, do not function without institutions. Following a definition developed by Douglass North almost two decades ago, institutions can be defined as the rules of the game according to which actors play.[10] Institutions are composed of formal rules (laws, regulations) and informal constraints (norms, conventions) and usually embrace some form of enforcement mechanism. The study of institutions is based on the recognition that markets would work perfectly only in the absence of transaction costs. As we do not live in such an ideal world, institutions are crucial in order to lower transaction costs and to set incentives for market participants to compete on price and quality.

A comprehensive typology of institutions in energy markets is beyond the scope of this volume, but in brief, institutions can be classified according to various principles, for example by source (public, private, or public-private), enforcement mechanism (on a continuum from legal fiat to voluntary compliance), and function (what they do or are supposed to do). For the purpose of this volume, we set out a functional categorization of institutions in global energy markets and use it as a purely heuristic device to highlight and emphasize the important role these institutions play in making energy markets tick. On the basis of such a functional categorization, institutions in international energy markets can be grouped into three types.

First, some institutions are designed to correct market failures. International oil and gas markets are no nearer perfect than any other market structure. As a prime example, and as also discussed in further detail in this volume, following the 1973–74 oil price shocks major energy-consuming nations established the IEA. In addition to acting as a source of energy market statistics, the IEA introduced distinct rules for two specific mechanisms of short-term supply (risk) management: the International Energy Program (IEP, founded in 1974, which established national emergency oil stocks among members) and the Coordinated Emergency Response Mechanism (CERM, founded in 1979). The linchpin of the framework is the reserve system of IEA member states, maintaining mandatory emergency oil reserves (strategic petroleum reserves, or SPR) equivalent to at least ninety days' worth of their respective oil imports.

10. North (1990).

The SPR enables a stock draw—the release of reserves—during a crisis, producing barrels immediately, with a simultaneous calming effect on global prices.[11]

Second, some institutions are designed to lower transaction costs (such as by sharing and disseminating information). Examples include mechanisms to foster consumer-producer dialogue, such as the International Energy Forum (IEF). As yet the IEF is a rather soft institution, with the role of promoting informal dialogue, as opposed to a forum for decisionmaking or negotiations. While producers and consumers usually disagree on price levels, both sides have a primary interest in promoting transparency. As is explained in further detail later in this volume, more transparency would reduce uncertainty in international energy markets and thus adjustment costs for both consumers and producers. The IEF enhances mutual understanding and allows the discussion of long-term issues between producers and consumers. The IEA's data-gathering and data-sharing activities are another example of lowering transaction costs. The database maintained by the IEA has emerged as a key tool with which market players can enhance their knowledge about present and (expected) future national, regional, and global consumption levels, thus fostering planning security.[12]

Third, some institutions are designed to set rules and standards for market exchange. These institutions prescribe, encourage, or constrain certain behaviors on the part of market participants. At the international level this includes rules set and surveyed by bodies such as the World Trade Organization (WTO). The primary objective of the multilateral trading system as established by the WTO is to provide mutual market access without barriers. Hence trade in energy goods is in principle covered by WTO rules.[13] In the past this has however been of little consequence, as is also further discussed in this volume.

The Energy Charter Treaty (ECT) is another rule-setting institution. The ECT, concluded in 1994, explicitly addresses the energy sector, especially natural gas, petroleum, and petroleum products, linking free-market policies with an open-access investment regime. The parties to the ECT include producing coun-

---

11. It is important to note that supply disruptions do not necessarily occur only as a result of market failure. As Hurricane Katrina and the First Gulf War reveal, natural disasters or political events may also disrupt supplies and require a release of strategic stocks to stabilize prices. Yet while these events can be regarded as wild cards exogenous to the market, the emphasis of our argument lies on the market structures as such and on the governance mechanism that characterizes them.

12. For a discussion, see Mitchell (2005).

13. For an overview, see Jiménez-Guerra (2001), pp. 191–218.

tries (such as Russia), consuming (European) countries, and transit countries (such as Ukraine). The ECT establishes a clearly defined set of rules for investment, transit, and trade in the energy sector, complemented by a dispute settlement mechanism. However, since some signatory states have yet to ratify the treaty, the ECT continues to be applied only provisionally by certain key actors, including the Russian Federation.[14]

In general, enforcement mechanisms vary across the rules of the game. Some institutions provide formal compliance mechanisms; others rely on voluntary commitments and peer pressure to promote implementation. However, all such mechanisms have an element designed to foster implementation and enforcement; this sometimes involves sanctions but in most cases is incentive based.

In sum, these rules of the game play important roles in determining outcomes in international oil and gas markets. Obviously, the historical evolution underlying these rules of the game to some degree reflects the realities of the cold war era—an era characterized by significant increases in the discovery of supply stocks (and by occasional supply shocks); intensifying conflicts between producer and consumer nations following decolonization and the formation of OPEC; and the geostrategic competition for influence on major supplier countries in the Middle East and in Africa as a direct consequence of the great-power conflict. Thus the structure of the rules of the game also reflects power differentials. Nonetheless, an exclusive focus on access to energy resources does not provide any guidance for analyzing current dynamics in international energy markets, nor does it provide a suitable lens through which to assess the implications of the fundamental shifts that are currently transforming these markets.

Rules under Pressure: Dwindling Low-Cost Reserves, the Rise of New Consumers, and the Lack of Investment

Despite the overall importance of markets and rules in global energy, popular debates on energy security have recently begun to move in a very different direction. In particular, intensifying concerns about security of supply have fueled great anxiety among consumer nations and have opened the field for state-centered energy policy formulas that many believed a thing of the past.

In essence, current fears of a supply crunch are fueled by three factors that are changing the dynamics of oil and gas markets: dwindling low-cost reserves, the

14. See, for example, the contributions in Wälde (1996).

rise of new consumers, and lack of investment.[15] After 150 years of constant supply increases, much of the world's low-cost conventional oil has been tapped, rendering exploration and production a progressively more demanding and thus
more expensive endeavor in deep sea waters such as those of the Arctic or in more
unconventional media such as tar sands. In addition, the input prices of drilling
technology, skilled labor, and equipment have soared as a result of both the
increasingly demanding exploration and production environments and market
shortages. As CERA's Upstream Capital Costs Index (UCCI) reveals, finding and
development costs in oil and gas have risen by a startling 210 percent since 2000,
adding a significant cost increment to crude supply.[16]

Although ample supplies of gas still exist, these too are often locked up in places
that are not easily accessible; what matters most in the case of Europe and much
of the emerging Asian economies, however, is that reserves are far away from their
consumer markets. Furthermore, as a consequence of their meteoric economic rise
during recent decades, China and India—certainly to be followed by other emerging economies—have virtually stormed global markets and have triggered a fundamental shift in the traditional consumer base of global oil. In fact, according to
some estimates, roughly 43 percent of the increase in global oil demand up to
2030 will come from China and 19 percent from India.[17] Finally, rising demand
and skyrocketing exploration and production costs are outstripping actual investment levels in upstream and infrastructure, which are estimated at US$6.5 trillion
up to 2030 in oil alone.[18] The main reason for this mismatch is identified as a rise
in resource nationalism and a lack of access to foreign capital in key producer
regions. In fact the IEA has repeatedly warned how little investment has gone into
exploration and development, as producers concentrate on the development of
aging fields.

Together, these factors have led to a resurgence of state-centered energy policy
programs aimed at rolling back the liberalization of oil and gas markets and

15. It is important to note that, while the predominant focus regarding consumption is on
emerging economies, additional trends need to be accounted for as well. In particular the growth
in energy consumption in oil-exporting countries, mainly encouraged by subsidies, might constrain their export capacities and even make some of these countries net oil importers in years to
come. See Mitchell and Stevens (2008). Additionally, while two-thirds of the projected global
consumption increment up to 2030 will be caused by emerging economies, the remaining third
still remains with importing industrialized economies, that is, the OECD world. See International
Energy Agency (2008).

16. See Cambridge Energy Research Associates, "IHS/CERA Upstream Capital Costs Index"
(http://ihsindexes.com/ucci-graph.htm).

17. International Energy Agency (2008), p. 77.

18. International Energy Agency (2008), p. 89.

shifting to mercantilist approaches to energy security. Cases in point are China's much-discussed quest for energy in Africa, Japan's renewed flirtation with a more assertive government role in securing energy supplies, and the newly emerging role in global energy of the NOCs, which have pushed private (Western) Big Oil out of the world's top fifteen oil and gas corporations in terms of reserves.[19] Alarmist voices warning of looming resource wars over dwindling reserves or urging that energy security matters be included within the remit of military alliances such as NATO add to an overall retrograde trend toward a world in which one country's access to energy is another country's lack thereof.[20]

This narrow geopolitical lens is reductive and fosters a zero-sum mentality, when in fact energy markets are quite complex and offer joint benefits from cooperation between producers and consumers. Despite the reemergence of state players and resource nationalism, markets matter more than ever in global oil and gas. While, for instance, Chinese-owned foreign assets contributed between 10 and 15 percent to China's crude oil imports in 2005, the remainder was purchased on the global market, a vital mechanism to satisfy the country's exploding demand.[21] In addition, most of the oil produced by ventures in which China's NOCs hold stakes is sold on world markets, not shipped back to China—a function of price differentials between global and domestic Chinese prices. Furthermore, in a high-price environment, financial markets will continue to play the key role in financing global oil and gas endeavors. Finally, continuing large-scale liberalization efforts, such as the current reform of the European gas market, are based on the insight that price formation is better left to markets and not to governments.

In all, and counter to popular perceptions, the energy world of the future is unlikely to be one that pits producers against consumers or old consumers against new ones. The main reason for this is that the interests of all actors in the energy domain overlap. Most fundamentally, the consumers' quest for supply security is met by the producers' quest for demand security. And while new consumers have an interest in overcoming the disadvantages they experience as latecomers on the global market, old consumers have an interest in accommodating them at least possible cost, which means in a conflict-free manner. Hence current public discussions about who wins and who loses are focusing on the wrong questions.

19. On China and Japan, see Downs (2005); Evans (2006).
20. Most notably, prominent Central European politicians have repeatedly called for an Energy NATO to secure future supplies. For a geopolitical perspective on energy, see Klare (2008).
21. Eurasia Group (2006), p. 3; U.S. Department of Energy (2006), p. 28. For an overview of Chinese foreign assets, see also KPMG International (2005).

Instead, the main question is how and in what ways we need to adapt the currently existing set of rules governing global energy relations to the realities of the twenty-first century.

The continuing process of climate change—affecting consumers and producers alike—is putting further emphasis on this fundamental question. Climate change is now an almost universally accepted fact; and according to most projections the process is picking up the pace, rapidly closing the window of opportunity for policymakers to put in place policy frameworks conducive to preventing greenhouse gas emissions rising to a level that would inflict the gravest economic, environmental, and social damage.[22] As discussed also in more detail in various chapters in this volume, one dimension of the climate change conundrum is how appropriate incentives can be set in markets to shift investments away from fossil fuels toward climate-friendly technologies. The current landscape is characterized by a patchwork of national and international policy frameworks that have engendered some results (such as a higher share of renewable energy in electricity production in some European countries) but that fall far short of the capacity to achieve change on the massive scale needed to transform the existing energy paradigm. In addition, as further discussed in this volume, the patchwork of national and international rules also results in investment uncertainty for private market actors.[23] Finally, the alternative fuels available to date are not without adverse effects, raising new environmental and developmental challenges.

Rather than pointing to geopolitical options, the answer to these challenges is that functioning markets play a key role and, if properly managed and structured through appropriate rules and institutions, can satisfy the needs of all players involved. Avoiding a return to an energy world of zero-sum games requires that the rules of the game in global energy markets be adapted along all three fronts sketched above: building and extending markets, addressing market failures, and setting standards. Here, as emphasized by the contributions to this volume, existing institutions need to be overhauled and made ready for the new energy realities.

Outline of This Book

As pointed out above, the importance of assessing the political economy of rules and institutions in global energy has not yet entered the mainstream discourse on

---

22. Stern (2007).
23. See also Blyth and Sullivan (2006).

energy security. This book offers a first tack at applying a governance lens in analyzing contemporary challenges in international oil and gas markets. Adopting an institutionalist perspective on global energy, the contributions to this volume focus on two questions:

—What are the functional logics of existing institutions governing global oil and gas on financial markets; on investment treaties and bilateral, regional, and global trade agreements; and on supply risk management?

—How do these institutions need to adapt in order to meet the challenges of the twenty-first century in terms of security of supply at affordable prices, environmental sustainability, and good governance?

The book thus complements existing analyses by explicitly focusing on the main institutional structures regulating global oil and gas markets and the extent to which they need to be adapted to changing framework conditions. The analyses of the institutions contained in this volume span the entire spectrum of the global energy arena and are consequently organized into four parts: part 1, Global Energy and Trade and Investment; part 2, Global Energy and Financial Markets; part 3, Short-Term Supply Management and Long-Term Energy Cooperation; and part 4, Emerging Issues and Outlook. Analytical chapters in each part are followed by summary chapters presenting a policy perspective.

Global Energy and Trade and Investment

At present there is no internationally agreed set of rules for trade of energy resources and investment flows. As a trend during the past twenty-five years, the political and economic mainstream promoted the liberalization of energy markets and the opening of investment opportunities to foreign actors on a nondiscriminatory basis. This has led to the establishment of multilateral institutions such as the World Trade Organization alongside regional arrangements such as the North American Free Trade Agreement (NAFTA), the Energy Charter Treaty, Asia-Pacific Economic Cooperation (APEC), accompanied by biregional forums such as the EU-Gulf Cooperation Council and the EU-Russian Dialogue. Today oil and gas are basically freely traded (though this is not based on international agreements), whereas related investment is mainly subject to national legal provisions. This patchwork of rules governing trade and investment of oil and gas is confronted with a variety of challenges, which are analyzed in this volume.

One challenge relates to the reemergence of energy diplomacy and its implications for trade and investment in oil and gas. Newly emerging consumer countries such as China, but also established market participants such as Japan, tend to increasingly flank energy contracts diplomatically to secure their rising energy needs. In turn producer countries such as Russia foster the expansion of their NOCs toward upstream assets and markets abroad. Both tendencies presumably undermine principles of free trade and lever out generally accepted rules of investment. In chapter 2 Andreas Goldthau addresses the question to what extent energy diplomacy challenges existing market structures in oil and gas. Drawing on anecdotal evidence from the cases of China's quest for oil and Russia's expansion into foreign gas assets, he discusses the motivations for and the various forms of energy diplomacy and analyzes how empirically significant the trend is. Goldthau then offers some counterintuitive results with regard to energy diplomacy's perceived effectiveness.

Another challenge is the ongoing trend toward a proliferation of regional and bilateral trade and investment agreements, which is taking place independently of efforts to strengthen multilateral institutions in order to govern oil and gas trade- and energy-related investments. In some areas these different regimes may complement each other; in others, they are at odds. In chapter 3 Yulia Selivanova analyzes the patchwork of existing international rules governing trade and investment in energy. She presents the various forms of regulatory structures that exist outside global trade agreements, mostly on a regional level, and analyzes the implications of the rise of bilateral treaties on the effectiveness of a global rules framework in the context of the WTO. Selivanova argues that the existence of such a patchwork is not necessarily to the detriment of international regulation of energy trade and investment. She identifies energy-specific forums such as the Energy Charter Treaty as potentially effective providers of rules and standards specific to energy trade, and she concludes by highlighting potential public policy options for transforming the current patchwork of rules governing trade and investment into a more coherent framework suiting the interests of both producers and consumers.

A third challenge relates to the impact of existing trade and investment rules on the environment. For example, WTO regulations as well as rules established by regional and bilateral trade and investment treaties are partially at odds with objectives of environmental protection. Regional and bilateral trade and investment treaties are often aimed at fostering energy relations and thus by definition favor fossil resources over renewables. Moreover, they may run counter to UN initiatives to secure the environment and to combat climate change.[24] In addition, WTO regulations treat major renewable energy sources such as biomass as agri-

24. See also Wälde (1996).

cultural products. Hence they are subject to a set of rules and regulations that are a political minefield, as the two dominating world markets—the EU and the United States—have established a variety of mechanisms to protect their producer companies.[25] Since the agricultural sector enjoys elaborate subsidy schemes on both sides of the Atlantic, agricultural products are regularly subject to heated trade disputes.

In chapter 4 Simonetta Zarrilli provides a governance perspective on the biofuels arena. Zarrilli presents recent data on production, consumption, and trade flows in biofuels, analyzes biofuels policies of leading producing and consuming countries, and evaluates to what extent those policies have contributed to the shortcomings experienced by the biofuels industry as well as to the recent political backlash against biofuels. Zarrilli also provides guidance for policymakers intent on maximizing the potential of biofuels while minimizing their negative side effects.

A concluding policy perspective for part 1 is offered by Ralf Dickel in chapter 5.

Global Energy and Financial Markets

Energy being a highly capital-intensive industry, all oil and gas businesses heavily rely on financial markets to facilitate exploration and production projects. Moreover, financial market instruments enable oil and gas companies to at least partially transfer certain types of risks from operators to investors, including currency, commodity price, and operating risks as well as risks of expropriation. From a financial market perspective, investments in the energy sector principally follow the logic of investments in any other sector: that is, invested money has to generate a certain payoff over a defined period of time. Unlike other investment projects, however, the energy sector (and the resource extracting industry in general) often also entails considerable political risk. It thus depends on the ability of financial markets to mitigate or hedge these risks: its underlying rules of the game determine which oil and gas investment projects attract financing and which do not. Similar to the rules governing trade and investment, the rules underlying financial markets with regard to the oil and gas business are confronted with a variety of challenges (addressed in this volume).

One challenge to existing rules governing financial markets relates to the ever more powerful role of state players in these markets. National oil companies now control the vast majority (over 80 percent) of proven oil and natural gas

25. For an overview see Desta (2002).

resources and will overwhelmingly dominate world oil production and pricing in the coming decades. The IEA projects that cumulative investment in the upstream oil and gas sector will amount to around US$8.4 trillion over 2007–30, or US$350 billion a year on average, to meet rising world demand for oil.[26] Despite these tremendous capital requirements, many governments intervene in energy markets in a manner that slows and even discourages this needed investment. Private sector firms that have in the past succeeded in amassing the capital required to make major risky and long-term investments in promising resources have been denied access to many of these promising regions. Generally speaking, resource development in the most prolific regions of the world, including the Middle East, Russia, and South America, can only proceed with adequate investment mobilized by national oil companies.

Hence the critical question for the immediate future is whether the world's major NOCs will be able to continue to invest adequate amounts to meet the projected rise in oil demand in the United States, Europe, China, and the emerging economies of Asia and elsewhere. This question is particularly pressing as governments have come to increasingly siphon off the NOCs' capital to meet domestic requirements for socioeconomic welfare priorities. Accordingly, chapter 6, by Amy Myers Jaffe and Ronald Soligo, investigates to what extent NOCs' state-backed finance or international credit markets finance their expansion programs. It then discusses how investment decisions and strategies of key NOCs are influenced by government preferences and assesses whether the pull of noncommercial obligations will continue to detract from the NOCs' abilities to tap rising revenues to foster adequate investment in oil and natural gas. The chapter concludes with a set of recommendations for international rules designed to increase the efficiency of the allocation of capital to oil and gas exploration and development projects given the dominance of NOCs in the sector.

A second challenge relates to climate change. While the rules governing trade and investment in conventional energy are incomplete and require reform, the rules governing the nascent carbon markets are at best embryonic. In chapter 7 William Blyth reviews the current state of existing carbon markets. Blyth argues that a top-down approach creating a global carbon market with universally accepted resource allocation is unlikely to emerge in the near future due to the political difficulties of making a global deal. Instead, national and regional carbon markets will continue to proliferate, resulting in a patchwork of systems

26. International Energy Agency (2008), p. 44.

and rules. Blyth posits, though, that this is not necessarily bad news. He suggests that tackling climate change needs a new multinational approach to assigning emissions rights and abatement responsibilities, building on the various bottom-up approaches in different jurisdictions, and in the medium to long term potentially culminating with a top-down approach to link these various schemes.

A third and related challenge lies in investments in low-carbon energy sources. Regarding increasing carbon emissions, the crucial question arises as to whether financial markets help to facilitate the necessary shift toward a low-carbon future. In recent years investments in alternative energy sources and environmentally sustainable projects have gained more attention on international financial markets. In fact the bond market has started to finance projects such as wind farms, and investment banks have become more interested in shares of companies active in the renewable sector.[27] It remains unclear however whether the price signals are strong enough to channel sufficient capital into environmentally sustainable energy projects (including solar power and biofuels). In chapter 8 Hillard Huntington and Christine Jojarth review technological, political, and economic factors that determine investments into alternative energy sources. Arguing that the recent credit crunch makes political action regarding the promotion of investments in low-carbon energy sources more necessary than ever, they identify various key arenas in which climate-friendly investment policies need to be promoted, including the introduction of an auction-based cap-and-trade-system, a shift in research and development expenditures, a review of energy policy (in particular price controls on coal, natural gas, and petroleum products), and a proactive harmonization of climate change and trade rules.

A concluding policy perspective for part 2 is offered by Joseph Stanislaw in chapter 9.

Short-Term Supply Management and Long-Term Energy Cooperation

In recent years the heightened global tensions emanating from the Middle East, as well as the oft commented on rise of India and China, have brought short-term risk management of global oil back to the forefront of global energy security. When added to the feared, though by no means agreed upon, impact of so-called peak oil, it is clear to see why the impacts of the 1973–74 oil crisis are being revisited and the mitigation mechanisms available to consumers dusted

27. For an overview on investment volumes, see REN21 (2006).

off and reassessed.[28] Following the 1973–74 oil price shocks, OECD members concluded that it was no longer sufficient for any single actor to protect itself in the global oil market, and they established specific mechanisms of short-term supply (risk) management within the realm of the IEA.[29] In addition, consumers took steps to institutionalize producer-consumer dialogue to facilitate greater market stability. The premier forum in this context is the International Energy Forum.

Governance structures for short-term supply management as well as for long-term energy cooperation are confronted with a variety of challenges, however. One prominent challenge stems from the fact that Chinese and Indian oil consumption represents a fundamental move away from the traditional consumer base. As these new consumers are not part of the institutional framework that encompasses short-term supply management mechanisms, they are excluded from the IEA's strategic petroleum reserves and other mitigation mechanisms. In addition, consumer country cooperation is required to effectively address the pressing problem of climate change. Starting from these observations, Wilfrid Kohl in chapter 10 first assesses the range of existing platforms, forums, and organizations mainly comprising consumer nations, including the IEA, the G-8, the EU, and global climate change regimes. He then assesses to what extent these forums are able to deal effectively with the effects of short-term supply disruption, to coordinate their policies, and to address climate change. Finally, he offers suggestions on how to foster consumer-consumer cooperation and how to accommodate the new consumer heavyweights in the existing structures of global oil governance, such as the IEA.

A second challenge relates to emergency risk management mechanisms in an emerging global gas market. Assessing the possible contribution of liquefied natural gas in supply risk management, Dick de Jong, Coby van der Linde, and Tom Smeenk, in chapter 11, review the role of LNG in the emergence of a globalized gas market. They show that flexible LNG could potentially play a role in addressing supply shortages in Europe and in lowering peak spot prices, but the authors also highlight the fact that the availability of LNG remains uncertain and that Europe is likely to be the least attractive market for suppliers. These authors' analysis also reveals that the changing nature of the natural gas business requires adjustment in gas market regulation. Given that price competition in the gas

---

28. Prominent studies in this field include Willenborg, Tönjes, and Perlot (2004); Kalicki and Goldwyn (2005); Emerson (2006).

29. Scott (1995).

market increasingly takes place on an international level, they argue that especially the EU needs to redesign its internal market. With regard to the issue of potential supply disruptions, the best option for policymakers may be to invest not in supply diversity but rather in diversification of the energy mix and in enhancing regional cooperation with neighbor countries.

A third challenge stems from the fact that, given that new consumers and major producing countries fail to publish crucial data on market fundamentals, markets are characterized by increasingly significant uncertainty. In chapter 12 Enno Harks focuses on the question of what contribution enhanced consumer-producer cooperation could bring to the table to tackle this problem. Thus far the IEF is the only place where producers and consumers engage in an institutionalized exchange on energy market developments and related policies. Harks argues that the IEF is likely to become central in providing the notoriously speculative oil market with more information given increasingly tight supply situations. Further, he identifies the IEF's Joint Oil Data Initiative (JODI) as an important instrument for rendering the oil market more transparent. Harks also explores the role the IEF plays in mitigating oil and gas market risks and offers policy options designed to strengthen its impact as a forum of dialogue between producers and consumers.

A concluding policy perspective for part 3 is offered by Albert Bressand in chapter 13.

Emerging Issues and Outlook

Part 4 considers emerging issues affecting the development of the international oil and gas markets and discusses their impact on global energy governance. In chapter 14 Thorsten Benner and Ricardo Soares de Oliveira focus on the efforts over the past ten to fifteen years to make good resource governance a part of the rules of the game for global energy governance. Whereas traditionally global energy governance was a value-blind enterprise dominated by crude realpolitik concerns in terms of profit, price, and security of supply, rhetorically at least a norm transformation has taken place. The G-8 declared that it "is in our common global interest that resource wealth be used responsibly so as to help reduce poverty, prevent conflicts, and improve the sustainability of resource production and supply. We firmly agree that significant and lasting progress in this area can only be achieved on the basis of transparency and good governance."

The chapter first analyzes the context and the drivers of the rise of good governance. The second part reviews the record of good governance reform initiatives. It analyzes voluntary transparency initiatives, chiefly the Extractive Industries

Transparency Initiative (EITI), and reviews its performance in crucial cases (Nigeria, Azerbaijan). It also looks at other institutional experiments, such as the Chad-Cameroon pipeline experience and the EITI++. The third part discusses the prospects for the role of the "good" in global energy governance. It argues that good governance is far from being anchored in the rules of the game of global energy governance due to the lack of political will on the part of Western political cal powers to mainstream the agenda into the financial system, the lack of coverage (that excludes major producers such as Saudi Arabia and Russia), and the lack of interest on the part of such new consumers as India and China, which never subscribed to the good resource governance reform agenda in the first place.

Chapter 15, by Jamie Manzer and Jan Martin Witte, focuses on the increasing importance of sovereign wealth funds in recycling petrodollars from producing countries. During the last decade oil price hikes have enabled producing countries such as Russia and Dubai to pile up enormous amounts of U.S. dollar reserves, a significant share of which are now stored in sovereign wealth funds. The rise of these state-owned investment vehicles has triggered a political backlash fueled by concerns over the accountability and transparency of these funds as well as the alleged propensity of government owners to utilize them for political-strategic rather than economic gain. Manzer and Witte analyze recent efforts under the auspices of the IMF to develop international rules of the game for the funds.

Andreas Goldthau, Wade Hoxtell, and Jan Martin Witte summarize the findings of the contributions in the book in chapter 16. They analyze the impact of the rise of new consumers, the reemergence of state players, and climate change for the three functional categories of institutions in global energy; they highlight key lessons learned from the various contributions to this book regarding the adjustment of the rules structuring global energy; and they elaborate on possible routes of further research to fully understand the key challenges and solutions for global energy governance in the twenty-first century.

References

Biolsi, Robert. 1995. "Spot, Options, and Futures Oil Markets." In *The New Global Oil Market: Understanding Energy Issues in the World Economy,* edited by S. Shojai. Westport, Conn.: Praeger.

Blyth, William, and Rory Sullivan. 2006. "Climate Change Policy Uncertainty and the Electricity Industry: Implications and Unintended Consequences." Briefing paper. Chatham, N.J.: Chatham House.

Desta, Melaku Geboy. 2002. *The Law of International Trade in Agricultural Products: From GATT 1947 to the WTO Agreement on Agriculture.* Norwell, Mass.: Kluwer.

Downs, Erica Strecker. 2005. *China's Quest for Energy Security.* Washington: Rand.

Emerson, Sarah. 2006. "When Should We Use Strategic Oil Stocks?" *Energy Policy* 34, no. 18.

Eurasia Group. 2006. *China's Overseas Investments in Oil and Gas Production.* New York: U.S.-China Economic and Security Review Commission.

Evans, Peter C. 2006. "Bracing for an Uncertain Energy Future." Energy Security Series, Japan. Brookings.

International Energy Agency. 2008. *World Energy Outlook.* Paris.

Jiménez-Guerra, Andrea. 2001. "The World Trade Organization and Oil." Oxford University, Institute for Energy Studies.

Kalicki, J. H., and D. L. Goldwyn, eds. 2004. *Energy and Security: Toward a New Foreign Policy Strategy.* Washington: Woodrow Wilson Center Press.

Klare, Michael T. 2008. *Rising Powers, Shrinking Planet: The New Geopolitics of Energy.* New York: Metropolitan Books.

KPMG International. 2005. *China Energy Outlook.* Hong Kong.

Mitchell, John. 2005. *Producer-Consumer Dialogue: What Can Energy Ministers Say to One Another?* London: Chatham House.

Mitchell, John V., and Paul Stevens. 2008. *Ending Dependence: Hard Choices for Oil-Exporting States.* London: Chatham House.

North, Douglass C. 1990. *Institutions, Institutional Change, and Economic Performance:* Cambridge University Press.

REN21. 2006. "Renewables Global Status Report: 2006 Update." Paris: Renewable Energy Policy Network for the 21st Century.

Scott, Richard. 1994. *IEA—The First Twenty Years: The History of the International Energy Agency, 1974–1994.* Paris: IEA/OECD.

Stern, Nicholas. 2007. *Stern Review on the Economics of Climate Change.* HM Treasury.

U.S. Department of Energy. 2006. "National Security Review of International Energy Requirements."

Wälde, Thomas, ed. 1996. *The Energy Charter Treaty: An East-West Gateway for Investment and Trade.* London: Kluwer Law International.

Willenborg, Robbert, Christoph Tönjes, and Wilbur Perlot. 2004. "Europe's Oil Defences: An Analysis of Europe's Oil Supply Vulnerability and Its Emergency Oil Stockholding Systems." The Hague: Clingendael Institute.

Yergin, Daniel. 2004. "Energy Security and Markets." In *Energy and Security: Toward a New Foreign Policy Strategy,* edited by J. H. Kalicki and D. L. Goldwyn. Washington: Woodrow Wilson Center Press.

PART ONE

Global Energy and Trade and Investment

2

Energy Diplomacy in Trade and Investment of Oil and Gas

Andreas Goldthau

To secure enough oil and gas for their rising energy needs, emerging consumer countries such as China increasingly enter into energy contracts using
state diplomacy. Even producer countries like Russia have adopted a state-backed
strategy to supplement their domestic energy sources. Both modalities have been
labeled *energy diplomacy*. The term commonly connotes the way countries give
their energy companies a competitive edge in bidding for resources by using the
state's power: consumer countries strengthen their supply situation by diplomatically flanking energy contracts, whereas producer countries use diplomacy to
enhance access to markets or reserves.

To be sure, the phenomenon of energy diplomacy is nothing new. Oil and gas
have always been politically charged commodities and, hence, have been subject
to significant government intervention. China and Russia are simply following a
path that the United States, Japan, and a number of European countries once
took.[1] Yet the current trend toward energy diplomacy coincides with the general
perception that global energy politics has become a zero-sum game, in which one

---

1. A case in point are the corporations dubbed the Seven Sisters, which dominated the world oil
market until the end of the 1960s and whose business activities abroad were clearly flanked and fostered
by U.S. legislation and policy. For a historical overview, see Yergin (1991).

country's energy security is another's lack thereof.[2] Energy diplomacy has thus emerged as a powerful concept in public discourse. But are the common perceptions of energy diplomacy correct? Is energy diplomacy effective? And does it necessitate adjusting the rules to curb the use of political influence in the energy business?

This chapter argues that the concept of energy diplomacy has clear empirical and functional limits and questions the assumption that diplomatic means can effectively secure supply or access to resources. While energy diplomacy is certainly not to be ignored, its impact is strongly moderated by the logic of market structures. Instead, it is argued that, by sidelining economic fundamentals, energy diplomacy disturbs the effective allocation of capital and decreases transparency in energy markets. Hence the challenge for global energy governance lies in strengthening mechanisms enhancing market transparency and allocation of investment, rather than in curbing the use of diplomatic means in energy relations.

This chapter reviews the trend toward energy diplomacy, drawing on anecdotal evidence from the cases of China and Russia and assessing the motivations for, and the various forms of, energy diplomacy. Further, it asks how empirically significant the current trend in fact is, both with regard to a major importing country aiming at securing its supplies (China) and with regard to a major producer country helping its energy companies to expand abroad (Russia). The discussion challenges some commonly held beliefs about energy diplomacy, examining whether energy diplomacy makes a difference and assessing the success or failure of state-backed efforts to facilitate or foster resource access. Energy diplomacy strategies are also examined in light of the imperatives stemming from existing market structures. On this basis, the chapter then addresses the question as to where and to what extent energy diplomacy challenges existing governing structures in global oil and gas. The chapter concludes by suggesting that emerging consumer nations may at some point develop an interest in reliable rules of access, thus eventually siding with the established Western consumer nations. The chapter also references the way the ongoing financial crisis may affect the calculation of governments and "their" national oil (gas) companies (NOCs).

Energy Diplomacy: The State of Affairs

Energy diplomacy has emerged as a buzzword. While widely used in political debate, its analytical content remains rather elusive. Therefore I begin by defining this rather fuzzy and often politically charged term.

2. *Energy security* is defined as reliable supply at affordable prices in the case of consuming nations and as reliable demand at sustainable prices in the case of producing nations.

Defining Energy Diplomacy

Throughout mankind's history, energy resources have been both the cause of or a proxy for foreign policy or even military actions. At the beginning of the twentieth century, British-Russian rivalry over the control of Persia is believed to have strengthened after the discovery of oil in the region. Italy's invasion of Abyssinia in 1935 was met with economic sanctions from the League of Nations, centrally targeting Italy's access to oil and other resources. The U.S. oil embargo against resource-poor Japan, aimed at forcing the country to withdraw its troops from occupied China, is widely portrayed as a primary cause for Japan's declaration of war against the United States in 1941. Germany's strong import dependency on overseas oil and the Soviet Union's dependency on Caspian oil reserves are believed to have been a core cause of Berlin's decision to invade the Soviet Union in 1941, in order to seize control of Caspian energy.[3] And recent projects such as the Baku-Tblisi-Ceyhan pipeline, built to provide (Western) access to Caspian oil reserves, would not have been realized without Washington's strong and outspoken diplomatic backing.[4] Hence the link between energy and diplomacy or even military action is not a recent phenomenon.

A decade-long period of oversupply on oil and gas markets and resulting low prices calmed public debate on these issues. It is only since the turn of the new millennium, when supply-demand balances both in global oil markets and in regional gas markets tightened again, that energy diplomacy has come to receive renewed attention. Despite a myriad of contributions linking the term to the nexus of energy, foreign policy, and supply security, there is no consensus on what exactly the term *energy diplomacy* means. A review of current debates on energy diplomacy reveals an assumed strong issue linkage, particularly between energy and development policy, bilateral trade, military aid, and foreign policy in general. As a general pattern, the term is used mostly in the geopolitics-informed debate on access to resources and points to a strategic and instrumental use of foreign policy to secure a country's energy supplies. References to China's oil diplomacy in Africa and the Kremlin's pipeline diplomacy in the Caspian region and Asia are cases in point. In addition, the rise of NOCs, together with ongoing efforts to marginalize private international oil companies in promising (foreign) development projects, is frequently cited as proof of revived

3. Crane and others (2009), p. 25f.
4. Jofi (1999).

state efforts in securing energy supplies or revenues stemming from resource extraction.[5]

While a generally accepted definition of energy diplomacy does not exist, it would seem appropriate to define the term as the use of foreign policy to secure access to energy supplies abroad and to promote (mostly bilateral, that is, government to government) cooperation in the energy sector. This definition suggests that the primary units of analysis are states or state actors; that the primary driver behind the conclusion of oil and gas deals is not necessarily maximizing business opportunities but national security goals; and that the underlying cost-benefit calculations do not follow an economic logic but rather a political one.

What are the motivations of conducting energy diplomacy, and what means are typically used? In what follows, the cases of China and Russia are used to illustrate the schemes that consumer and producer nations employ in their efforts to give their NOCs an edge. China's quest for energy, most prominent in Africa, has almost become legend and offers insight into the country's mercantilist approach to energy security. Russia, on the other hand, a top oil and gas producer since the turn of the new millennium, is backing the strong expansion course of state-owned gas monopolist Gazprom, both on domestic and on foreign markets.

State Efforts to Secure Supply: China's Quest for Energy

An examination of China's mercantilist approach to securing resources allows analyses of the motivations for and specific patterns of energy diplomacy in an import-dependent consumer country. Unlike fully industrialized nations, China has not yet decoupled economic growth from energy consumption. Indeed, despite its two-decade-long economic rise, the country's energy demand is set to continue on its steep upward slope in the years ahead. While China will be able to cover most of its power production through domestic coal and gas (for both of which there are sufficient reserves for decades to come), oil has emerged as the country's Achilles' heel (box 2-1). In fact, according to the projections by the International Energy Agency, China could rely on imports for as much as 85 percent of its overall oil consumption by the year 2030.[6] Against this backdrop, a number

5. For recent analyses on China's Africa policy on the resource nexus, see, among others, Alden (2007), Konings (2007), Holslag (2006), Tull (2007), Taylor (2006), and Downs (2005). Pars pro toto on Russia, see Smith (2006), Norman (2005), and Champion and Chazan (2006). For a counter perspective, see Noel (2008) and Goldthau (2008a). On "pipeline diplomacy," see Socor (2005), Stulberg (2008), Lall (2006), and Bahgat (2003). In the remaining parts of this chapter, for the sake of simplicity, the term *NOC* is also used to mean national gas companies.

6. International Energy Agency (2007), p. 124.

Box 2-1. *A Primer on Chinese Energy*

Having become a net importer of oil in 1993, China can no longer cover domestic demand through its generic reserves, amounting to a mere 1.3 percent of the world's total. The country consumed 7.45 million barrels a day in 2006, about twice its domestic production and 9 percent of global demand. The majority of China's producing oil fields have matured. While China's decreasing domestic oil production may be partially compensated by increased volumes generated by coal-to-liquid (CTL) plants, overall import shares will rise from 51 percent in 2004 to 85 percent in 2030. By that time China is expected to be both the world's second-largest oil consumer (behind the United States and before the European Union) and the world's second-largest oil importer.

As for gas, China is projected to increase both consumption and imports. Yet as the country's electricity generation and power sector relies mainly on large generic coal reserves, demand for gas is not projected to increase as steeply as for oil. As the International Energy Agency estimates, the Chinese import market will not expand beyond 106 billion cubic meters by 2030.

Source: BP (2007); International Energy Agency (2007), pp. 105, 118.

of intertwined factors render energy diplomacy an attractive and to some extent imperative policy option for Beijing.

First, China's elite crucially depends on continued economic growth in order to maintain social and political stability and to legitimize the rule of the Communist Party—with a reliable supply of energy being a precondition thereof. Trying to secure constant and reliable oil imports is thus a highly rational move. Given Beijing's historic penchant for controlling the way oil supplies are generated, markets appear a rather unreliable mechanism.[7]

Second, China is a latecomer to the international oil business. After being self-sufficient for large parts of its postrevolution industrialization phase and its market-based catch-up period after the 1978 Great Leap Forward, the country entered the global oil market only in the early 1990s. Yet as the U.S. Department of Energy pointedly notes, few untapped areas for petroleum investment are available to latecomers such as China.[8] Moreover, as the structure of the global oil

7. See for example Lieberthal and Herberg (2006).
8. U.S. Department of Energy (2006), p. 32.

market has traditionally been shaped by established (Western) market actors, China has to play according to rules of the game which may not necessarily be perceived suiting its interests. In addition, Western, especially U.S., international oil companies (IOCs) have a historic advantage in tapping and operating reserves in key producer regions such as the Persian Gulf. Hence in the view of Beijing effective supply security is not guaranteed by the existing market structure, which is seen as biased toward established players. From this angle, public intervention, in the form of Chinese NOCs sent abroad in order to directly tap reserves, would appear justified. As a consequence, China has turned to regions whose reserves have been opened up to foreign exploration and production only fairly recently and that are characterized by relatively low American corporate, government, and military presence. Africa and Central Asia both fulfill these characteristics.[9]

Third, however, it is important to acknowledge the role that Chinese NOCs themselves are playing in driving China's outreach. In fact it is argued that the restructuring of the domestic oil and gas sector in 1998 motivated Chinese NOCs to maximize their commercial interests, improve their performance, and expand their business.[10] Further, against the backdrop of limited and declining domestic reserves, and given that Chinese NOCs face strong limitations on growth through mergers and acquisitions, they have an additional incentive to expand their business by growing abroad, even if this implies accessing politically and technologically demanding regions.[11] Adding to this, their status as latecomers forces them to tap countries where the IOCs' activities are legally restricted or politically infeasible, such as Sudan, Burma, and Iran. In all, as Trevor Houser argues, "though Beijing actively encouraged overseas investment in the past, the [NOCs] are taking the lead today . . . to suit economic interests."[12] In other words, rather than Beijing's solely designing China's global strategy, it is also Sinopec, the China National Petroleum Corporation (CNPC), and the China National Offshore Oil Corporation (CNOOC) that use government support to flank their expansion efforts and shape policy.[13]

In sum, China's energy diplomacy efforts are driven by both the government's strategic considerations and the NOCs' commercial motives. Both are deeply intertwined. But the NOCs appear to be increasingly in the driver's seat.

9. Crane and others (2009), p. 38.

10. Chen (2008), p. 91.

11. CNOOC's failed attempt to take over UNOCAL in 2005 is a case in point; Chen (2008), p. 91; Houser (2008), p. 158; for a comparative perspective, see Paik and others (2007).

12. Houser (2008), p. 156.

13. On incentives for Chinese NOCs to go abroad, see also Downs (2004); Xiaojie (2007); on the relationship between the oil companies and the government, see also Lieberthal and Herberg (2006).

State Intervention to Secure Reserves and Markets: Russia's Lock-Up Efforts

While it may appear somewhat straightforward for a major, import-dependent consumer nation such as China to recur to foreign policy support in securing access to energy supplies, what are the motivations for a major producer such as Russia to engage in energy diplomacy? In fact, Russia is the largest holder of world gas reserves and has also emerged as one of the globe's top oil producers in recent years. While its oil reserves are comparably limited, its gas supply is abundant, totaling 26 percent of global reserves (box 2-2).[14]

Yet, and somewhat counterintuitively, it is mainly foreign gas reserves and infrastructure that are the primary target of Russian energy diplomacy efforts, areas in which the Russian industry already is in a strong position. In recent years Russia has tended to not only diplomatically flank Gazprom's expansion strategies abroad but also to take the lead in establishing bilateral business relations in the gas sector, most prominently in the Caspian region, Central and Eastern Europe, and North Africa. The reasons for Russia's diplomatic efforts to strengthen Gazprom's presence in these regions are manifold and reflect the coinciding yet not necessarily identical interests of the Kremlin and the Russian gas industry.

First, given that Gazprom accounts for almost a third of overall state revenues during the last years, it is imperative for Moscow to ensure a strong development of this vital corporation. Expanding Gazprom's business both within and outside Russia has thus been openly declared a core policy goal.[15] In addition, Moscow's recent rhetoric seems to suggest that natural gas is also regarded as a potential tool in fostering foreign policy objectives. Feasible or not, given the strong bilateral interdependency in Eurasian gas market structures, such an approach requires a strong position of the gas sector in key markets, an additional incentive to diplomatically flank its expansion strategy.

Second, Gazprom itself has a strong incentive to go abroad. Given a strongly regulated domestic market, which allows for only modest price increases, the company can grow only in foreign markets. Hence it has adopted a growth strategy targeting key consumer regions, notably Central and Eastern Europe. Given the largely locked up European downstream sector, strongly guarded by national governments, political support is a welcome factor when cutting deals.

14. BP (2007).
15. For an overview of the role of Gazprom and energy in the Russian economy, see Gaddy and others (2008) and Stern (2005).

Box 2-2. *A Primer on Russian Energy*

Russia is one of the most resource-rich countries on earth. It owns one-fourth of global gas reserves compared to only 6.6 percent of oil reserves. In 2007 Russian crude oil output amounted to more than 8 percent of global production, rendering the country the world's largest oil producer after Saudi Arabia. While the Russian state has recently strengthened its grip on the oil sector, most prominently by taking over formerly private Yukos, the bulk of the industry remains in private hands. Russia's gas production and export is dominated by the state-controlled monopoly OAO Gazprom, which accounts for around 85 percent of domestic gas production and also controls the domestic pipeline system. As gas makes up more than half of Russia's primary energy consumption, the Russian gas market is highly regulated. Out of more than 650 billion cubic meters of annually produced gas, around 444 billion cubic meters are used domestically. As a consequence of strict domestic price regulation, Gazprom earns more than 80 percent of its profits from exports to Western Europe, although this market accounts for only 30 percent of the company's total production.

As political actors tend to be deeply involved in the Russian gas sector—most evidently represented by Dmitry Medvedev, former chairman of Gazprom's board and now Russian president—the company has come to be portrayed as the Kremlin's foreign policy arm. The recent financial crisis has put severe financial strains on Gazprom, which lost around three-quarters of its stock market value in 2008 and now faces difficulties in raising money to service its debt and tackle demanding investment projects such as the multibillion-dollar gas fields of Shtokman and Yamal.

Source: BP (2007); International Energy Agency (2008); International Herald Tribune (2008a).

Third, given that generic Russian gas production is falling, mainly due to under-investment and a regulatory framework disincentivizing production by independent producers, Gazprom needs to tap foreign reserves to satisfy growing domestic demand and to at the same time serve its export commitments.[16] To make up for perceived shortages in domestic production and to improve its gas balance, Gazprom's strategy has been to cut openly state-backed deals with resource-rich

16. Goldthau (2008b). Note that the gas market has changed into a soft market since the end of 2008, endangering Gazprom's export revenues rather than putting in question the supply side.

nations in Central Asia and has even approached major African exporters such as Algeria. In that it has sought to lock up reserves in producer regions, which could eventually become alternative and rivaling gas suppliers for Europe, Gazprom's vital key market.

Fourth, Gazprom has sought to gain (or regain) control over pipeline infrastructure in the Commonwealth of Independent States and parts of Central and Eastern Europe, which would enable the company to control export routes to Western consumers. Gazprom has frequently accepted infrastructure assets as compensation for outstanding debt and thus has gained ownership over pipeline and transport networks in these regions.

To be sure, Gazprom's moves—such as securing markets instead of enhancing product quality or output and marginalizing competitors by controlling market access and infrastructure—fulfill the criteria of a textbook monopolist rather than point to politicized motives. Recently initiated large-scale pipeline projects such as Blue Stream (transporting gas under the Black Sea to Turkey), South Stream (supplying Italy and Hungary through Greece, Bulgaria, and Serbia), and Nord Stream (a direct Russian-German connector under the Baltic Sea) fit well into this picture. These projects, often dubbed pipeline diplomacy, aim to neutralize Western European efforts to diversify supply routes. In that they are a purely rational move by a market actor aiming at exclusive delivery to a profitable market. Yet as this example reveals, corporate interests overlap and coincide with the Kremlin's goals, which renders mutual relations mostly symbiotic.

Again, however, as in the case of China, there remains the question of who in fact sits in the driver's seat. While the underlying rationales of Gazprom's 2009 gas dispute with Ukraine's state oil company, Naftohaz, remain somewhat blurred, especially given the lose-lose outcome for both sides, the 2006 gas dispute with Belarus has revealed Gazprom's and the Kremlin's diverging interests. The push for an increase of margins and enhanced control of infrastructure in a key transit country was not necessarily congruent with the country's foreign policy interests in Central Europe, and the move eventually deprived Moscow of the last remaining ally in the region. Hence while Russia's expansion in the energy business is never apolitical, politics may occasionally just provide a useful narrative when, in fact, economic interests take over.

This quick assessment of China's and Russia's motivations for engaging in energy diplomacy challenges the assumption that the primary driver is national security. Rather, both strategic government goals and corporate business interests—which may often coincide but not necessarily be identical—are reflected in energy diplomacy. As the cases of China and Russia reveal, the driving force of (energy-related) foreign policy is not necessarily only the Kremlin or the Chinese presidency but may be also the headquarters of Gazprom or PetroChina.

Modes and Forms of Intervention

What forms of intervention can be observed in energy diplomacy? In general both China and Russia use similar instruments, though in different configurations and intensities.

In China, linking development assistance and resource access is the dominant pattern, particularly with African countries. Through its aid-for-oil approach to development cooperation, Beijing has granted significant financial assistance to African countries, mostly through preferential loans, loans turned into grants, and debt relief. In fact as Oxford's Ngaire Woods notes, China has written off total debts of more than US$2 billion for forty-four recipient countries, the bulk of which are African.[17] Moreover, funding instruments such as the US$5 billion China-Africa Development Fund have turned China into one of Africa's most important donor countries.[18] As China tends to grant financial aid largely without setting conditions on domestic governance, it provides access for African countries, such as the repressive Sudan and Zimbabwe, that usually fail to meet the conditions of good governance posed by major Western donor organizations. In addition, Chinese development-related efforts in Africa include various forms of nonfinancial assistance, such as construction of hospitals, malaria prevention centers, schools; improvements in roads and infrastructure; and stipends for African students to study in China.[19]

As for political support at the international level in exchange for favored access to resources, China's obvious protection of Sudan in the UN Security Council is a frequently cited example. The oil-rich pariah state is one of China's main oil suppliers and accounted for around 5 percent of China's imports in 2006.[20] In addition to paralyzing collective international action on Sudan, Chinese trade with this country, mainly in oil, is widely believed to lighten pressure on the Sudanese government to end the Darfur crisis. China's Sudan policy also seems to fit the larger

17. Woods (2008).
18. See www.cadfund.com.
19. Yet it is important to note that, while China's provision of unconditional development assistance is widely interpreted through the prevalent quest-for-energy lens, this approach is not entirely new. Nonconditional aid has been the trademark of Chinese development assistance since the 1960s. Long before China became a net importer of oil and other resources, development policy was used to promote their One China policy.
20. Energy Information Administration (2006); see also Large (2007).

picture of trying to buy friends in the region by granting unconditional support.[21] Finally, military cooperation and arms sales tend to accompany political support, with China's arms sales to oil-rich Nigeria being a case in point.[22]

In contrast to China's development-centered approach, Russia tends to rely more on subsidies and price incentives, preferential ties with states of the former Soviet Union, and occasional military cooperation. After the dissolution of the Soviet Union, Russia has used preferential oil and gas agreements as a primary instrument to procure access, transit, and allies. This barter practice, inherited from Soviet times, has been used in such different cases as the Ukraine (in-kind gas payments in exchange for gas transit), Armenia (subsidized gas deliveries in exchange for political support), and Belarus (both transit and political support, and both in oil and in gas). More recently Russia has started to reduce subsidies and swap outstanding debt against pipeline and transport infrastructure and access to the downstream sector.[23]

Regarding energy supplies in Central Asia, Russia has used historic political ties, price incentives, and the region's restricted export infrastructure to foster privileged access. In 2003, for instance, Moscow took advantage of both Turkmenistan's lack of alternative export routes and its need for stable markets and managed to make Ashgabat commit its entire gas export capacity to Gazprom for the following twenty-five years. In addition to monopolizing Turkmen gas transit and exports, a 2007 agreement ensures that Kazakh gas exports to Western Europe will continue flowing through the restored CAC gas pipeline system, a pipeline route from Turkmenistan through Kazakhstan to Russia.[24] The Kremlin was represented in all these deals by Vladimir Putin, who was president of Russia at the time. Further, Russian pipeline diplomacy (efforts to circumvent transit countries and exclusively deliver gas to Western European clients) was supported by high-level visits by Russian officials to critical partner countries. As for military cooperation, a joint Russia-Venezuela sea maneuver at the end of 2008, and recent Russian-Libyan arms deals are widely regarded as efforts to foster collaboration in the field of energy.[25] Finally, Russia's ongoing assistance to Iran in the field of nuclear technology, most notably regarding the construction of a nuclear power plant at Bushehr, and its

21. Beijing's long-term support of Mugabe's authoritarian regime in Zimbabwe is a prime example.
22. See, among others, Human Rights Watch (2003); and Taylor (2007).
23. This policy triggered a series of "gas disputes" with neighboring CIS countries. See for instance Stern (2006).
24. *International Herald Tribune* (2007); Torbakov (2003).
25. Among others, *The Economist* (2008); Agence France-Presse (2008); and *International Herald Tribune* (2008b).

support for Iranian missile technology are believed to be linked to a Russian-Iranian rapprochement in the gas sector.[26]

In sum, China and Russia use various forms of energy diplomacy, ranging from development assistance and aid to bilateral subsidies and preferential loans, political support on an international level, and even military cooperation and arms sales. While China's activities tend to focus on oil, Russia's main efforts are in the gas sector. Yet it has to be noted that the use of these instruments is neither new nor unique to these two countries. In fact almost all major Western industrial nations have historically used development assistance, arms sales, and financial aid to either forge the interests of their "national champions," or to secure supplies, or both. Cases in point here include not only Great Britain in Persia but also other OECD nations such as Japan. Japan has a long and established history in energy diplomacy following World War II and for a long period sought to secure supplies through state-owned Japan National Oil Corporation. Having abandoned this approach for the last two decades, it is only recently that Tokyo adopted a new energy strategy, which de novo aims to increase Japanese companies' share of oil imports (to 40 percent by 2030, up from the current level of 15 percent).[27]

Does Energy Diplomacy Make a Difference?

As indicated in the beginning, common preconceptions on energy diplomacy center upon one main assumption, namely that both producing and importing countries can improve their position vis-à-vis competitors by giving their countries' companies a competitive edge in bidding processes. Yet are these assumptions justified?

Diplomacy and Access

Evidence seems to show clear limits for diplomacy when it comes to securing energy supplies or access. Supporting the opposite side, some of China's development assistance and political support is believed to having facilitated successful bids of Chinese NOCs abroad. As Brookings's Erica Downs notes, the Angolan decision to award two concessions to Sinopec in 2004 seems to be linked to a prior US$2 billion infrastructure loan granted by China's ExIm Bank.[28] Further, CNPC's successful bid for four oil concessions in Nigeria in May 2006 apparently occurred after President Hu Jintao's visit to Abuja a month earlier, which featured an agree-

26. See also recent discussions on the "Gas Troika," involving Russia, Iran, and Qatar: *International Herald Tribune* (2008c).
27. Evans (2006), pp. 8ff.
28. Downs (2007), p. 52.

ment on a Chinese multibillion-dollar infrastructure investment.[29] Finally, China's successful buy-in into Sudan's Greater Nile Petroleum Operating Company and the 2002 replacement of some Western oil companies (in promising Sudanese exploration projects) by Chinese companies seem to prove energy-related motives behind Beijing's support of Khartoum in the UN Security Council.[30]

Yet as observers note, the link between development assistance and access to oil is often less robust than usually assumed, suggesting that China's engagement in Africa also follows other, nonoil-related—and at least partly humanitarian—motivations.[31] In addition, while Chinese outward foreign direct investment (FDI) has grown substantially over the last years, from US$5.4 billion in 2004 to more than US$25.5 billion in 2007, only a fraction of these capital flows appears to be directed toward the oil, gas, and mining sectors.[32] According to the Chinese Ministry of Commerce, Chinese outward FDI in oil, gas, and mining amounted to US$1.8 billion and US$1.7 billion in 2004 and 2005, respectively; it spiked in 2006 to some US$8.5 billion and then fell in 2007 to US$4.0 billion.[33]

Thus although mining indeed holds a prominent position in Chinese outward FDI, it is only fourth in volume after wholesale and retailing, leasing and business services, and transport. In addition, most of Chinese outward capital flows have traditionally been directed toward Asia, not Africa. Cumulative FDI stocks from 2004 through 2007 are dominated by Asia (67.0 percent) and Latin America (20.1 percent), with the remaining marginal percentages going to Europe (3.8 percent), Africa (3.8 percent), and North America (2.75 percent).[34] Moreover, Chinese companies active in Africa have experienced the negative effects that domestic turmoil can have on investment projects, as incidents in Sudan and elsewhere have shown.[35] China's engagement in these regions is thus likely to face significant limits. Further, Beijing has come to face strong international attention on and opposition to its military assistance and its unconditional support of certain, mostly African, authoritarian regimes.[36]

Given this policy's negative impact on China's international standing, Beijing has apparently started to change its approach toward not only oil-rich Sudan but

29. Evans and Downs (2006), p. 3.
30. Eurasia Group (2006), p. 4; Human Rights Watch (2003).
31. Downs (2007); Houser (2008), p. 158; Taylor (2006); Woods (2008).
32. Ministry of Commerce of China (2008), pp. 59ff.
33. Ibid.
34. Ibid.
35. See, for instance, *New York Times* (2008).
36. Among others, *New York Times* (2007)

also other outlaws such as Zimbabwe. Finally, the share of equity oil (the amount of crude generated by Chinese foreign assets) in overall Chinese crude imports has long been unimpressive. It is true that Chinese NOCs have invested in exploration, development, and pipeline and refinery projects in such varying places as Iran, Sudan, Kazakhstan, and Kuwait, but equity oil—the key indicator for a 'successful' going abroad policy—has hovered around some 15 percent until 2005, and reached 26 percent only in 2007.[37] Still, equity oil accounts for only about 12 percent of China's oil consumption and a mere 1 percent of global oil production.[38]

As for Russia, and despite the country's successful buy-ins in Central and Eastern Europe and Central Asia, its overall record also appears somewhat mixed. Its policy of swapping outstanding debt against infrastructure assets and downstream access was generally successful in Belarus, which sold a majority stake in Beltransgaz, the state-controlled gas network, and in Moldova, which allowed Gazprom to further increase its (already majority) share in Moldova's national gas company, MoldovaGaz. Yet it was only partially successful in Ukraine, a crucial transit country for around 80 percent of Russian gas exports. Kyiv used its geographical monopoly as a bargaining chip and negotiated extended gas deliveries at preferential prices.[39] The 2009 gas dispute only confirmed this finding.

Regarding access, although Russia has secured Turkmen exports, this has not yet translated into real upstream capacities, due to a lack of capital and a poor investment climate in this country.[40] Gazprom has also by and large failed to claim control over Azerbaijan's pivotal energy resources. Despite a recent agreement on gas deliveries to Russia and the growing role of state-owned SOCAL in upstream projects, Baku has kept the country open for foreign companies such as BP. Kazakhstan, in turn, keeps its options open to export natural gas to China and has recently joined a consortium constructing a pan–Central Asia pipeline to be opened in 2013. Bypassing Russia, the gas link also involves Uzbekistan and Turkmenistan and is planned to eventually bring net volumes of 30 billion cubic meters to China.[41]

All of these factors reveal the riskiness of Gazprom's business strategy, which relies on Central Asian reserves to satisfy both domestic demand and export

37. Wu (2008), p. 6; Eurasia Group (2006), p. 3; U.S. Department of Energy (2006); KPMG (2005).
38. Wu (2008), p. 6.
39. Crane and others (2009), pp. 30ff.
40. *International Herald Tribune* (2008d).
41. Reuters (2008).

commitments. In addition, Gazprom's Kremlin-backed strategy to secure foreign markets and strategically lock up reserves has apparently pushed the company to its financial limits. In late 2008 Gazprom faced liabilities of US$49.5 billion, compared to a stock market value of US$85 billion, a trend unlikely to turn any time soon, given the gloomy prospects of the Russian domestic market and falling oil prices.[42] These numbers put in question the realization of the Shtokman and Yamal exploration and production projects, which are needed to make up for falling domestic output.[43] Finally, Russian attempts to use regional forums such as the Shanghai Cooperation Organization for energy-related political purposes were blocked by other member states, especially China, which feared Russian dominance.[44]

In all, anecdotal evidence seems to reveal that there are clear limits for diplomacy when it comes to securing energy supplies or access. Maybe even more important, however, the functioning logic of existing market structures in oil and gas call into question the assumption that countries can improve their competitive position by diplomatic efforts.

Diplomacy versus Market Structures

The market for oil is both global and liquid. These aspects of the oil market have certain implications for energy diplomacy. A change in global supply, for example, translates into a change in prices on a global scale and for all market actors. In other words, it does not matter who gets the crude out of the ground but how much oil is globally available.

Applied to the case of a large consumer country such as China, this fact means that China's investing in foreign reserves will improve the global supply of oil and have a positive effect on the global offer-and-demand balance, regardless of whether the crude is bilaterally contracted or not. If it is bilaterally contracted the additional equity oil (generated by Chinese NOCs and consumed by Chinese consumers) takes pressure off the market, as global demand rises less steeply. If it is not bilaterally contracted, it still enhances the global supply situation and thus has a positive price effect. Hence energy diplomacy would only be detrimental to the liquidity of global markets if it intends to contract and lock up reserves without eventually tapping them, which is hardly the goal of Beijing's energy diplomacy.

42. After temporarily peaking at US$300 billion, Gazprom's stock market value dropped by some 75 percent by the end of 2008. See the *International Herald Tribune* (2008e).

43. See Goldthau (2008b) for a summary assessment of Russia's gas balance.

44. RIA Novosti (2006).

Moreover, because China's energy diplomacy tends to target reserves, which Western IOCs would abstain from addressing for political reasons or because such reserves lack profitability, the price of this additional supply may well bear an additional premium. This premium would translate into a higher price for the barrel compared to the world market price, since exploration and production costs are comparably higher, with projects producing a comparably smaller outcome in terms of equity oil or generating a comparably smaller return on investment; in addition, it translates into—though nonfinancial—political costs; or it does even both. In short, market logic implies that energy diplomacy in oil can easily translate into not only a money loss.[45]

Energy diplomacy targeting foreign supplies makes no difference for producing countries, either. As long as the crude finds its way to global markets—which it usually does unless there is the exceptional situation in which a number of producer countries manage to effectively cartelize the market—ownership does not influence market fundamentals. Upstream projects run by Rosneft instead of, say, BP therefore just imply a larger share of revenues being rechanneled to Russian state pockets instead of to BP's private shareholders. The ownership of these projects does not, however, affect supply or prices. In other words, the globalized character of the oil market balances out attempts to secure supplies by diplomatic means.

Natural gas, by contrast, has very much remained a regionally traded commodity, primarily as a result of its pipeline-based delivery. The share of liquefied natural gas in total global gas trade is projected to strongly increase throughout the next decades, a trend that makes observers suggest that a liquid, globalized market for natural gas could replace the established bilateral system. Yet due to extremely high upfront costs, most LNG contracts are long term, a characteristic that will change only gradually.[46] Gas trade is still by and large restricted to exchange within Eurasia, North America, and the Asia-Pacific region. As a consequence, and with the notable exception of the United States, markets for gas have been slower to liberalize, and much of gas trading is tied to long-term bilateral deals entailing destination clauses. Most contracts peg the price of gas to the price of oil, hence splitting the price risk (remaining with the producer) and the volume risk (remaining with the consumer). This is a result of high upfront costs in exploration

---

45. For a pointed critique of the preconceptions on Chinese bilateral energy deals, see also Press and Gholz (2007); for the opposite perspective, see Stevens (2008).

46. International Energy Agency (2008), pp. 115ff; see also chapter 11, this volume.

and production and a high degree of mutual dependency.[47] Three consequences follow from this prevalent market structure.

First, there is a strong path dependency in mutual gas relations, which is hard to leave. After three-decade-long contractual relations with Central and Western Europe, Russia finds itself firmly tied to these export markets and will remain tied to them for years to come. Serving alternative export markets such as, say, China requires significant investments in additional, yet nonexisting, pipeline infrastructure, which are characterized by long lead times. In turn, while European consumers have the option to contract additional sources, they cannot easily diversify their imports away from Russia.

Second, consumer countries do indeed have an incentive to contract supply on a bilateralized basis and to cut individual deals in order to secure needed gas supply. Gas producers, by the same token, have an incentive to contract with and to exclusively serve individual consumer markets, as this is the only way to secure a stable stream of revenues. Caspian producer countries, for instance, have already started to look eastward and to diversify their customer base. Russia may follow suit.

Third, both producers and consumers have an incentive to buy into gas-rich regions. Producers can strengthen their position as suppliers to large export markets. Russia has pursued this strategy, notably in the Commonwealth of Independent States and particularly the Caspian region. Consumers, in turn, can broaden their import portfolio.

In view of all this, flanking bilateral contracting efforts diplomatically may appear an attractive option for both gas producers and consumers. Yet at least for the Eurasian gas market, two observations raise doubts about both the market power of a dominant supplier and the probability of a rat race among consumers.

First, even if Russia successfully locked up Caspian reserves, this dominant market position does not necessarily translate into a supply or price problem for European consumers. The simple reason for this is that the market structure prevents Moscow from being able to dictate prices, which are pegged to crude oil and thus are beyond the control of the producer. Rationing supply for strategic business or even for political reasons would thus not translate into higher prices but would (while presumably also hurting consumer economies) first and foremost ruin Russian state finances. Hence there is no incentive to translate a dominant position on the supply side of the gas market into limiting the actual offer.

---

47. For contractual details and pricing mechanisms, see ECTS (2007).

Second, competition among consumers for natural gas reserves may be less pronounced than assumed when one takes into account actual demand developments. European demand will increase from around 540 billion cubic meters a year to some estimated 700 billion cubic meters a year in 2030, 477 billion of which will be imports.[48] China, by contrast, is assumed to have a much lower import demand (106 billion cubic meters a year), since the country has decided to base most of its power generation on abundant domestic coal reserves and not on gas.[49] So despite the fact that China has started to buy into Caspian reserves and has announced (though never realized) a large-scale deal with Russia that would bring gas from fields in West Siberia and the Russian Far East, chances are that competition over reserves may turn out to be much less pronounced that commonly assumed, at least among major consumers.[50]

To sum up: energy diplomacy does not really make a difference when it comes to securing supply in oil. Although securing supply is certainly possible in physical terms, a consumer country runs the risk of generating its own supply at significantly higher costs than if the crude was instead bought on world markets. This being said, it however remains to be seen what effects the ongoing financial crisis has on world market structures. The recent Sino-Russian deal on a twenty-year oil delivery of 15 million tons a year in exchange for a Chinese US$15 billion loan to the Russian state-owned oil company Rosneft and a US$10 billion loan to Russian state-owned Transneft (running the country's pipeline infrastructure) might remain an outlier case.[51] It may also stand for a new form of bilateral deal, whose rationale is primarily informed by adverse domestic impacts stemming from the global financial meltdown.

As for gas, diplomatic efforts may in fact facilitate access and thus have an influence on the supply side, although it appears not very likely that a producer can translate control over supplies into market power, while competition among consumers over access may be moderate on Eurasian gas markets—at least under the prevalent market structure, which is characterized by take-off agreements, which all market participants have an incentive to adhere to. It remains to be seen, however, what impact the emerging LNG market has on prevalent market structures. Cartelization is by no means excluded, though it would not take place

48. International Energy Agency (2008), pp. 110, 118.
49. International Energy Agency (2008), p. 118.
50. See, for instance, *Financial Times* (2006); Zang (2008).
51. Reuters (2009).

within the "Gas Troika," but rather on the industry level (such as between Gazprom and Sonatrach).

Implications for Global Governance: Energy Diplomacy in Oil and Gas

As shown, both producing and importing countries face limits when it comes to improving their position vis-à-vis competitors by means of energy diplomacy, regarding supply or access, or both. As history shows, reflexes recurring to diplomatic means, including the strategic use of development assistance or military cooperation, tend to occur in times of high commodity prices. During low-price periods, when capital becomes scarce in producer nations and global energy turns into a consumer market, access both for oil and for gas tends to become easier and foreign investment more welcome. Hence the present trend toward enhanced state efforts to flank energy deals does not necessarily challenge existing market structures the way it is suggested in current public debates; in the end, it probably does not require a fundamental reassessment of the rules of the game in global energy. Yet energy diplomacy may exert some negative side effects on two crucial aspects of global energy: investment and transparency. Here energy diplomacy may in fact have significant policy implications and may require action.

As stressed earlier, investment decisions based on political calculations tend to ignore some of the underlying economics. As Chinese upstream investments in Africa reveal, political opportunity may influence both investment location and volume; this often implies a lower return on investment compared to exploration and production projects driven by hard business fundamentals. As a consequence, energy diplomacy entails the risk of money flowing into the "wrong" projects and thus negatively affecting allocation of investment.

For an individual consumer such as China, this may imply just a suboptimal deal and simply put an additional chunk on the price for a barrel—which may be bearable from a political point of view, where the primary goal is to secure supply and not to optimize costs. Yet if this strategy is pursued by a large number of market participants, including producers, the overall effect can be highly detrimental on an aggregate, global level, as the resulting suboptimal allocation of capital implies a suboptimal development of available supply and may eventually translate even into a supply gap. In addition, politically driven or flanked exploration and production projects may crowd out private sector investments, adding to the overall negative supply effect. In sum, energy diplomacy could prevent supply from developing as it would if market signals were the drivers.

In addition, politically driven or flanked investments decrease market transparency, a crucial problem in global oil. To be sure, uncertainty and lack of transparency are nothing new in the oil sector. For decades the bulk of market participants (except for OECD member states) have failed to provide detailed information on their supply and demand developments. Major producer countries such as Saudi Arabia keep information on their upstream capacities undisclosed, while major consumers such as China do not reveal data on their real consumption.[52] As a consequence, and put simply, the oil price is formed on educated guesses rather than on real market fundamentals, a fact some observers blame for price volatility.[53] When upstream deals are flanked politically or even backed financially by state capital or guarantees, financial markets may no longer finance large-scale projects, decreasing transparency regarding not only volume of investment but also business fundamentals.[54] Both suboptimal allocation of capital and decreased transparency affect supply, price, and volatility.

In view of this, the challenge for global energy governance is to strengthen the mechanisms that enhance market transparency and improve allocation of investment. Major producers such as Russia obviously have very little incentive to join in global efforts targeting binding investment conditions, for this would affect their domestic regulatory framework. Yet major consumer nations such as China and India may indeed develop an interest in leveling the playing field. Their NOCs could become the drivers of such a process, as their growth potential faces limits in regions in which their private Western counterparts have already been excluded. Chinese oil companies' strategic decisionmaking appears at least partly driven by a desire to maximize profit. Hence, China and India may at some point develop an interest in reliable rules of access as well, thus eventually siding with the established Western consumer nations.

Finally, it also remains to be seen what impact the financial crisis, which started in 2008 and is likely to continue for some time, will have on the allegedly mighty NOCs. Chances are that, voluntarily or not, their cost-benefit calculations might alter rather profoundly.[55]

---

52. See chapter 12, this volume.
53. Tempest (2001); Brook and others (2004).
54. See, for instance, Evans and Downs (2006).
55. The *Financial Times* (2007) recently identified Saudi Aramco (Saudi Arabia), Gazprom (Russia), CNPC (China), NIOC (Iran), PDVSA (Venezuela), Petrobras (Brazil), and Petronas (Malaysia) as the "New Seven Sisters." Gazprom has recently announced a cut of RUR 200 billion (or EUR 4.4 billion) out of initially planned RUR 920 billion investments in 2009, a function of faltering oil prices and reduced demand (Kommersant 2009). Chinese NOCs, by contrast, have started buy-ins into Western resource companies such as Rio Tinto, with energy companies likely to follow suit.

References

Agence France-Presse. 2008. "Russia and Venezuela Ink Energy Pacts, Eye 'Counterweight' to US." September 25.

Alden, Christopher, Daniel Large, and Ricardo Soares de Oliveira. 2007. *China Returns to Africa: A Rising Power and a Continent Embrace.* London: C. Hurst.

Bahgat, Gawdat. 2003. "Pipeline Diplomacy: The Geopolitics of the Caspian Sea Region." *International Studies Perspectives* 3 (3): 310–27.

BP. 2007. *Statistical Review of World Energy 2007.* London.

Brook, Anne-Marie, Robert Price, Douglas Sutherland Niels Westerlund and Christophe André. 2004. *Oil Price Developments. Drivers, Economic Consequences, and Policy.* OECD Working Paper 412. Paris: OECD.

Champion, Marc, and Guy Chazan. 2006. "Russia's Gas Diplomacy Fuels Realignment of Former Soviet Bloc." *Wall Street Journal,* January 30.

Chen, Shaofeng. 2008. "Motivations behind China's Foreign Oil Quest: A Perspective from the Chinese Government and the Oil Companies." *Journal of Chinese Political Science* 13, no. 1.

China Daily. 2006. "China's Overseas Investment to Reach US$60 Bln in 2010." September 10.

Crane, Keith, and others. 2009. "Imported Oil and U.S. National Security." Washington: RAND Corporation.

Downs, Erica. 2004. The Chinese Energy Security Debate. The China Quarterly 177:21–41.

———. 2005. *China's Quest for Energy Security.* Washington: Rand.

———. 2007. "The Fact and Fiction of Sino-African Energy Relations." *China Security* 3, no. 3: 42–68.

The Economist. 2008. "Venezuela and the Kremlin: The Russians Are Here." September 11.

ECTS. 2007. *Putting a Price on Energy: The International Pricing Mechanisms for Oil and Gas.* Brussels.

Energy Information Administration. 2006. *Sudan: Country Analysis Brief.*

Eurasia Group. 2006. *China's Overseas Investments in Oil and Gas Production.* New York: United States—China Economic and Security Review Commission.

Evans, Peter, and Erica Downs. 2006. "Untangling China's Quest for Oil through State-Backed Financial Deals." Policy Brief 154. Brookings.

Evans, Peter. 2006. *Japan: Bracing for an Uncertain Energy Future.* Brookings.

Financial Times. 2006. "Russia Pledges Gas Pipelines to China." March 21.

———. 2007. "The New Seven Sisters: Oil and Gas Giants Dwarf Western Rivals." March 11.

Gaddy, Clifford, and Barry W. Ickes. 2008. *Russia's Addiction. The Political Economy of Resource Dependence.* Brookings.

Gazprom. 2007. *Annual Financial Report 2006.* Moscow.

Goldthau, Andreas. 2008a. Resurgent Russia? Rethinking Energy Inc. Five Myths about the "Energy Superpower." *Policy Review* 147: 53–63.

———. 2008b. "Rhetoric Versus Reality: Russian Threats to European Energy Supply." *Energy Policy* 36: 686–92.

Holslag, Jonathan. 2006. "China's New Mercantilism in Central Africa." *African and Asian Studies* 5, no. 2: 133–69.

Houser, Trevor. 2008. "The Roots of Chinese Oil Investment Abroad." *Asia Policy* 5 (January).

Human Rights Watch. 2003. *Sudan, Oil and Human Rights.* New York.

International Energy Agency. 2007. *World Energy Outlook 2007.* Paris.

———. 2008. *World Energy Outlook 2008.* Paris.

International Herald Tribune. 2007. Russia, Kazakhstan and Turkmenistan Sign Caspian Gas Pipeline Deal. December 20.

————. 2008a. Gazprom Pays Price for Its Aggressive Takeovers. December 30, 2008.

————. 2008b. Libya's Gaddafi Visits Russia on Arms Drive. October 29.

————. 2008c. Russia, Iran, and Qatar Move toward Forming Gas Cartel. October 22.

————. 2008d. Audit Firm Confirms Huge Turkmen Gas Reserves. October 14

————. 2008e. Gazprom, Once Mighty, Is Reeling. December 29.

Jofi, Joseph. 1999. "Pipeline Diplomacy: The Clinton Administration's Fight for Baku-Ceyhan." Princeton University (www-03wws.princeton.edu/research/cases/pipeline.pdf).

Kang Wu. 2008. "China's Overseas Oil and Gas Investment: Motivations, Strategies, and Global Impact." *Oil and Gas Energy Law* 6, no. 1: 1–9.

Kommersant. 2009. "Gasprom upal do $25 sa barrel," 25 February. (www.kommersant.ru/doc.aspx?DocsID=1125617).

Konings, Piet. 2007. "China and Africa." *Journal of Developing Societies* 23, no. 3: 341–67.

KPMG. 2005. *Energy Outlook for China.* Hong Kong.

Lall, Marie. 2006. "Indo-Myanmar Relations in the Era of Pipeline Diplomacy." *Contemporary Southeast Asia: A Journal of International and Strategic Affairs* 28, no. 3: 424–46.

Large, Daniel. 2007. "China and the Changing Context of Development in Sudan." *Development* 50, no. 3: 57–62.

Lieberthal, Kenneth, and Mikkal Herberg. 2006. "China's Search for Energy Security: Implications for U.S. Policy." Occasional Paper 17. Seattle: National Bureau of Asian Research.

Ministry of Commerce of China. 2008. *2007 Statistical Bulletin of China's Outward Foreign Direct Investment.* September 28 (http://hzs2.mofcom.gov.cn/accessory/20080928/1222502733006.pdf).

New York Times. 2007. "Darfur Collides with Olympics, and China Yields." April 13.

————. 2008. "Sudan: Kidnappers Kill 5 Chinese Oil Workers." October 27.

Noel, Pierre. 2008. "Beyond Dependence: How to Deal with Russian Gas." Policy Brief 7. New York: European Council on Foreign Relations.

Paik, Keun-Wook, and others. 2007. "Trends in Asian NOC Investment Abroad." Working Background Paper. London: Chatham House.

Press, Daryl G., and Eugene Gholz. 2007. "Energy Alarmism: The Myths That Make Americans Worry about Oil." Policy Analysis Series. Washington: Cato Institute.

Reuters. 2008. "Kazakhstan Starts Building Gas Pipeline to China." July 9.

————. 2009. "China Lends Russia $25 Bln to Get 20 Years of Oil." February 17 (http://uk.reuters.com/article/marketsNewsUS/idUKLH44422920090217).

RIA Novosti. 2006. "Putin Proposes Shanghai Cooperation Organization (SCO) Energy Club." June 15.

Simpson, Emma. 2006. "Russia Wields the Energy Weapon." BBC News.

Smith, Keith. 2006. Defuse Russia's Energy Weapon. *International Herald Tribune.* January 16.

Socor, Vladimir. 2005. "Eurasia: The Great (Pipeline) Game." *Wall Street Journal.* October 7.

Stern, Jonathan P. 2005. *The Future of Russian Gas and Gazprom.* Oxford University Press.

————. 2006. *The Russian-Ukrainian Gas Crisis of January 2006.* Oxford Institute for Energy Studies.

Stevens, Paul. 2008. "National Oil Companies and International Oil Companies in the Middle East: Under the Shadow of Government and the Resource Nationalism Cycle." *Journal of World Energy Law and Business* 1, no. 1.

Stulberg, Adam N. 2008. *Well-Oiled Diplomacy: Strategic Manipulation and Russia's Energy Statecraft in Eurasia.* SUNY Press.

Taylor, Ian. 2006. "China's Oil Diplomacy in Africa." *International Affairs* 82, no. 5: 937–59.

———. 2007. "Arms Sales to Africa: Beijing's Reputation at Risk." *China Brief* 7, no. 7.

Tempest, Paul. 2001. "Distortion, Illusion and Confusion: How to Improve Global Oil Market Data." *Energy Policy* 29, no. 5: 341–43.

Torbakov, Igor. 2003. "Russian-Turkmen Pacts Mark Strategic Shift for Moscow in Central Asia." *Eurasia Insight,* April 15.

Tull, Denis. 2007. "China's Engagement in Africa: Scope, Significance and Consequences." *Journal of Modern African Studies* 45, no. 3: 459–79.

UNCTAD. 2006. *World Investment Report.* New York: United Nations.

U.S. Department of Energy. 2006. Energy Policy Act 2005, Section 1837. "National Security Review of International Energy Requirements."

Woods, Ngaire. 2008. "Whose Aid? Whose Influence? China, Emerging Donors, and the Silent Revolution in Development Assistance." *International Affairs* 84, no. 6: 1205–21.

Wu, Kang. 2008. "China's Overseas Oil and Gas Investment: Motivations, Strategies, and Global Impact." *Oil and Gas Energy Law* 6, no. 1.

Xiaojie, Xu. 2007. Chinese NOCs' Overseas Strategies: Background, Comparison, and Remarks. Houston: James A. Baker III Institute for Public Policy, Rice University.

Yergin, Daniel. 1991. *The Prize: The Epic Quest for Oil, Money, and Power.* New York: Simon and Schuster.

Zang, Kelly. 2008. "Russia to Delay Construction of Proposed Gas Pipeline to China." *Thomson Financial News.*

Ziba, Norman. 2005. "Russia's Gas Weapon." *International Herald Tribune,* December 21.

3

Managing the Patchwork of Agreements in Trade and Investment

Yulia Selivanova

E nergy markets are constantly evolving, making it difficult to adopt international rules for each new circumstance. However, current trends toward
tighter supply and increased demand require a reliable framework for trade and
investment in oil and gas. The energy sector accounts for the biggest share of trade
flows (20 percent in 2007) and is set to grow further in the future.[1] At the same
time, bilateral disputes, related mainly to the gas trade, have prompted the question whether any international rules could reduce tensions and provide speedier
resolution to disputes.

Energy is different from any other commodity for a number of reasons. First,
energy is more vital to the economic and social development of the modern world
than any other good. Second, hydrocarbon resources are distributed very unevenly
throughout the world. Third, energy trade is often linked to the fixed infrastructure necessary for the transportation of hydrocarbons and electricity. In addition,
pipelines and transmission grids require substantial investments of high specificity,
that is, such transportation networks can be used only for transportation of specified energy products.

---

1. "Trading in a Globalising World," *World Trade Report* (www.wto.org/english/res_e/
booksp_e/anrep_e/world_trade_report08_e.pdf [February 2009]).

Moreover, concerns over security of energy supply and demand, both accentuated by the recent unprecedented fluctuations of the oil price, put a special premium on investment rules.[2] While the demand for energy is set to grow in the long term and new major consumers in emerging economies are contributing to demand growth, there has been no parallel response on the supply side: investments in exploration and production are lagging behind. Compounding this problem, the ongoing global financial crisis will surely put an additional constraint on investment in energy projects. However, even before oil prices plummeted to US$40 a barrel, there was a sense that investments were not flowing into energy projects at the rate that would ensure adequate supply. Moreover, growing resource nationalism prompted a number of disputes between investors and host governments and a consequent reversal of investment contracts.

National oil companies (NOCs) in producing states are growing and are increasingly competing with international majors. Such newly emerging giants are interested in investment abroad, both upstream and downstream. These companies also emphasize the need for fairer trade in state-of-the-art technologies. The issue of technology transfer increasingly influences investment decisions. In addition, the challenge of climate change necessitates an adequate response to increased energy consumption. Investment in and trade of renewable energy technologies, as well as state-of-the-art and more efficient conventional energy technologies, may require an adjustment of existing multilateral trade and investment rules.

These trends call into question the present institutional structure, which is characterized by multilateral, plurilateral, regional, and bilateral treaties that cover differing and sometimes overlapping spheres of energy trade and investment. The rules of the multilateral system embodied in the World Trade Organization (WTO) were for a long time perceived to leave the energy sector outside of its scope. It is, however, without doubt that these rules do indeed cover trade in energy, although they do not specifically address major issues in energy trade (given that discussions on the creation of such specific rules were stalled in the General Agreement on Tariffs and Trade, or GATT). Although this fact may reduce the relevance of WTO rules for energy trade, it certainly does not exclude energy from WTO coverage in general. The existing GATT-WTO agreements do, however, entail a traditional bias toward market access and thus do not fully address the issues of export restrictions and investment protection, commonly regarded as the most crucial challenges in oil and gas.

2. Oil prices increased from US$3 a barrel in the early 1970s to a record high in mid-2008. On July 3, 2008, West Texas Intermediate (WTI) oil reached US$146.69; this was followed by a declining trend, leading to WTI trading at US$40.04 on February 26, 2009.

The major existing plurilateral example of a comprehensive energy trade and investment agreement is the Energy Charter Treaty (ECT). Composed of fifty-two member states, the ECT includes in its membership countries across the Eurasian continent, including those of the European Union, former Soviet Union republics, and Japan. Moreover, the importance of the ECT is highlighted by its including not only producer and consumer countries but also transit states. Furthermore, the ECT includes among its members countries that are not yet WTO members. Finally, it is the only international treaty that sets legal norms specific to energy trade and investment. This last element—investment rules enforceable through a dispute settlement system—makes the ECT the only international energy investment treaty. Regarding energy trade, it has been questioned what role the ECT should play, considering the parallel WTO framework.

Some regional trade agreements include specific rules on energy trade and investment; for instance, the North American Free Trade Agreement (NAFTA) contains a chapter on energy. Moreover, a multitude of bilateral trade and investment treaties cover the energy sector. However, the effectiveness of such regional and bilateral agreements for regulation of energy trade and investment has been questioned. First, these are general agreements that cover trade and investment across sectors, so they do not provide specific rules for energy commodities. Second, these agreements often contain exemptions precisely with respect to energy. Third, such important aspects of energy trade as transit cannot be regulated by bilateral treaties, and regional treaties only partially fill the gap. Fourth, many regional and bilateral treaties lack an effective enforcement system.

Despite an acknowledgment of the importance of rules governing energy trade and investment, the above issues make negotiations of such binding rules very difficult. Despite their obvious interdependence, the interests of consuming and producing countries differ significantly, and finding common ground is challenging. These distinctive features lead to the question of whether energy trade and investment can be effectively regulated by a general international legal framework or whether a more specialized framework is needed. Increasing reliance on internationally traded energy, considerations of security of supply and demand, and the need for adequate investment require predictability and transparency, which could be achieved most effectively through a multilateral legal framework.

The Existing Framework

The current international energy trade and investment framework consists of multiple agreements regulating international trade relations on multilateral, regional, and bilateral levels.[3] These agreements rarely contain rules specific to trade in energy products and materials. Those few regional or bilateral trade agreements that address energy specifically normally contain reservations with respect to investments in the energy sector.[4]

At several points during the past couple of decades energy-specific international forums multiplied, most notably in the aftermath of the oil crises of the 1970s. Most regional agreements reached in these forums set forth cooperative frameworks rather than rules to regulate energy trade.[5] The role of such cooperative frameworks should not be underestimated, especially in the energy sector, as energy has been treated in a political context for quite some time. Nevertheless, legally binding international norms that can be enforced have become ever more important.

Issues related to energy were not extensively discussed during the formation of GATT. Trade in commodities was, however, generally addressed during negotiations on the creation of the International Trade Organization.[6] One of the likely reasons for the absence of energy-specific rules in GATT is that energy-exporting countries were not among the founding contracting parties of the agreement.[7] Furthermore, energy had been treated in a political context for a long time likely due to its strategic nature, and therefore many countries were apprehensive about negotiating international, legally binding, rules. During the Tokyo (1973–79) and Uruguay (1986–94) rounds, GATT contracting parties attempted to address energy-related issues such as natural resource subsidies and energy dual

3. Multilateral agreements are included in the WTO framework; the agreements are both general (GATT, TRIPs, Agreement on Technical Barriers to Trade) and sector specific (Agreement on Agriculture, Agreement on Trade in Civil Aircraft). Regional agreements are meant to increase liberalization level among the trade partners.

4. Selivanova (2007), p. 9.

5. For instance, the Association of Southeast Asian Nations (ASEAN) countries signed the Agreement of ASEAN Energy Cooperation, which covers development and use of all forms of energy, including renewables.

6. United Nations (1948). The Havana Charter initially contained an extensive chapter on intergovernment commodity agreements, including control agreements that involve regulation of production, regulation of prices, and quantitative control of exports and imports of primary commodities. Moreover, the text of the Havana Charter emphasizes the role of natural resources in economic development. For instance, members can adopt measures that are necessary to promote the establishment or development of a particular industry for the processing of primary commodities for "fuller and more economic use of the applicant Member's natural resources."

7. Although Norway, the Netherlands, and the United Kingdom are founding contracting parties to GATT, their energy resources were discovered at end of the 1950s and the beginning of the 1960s.

pricing, export restrictions, and export taxes, but energy-endowed countries resisted.[8]

Although there was a period of misperception that energy was out of the scope of the multilateral trade system, it is now commonly accepted that WTO agreements apply equally to energy as to any other product.[9] However, these general rules are arguably not designed to tackle some of the issues pertinent to energy trade. Trade-restrictive practices related to energy are mainly found on the export side, while multilateral trade rules have been devised in a manner to address import barriers to a larger extent than export barriers.

The traditional focus of GATT has been foreign market access for domestic products rather than access to foreign supplies. This focus may be because these rules were meant to deal with manufactured products that could be normally produced without limitation in many countries, due account being made to the theory of comparative advantage.[10] But manufactured goods do not encounter natural endowment constraints as do hydrocarbons, which are finite resources and unequally distributed around the world. Countries that possess such finite resources are usually driven in their development and exploration decisions by three domestic policy considerations. One, they want to ensure maximum rent from their development and exploration. Two, they want to use their natural resources to promote domestic industrialization. Three, they want to promote certain social policy objectives. These domestic policy considerations have provoked controversies in the WTO (for instance, dual pricing has been perceived by some WTO members to be inconsistent with WTO rules).[11]

Some features of the energy sector point to the need for energy-specific rules. The need for energy security and for solutions to climate change problems call into question how WTO rules can address these challenges.

---

8. Uruguay Round, Group of Negotiations on Goods, Negotiating Group on Natural Resource–Based Products, Meeting of February 11, 1987, Note by the Secretariat, MTN.GNG/NG3/1 (February 26, 1987), para. 10-11; see also Uruguay Round, Trade Negotiations Committee, Subsidies and Countervailing Measures, Communication from the Permanent Delegation of Mexico, MTN.TNC/W/38 (November 26, 1990).

9. Several WTO agreements are directly relevant to trade in energy: GATT, General Agreement on Trade in Services, Agreement on Technical Barriers to Trade, Agreement on Trade-Related Investment Measures, Agreement on Subsidies and Countervailing Measures, Agreement on Government Procurement. World Trade Organization (2000).

10. The theory of comparative advantage suggests that it is more efficient for countries to specialize in production of those goods that they can produce relatively more cheaply compared to other countries and other products. Mankiw (1998), pp. 54–55.

11. Selivanova (2004), pp. 559–602.

Challenges for the Existing Framework

The challenges facing the existing framework are linked to the reliance of the energy trade to fixed infrastructure; the transit of energy through other countries; and the environmental implications of energy use.

Fixed Infrastructure

A significant part of international energy trade is linked to fixed infrastructure built specifically for the purpose of carrying hydrocarbons or electricity. The network dependence of energy implies that the elimination of import barriers alone is not enough for effective liberalization. This link between energy trade and fixed infrastructure puts an additional emphasis on two issues: the framework for investment in highly capital-intensive infrastructure and the conditions for access to this infrastructure, neither of which is addressed in a meaningful way by WTO rules.[12]

Discussions regarding the creation of an investment framework were held in the WTO in the initial stage of the Doha round, but this topic was eventually excluded from negotiations at the Cancun ministerial in 2003. Arguably, through the General Agreement on Trade in Services (GATS), these investment issues have been addressed to a limited extent; this coverage is not sufficient, however. Many disciplines of GATS cover issues with specific commitments by WTO members in various services sectors. The problem is that very limited commitments were taken in energy services. When relevant commitments are undertaken and GATS disciplines do apply, they are limited to the services sector. However, the energy trade is not limited to aspects of energy services. An energy investment framework is needed that goes beyond services.

The issue of access to energy transportation and distribution infrastructure is also not addressed by WTO rules. Such access is often controlled not by governments themselves, but by powerful incumbent companies that are often monopolies supplying energy to the national market. These companies can claim lack of capacity and charge transportation fees that far exceed the cost of services rendered. Although the behavior of so-called state trading enterprises is addressed in Article XVII of GATT, the coverage is limited to nondiscrimination of purchases or sales by such enterprises.[13] Furthermore, while GATS contains provisions that

---

12. Mernier (2008), p. 43.

13. The definition covers companies that were granted, formally or in effect, exclusive or special privileges. Arguably, control over energy transportation infrastructure qualifies as such privilege.

deal with the conduct of monopolies and exclusive service suppliers, these provisions are limited to the services sector.[14]

The WTO does, however, have a successful example of negotiating a sector agreement that covers access to infrastructure, namely the GATS Agreement on Basic Telecommunications Services and its Reference Paper. The United States and Norway proposed to devise a reference paper for energy services modeled on this Reference Paper and to develop rules for cross-border energy trade. The purpose of the energy services reference paper would have been to ensure transparency in the formulation and implementation of rules; nondiscriminatory third-party access to and interconnection with energy networks and grids; nondiscriminatory objective and timely procedures for the transportation and transmission of energy; and requirements preventing certain anticompetitive practices for energy services in general. The negotiations did not, however, succeed.[15]

Although the idea of a reference paper in the energy sector is pertinent, despite similarities between the telecommunications and energy sectors (highly regulated markets characterized by large incumbent suppliers and regulation), there are important differences between telecommunications and energy that need to be taken into account. Most significantly, the energy sector requires more sophisticated regulation due to possible impact on the environment and to issues related to energy efficiency and security of supply (including noninterruption of energy flows).[16]

Energy Transit

Energy transit is commonly understood as energy originating in one country (exporter), transiting at least one other country (transit country), and then entering the destination country (importer). Secure transit through the territory of other states is crucial for cross-border trade in energy. Energy transit is different from transit of most other goods in that it is often grid bound and thus capacity restricted. In the transit of most goods (transported in vessels, trucks, or railway cars through a common carrier infrastructure) the issue of capacity constraints can

---

14. See Articles VIII and IX of GATS. Article VIII is especially relevant to gas transportation and distribution services; it requires members to ensure that the incumbent natural monopolist in the transportation and distribution market does not act in a manner inconsistent with the most-favored-nation principle and with the member's specific commitments. In addition, if such a monopoly supplier competes in the supply of a service outside the scope of its monopoly rights, the member has to ensure that the incumbent monopoly does not abuse its position subject to the member's specific commitments.

15. Selivanova (2007), p. 22.

16. Selivanova (2007).

be solved by queuing, without adverse implications, as the goods can usually be easily stored. The time-capacity factor does not adversely affect transit.

But because energy transportation is capacity restricted and energy is more difficult to store, the time aspect matters. Energy transit normally requires the creation of infrastructure built specifically for this purpose. Volumes are programmed on a long-term basis, since pipelines have a limited use for transporting a specific fuel and involve significant investments. (No excess capacity is normally built without being backed by available supplies.) Freedom of energy transit is thus linked not just (and not so much) to the nondiscriminatory use of existing infrastructure as to creating additional transit capacity.

Although GATT Article V establishes a general rule of freedom of transit (including energy transit) based on nondiscrimination, it does not address issues that are crucial for energy flows, such as noninterruption of transit flow and nonimpediment of building new infrastructure if available capacity is not sufficient.[17] For the latter an effective investment framework is needed. Moreover, the energy sector is dominated by monopoly enterprises that could obstruct access to transit infrastructure, and it is not clear how their behavior can be tackled under general WTO rules.[18] Article V remains one of the provisions little tested in the dispute settlement, although there are many cases in which transit, in particular of energy, has been used by the transit state to extract excessive transit fees or otherwise obstruct

---

17. It sets forth, inter alia, that "there shall be freedom of transit through the territory of each contracting party, via the routes most convenient for international transit, for traffic in transit to or from the territory of other Contracting Parties." Article V further states that "except in cases of failure to comply with applicable customs laws and regulations, such traffic coming from or going to the territory of contracting parties shall not be subject to any unnecessary delays or restrictions and shall be exempt from customs duties and from all transit duties or other charges imposed in respect of transit, except charges for transportation or those commensurate with administrative expenses." Only reasonable, cost-related charges are thus allowed. World Trade Organization (2000).

18. Most WTO provisions, including those contained in Article V, are primarily directed at governments. Certain provisions of GATT and GATS, however, require WTO members to ensure the conformity of their monopoly suppliers with provisions of WTO agreements. For instance, Article XVII requires that state trading enterprises, in their purchases or sales involving either imports or exports, act in a manner consistent with the general principles of nondiscriminatory treatment. Furthermore, Article XVIII obliges members to ensure that their monopoly suppliers, which compete in the supply of service outside of their monopoly rights, do not abuse their monopoly position. The scope of this obligation is limited to the extent to which members undertook specific commitments, and those are arguably not extensive in the field of pipeline transportation. Moreover, transit of energy by pipeline is distinct from providing the services of pipeline transportation, as normally energy companies do not provide these services but rather seek pipeline access to supply their energy to a distinct market.

energy trade, in particular in the case of states that are dependent on transit. The lack of GATT and now WTO disputes with respect to transit may reflect the fact that many of the states where transit problems occur are not yet members of the WTO.[19]

In summary, energy transit, when it is linked to fixed infrastructure, is very different from transit of other goods and requires additional disciplines at the multilateral level. The dependency of energy trade on fixed infrastructure, inter alia in the context of transit, also makes it less sensible to shift energy trade from a multilateral framework and try to regulate it at a bilateral level.

Environment and Climate Change

Another aspect of energy production and use that puts a high premium on multilateral engagement is the environmental and especially climate implications of energy use. While environmental challenges can be tackled at a local level, an approach to the climate change problem requires a multilateral response. While the Kyoto Protocol sets up a framework for addressing climate change, policies to pursue the goals set out in the protocol are to be designed at a national level. Moreover, the forthcoming negotiations are aimed at setting the post-Kyoto framework for climate change mitigation.

These policies have a certain dimension that may have implications for energy trade. To what extent can national climate change policies be obstructed by multilateral trade rules? It is true that the GATT-WTO rules were negotiated when the problem of changing climate was not as acute as it is now. Policies aimed at solving the climate change problem would be easier to implement if adjustments in the multilateral trade rules were made. For instance, in the context of climate change, interest in the development of new sources of energy and cleaner technologies and equipment has prompted a question as to whether, in the trade system, a different subset of rules and disciplines should apply to clean energy.

How can policies to combat climate change be affected by the WTO rules?[20] There indeed are some issues to consider; for example, financial support for pro-

---

19. Selivanova (2007), p. 18.
20. Article 3, paragraph 5, of the UNFCC provides that "measures taken to combat climate change, including unilateral ones, should not constitute a means of arbitrary or unjustifiable discrimination or a disguised restriction on international trade." The protocol (article 2) provides that its parties "shall strive to implement policies and measures . . . in such a way as to minimize adverse effects, including . . . effects on international trade."

ducers of renewable energy might fall under WTO subsidies rules.[21] Furthermore, the requirement that energy taxes and all domestic laws and regulations should not be applied in a discriminatory manner might impede promotion of cleaner energy technologies.[22] Technical regulations and standards to promote the efficient use of energy should be nondiscriminatory and cannot constitute unnecessary obstacles to trade.[23] Therefore, for the promotion of clean energy, the development of international standards is important, as such standards would facilitate nondiscriminatory market access and consequently promote the spread of clean energy products and technologies.

CARBON TAX

One of the policies used to address climate change is a carbon tax. Carbon dioxide and energy taxes can be applied directly to fuels, to electricity, and to downstream industries that use energy as input on the basis of the amount of carbon dioxide emitted or energy consumed in their production.[24]

The pertinent question arises if countries pursuing environmental objectives could discriminate among energy goods and materials on the basis of the technologies used in the production of such goods. They might wish to impose lower taxes on goods and materials that have been produced using environmentally friendly technologies. The answer to this question is not straightforward. This case appears to be especially complicated if final goods possess identical physical characteristics and have the same end use, such as electricity generated by nuclear power and that generated by renewable sources. In this case, it would be difficult

---

21. As set forth in the Agreement on Subsidies and Countervailing Measures.

22. According to GATT's article 3, "The products of the territory of any contracting party imported into the territory of any other contracting party shall not be subject, directly or indirectly, to internal taxes or other internal charges of any kind in excess of those applied, directly or indirectly, to like domestic products." The national treatment requirement exists with respect to internal taxes and charges, laws and regulations. Internal taxes for imported energy materials and products have to be not higher than for like materials and products that are domestically originated. National treatment applies after the product has been imported into the territory of the respective state. The requirement is applicable to nondiscriminatory treatment of like products. Exported products can be taxed differently from products destined for domestic consumption. The likeness of products is determined based on several factors: physical characteristics, end uses, consumers' tastes and preferences, and tariff classification. The Appellate Body mandates nonlike differentiation of products based on health risks, as such risks are related to physical properties and affect consumers' tastes and habits. World Trade Organization (2001). ("EC—Measures Affecting the Prohibition of Asbestos and Asbestos Products," WT/DS135/AB/R, para. 113).

23. Article 2 of the Agreement on Technical Barriers to Trade (1999, p. 122).

24. Trade Agreements, Petroleum and Energy Policies, UNCTAD, UNCTAD/ITCD/TSB/9 (2000).

to argue that differently generated types of electricity are not like products and can be treated differently for the tax purposes.

Several WTO disputes dealing with environmental taxes have been considered in the WTO dispute settlement system. For instance, the European Commission (EC) brought a claim against the U.S. tax on automobiles.[25] The tax's objective was to create an incentive to purchase more fuel-efficient cars. The EC argued that the tax was inconsistent with Article III, paragraph 2, of GATT, since most cars affected by the measure were European. The panel concluded, however, that fuel-inefficient imported cars could be treated less favorably, as they were not like fuel-efficient domestic cars.[26] In another case, called the Superfund case, the panel examined the U.S. tax on petroleum imposed with the aim of financing the cleanup of hazardous waste sites.[27] In this case the panel allowed the imposition of domestic environmental taxes, although it found that some aspects of the U.S. law were inconsistent with Article III of GATT.

Without doubt the WTO framework allows room for environmental tax measures. However, taxes related to processes that do not affect physical characteristics of products (such as taxes on carbon dioxide emission during the production process) remain controversial.

Border Tax Adjustments

Border tax adjustments are used to refund domestic taxes to companies upon exportation in countries with high environmental standards, as the energy-intensive products produced in these countries become less competitive compared to foreign products that are not subject to such regulations. However, there are no clear-cut criteria in WTO agreements for defining the eligibility of some border tax adjustments. According to the Subsidies and Countervailing Measures (SCM) Agreement, prior-stage cumulative indirect taxes can be exempted at the border when levied on inputs that are consumed in the production of the exported product; this includes inputs that are physically incorporated, energy, fuels, and oil used in the production process.[28] The adjustment does not pose a problem when it is an energy tax on the product itself being levied or reimbursed at the border, for instance a tax on an energy material or product.

25. GATT (1994).
26. GATT (1994), US—Autos, paragraphs 5.24–5.26.
27. GATT (1987), US—Superfund.
28. SCM Agreement, Annex A: Guidelines on Consumption of Inputs in the Production Process.

Opinions are divided whether border tax adjustments are permitted under WTO law for taxable inputs that are not physically incorporated in the final product.[29] For instance, it is not clear if a tax on carbon dioxide emissions during production can be adjusted, an issue that needs clarification.

SUBSIDIES TO CLEAN ENERGY

The fact that many renewable technologies are not commercially viable puts an additional premium on the issue of public support for development of such technologies and production. Subsidies can be used for promotion of energy efficient methods of production. The question of use of different support schemes is especially important as governments seek to use different policies to support domestic producers of renewable energy.

The SCM Agreement prohibits support of programs that are contingent upon export performance. Furthermore, if such subsidies are specific to certain enterprises, industries, or groups they would be considered actionable. This means that products benefiting from such subsidies can be subject to countervailing duties. If they cause adverse affects, a WTO member can request a withdrawal of such subsidies.[30] The so-called green, or nonactionable, subsidies—for example, subsidies granted for research and development—were not continued by WTO members. Support programs that are limited to producers of renewable energy would likely meet the specificity criterion of actionable subsidies. If the government, for example, decides to grant financial support to energy production plants using renewable energies, this program would most likely constitute an actionable subsidy.

It is therefore important to design the programs aimed at environmental objectives in a WTO-consistent way, without the risk that products benefiting from such support will be countervailed. One solution could be to devise programs based on horizontal objective criteria of the eligibility for, and the amount of, a subsidy, making eligibility automatic and monitoring compliance. Such criteria and conditions must be transparent: for instance, requiring that carbon dioxide emissions during production not exceed a certain level. It is generally possible to devise programs encouraging energy-efficient use. However, direct support of renewable industries is likely to be considered an actionable subsidy. In the long run negotiating exceptions from subsidy disciplines, similar to green subsidies, should be considered so as to support clean energy technologies, including renewable energy.

29. Selivanova (2007), p. 28.
30. SCM Agreement, Articles 5—7. Clarke and Horlick (2005), p. 686.

REGULATION OF ENERGY TRADE THROUGH A MULTILATERAL FRAMEWORK

Although energy is covered by general WTO rules, these rules are not designed to address the most acute energy problems: the transit rules do not address problems arising during energy transit; there is no investment framework; and climate change requires the adjustment of existing trade rules (which should arguably take place after the post-Kyoto framework is created).

The current Doha round mandate covers energy-related issues only to a limited extent, most notably in the area of energy services and the liberalization of environmental goods and services. Moreover, attempts have been made to specify rules on transit to explicitly include transit through fixed installations such as pipelines, although no crucial additional disciplines are proposed to tackle energy transit problems. In general, if the round succeeds, energy trade is likely to gain from new provisions on trade facilitation.[31]

The most pertinent issues to be addressed include access to fixed infrastructure and the climate change–trade interface. These issues are difficult to tackle on a bilateral or regional basis because they are global and thus need attention in the multilateral forum. Considering the state of play in existing negotiations and also the increasingly differing positions of energy-producing and energy-consuming states, these issues may remain unresolved for many years. The question arises whether regional energy agreements can fill the gap. As noted above, regional trade agreements, with rare exceptions, do not address energy issues beyond the cooperative level; and if they contain energy-related provisions, they are generally restrictive. There is a notable exception though: the Energy Charter Treaty, described below.

Energy Charter Treaty

The ECT is the only intergovernment agreement in the energy field that has legally binding rules backed up by a dispute settlement mechanism; it is the first binding multilateral agreement for the promotion and protection of foreign investment in the energy field; and it is the first multilateral instrument that sets forth detailed principles of energy transit.

The process that resulted in the ECT started after the tearing down of the Berlin Wall. There was a need for energy resources in Western Europe as well as a need of the former Soviet republics for investments to exploit their

---

31. See www.wto.org/english/tratop_e/dda_e/negotiations_summary_e.htm. The impact of additional clarifications of GATT Article V for energy transit is likely to be quite limited.

resources. For energy-producing countries in the territory of the former Soviet Union, the export of energy was the major source of revenue. The European Energy Charter declaration of 1991 set the framework for cooperation based on the principles of nondiscrimination, sovereignty over natural resources, and development of open and efficient energy markets. Furthermore, a legally binding international framework was created in December 1994 with the signing of the ECT, which includes unique international rules in the areas of investment protection, trade, transit, dispute settlement (including investor-state arbitration and interstate arbitration), and energy efficiency.[32] Furthermore, the ECT contains "soft law" provisions on competition, transfer of technology, and access to capital.

The importance of the ECT's role is accentuated by the fact that it is the only forum that is open to all countries along the energy chain: producers, consumers, and transit states as well as industrialized, transition, and developing economies. Furthermore, the ECT includes a significant global dimension: Japan, Mongolia, and the Central Asian states of Kazakhstan, Kyrgyzstan, Tajikistan, Turkmenistan, and Uzbekistan are members. The latest signatories are Pakistan, Afghanistan, and Jordan.

One of the remarkable features of the treaty is its provision confirming the principle of national sovereignty over energy resources (article 18). However, it is also important to note what the ECT does not do. The ECT does not prescribe the structure of the domestic energy sector or the ownership of energy companies or oblige member countries to open their energy sector to foreign investors. In addition, the ECT does not impose mandatory third-party access to energy infrastructure.

TRADE REGIME

A distinctive feature of the ECT is that its rules cover the entire energy chain, including not only investments in production and generation but also the terms under which energy can be traded and transported across various national jurisdictions to international markets. The ECT trade framework is based on the rules of the multilateral trade system as set forth in GATT and other WTO agreements. The nonderogation from the multilateral trade rules is the cornerstone of the ECT.

---

32. The Protocol on Energy Efficiency and Related Environmental Aspects entered into force simultaneously with the treaty, on April 16, 1998.

Moreover, the ECT extends WTO rules for the energy sector to contracting parties that are not yet members of the WTO. Through a "GATT by reference" approach, the ECT made applicable GATT rules to energy trade relations between its contracting parties, at least one of which is not a WTO member.[33]

TRANSIT

During ECT negotiations many felt that general provisions on transit contained in GATT were not sufficiently detailed, because transit transactions in the energy sector are becoming more and more complex. This is especially true with respect to transit fees and access to transit pipelines.[34] More elaborate rules were thought to be needed in addition to GATT Article V to ensure transit on reasonable terms based on the balance between the sovereign interests of states and the need for security and stability of transit. The treaty therefore addresses in a detailed manner the important strategic issue of energy transit. Although ECT provisions on transit essentially reiterate the principle of freedom of transit contained in GATT Article V, they are more detailed and oriented toward energy-related transit issues. Similar to GATT Article V, current treaty transit provisions contained in the ECT Article 7 oblige participating states to take the necessary measures to facilitate transit of energy, consistent with the principle of freedom of transit, and to secure established energy flows.

In addition, the ECT transit regime contains several elements that are absent in the more general GATT framework. For instance, ECT members are under obligation not to obstruct creation of new capacity if transit cannot be carried out through existing infrastructure due to lack of capacity. Transit countries are also under an obligation not to interrupt or reduce transit flows, even if they have disputes with another country concerning this transit. There is a special conciliation procedure for resolution of transit disputes.[35]

The transit protocol to the ECT, the negotiations of which are pending, would elaborate in more detail some specific aspects of energy transit, such as conditions for access to networks and methodologies for calculation of transit tariffs.

33. As of August 2008 this was relevant for eight member countries of the Energy Charter Treaty that are not yet members of the WTO. The ECT thus governs relations between WTO members and non-WTO members as well as between non-WTO members. In relations between two ECT members that are also WTO members, WTO rules apply.

34. Energy Charter Secretariat (2002), p. 29. This paragraph and the following paragraph reference this work extensively, especially Article 7 of the treaty.

35. Energy Charter Secretariat (2002), Article 7, paragraph 7.

INVESTMENT

The need for stability in the relationship between investors and host governments is particularly acute in the energy sector, where projects tend to be long term and highly capital intensive. The ECT takes a balanced approach to investors' access to resources. On the one hand, the treaty is explicit in confirming national sovereignty over energy resources. On the other hand, there is a requirement that rules on the exploration, development, and acquisition of resources are publicly available, nondiscriminatory, and transparent. The treaty provides a reliable and stable interface between this investment and the host government. Once a foreign investment is made, investors are protected against the most important political risks, such as discrimination, expropriation, nationalization, breach of individual investment contracts, damages due to war and similar events, and unjustified restrictions on the transfer of funds.[36] Host states are obliged to grant to investments from other ECT members—as well as to related activities such as management, maintenance, use, enjoyment, and disposal—treatment at least as favorable as that they accord to the investments of their own investors or of investors of other countries.

The nondiscrimination obligation is applicable only to the postinvestment stage—to investments already made. Regarding the process of making investments, there is only a "best endeavor" obligation to grant nondiscriminatory treatment.[37] Furthermore, ECT members undertook not to introduce new restrictions for foreign investors concerning the making of an investment (standstill) and to progressively reduce remaining restrictions (rollback).

Considering that WTO agreements (except to a limited extent through GATS) do not deal with investment policy and only prohibit those investment measures that are inconsistent with obligations of national treatment and prohibition of quantitative restrictions, the investment provisions of the ECT provide an important addition to the WTO framework.[38]

---

36. Article 13 prescribes certain conditions for expropriation. Expropriation needs to be in the public interest, nondiscriminatory, and carried out under due process of law; and a prompt, adequate, and effective compensation needs to be paid. Such compensation has to be calculated at the full market value at the time immediately preceding the announcement of the expropriation; breach of individual investment contracts by a host country that is an ECT member is considered a violation of the treaty. The investor can bring a dispute settlement claim directly against the host state under article 26 of the treaty.

37. Considering the importance of nondiscrimination at the preinvestment stage, negotiations for the supplementary treaty were launched in 1995. Although the text of the agreement was elaborated, political issues prevented a conclusion of negotiations.

38. Selivanova (2007), p. 7.

Disputes

The ECT contains a comprehensive system for settling disputes. The two basic forms of binding dispute settlement are state-to-state arbitration on the interpretation or application of almost all aspects of the treaty (except for competition and environmental issues) and investor-state arbitration for investment disputes.[39] Dispute settlement provisions make a significant contribution to investor confidence and to a more reliable investment environment. There are special provisions, based on the WTO model, for the resolution of interstate trade issues. The treaty also offers a conciliation procedure for transit disputes.

The starting point for all of these mechanisms is the desirability of an amicable agreement between the parties to any dispute. However, in the event that this does not prove possible, the treaty opens a number of additional avenues to promote and reach a settlement.

ECT's Role

The ECT has a unique role as the only energy-specific multilateral agreement that covers all major aspect of international energy turnover: trade, transit, investment, and energy efficiency. It could be argued that the ECT framework is not as complete as it might be and that more detailed rules on transit (emerging in the transit protocol) as well as preinvestment rules are needed. The value of the treaty should not be however underestimated.

The ECT adds value to the existing general WTO framework, which has a much larger constituency. The investment framework and more elaborate transit rules are valuable features, which have not been negotiated in a detailed manner within the WTO. The cornerstone of the ECT is nonderogation from the WTO. Rather, the ECT and WTO frameworks complement each other, creating synergies without unnecessary duplications.

Apart from the legal provisions, the charter process plays an important role in contributing to the dialogue between different groups of players. From this point of view, the ECT has a distinctive role: no other energy-related organization

---

39. If an investor chooses to bring a dispute to arbitration, there are three possible avenues: the International Centre for the Settlement of Investment Disputes, an autonomous international institution with close links to the World Bank; a sole arbitrator or an ad hoc arbitration tribunal established under the rules of the UN Commission on International Trade Law; or an application to the Arbitration Institute of the Stockholm Chamber of Commerce. International arbitral awards are binding and final, and each contracting party is obliged to make provision for the effective enforcement of such awards in its area.

provides a common platform for the development and implementation of binding disciplines among these stakeholders, consumers, producers, and transit states.

Bilateral Agreements

Free trade agreements rarely contain provisions specific to the energy sector. The North American Free Trade Agreement (NAFTA) contains an energy chapter, which applies to measures relating to energy and basic petrochemical goods and covers measures relating to investment and to cross-border trade in services associated with such goods. Energy regulatory measures are subject to national treatment requirements.

NAFTA interprets GATT rules in a stricter way than has been the case in the past and builds upon them, for instance in the area of export duties and restrictions.[40] For instance, parties state their understanding that provisions of GATT incorporated in NAFTA prohibit minimum or maximum export price requirements and minimum or maximum import price requirements in circumstances where any other quantitative restrictions are prohibited.

NAFTA parties may adopt restrictions otherwise justified under GATT with respect to the export of energy or basic petrochemical goods only if they do not impose a higher price for exports of energy or basic petrochemical goods than that charged when such a good is consumed domestically. This requirement covers licenses, fees, taxation, and minimum price requirements.

Mexico has made a number of reservations. It reserved for itself the following activities (including investment and the provision of services): first, exploration and exploitation of crude oil and natural gas; refining or processing of crude oil and natural gas; production of artificial gas and basic petrochemicals and their feedstock and pipelines; and second, foreign trade, transportation, storage, and distribution, up to and including the first-hand sales of crude oil, natural and artificial gas, and basic petrochemicals. The coverage of NAFTA with respect to energy has been substantially limited through these important exemptions by Mexico.

On a regional level, most agreements set forth a framework for cooperation in the energy sector, rather than a legal framework. For instance in 1986 member countries of the Association of Southeast Asian Nations (ASEAN) signed a special Agreement on ASEAN Energy Cooperation. The agreement provides for cooperation in development and use of all forms of energy, including renewables.

---

40. UNCTAD (2000).

The scope of cooperation covers resource investigation, exploration, development, technology transfer, energy conservation techniques, energy security arrangements for emergency situations, and sharing of methodologies.

Very few bilateral trade agreements address energy specifically. Those few that address energy mostly contain reservations with respect to investments in the energy sector. For instance, the free trade agreement between Chile and Mexico contains a number of important exemptions with respect to energy. Chile has reserved national treatment and performance requirements in energy investments in exploration, exploitation, and benefits from hydrocarbons in liquid and gas form. The reservation does not cover storage, transport, and refining of energy materials. Mexico also has made reservations with respect to the energy sector. Only Mexican nationals can acquire, establish, and operate gasoline stations. A similar exemption was made with respect to distribution, transportation, storage, and sale of gas and petroleum. Moreover, there is a 49 percent ceiling on foreign participation in the Mexican companies supplying combustibles and lubricants used by ships, airplanes, and trains. Finally, Mexico has reserved exclusive rights to deny and authorize investments in exploration, exploitation, refining, and processing of crude petroleum and natural gas; production of basic petrochemicals; transportation, storage, distribution, retail, and external trade of crude petroleum, gas, basic petrochemicals; and energy materials and products produced from crude oil.

The free trade agreement between Canada and Chile provides that, in the application of energy regulatory measures, regulatory bodies avoid disruption of contracts to the maximum extent possible. The parties should also seek to implement regulatory measures equitably. The agreement does not pose, however, a positive obligation on its parties with respect to the above matters.

The energy cooperation agreement Petrocaribe was established to facilitate the development of energy policies and plans for the integration of Caribbean countries. The parties agreed to coordinate and harmonize their energy policies on oil and oil derivatives, gas, and electricity and the efficient use of these resources; to advance technological cooperation, training, and development of energy infrastructure; and to promote alternative sources of energy, such as renewable energy. Venezuela has extended credit for supplies of energy with payment periods up to twenty-five years on favorable conditions. Some portions of credit can be paid with goods and services.

However, as stressed above, relatively few bilateral and regional trade agreements contain rules specific to the energy sector. Energy-endowed states appear to be apprehensive about opening their energy sector through international agreements. This is understandable, as they are interested in retaining control over natural resources and increasing their political leverage.

Beyond Patchwork

The increasing reliance on internationally traded energy, considerations of security of supply-demand, and need for investment make a multilateral legal framework ever more pertinent for the regulation of energy. These trends however also challenge the existing rules.

The competition for access to energy resources prompts many consuming countries to favor bilateral agreements with energy producers. Efforts to regulate energy trade and investment on the bilateral level are not likely to be effective. Energy trade has a global or at least a regional character and thus cannot be effectively tackled on a bilateral basis. For instance, serious problems in energy cross-border trade recently have been linked to transit. Transit relations involve at least three states, and often energy flows have to cross several countries to reach the consumer. Therefore the most effective way to deal with cross-border energy flows is to address the issue at a multilateral level. The same holds true for other aspects of energy production and trade.

As far as investment is concerned, a far-reaching plurilateral or bilateral framework in energy would create ambiguity in terms of consistency with WTO rules. There is also the problem of free riding, because favors granted under such deals may necessitate being extended on an MFN basis to all members of the WTO. Further, investors are hesitant to invoke dispute settlement mechanisms in the context of bilateral agreements on energy investments. Although it is not always true that compliance will be better in a multilateral setting, multilateral obligations arguably put more pressure than bilateral obligations on states considering deviation from rules. Also, a multilateral dispute is a matter of government settlement, and a government has more leverage against another state than a foreign investor company would.

The multilateral rules and disciplines that apply to energy trade are thus of great strategic significance. Existing GATT-WTO agreements, however, appear not to be designed to provide for such a framework. They focus on traditional issues of market access and thus do not fully address issues of export restrictions and investment protection, commonly regarded as the most crucial challenges in oil and gas. Existing multilateral trade rules do not address problems related to transit, access to transportation networks, restrictive practices by exporting countries, and monopolistic energy enterprises. Another issue that existing rules are not equipped to address are the implications of environmental damage and climate change. Synergies between an international climate change framework and a multilateral trade framework need to be formed.

With respect to the latter, arguably the most important adjustment, the post-Kyoto Agreement should include all major emitters. The WTO framework should then be adapted to climate change rules. For policies necessary for attainment of climate change objectives, WTO members might consider a dispensation from restrictive WTO provisions on subsidies, taxes, and similar disciplines. This would require at a minimum the political will of all major trading countries, including the United States (which decided not to participate in the Kyoto process). Moreover, the participation of the major emerging economies and emerging major emitters appears necessary both for the agreement on climate change and the adaptation of the WTO rules to any climate change agreement.

Although adaptation of a multilateral framework to current trends is necessary, there may be some limitations. Considering the deadlock in the Doha negotiations, it would certainly be a long-term task and not easy to accomplish. Liberalization of energy services and environmental goods and services are part of the existing WTO agenda. Although the issue of transit has been addressed by several WTO members in the course of trade facilitation discussions, their proposals have been limited to reconfirming the coverage of GATT transit provisions to apply to energy. These proposals did not address crucial issues such as congestion management and creation of additional transportation capacity. At the same time, energy markets and trade are constantly evolving, so it is a real challenge to negotiate multilateral rules for energy trade.

Efforts to regulate the international energy sector in the same way as any other internationally traded commodity are likely to face difficulties.[41] Fossil fuels are finite, and nonrenewable and vital to economic and social development. Moreover, they are under the sovereign control of a relatively small number of resource-owning countries. This means that there is an irreducible political element in international energy trade and that respective policies are controversial because of the strategic importance of fossil fuels.

Most important, the trade system would need to balance the opposing interests of both energy-importing and energy-exporting states. To achieve this balance, it will be necessary to look at the shared principles and interests of countries along the energy value chain, including both producers and consumers.[42] Deci-

---

41. Mernier (2008), p. 43.
42. Mernier (2008).

sions on depletion policy—on whether and how fast national resources are to be developed—are matters for resource-owning governments.[43] International regulation is not likely to succeed if it tries to infringe on these national prerogatives.[44] This was the experience during the preceding rounds of trade negotiations. In fact, all attempts to introduce energy-specific rules in GATT during the Tokyo and Uruguay rounds were resisted by producing countries.

If the interests of producers and consumers of energy are so divergent, is there a chance to adapt a multilateral trade framework to current energy trade and investment trends? The good news is that the interests of all countries across the energy chain are converging. Consumers are interested in a secure supply, producers should be interested in keeping their supply obligations, and transit countries are interested in continuing to benefit from their transport infrastructure. Furthermore, a transparent investment framework would also benefit all. Producers need capital and technology for exploration and development of deposits. Moreover, many NOCs have developed or are developing into global players. These companies are competing increasingly with international majors and are moreover interested in investment downstream and in other producing regions. On one of the most crucial and urgent issues, namely climate change, all countries should find benefit in cooperation, as climate change is a global phenomenon and will affect all countries on the planet, no matter where the emissions are produced.

As for the coexistence of several regional and plurilateral frameworks for energy trade and investment, there is no seeming duplication that renders such coexistence detrimental. Both NAFTA and the ECT build on WTO provisions as far as energy trade is concerned. Moreover, the ECT has an effective investment framework that is backed up by a dispute settlement protocol. Although the transit protocol is still being negotiated, the ECT already provides detailed regulation of transit relations. Furthermore, the intricacies of energy transit seem to necessitate the regulation of this sphere of energy trade by a specialized agency.

Conclusions

The current trends in energy trade necessitate an effective international regulatory framework. Challenges linked to energy trade are of global character, and

---

43. See UN Resolution 1803, December 18, 1962, On permanent sovereignty over natural resources.
44. Mernier (2008), p. 43.

bilateral regulation of such trade would not address pertinent problems. The existing multilateral trade framework is focused on market access and is not designed to tackle energy trade and investment. Transit, access to transport infrastructure, and policies of energy incumbents are among issues that are not substantially addressed by WTO rules. The challenge of adaptation of these rules to current trends should not be underestimated.

Previous attempts to regulate energy through the WTO were resisted by energy-producing countries. Technical aspects of energy trade make the task of adaptation even more difficult. Considering these factors and the stalled Doha negotiations, the question arises, What is the most efficient way for the WTO to address energy issues? The WTO has a focus on trade liberalization and market access. The obvious areas where energy trade would benefit are in liberalization of energy services and energy-related environmental goods and services, issues already included in the current negotiations mandate. After a climate change agreement is reached, there would be an urgent need to adapt a multilateral framework to such an agreement.

Other issues that would be more difficult to address in the WTO are linked to the fact that energy trade depends on fixed infrastructure. This includes but is not limited to transit. Considering the difficult decisionmaking process in the WTO and the fact that interests of its membership are diverging, energy-specific forums like Energy Charter are likely to be more effective in addressing such issues specific to energy trade. The patchwork of organizations is thus not to the detriment but to the help of international regulation of energy trade and investment.

References

Clarke, Peggy A., and Gary N. Horlick. 2005. "The Agreement on Subsidies and Countervailing Measures." In *The World Trade Organization: Legal, Economic, and Political Analysis,* edited by P. F. Macrory, A. E. Appleton, and M. G. Plummer. New York: Springer.

Energy Charter Secretariat. 2002. *The Energy Charter Treaty: A Reader's Guide.* Brussels.

GATT (General Agreement on Tariffs and Trade). 1987. *United States—Taxes on Petroleum and Certain Imported Substances* ("Superfund"), BISD 3 US/13b, L/6175 (June 5).

_____. 1994. *United States—Taxes on Automobiles*, DS31/R, Report of the Panel (October 11).

Mankiw, N. Gregory. 1998. *Principles of Economics.* New York: Dryden.

Mernier, André. 2008. "Setting the Rules of Energy Trade." In *Fundamentals of the Global Oil and Gas Industry.* London: Petroleum Economist.

Selivanova, Yulia. 2004. "World Trade Organization, Rules and Energy Pricing: Russia's Case." *Journal of World Trade* 38, no. 4.

_____. 2007. "The WTO and Energy: WTO Rules and Agreements of Relevance to the Energy Sector." In *Trade and Sustainable Energy Series*. Geneva: International Centre for Trade and Sustainable Development.

UNCTAD. 2000. *Trade Agreements, Petroleum, and Energy Policies*. New York: UN Conference on Trade and Development.

United Nations. 1948. Final Act and Related Documents. Havana Charter for an International Trade Organization. New York: UN Conference on Trade and Employment.

World Trade Organization. 2000. *The Legal Texts: The Results of the Uruguay Round of Multilateral Trade Negotiations*. Cambridge University Press.

_____. 2001. "European Communities—Measures Affecting Asbestos and Asbestos-Containing Products." *Appellate Body Report*, WT/DS135/AB/R.

_____. 2009. *Analytical Index: Guide to WTO Law and Practice*. 2nd ed. Cambridge University Press.

4

Development of the Emerging Biofuels Market

Simonetta Zarrilli

Growing concerns about oil price volatility, independence on foreign oil supplies, and the climate change ramifications of fossil fuel use have drawn substantial attention to renewable energies—including biofuels—as alternatives to meeting the world's energy demand.

Both supply and demand of biofuels are expected to rise dramatically in the coming years, and according to many, the unfolding of this energy revolution may have far-reaching consequences for agricultural production, world trade, and development. Biofuels present many opportunities, especially for those developing countries with land to devote to feedstock production, a favorable climate to grow them, and abundant farm labor. Positive economic, social, and environmental objectives could be fulfilled by increased production, use, and international trade of biofuels.

However, biofuels also raise concerns related to food security, rising food prices, and environmental conservation. Guiding biofuel development to realize multiple potential benefits while minimizing the equally multiple risks requires the implementation of well-tailored policies. The production, trade, and use of

The author wishes to express her thanks to Ron Steenblik and to an anonymous referee for helpful comments on a draft of this chapter.

73

biofuels thus has emerged as one of the key challenges in global energy governance today. While putting the right policy in place is essential for all countries and regions, it is particularly important for developing countries, given that many of them are vulnerable to climate change, are highly dependent on oil imports, have limited capacity to modify their energy portfolio, have huge food-security challenges, and have experienced slow progress in introducing policies that make international trade an effective mechanism for poverty reduction.

The purpose of this chapter is to analyze recent developments in the biofuels sector; present data on production, consumption, and trade flows; analyze current biofuel policies (especially those put in place by leading biofuel-producing and -consuming countries); and examine to what extent these policies have contributed to the shortcomings experienced by the biofuels industry and the recent backlash against them. Some suggestions on governance mechanisms that could make biofuels fulfill their environmental, energy, and developmental goals while minimizing their actual or potential negative side effects are presented.

Explaining Biofuels

The term *biofuels* is commonly used with reference to liquid transportation fuels, that is, ethanol and biodiesel, derived from agricultural, forest, or any other organic material (feedstock). There are several reasons that biofuels have emerged as an alternative source of energy, the most considerable among them being widespread concerns about fossil fuel prices and availability.

While high and volatile oil prices have micro- and macroeconomic effects on all countries, for many developing countries their energy import bills have become unaffordable, and they actively pursue strategies to partially replace imported oil and oil products with domestically produced energy. Also, concerns about high and extremely volatile oil prices as well as long-term oil availability have triggered a renewed quest by many countries to reduce their dependence on foreign sources. The relative abundance of feedstocks in all regions—as opposed to fossil fuels, which are concentrated in a limited number of countries—makes it possible to produce biofuels in all countries and regions that have some agricultural and forest resources. Around sixty countries in the world produce biofuels, particularly for use in the transport fuel sector (these include the United States, Brazil, the European Union, Japan, Malaysia, Indonesia, India, South Africa, Colombia, and the Philippines). Those countries that cannot produce biofuels themselves at least have many potential suppliers.

Additional benefits linked to biofuels are their potential to reduce emissions of greenhouse gases (GHG) by displacing fossil fuels. While actual emissions' reduction calculated through the life cycle of the product leads to different results depending on the feedstock and the industrial conversion process used, large reductions are estimated for sugar cane ethanol and for second-generation biofuels. From an economic perspective, biofuels have the ability to offer a new end market for agricultural commodities and to become an important source of export income for several developing countries. Participating in the global economy through exports is a crucial part of the economic process and a way to attract investment and upgrade technological capacity. Last but not least, biofuels have the advantage of easy utilization in combustion engines for transportation, contrary to many of the alternatives. While there are many substitutes for oil in the heating and manufacturing sectors, this is not the case in the transportation sector, even though we may assume that other energy sources in all sectors will increasingly be substituted for oil.

Ethanol—an alcohol produced by the biological fermentation of carbohydrates derived from plant material, mainly grains and sugar crops—can be used directly in cars designed to run on pure ethanol (hydrated ethanol, which usually has about 5 percent water content) or on ethanol blended with gasoline (at up to 25 percent) to make gasohol. Dehydrated (anhydrous) ethanol is required for blending with gasoline. No engine modification is typically needed to use the blend. Ethanol can be used as an octane-boosting, pollution-reducing additive in unleaded gasoline, thereby substituting for chemical additives such as MTBE (methyl tertiary butyl ether).[1]

At present, Brazil is the only country that uses ethanol both as a 100 percent substitute for gasoline and in blends. In all other countries that use biofuels, ethanol is blended with gasoline in differing proportions. Ethanol is also used as a solvent in industrial applications, while its oldest and most traditional use is in making spirits or alcoholic beverages.

Biodiesel is a synthetic diesel-like fuel produced from vegetable oils, animal fats, or recycled cooking grease. It can be used directly as fuel, which requires some engine modifications, or blended with petroleum diesel and used in diesel engines with few or no modifications. Biodiesel is made through a chemical process called transesterification. The process leaves behind two products: methyl esters (the

---

1. MTBE, which used to be a leading gasoline additive, was banned in the states of California and New York in 2004 and later on in many other states of the United States, due to groundwater pollution problems arising from its use and storage.

Figure 4-1. *World Production of Ethanol, by Country or Region, 2007*[a]

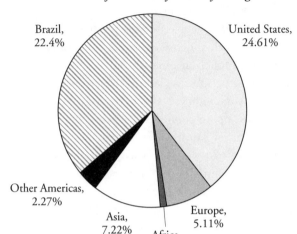

Brazil,
22.4%

United States,
24.61%

Other Americas,
2.27%

Asia,
7.22%

Africa,
0.694%

Europe,
5.11%

Source: Nastari (2008).
a. Total 2007 = 62.3 billion liters.

chemical name for biodiesel) and glycerin, a by-product used in food and cosmetic products.

Production and International Trade

Annual world ethanol production (for all uses) grew between 2000 and 2007 by 12.2 percent on average, totaling roughly 62.3 billion liters in 2007 (figure 4-1). With global fuel demand forecast to grow by about 40 percent between 2000 and 2020, there is plenty of room for the biofuels market to grow.[2] In fact, global ethanol production is estimated to have totaled 79 billion liters in 2008 and is projected to reach about 148 billion liters in 2018.[3]

Until 2005 Brazil was the world's leading ethanol producer. By 2006 the United States replaced Brazil as the top producer, with U.S. ethanol production reaching 24.6 billion liters in 2007, compared to 22.4 billion liters in Brazil. The European Union (EU) holds a distant but significant third place in world rankings, followed by China, Canada, Thailand, Colombia, India, and Australia.

2. Nastari (2008).
3. OECD-FAO (2009).

Still, the international ethanol market thus far remains small and volatile with only around 10 percent of world production traded internationally. The largest ethanol exporter is Brazil, which from October 2006 to September 2007 accounted for 63 percent of global ethanol exports (to forty-four countries). The largest ethanol importer is the United States, with 1.7 billion liters imported in 2007, roughly corresponding to 6 percent of its domestic consumption. The United States is followed by Japan, Germany, and the Netherlands.[4] The bulk of U.S. ethanol imports have been supplied by Brazil, either directly or through Caribbean and Central American countries, taking advantage of the duty-free treatment under the Caribbean Basin Initiative.[5] The United States also imports ethanol from Canada and China. As more countries put in place policies that mandate the use of biofuels, international trade in ethanol is expected to grow, reaching 6 billion liters in 2010 and 13 billion liters in 2018. Trade flows are expected to follow the usual path, from Brazil to the EU and the United States.[6]

Production of biodiesel started in Western Europe, while the industry outside of Europe remained insignificant until around 2004. Since then, governments around the world have put in place policies to encourage the development of the industry, and new capacity is now available in North America, Southeast Asia, and Brazil.[7] As a result, between 2000 and 2007 biodiesel production grew from less than 1 billion liters to almost 11 billion liters.[8] In 2007 the EU still accounted for 68 percent of total biodiesel production. In the same year 2.6 percent of the total transport fuel consumed in the EU was biofuels, of which about 76 percent was biodiesel.[9] However, the United States, which produced around 1.7 billion liters in 2007, is scaling up production at a faster rate than Europe and is increasingly exploring new technologies and new feedstocks for its biodiesel production. According to some projections, however, Brazil is expected to surpass U.S. and EU production by 2015.[10] Global production may reach 44 billion liters by 2018.[11]

4. Steenblik (2007); Renewable Fuels Association (2009).

5. The Caribbean Basin Initiative (CBI) is a unilateral concession by the government of the United States for tariff exoneration for a large portion of the products of the Caribbean region. Launched in 1983 through the Caribbean Basin Economic Recovery Act, and substantially expanded in 2000 through the U.S.–Caribbean Basin Trade Partnership Act, the CBI has currently nineteen beneficiary countries.

6. OECD-FAO (2009).

7. Steenblik (2007).

8. OECD-FAO (2009).

9. Garofalo (2009).

10. Emerging Markets Online (2008).

11. OECD-FAO (2009).

While there is little international trade in biodiesel at present, the development of the industry in several regions and ambitious government targets in several countries are expected to lead to more international trade in the future, especially if alternative feedstocks, such as jatropha oil, can be produced on a large scale. Moreover, the need for a number of non-self-sufficient countries to meet biofuels utilization mandates will also likely contribute to the expansion of international trade.

In collecting and analyzing data on trade flows in biofuels and tariff regimes, some basic difficulties are encountered: first, a lack of commodity classification codes for distinct biofuels; and second, the multiple potential uses of feedstocks, which makes it difficult to track the percentage of agriculture production devoted to biofuel manufacturing as opposed to feed and food consumption or other industrial uses.[12] Breakdowns of final uses of feedstocks are carried out by some countries at the national or regional levels. There is currently no specific customs classification for ethanol in biofuel production, as opposed to ethanol for other uses, especially alcoholic beverages. Ethanol is classified as an agriculture product, ethyl alcohol; biodiesel is classified as a chemical product.[13]

Instruments for Promoting Biofuels Production

As mentioned above, some fundamentals, namely the quest for energy security, as well as the need for climate change mitigation and rural development, have pressed countries to promote biofuels as a new or expanding component of their energy mix. These fundamentals persist. Countries that have embarked on biofuels production and use have relied upon a variety of policy instruments to make the biofuels industry start and flourish. These policies are expected to spur a sustained worldwide demand and supply of biofuels in the years to come. This in turn may trigger a profound change in the world agricultural economy.

12. Products traded internationally are classified according to the Harmonized Commodity Description and Coding System (HS), an international nomenclature developed by the World Customs Organization.

13. Ethyl alcohol product is classified under HS code 2207, which covers undenatured (HS 2207 10) and denatured alcohol (HS 2207 20). While both denatured and undenatured alcohol can be used for biofuel production, undenatured alcohol is more suitable for use as a fuel, while denatured ethanol is often used as a solvent; in March 2005 the World Customs Organization classified biodiesel under the HS code 3824 90, an industrial code that includes a large spectrum of chemical products and preparations of the chemical or allied industries (including those consisting of mixtures of natural products) not elsewhere specified or included. Biodiesel was previously classified as an oil, that is, an agricultural product. For both ethanol and biodiesel, however, countries are using at the national level tariff classifications that go beyond the six-digit level of the HS in order to distinguish the different final uses of the products.

Mandated Amounts, Percentages, and Blending Targets

One of the most common tools for creating a biofuel industry is the imposition of a prescribed amount of biofuels to be put into the market, a measure that automatically generates a market for biofuels. As of June 2009 around forty countries had introduced or were considering introducing the mandatory use of biofuels.[14]

The mandatory use of certain amounts or percentages of biofuels in transportation fuels not only creates a market of a certain size but also ensures stability and predictability for new investments. It also helps ensure the growth of the biofuels sector, sets demand ahead of supply, and induces investments to close the gap. This policy may have disturbing implications when the targets are set beyond the capacity of the industry to produce biofuels at a reasonable price and according to sustainable agricultural practices. Aggressive targets could also induce speculative behavior in agricultural commodity markets, as investors gauge the ability of the agricultural sector to meet additional demand and transfer the expectations for increasing demand for agricultural products into commodities futures markets.[15]

Support Measures

Subsidies and tax rebates to biofuel production, support for construction of refineries, and support for production of feedstocks are major instruments used by several developed countries at the national, subnational, and even local government levels to make it possible for the domestic biofuel industry to exist and prosper.

Governments support the biofuels industry through a multiplicity of policies and instruments. At the beginning of the supply chain are subsidies for those goods and services consumed in the production process. Among the largest of these subsidies are measures supporting the producers of biofuel feedstocks. These subsidies are often accompanied by grants, or reduced-cost credits, for building the necessary infrastructure to convert feedstocks into fuels, namely ethanol refineries and biodiesel manufacturing plants. Such subsidies have the effect of lowering fixed costs, lowering investor risks of new plants, and improving return on investment.

Moreover, there are the subsidies directly linked to the volumes produced or used. Biofuel producers benefit from exemptions from fuel excise taxes and from grants or tax credits related to the volume of biofuels produced, sold, or blended

14. The mandatory use of biofuels could take the form of a mandatory blend of biofuels and fossil fuels per unit of fuel sold, as in Brazil; or a mandatory target of biofuels that refiners and blenders have to meet over the course of a year, as in the United States.

15. UN Conference on Trade and Development (2009).

with fossil fuels. Tax credits are specific allotments of money given to oil companies when they blend biofuels into their fossil fuels or to the biofuels industry. In
the United States, for example, companies that blend ethanol into gasoline,
including imported ethanol, benefit from a volumetric ethanol excise tax credit
of US$0.45 a gallon. Companies that blend biodiesel, excluding imported
biodiesel, into diesel fuel benefit from a volumetric biodiesel tax credit of
US$1.00 a gallon. Producers of cellulosic ethanol benefit from a production tax
credit of US$1.01 a gallon.

Support is also provided to the downstream segment of the biofuels market
through grants, tax credits, and loans to build the infrastructure needed for storing, distributing, and retailing biofuels and for purchasing fleets that can transport them.[16] Finally, government procurement programs may give preference to
the purchase of biofuels.[17]

In the United States virtually every production input and production stage of
biofuels is subsidized, and in many locations producers could tap into multiple
subsidies at once. In 2008 U.S. subsidies to biofuels were worth more than
US$9.5 billion. As the Energy Bill requires more and more biofuels to be consumed
each year, the cost for public budgets to support the biofuels industry is rising
sharply.[18]

At the same time, these support measures in developed countries have implications for developing country producers, including reducing their competitiveness, creating global inequalities, and distorting international trade.

Import Tariffs

Biofuels, in particular ethanol, face high most-favored-nation (MFN) tariffs in
industrialized markets. In the EU, trade of ethanol is subject to specific import
duties of EUR 0.102 a liter on denatured alcohol and EUR 0.192 a liter on
undenatured alcohol (box 4-1). The United States imposes import duties of
US$0.54 a gallon (US$0.1427 a liter) plus a 2.5 percent ad valorem tariff on fuel
ethanol (box 4-2). Japan imposes an ad valorem tariff of 27.2 percent on ethanol
intended for beverage use, but the same tariff also applies to ethanol for fuel. Australia applies an ad valorem tariff of 5 percent plus a specific import duty of
AU$38.143 a liter. Canada applies a specific duty of C$0.0492 a liter. Switzerland applies a specific import duty of CHF 35/100 a kilogram (equivalent to CHF
0.277 a liter); however, it actually applies this tariff to only a few countries; numer-

16. Koplow (2009).
17. Koplow (2006); Doornbosch and Steenblik (2007), pp. 24–25.
18. Koplow (2009).

Box 4-1. *Biofuel-Related Trade Regimes, European Union*

Most-favored-nation (MFN) trade in ethanol is subject to specific import duties of EUR 0.102 a liter on denatured alcohol (HS 2207 20) and EUR 0.192 a liter on undenatured alcohol (HS 2207 10). Brazil is the largest ethanol exporter to the European Union, with all of its exports subject to MFN tariffs.

Several preferential trade arrangements concluded in the past by the EU with developing countries foresaw either no duties or reduced tariffs for ethanol, including the Generalized System of Preferences (GSP, which applies to many developing countries), the Cotonou Agreement (African, Caribbean, and Pacific countries; or ACP Group), the Everything But Arms (EBA) initiative (for the Least Developed Countries, LDCs), among others. Pakistan, with a 20 percent share of EU ethanol imports, was the largest exporter under preferential trade arrangements. Other ethanol-exporting developing countries that benefited from EU trade preferences are Guatemala, Peru, Bolivia, Ecuador, Nicaragua, and Panama (which benefited from unlimited duty-free access accorded under special drug diversion programs); Ukraine and South Africa (under the GSP); Democratic Republic of the Congo (under the EBA); Swaziland and Zimbabwe (as ACP countries); and Egypt (under the Euro-Mediterranean Agreement).

The GSP that applied from January 1, 2006, to December 31, 2008, no longer provided for any tariff reduction for ethanol. The situation has not changed with the new GSP, which entered into force on January 1, 2009, and will remain in operation until the end of 2011. However, the special incentive arrangement for sustainable development and good governance, known as GSP+, which offers additional tariff reductions to support "vulnerable" developing countries in their ratification and implementation of international conventions in the fields of human rights, sustainable development, core labor standards, and good governance, provides unlimited and duty-free access to ethanol. Sixteen beneficiary countries have qualified to receive the additional preferences: Armenia, Azerbaijan, Bolivia, Colombia, Costa Rica, Ecuador, El Salvador, Georgia, Guatemala, Honduras, Mongolia, Nicaragua, Paraguay, Peru, Sri Lanka, and Venezuela.

An important feature of the GSP is that, whenever an individual country's performance on the EU market over a three-year period exceeds

(continued)

Box 4-1. *Biofuel-Related Trade Regimes, European Union (continued)*

or falls below a set threshold, preferential tariffs are either suspended or reestablished. This graduation mechanism is relevant only for GSP and GSP+ preferences, while access for LDCs under EBA is not affected. Pakistan, one of the most competitive ethanol producers and exporters, lost its privileged status under the GSP in October 2005 and appears to be unable to overcome the tariff barrier in the European market.

Duty-free and quota-free access is granted to LDCs under the EBA Initiative. While exports of ethanol from EBA countries have so far been negligible, new opportunities may emerge in those countries, particularly as a result of increased sugar cane cultivation and foreign investments, including from Brazil.

Under the Cotonou Agreement, ACP countries qualified for duty-free access to ethanol. However, imports of ethanol from South Africa, which exported on average approximately 5 million liters a year to the EU during 2002–04, have been subject since January 1, 2006, to the full MFN duty. Starting January 1, 2008, new agreements on trade and economic cooperation (the Economic Partnership Agreements) have started replacing the Cotonou Agreement and will govern trade relations between the ACP and the EU.

EU imports of biodiesel are subject to an ad valorem duty of 6.5 percent. To relax pressure on domestic rapeseed oil production, European biodiesel producers have begun getting feedstocks from foreign sources. Between 1999 and 2005, EU imports of palm oil (primarily from Malaysia) more than doubled; they reached 4.65 million tonnes in 2007. Since January 1998 Indonesia and Malaysia have been excluded from GSP benefits for all products of HS chapter 15 (animal and vegetable fats and oils), including palm oil.

In March 2009 the EU imposed temporary antidumping and counter-vailing duties, ranging from EUR 21 to EUR 41 per 100 kilograms, on imports of biodiesel from the United States. In July 2009 the temporary duties were made definitive for a five-year period. The reason for these measures is a subsidy available in the United States since 2004 that offers a tax credit of US$1 a gallon of biodiesel blended with mineral diesel. The benefit of the subsidy is not limited to biodiesel produced and consumed in the United States but is also available on export. It applies without limitation in terms of biodiesel content; therefore, even by adding a "drop" of mineral diesel to biodiesel, the blend is eligible for subsidy.

Box 4-1. *Biofuel-Related Trade Regimes, European Union (continued)*

According to EU authorities, the 2004 U.S. measure resulted in a surge of underpriced exports of "B99"(99 percent biodiesel, 1 percent mineral diesel) from the United States to the EU and caused European producers to lose substantial market share. On top of this, a triangular trade referred to as "splash and dash" also developed, whereby foreign producers (for example, in Indonesia, Malaysia, Argentina) were taking advantage of the U.S. biodiesel subsidy before shipping their commodities to Europe. The splash and dash scheme, however, never represented more than a marginal share of the total B99 volumes entering the EU, and the subsidy was removed by the U.S. Congress in October 2008.

Sources: Zarrilli (2006), European Biodiesel Board (2009, 2009a)

---

ous nations enjoy duty free or reduced import duties under preferential tariff arrangements.

In conclusion, the competitiveness of domestic biofuels in industrialized countries depends by and large on the fact that they are shielded by subsidies and import tariffs. Such instruments offset lower production costs in other countries and represent a significant barrier to imports as well as a tool to guarantee a captive market for domestic biofuels producers.

Biofuels at a Crossroads

Biofuels are at a crossroads. Public opinion has shifted from the hearty enthusiasm of a few years ago to skepticism or open condemnation. A number of concerns are being voiced, including food security, commodities prices, effect on overall carbon emissions, and other environmental impacts.

Food Security and Commodities Prices

The rapid increase in agricultural and food prices, partially fueled by the use of grains and oilseeds for the production of ethanol and biodiesel, is calling into question the ethics of diverting land and crops to energy production. Prices for food traded internationally increased almost 60 percent during the first half of 2008, with basic staples such as grains and oilseeds showing the largest increases. The fall in energy and fertilizer prices during the second half of 2008 partially reversed

Box 4-2. *Biofuel-Related Trade Regimes, United States*

The United States imposes a most-favored-nation (MFN) import duty of $0.54 a gallon ($0.1427 a liter) plus a 2.5 percent ad valorem tariff on fuel ethanol. A limited amount of ethanol may be imported duty free under the Caribbean Basin Initiative (CBI), even if most of the steps in the production process were completed in other countries.

More specifically, if produced from at least 50 percent local CBI feedstocks, ethanol may be imported duty free into the U.S. market. If the local feedstock content is lower, limitations apply on the quantity of duty-free ethanol. Nevertheless, up to 7 percent of the U.S. market may be supplied duty free by CBI ethanol containing no local feedstocks. In this case, hydrous ethanol produced in other countries (mainly Brazil) can be shipped to a dehydration plant in a CBI country for reprocessing. After the ethanol is dehydrated, it is imported duty free into the United States. Until the present, imports of dehydrated (anhydrous) ethanol under the CBI have been far below the 7 percent cap (3.0 percent in 2006 and 3.6 percent in 2007), though the situation may change as agribusinesses, some of them North American, invest in ethanol plants in the Caribbean. Dehydration plants are operating in Jamaica, Costa Rica, El Salvador, and Trinidad and Tobago.

Duty-free ethanol imports have also played a role during the negotiations of the U.S.–Central America Free Trade Agreement (U.S.-CAFTA). However, CAFTA did not introduce major changes. It does not increase overall preferential access to the U.S. ethanol market, but it does establish country-specific shares for El Salvador and Costa Rica within the existing CBI quota. The other CAFTA countries retain existing CBI benefits on ethanol. Under the Andean Trade Preferences Pact, Peru, Bolivia, Colombia, and Ecuador also enjoy duty-free access to the U.S. market.

In some bilateral or regional trade agreements, like the U.S.-Israel Free Trade Agreement and the North American Free Trade Agreement (NAFTA), ethanol that is fully produced with feedstocks from those countries is allowed to enter the U.S. market duty free.

There is support in some quarters to eliminate tariffs on imported ethanol so as to increase supply and mitigate spikes in both fuel and food prices. Duty-free treatment of ethanol in the United States has, however, raised concerns. The generous subsidies provided to the local biofuel industry coupled with the market protection provided by import tariffs have shielded domestic producers from foreign competition and created strong vested interests. Reforming such a system implies strong political willingness.

Source: Zarrilli (2006).

this trend, but in the immediate future, food prices are expected to remain much higher than during the 1990s.[19]

While there is consensus that the world has the capacity to produce enough food to feed everyone, at present there are more than a billion undernourished people. The obstacles to sufficient nutrition in most cases lie not in production but in food distribution and affordability. Increasingly, the poor do not have the incomes to pay for food.

Rapid growth in demand for energy feedstocks could divert too much cropland to fuel crops and imperil food security. According to the Food and Agriculture Organization, a UN body, major agricultural producers such as Brazil, the United States, the European Union, and Canada are expected to reduce exports of basic feedstock commodities (cereals and oilseeds) for use in domestic biofuels industries or to increase imports of biofuels—or both.[20] This expectation has serious food security implications for developing countries, particularly those with large proportions of poor, urban, hungry people. This concern is especially relevant in relation to first-generation biofuels, which are mostly processed from edible plant material; the relevance should be less significant for second-generation biofuels, which are expected to be produced from lignocellulosic biomass, enabling the use of lower-cost, nonedible feedstocks and thereby limiting direct food-versus-fuel competition.

A related issue is the impact of increasing agricultural commodity prices on certain segments of the population in developing countries. While the increase in agricultural prices could potentially benefit some of the 2.5 billion people whose livelihood depends on the agricultural sector, small landholders, rural landless workers, and the urban poor could be at significant risk, at least in the short term. As mentioned above, the impact of higher food prices on the world's poor and developing economies is particularly significant. For example, the increase in food prices since 2007 is likely to have increased poverty for 130 million to 155 million people, or by around 1.3 to 1.5 percent.[21]

Emissions Reduction

While one of the aims of transitioning to bioenergy is to reduce GHG emissions, biofuels are not necessarily carbon neutral. There are emissions associated with feedstocks production and transport, and some aspects of biofuels production may also contribute significantly to GHG emissions, especially if fossil fuels are used

19. World Bank (2009).
20. Food and Agriculture Organization (2007).
21. World Bank (2009).

to power ethanol refineries or the biodiesel manufacturing plants. Land conversion for the purpose of producing feedstock—so-called direct land use change—may contribute to GHG emissions because when forest and grasslands are cultivated, carbon that is stored in the plants and the soil is released. There is also the forgone carbon sequestration that would have otherwise occurred in the absence of biomass production.[22] Additionally, nitrous oxide (N_2O) emissions resulting from the production and use of fertilizers used in feedstock cultivation could partially offset the benefits from reduced carbon emissions.[23]

Production of feedstocks in a new geographical area may cause undesirable effects from the so-called indirect land use change. For example, the energy demand for palm oil could be supplied from an existing plantation that used to supply the food market. The shortage created in the food market will over time result in the creation of a new palm oil plantation elsewhere. It is also possible to have a combination of direct and indirect land use changes. For example, rapeseed cultivation, aimed at biodiesel production, may replace wheat cultivation on a plot of land. This leads to a direct land use change, rapeseed instead of wheat, and an indirect land use change: the decrease in wheat production will need to be compensated by an increase in wheat production somewhere else. As such, land use changes represent a serious threat to large-scale feedstock production for biofuels.[24]

While a scientific assessment of the issues of land use change is urgently needed in order to design policies that prevent unintended consequences from biofuel production, there remains much ambiguity and uncertainty as to how different biofuel GHG analyses are conducted, rendering it difficult for any reliable comparisons to be made between biofuels on the basis of their GHG performance.

Environmental Concerns

Large-scale biofuel feedstock production could lead to considerable environmental degradation, including loss of biodiversity, overuse of water, and excessive use of pesticides. Further concerns relate to the introduction of invasive species, large-scale monocropping practices, and genetically modified plants.

Many feedstocks—including sugar, palm oil, and maize—are water intensive. Their expansion into regions where they are not rain fed is likely to create great competition for water, making it an increasingly scarce and precious resource. Feedstock production also affects downstream water quality through runoff of fer-

22. Timothy Searchinger and others, "Use of U.S. Croplands for Biofuels Increases Greenhouse Gases through Emissions from Land Use Change," *Science Express*, February 7, 2008.
23. Fritsche and others (2006).
24. Dehue, Meyer, and Hamelinck (2007).

tilizers and agrochemicals. Finally, feedstock production may cause soil erosion if poor farming techniques are employed.[25]

There are also claims that current biofuel policies discourage energy conservation. Indeed, biofuels could end up encouraging more fossil fuel consumption in the transportation sector, both because they may lower the price of fuels and because the presence of even tiny percentages of biofuels in the fuel mix may give consumers the false impression that driving does not contribute to GHG emissions.

Addressing Existing Policies

The possible undesirable side effects of biofuels production, described in the section above, should be interpreted as a policy failure rather than an unavoidable consequence of producing and consuming biofuels.

Whether biofuels will move ahead of the current deadlock will largely depend on the decisions that governments make. The path each country chooses will ultimately determine the costs and benefits of biofuels for individual countries and for the world. An assessment of biofuel policies and market instruments may be instructive as to how to reach energy, environmental, and rural development goals.

Mutually Supportive Policies

In its 2007 Energy Bill the United States introduced ambitious utilization levels of biofuels for transport—namely 9 billion gallons in 2008, rising to 36 billion gallons (136 billion liters) by 2022—which go far beyond those included in previous legislation (7.5 billion gallons in 2011). In addition, the European Union has set a very high target for biofuels use, which is beyond the capacity of its agricultural sector, namely a 5.75 percent mix of biofuels with fossil fuels by 2010. New legislation has raised the blending rate to 10 percent by 2020.[26] In addition, the United States and the European Union impose tariffs on imported biofuels and require adherence to technical requirements. These instruments, combined with a range of subsidies, result in a strong preference for domestically produced feedstocks. Such policies may well put pressure on agricultural prices and induce land use changes, with reverberating effects on global markets.[27]

25. Some tillage techniques can leave less than 15 percent of crop residues on the soil. Food and Agriculture Organization (2007), pp. 7–8.

26. Directive 2009/28/EC on the promotion of the use of energy from renewable sources and amending and subsequently repealing directives 2001/77/EC and 2003/30/EC, L 140/16, June 5, 2009.

27. UN Conference on Trade and Development (2008).

Indeed, increased biofuels production has been, for certain crops and certain countries, a driver of food price inflation, even though not the dominant one. Long-term factors—such as the failure to give the agricultural sector the attention it deserved during the last decades, lack of investments in productive capacity and infrastructure, distorted agricultural markets, and the dismantling of support policies for domestic markets in developing countries—seem to be the main reasons behind the present food crisis. These long-term factors have combined with unfavorable weather conditions in key food-producing countries (possibly due to the effects of climate change), a strong increase in energy prices (until mid-2008), the imposition of export bans or restrictions for some staples, and speculation in agricultural markets.[28]

To restore a natural market balance it would be suitable for the United States, the EU, and any countries that have mandated the use of biofuels to introduce flexibility into such measures and make them less ambitious. When biofuels are mandated, biofuel producers can outbid other consumers of feedstocks. Moreover, mandated volumes give rise to investor expectations about the future of the industry, further adding pressure to prices. Dropping barriers to the importation of biofuels would also contribute to a more properly functioning market. Allowing more trade in biofuels would reduce not only the price pressures on the feedstocks currently used (maize in the United States and oilseed crops in the EU) but also the costs of achieving the targets. Moreover, it would create opportunities for developing countries to produce and export biofuels to countries that need them.

In addition to such immediate responses, additional measures are needed to ensure that the biofuels industry develops in an economically and environmentally sound manner. Investments are needed to enhance the agricultural productivity of developing countries, particularly that of small farmers. Moreover, investments should increase the ability of farmers to capture a larger share of agricultural revenues from biofuel production.

Governments, especially in developing countries, should continue to invest in their distribution infrastructure for agricultural products so as to reduce transactions costs between farmers and the end market. If a reduction in marketing costs is not addressed, there is a risk that price increases for agricultural commodities will be captured mostly by the marketing system and will be of little consequence for rural producers. Conversely, it is necessary that a significant share of the generated value added reaches farmers and rural areas, as this would open up opportunities in other economic sectors. In the case of small landholders, the absence

28. UN Conference on Trade and Development (2008).

of clear property rights and enforcement mechanisms could lead to their displacement by large and powerful interests. Enhanced opportunities for local ownership and an emphasis on sustainable development are therefore key elements to ensuring the participation of rural entrepreneurs in this emerging sector. Government incentives, if implemented, should be biased in favor of ownership and a scale that benefits rural communities.[29]

The adoption of good agricultural practices—retention of soil cover, appropriate crop choice, crop rotation—can mitigate negative impacts on carbon, soil, and water and also can reduce the threat to biodiversity. Promoting integrated local food-energy production systems can avoid waste and increase the overall system productivity for food and energy.[30]

Biofuel policies, then, should be reassessed, considering the actual or potential impact of biofuels production on the price and availability of agricultural commodities for food production as well as the actual or potential impact of the price and availability of agricultural commodities on the viability of the biofuels sector.[31]

Biofuels Certification

To control the undesirable side effects that the expansion of the biofuels industry is provoking directly or indirectly, discussions are ongoing on developing certification programs that encourage sustainable biofuels production. The numerous public and private initiatives being undertaken are in various stages of development.[32]

Certification is a form of communication that permits the buyer to be assured that the supplier complies with certain requirements. Certification allows product differentiation and provides information about certain characteristics of a product, in this case its sustainability. Depending on how sensitive a market is to certain product attributes, certification may have a significant market impact, affecting both domestic and imported products. Moreover, for biofuels certification schemes sponsored by governments, certification is in most cases linked to tax breaks and other incentives, or it is the precondition for biofuels to be counted toward national or regional utilization targets. All this makes certification a crucial attribute for biofuels.

The development of a certification scheme starts with the establishment of general principles that describe the objectives of certification. Among the general principles considered for biofuels is that the GHG emissions of the biofuel throughout

29. De La Torre Ugarte (2008).
30. Food and Agriculture Organization (2007).
31. UN Conference on Trade and Development (2008).
32. Zarrilli (2008).

its life cycle must be less than those of the fossil fuel it displaces. Another is that biofuel production must not impair food security. These general principles are then translated into specific requirements in the form of criteria.

For example, the general principle that biofuels production not impair food security is spelled out in two criteria: that biofuel producers assess the status of local food security and not replace staple crops if there are indications of local food insecurity; and that biofuel production minimize negative impacts on food security by giving particular preference to the following: waste and residues as input; degraded, marginal, or underutilized lands as sources; and yield improvements that maintain existing food supplies.[33]

Indicators or verifiers are tools to test that the products actually meet the criteria. For example, the general principle that biofuels production must not negatively affect biodiversity is spelled out in the criterion that in new developments there should be maintenance or recovery of biodiversity within biomass production units. This criterion is then translated into the need to prove how fragmentation is discouraged, that ecological corridors are maintained, and that the restoration of degraded areas is taking place.[34]

The development of sustainable biofuels certification systems has involved four stakeholder groups: national governments and regional groupings, namely Belgium, the Netherlands, Germany, the United Kingdom, Switzerland, Brazil, Canada, the United States, and the European Commission; companies, such as Cargill, BP, Shell, and Electrabel, to mention a few; nongovernmental organizations, such as the World Wildlife Fund; and international organizations and initiatives, such as the Roundtable on Sustainable Biofuels.[35] The many certification initiatives reflect the fact that certification has been selected by governments, private companies, and NGOs as a suitable and effective tool to encourage sustainable biofuels production.

Certification initiatives, however, also raise a number of concerns. Proliferation of individual sustainability schemes may damage the efficiency and credibility of certification and create market segmentation and opacity. The principles and criteria on which the different certification schemes are based are diversified and often far reaching. All schemes put emphasis on GHG emissions reduction;

---

33. Roundtable on Sustainable Biofuels (2008).
34. The example comes from the "Testing Framework for Sustainable Biomass," developed in the Netherlands by the Cramer Commission.
35. On biofuels certification, see Van Dam and others (2008), pp. 749–80; Lewandowski and Faaij (2006), pp. 83–104.

others also tackle issues such as biodiversity preservation, land use changes, food security, social well-being, and local prosperity. Evaluating the macroeconomic effects of biofuels production may be a complex and lengthy process. Hence a balance should be struck between the comprehensiveness of the requirements included in the schemes and the technical and administrative feasibility of applying them.

Sustainability certification will add significant costs to biofuels production. These expenses are associated with both upgrading production to meet sustainability requirements and proving compliance. Costs will be highly dependent on the number, strictness, and inclusiveness of the requirements established by the certification system. They will likely be greater for developing countries than for industrialized countries and for smaller producers than for large-scale producers. Furthermore, concerns remain regarding developing countries' ability to effectively participate in the process of standards development and regarding the risk of domestic producers playing a disproportionately influential role in the establishment of sustainability requirements.

The legal implications of certifying biofuels and distinguishing them on the basis of sustainability are complex. World Trade Organization (WTO) rules contain some loopholes and grey areas on issues of relevance for biofuels certification schemes, starting with the fundamental question of whether such schemes, when developed by private bodies, are covered by WTO rules or, conversely, should be regarded as private marketing schemes outside the scope of WTO rules.

Another question refers to certification schemes developed by hybrid international entities (such as the Roundtable on Sustainable Biofuels) composed of representatives of public and private entities, international organizations, and NGOs. It is unclear whether such entities can be regarded as international standardization bodies. If this were the case, the principles and criteria they develop should be regarded as international standards and should be covered by a presumption of conformity with the Agreement on Technical Barriers to Trade (TBT Agreement).[36] On the other hand, if these initiatives are regarded as private schemes that fall outside the scope of the TBT Agreement, they escape from multilaterally agreed trade rules, such as nondiscrimination, abstention from

36. According to the TBT Agreement, annex 1, Terms and Definitions, international bodies or systems are those whose membership is open to the relevant bodies of at least all WTO members. This definition is not detailed enough to be of practical use.

creating unnecessary obstacles to trade, proportionality, and transparency. Nevertheless, they could have a significant impact on trade flows.

Another crucial aspect of biofuels certification that needs to be scrutinized under WTO law is the legitimacy of product differentiation based on how goods have been manufactured and on their impact through the life cycle. In other words, the question is whether certified biofuels and noncertified biofuels may or may not be regarded as the same products—"like" products, in WTO legal jargon.

The General Agreement on Tariffs and Trade (GATT), Article III, requires imported goods, once they have entered the country and cleared customs, to be treated no worse than domestically produced like goods, especially with regard to internal taxes and regulations. The purpose of the rule is to prevent domestic tax and regulatory policies from being used as protectionist measures and nullify the benefits of tariff concessions. In the *Asbestos* ruling, the Appellate Body established links between the "likeness" of two products and their respective impact on health.[37] This finding has important implications, especially if we assume that other nontrade concerns, such as environmental protection and climate change mitigation, could also be used as elements to be taken into account when assessing whether two products are like.

For biofuels, this approach might allow a distinction based on the contribution of sustainable (as opposed to nonsustainable) biofuels and feedstocks to mitigating the environmental and health problems related to carbon emissions. In the Appellate Body's reasoning in the *Asbestos* case, however, the health implications of a product become a relevant element to consider when they lead to the perception among consumers that products are different—one actually or potentially being dangerous to health and the other not. Hence a particular emphasis should be placed on how the domestic market treats certified (presumably sustainable) biofuels and feedstocks and uncertified ones, what their competitive relationship in the marketplace is, and whether consumers perceive them as distinct products. Market studies on cross-price elasticity of demand and any other evidence indicating to what extent the products involved are, or could be, in a competitive relationship in the marketplace would be among the evidence relevant for determining likeness under GATT Article III:4.

37. WTO. Report of the Appellate Body (2001). *Asbestos*, paragraph 113.

The case of biofuels and feedstocks certification presents an additional complexity, since products may be distinguished not only on the basis of their possible impact on health and the environment but also on the basis of labor and other social standards. The issue of trade and labor standards has been with the WTO since its birth. However, at the first WTO Ministerial Conference, in Singapore in December 1996, it was agreed that market access should not be linked with labor standards. While WTO jurisprudence has evolved to become more sensitive to nontrade concerns, especially in the health and environmental fields, it is questionable whether it would be equally open to accept trade discrimination linked to labor and other social conditions.

A number of steps may contribute to making certification work for sustainable biofuel production. Efforts should be made toward the convergence of existing programs and the formulation of internationally agreed upon principles and criteria. These principles and criteria should be flexible enough to accommodate the varying environmental and socioeconomic conditions of producing countries but also quantifiable, verifiable, and scientifically informed. They should be the result of an inclusive process, wherein stakeholders from various regions are effectively represented. Existing forums and ongoing initiatives may be used for the purpose of developing genuine international standards and to thus complement the existing patchwork of global energy governance with an internationally agreed approach to certification.

Certification programs should help small producers, especially in developing countries, comply with sustainability requirements. Compliance could be linked to certain benefits, such as access to microcredit or support services, to encourage producers to engage in sustainable production. Developing countries also must be helped to issue credible declarations of conformity and to test products. It is further crucial to assess what kind of product differentiation is suitable, WTO-consistent, and instrumental in the fulfillment of sustainability goals.

Second-Generation Technologies

The shift from current to more advanced biofuel technologies may alleviate some of the most serious side effects that the biofuel industry has engendered. Those technologies used so far to produce first-generation biofuels—made from grains, oilseeds, and sugar crops—are mature and rather simple technologies that developing countries can easily accommodate to domestic needs. However, a shift toward second-generation biofuels, made from lignocellulosic biomass (crop residues, purpose-grown grasses, woody crops), is taking place. This shift, in principle, would limit direct food-versus-fuel competition.

Second-generation biofuels can be further classified in terms of the process used to convert the biomass to fuel, either biochemical or thermochemical. Second-generation biofuels, compared to first generation, require more sophisticated processing equipment, more investment per unit of production, and larger-scale facilities (to capture capital cost scale economies). In addition, to achieve the commercial energy and (unsubsidized) economic potential of second-generation biofuels, further research, development, and demonstration work is needed on feedstock production and conversion.[38] Currently, second-generation biofuels are being produced only in pilot plants, and their share is only about 0.1 percent of total biofuels production. The first commercial plants are unlikely to come on line before 2013–15, and no large contribution is expected before 2030. According to U.S. analysts, many second-generation biofuel plants remain prohibitively expensive, especially with petroleum prices considerably lower than the highs of August 2008.

Second-generation biofuel technologies are being developed primarily in industrialized countries. Therefore, to capitalize on their comparative advantages of better growing climates and lower labor costs, developing countries will need to adapt such technologies to their own conditions. This raises issues of technology transfer, intellectual property rights, and the overall capacity for technological innovation. For successful technology adoption and adaptation, it will be essential to have a technology innovation system in place in a country or region.[39] Technology innovation would ideally begin with involvement in the earliest (precommercial) stages of technology development. Such an innovation system is one of the key reasons for the success of the Brazilian ethanol program.[40]

Opportunities in WTO Negotiations

The ongoing WTO negotiations on environmental goods within the framework of the Doha Development Agenda (DDA) could in principle provide a path for correcting some of the shortcomings of present policies, especially high tariffs and nontariff barriers affecting biofuels and in particular ethanol; the result could be a more conducive global governance framework for this emerging energy source.

38. Larson (2008).
39. An innovation system refers to people involved in a broad set of activities and institutions, including research universities and institutes generating fundamental knowledge and assimilating knowledge from the global community; industries with capacity to form joint ventures with foreign companies and to introduce innovation and learning into shared technologies; government agencies able to recognize and support the required research and technology adaptation needs; and a technology-informed policymaking system.
40. Larson (2008).

However, the difficulties and delays that WTO members are encountering to successfully conclude the Doha negotiations and the limited momentum gained by the specific negotiations on environmental goods may make this avenue of little practical use for the time being.

The DDA has launched negotiations on "the reduction or, as appropriate, elimination of tariff and non-tariff barriers to environmental goods and services."[41] Negotiations on environmental goods have been carried out by the Committee on Trade and Environment Special Session and by the Negotiating Group on Non-Agriculture Market Access. Negotiations on environmental services have been conducted within the Special Sessions of the Council for Trade in Services.

Most of the environmental goods negotiations have focused on how to define and identify environmental goods and how to attain trade liberalization in the area. It is worth noting that while the aim of the Doha mandate for environmental goods and services is to liberalize trade, it provides no indication of the pace, depth, or sequencing of such liberalization.

Several approaches have been proposed for identifying environmental goods. One suggestion is to establish a list based on national submissions. This approach triggers the criticism that the products included in the list would be by and large high-technology products, giving developed countries a leading role as producers and exporters. Moreover, a question was raised early on in the negotiations about how to deal with goods having dual uses (having both environmental and non-environmental final uses) and how to classify and distinguish them at the border in order to apply differentiated trade regimes.

In response, India proposed an environmental project approach, under which environmental goods and services would be liberalized within the framework of environmental projects undertaken at the national level and approved by national authorities. However, several WTO members find this approach too complex to become operational. Argentina proposed combining the environmental project approach with the list approach (integrated approach), whereby countries would identify environmental activities and then draw up a list of public and private entities that carry out these activities. These lists would be negotiated, the WTO would be notified, and all goods imported by the notified entities for use in the agreed activities would be granted preferential tariff treatment. The approach championed by Brazil would use a "request and offer" method. Under this approach, countries would request specific liberalization commitments from each other and then extend the tariff cuts they deemed appropriate to all WTO members.

41. Doha Development Agenda, paragraph 31 (iii).

A variant of the list approach, proposed by the EU and the United States, would involve identifying environmental goods, services, and technologies that address climate change and eliminating tariffs on them. Criticisms of the EU-U.S. approach include that the dual-use classification problem would not be solved; that the items identified in the proposal are largely of interest and relevance to developed countries only; and that ethanol is not included in the list under the pretext of being an agricultural good.

According to some countries, the definition of environmental goods should cover, inter alia, renewable energy products, which include ethanol and biodiesel and related products. Improved market access for products derived from or incorporating cleaner technologies, such as "flexifuel" engines and vehicles, could also be pursued.[42] Moreover, parts and components of biodiesel and ethanol plants could be classified as environmental goods. As mentioned above, while biodiesel is classified as an industrial product, ethanol is classified as an agricultural product. According to some countries, therefore, trade liberalization in ethanol should be negotiated as part of the separate WTO market access negotiations for agricultural goods.

Disagreements among countries on the identification of environmental goods and on the scope and approach to take to liberalize trade in such products have undermined the chances of generating any conclusive results. These specific problems, along with the overall difficulty in finding an agreement on the DDA package as a whole, may likely prompt countries to look to bilateral and regional agreements as faster and more predictable tools to remove tariffs and nontariff barriers affecting international trade in biofuels and related technologies. Moreover, the risk exists that, lacking progress through WTO negotiations, countries may also increasingly look at the dispute settlement mechanism of the WTO as a way to resolve problems, including the high tariffs applied to ethanol imports.

Conclusions

The expansion of the biofuels sector has triggered some unwanted results. It has contributed to spikes in the prices of grains, oilseeds, and some livestock products; in some regions feedstock production has contributed to deforestation; in some countries the GHG emissions reduction achieved through the use of biofuels has been minimal compared with fossil fuel use; in some countries the amount of subsidies granted to the industry has made biofuels an extremely expensive way to

---

42. A flexifuel vehicle runs on gasoline and ethanol or on any blend of gasoline and ethanol, using a single fuel tank. Flexifuel vehicles were introduced in the United States in the 1990s and in Brazil in the early 2000s. WTO (2005). Submission by Brazil, paragraphs 10-11.

diversify the energy mix, reduce GHG emissions, and improve energy security. However, such undesirable outcomes should not been seen as intrinsic to biofuels but rather as the result of poor policies.

Countries will probably have to reassess their biofuels policies, replacing them with policies that are less ambitious and more flexible. Such policies may specifically reduce subsidies and allow more international trade in biofuels. Such measures would lessen the undesirable pressure on agricultural commodity prices and encourage biofuel production in countries with more favorable climates, more available land, and less expensive labor.

Furthermore, the shift to second-generation biofuels has the potential of avoiding several of the adverse consequences of first-generation biofuels. Support of research and development through national and regional innovation systems would facilitate that shift and make it happen earlier. It would also ensure that developing countries benefit from it. Certifying biofuels on the basis of their sustainability may encourage sustainable production worldwide. Countries should avoid putting in place certification schemes that are burdensome and complex and that may become an obstacle to international trade. Ongoing multilateral trade negotiations may represent an opportunity for agreeing on tariff reductions on biofuels, and a more precise customs classification of biofuels could be instrumental to it. However, the impasse faced by the Doha trade talks may encourage countries to look at bilateral or regional negotiations as more promising avenues for reducing tariffs on biofuels and boosting international trade.

The potential benefits that biofuels hold, especially for developing countries, are numerous. However, sound policies and careful strategies are needed for such benefits to materialize.

References

Dehue, B., S. Meyer, and C. Hamelinck. 2007. *Toward a Harmonised Sustainable Biomass Certification Scheme.* Utrecht: Ecofys Netherlands BV.

De La Torre Ugarte, D. 2008. "Opportunities and Challenges of Biofuels for the Agricultural Sector and the Food Security of Developing Countries." UN Conference on Trade and Development.

Doornbosch, R., and R. Steenblik. 2007. "Biofuels: Is the Cure Worse than the Disease?" In *OECD Round Table on Sustainable Development.* Paris.

Emerging Markets Online. 2008. "Biodiesel 2020: Global Market Survey, Feedstock Trends, and Market Forecasts" (www.emerging-markets.com/PDF/Biodiesel2020Study.pdf).

European Biodiesel Board. 2009. *Subsidised and Dumped Biodiesel from the USA ("B99")— Mechanism and Impact for EU Industry.* Background Note.

————. 2009a. "EU Ministers Endorse Definitive Measures against US Biodiesel—EBB Praises Critical Decision for EU Producers." Press Release 672/COM/09.

Food and Agriculture Organization of the United Nations. 2007. "Food Security and Bioenergy." In *First FAO Technical Consultation on Bioenergy and Food Security*. Rome.

Fritsche, U. R., and others. 2006. *Sustainability Standards for Bioenergy*. Frankfurt am Main: WWF Germany.

Garofalo, R. 2009. "EU Biodiesel Potential." Paper prepared for Europe Stakeholder Outreach Meeting, Brussels, March 19 (http://cgse.epfl.ch/webdav/site/cgse/shared/Biofuels/Regional%20Outreaches%20&%20Meetings/2009/Europe%2009/Raffaello%20Garofalo%20-%20EBB.pdf).

Koplow, D. 2006. "Biofuels: At What Cost? Government Support for Ethanol and Biodiesel in the United States." Global Subsidies Initiative of the International Institute for Sustainable Development. Geneva.

————. 2009. *A Boon to Bad Biofuels*. Washington: Earth Track and Friends of the Earth.

Larson, E. 2008. "Biofuel Production Technologies: Status, Prospects, and Implications for Trade and Development." UN Conference for Trade and Development.

Lewandowski, I., and A. Faaij. 2006. "Steps toward the Development of a Certification System for Sustainable Bioenergy Trade." *Biomass and Bioenergy* 30, no. 2.

Nastari, P. M. 2008. "Global View on Biofuels." Paper prepared for Building the Bellagio Consensus. Bellagio.

OECD-FAO (Organization for Economic Cooperation and Development and Food and Agriculture Organization of the United Nations). 2009. *Agricultural Outlook 2009-2018: Highlights* (www.agri-outlook.org/dataoecd/2/31/43040036.pdf).

Renewable Fuels Association. *Ethanol Facts: Trade* 2009 (www.ethanolrfa.org/resource/facts/trade/).

Roundtable on Sustainable Biofuels. 2008. "Version Zero of the RSB Principles and Criteria." Lausanne.

Steenblik, R. 2007. *Biofuels: At What Cost? Governmental Support for Ethanol and Biodiesel in Selected OECD Countries*. Global Subsidies Initiative of the International Institute for Sustainable Development. Geneva.

UN Conference on Trade and Development. 2008. "UNCTAD's Position on Biofuels Policies and the Global Food Crisis" (www.unctad.org/Templates/Page.asp?intItemID=4526&lang=1).

————. 2009. *The Biofuels Market: Current Situation and Alternative Scenarios: Chapter 1*.

World Bank. 2009. "Global Economic Prospects 2009: Commodities at the Crossroads." Washington.

WTO (World Trade Organization). Report of the Appellate Body. 2001. *European Communities—Measures Affecting Asbestos and Asbestos-Containing Products*. WT/DS135/AB/R.

————. 2005. *Environmental Goods for Development—Submission by Brazil*, TN/TE/W/59, July 8.

Van Dam, J., and others. 2008. "Overview of Recent Developments in Sustainable Biomass Certification." *Biomass and Bioenergy* 32, no. 8.

Zarrilli, Simonetta. 2006. "The Emerging Biofuels Market: Regulatory, Trade, and Development Implications." UN Conference on Trade and Development.

————. 2008. "Making Certification Work for Sustainable Development: The Case of Biofuels." UN Conference on Trade and Development.

5

Trade and Investment in Global Energy: A Policy Perspective

Ralf Dickel

The previous chapters, part 1 of this volume, deal with the regimes for energy trade and investment flows across borders and the development and transfer of new technologies, that is, instruments to overcome restrictions created by the existence of national states and borders. This chapter addresses two questions: whether these regimes are sufficient to govern supply and demand of energy and its price formation on a global basis; and what role international organizations and national governments play or should play in defining and monitoring the balance of supply and demand and price formation.

The year 2008 saw unprecedented price movement in energy, especially for crude oil: oil prices during the 1990s averaged $20 a barrel, rose to $30 a barrel until 2004, broke the $100-a-barrel mark in December 2007, passed the $140-a-barrel mark in July 2008, and fell back to $40 a barrel at the end of 2008. The beginning of the development seemed to reflect fundamental changes in the balance of global energy supply and demand: oil and gas production and remaining reserves are increasingly concentrated in just a few countries, while rapidly growing, highly populated economies drive the fast increase in global energy demand.

In hindsight, however, it seems that the influence of speculation was larger than commonly believed, as prices increased in 2007 and 2008. The strong increase in the number of noncommercial, nonreportable market participants, combined with loopholes in the U.S. reporting system on positions taken, allowed for the flow of noncommercial money into the energy sector. This combination contributed substantially to driving oil prices up and, in consequence, to the subsequent price collapse, for reasons beyond the fundamentals of the energy industry and energy trade. Several loopholes in the U.S. reporting system were addressed by the Commodity Futures Trading Commission in 2008, though regulatory reform stalled in the autumn of 2008 in the wake of the banking and economic crisis.

Previous chapters show that the current system of governance in the financing and trading of global energy resembles a patchwork and lacks coherence. Yet rules do exist and allow for a functioning and liquid market, most obviously in the case of oil. The principal problem, however, lies in the fact that not every market necessarily yields an economic optimum; markets may generate results that are in the interest of neither producers nor consumers. Externalities such as greenhouse gas (GHG) emissions are not necessarily priced in effectively. Hence, and taking a broader perspective, this chapter assesses what determines energy supply and demand in the context of globalization; and what policies should follow from this in order to curb obvious market failures.

The Challenges of Globalization

Today the energy equation is a truly global one: finite fossil fuels are under national control, globally available renewable resources are converted into energy services, and globally available technologies are utilized to satisfy the demands of worldwide economic growth, which generates the negative side effects of the planet's pollution and global warming.

Some of the issues related to global supply and demand of energy can be ruled by multinational contractual arrangements, wherein national states give up, on a reciprocal basis, some of their sovereign rights to create a win-win situation, for example in trade and investment and transfer of technology. Some issues, most important the depletion policy of energy resources, remain in the hands of national states. New multinational organizations were created in the first half of the 1990s to address the trade-and-investment-related challenges of globalization: some of a generic nature like the World Trade Organization (WTO); some of a specific nature, like the Energy Charter Treaty (ECT) and the International Energy Forum (IEF). The ECT, partly by recourse to WTO rules, defines rules for the flow of energy trade, investment, and technology transfer across borders, while the IEF is a platform for a regular high-level producer-consumer dialogue.

Since the turn of the new millennium, the issue of GHG emissions has gained increasing public awareness, which is strongly linked to global energy governance, as about 80 percent of energy use stems from fossil fuels (which accounts for about 60–70 percent of GHG emissions). The issue of GHG is addressed by another set of global organizations, which were created in the beginning of the 1990s: the UN Framework Convention on Climate Change (UNFCCC) and related UN organizations like the Intergovernmental Panel on Climate Change.

Given this net of governance structures, it is fair to say that supply and demand of energy can be balanced by global trade among market players without undue restrictions caused by national borders. Oil and coal are governed by a global market, while the cross-border trade of gas is still dominated by pipelines and is more regional in character, although trade in liquefied natural gas is increasingly global. This might suggest that supply and demand of energy on a global basis can be left to the rules of market mechanisms, with price as the main regulating instrument.

Yet the present world order continues to be defined by sovereign national territorial states, many of which were formed after World War II and followed the creation of the United Nations and its suborganizations. The end of the colonial system in the late 1950s and early 1960s and the breakup of the Soviet Union in the early 1990s resulted in a large number of new sovereign states. Since then the habitable surface of the world is almost exclusively covered by sovereign national territorial states. In comparison to the world only some twenty years ago, today there is no more direct influence by governments on the setting of energy prices on a global level.

However, both production and consumption continue to be strongly influenced by national governments and occasionally by international organizations created to bundle interests in the energy sector. These include the Organization of Petroleum Exporting Countries (OPEC), created at the end of colonialism, and the International Energy Agency, created in response to OPEC. While producing states determine directly or indirectly the level of exploration and production on their territory, the level of consumption is mainly a function of economic activity and wealth. Here, consuming countries' governments have a multitude of instruments to influence the level of energy consumption and the energy mix.

Government Influence on the Supply Side

On the supply side—with the prominent exception of large parts of the United States—governments are the owners of resources on their territory. UN Resolution 1803 of 1962 declares that "the right of peoples and nations to permanent sovereignty over their national wealth and resources must be exercised in the interest of their national development and of the well-being of the people of the state concerned." This issue is also addressed in article 18 of the ECT (Sovereignty over Energy Resources). Both texts leave, within the rules of international law, the right of each country to determine exploration, development, and disposition of energy resources as well as the structure of the sector and the rent-taking regime. Article 18 of the ECT also stipulates that resource-owning countries will facilitate access to energy resources inter alia by allocating concessions in a nondiscriminatory manner on the basis of published criteria.

Taking compensation for the depletion of an exhaustible resource (a depletion premium) may not matter too much for domestic use, as the country and its population could benefit directly from the domestic resource. However, for exports, countries will try to maximize the depletion premium to exercise their sovereignty in the interest of their national development.

While the essential decision of resource depletion policy is in the hands of the government, capital and technology are needed to develop the resources. Especially during periods of relative low energy prices, resource-owning governments may have to compete for capital and technology providers and attract international companies for exploration and production. Insurance on the stability of the investment frame for investors, as is provided by part 3 of the ECT, is an important element in attracting investors at more favorable conditions for the country. At the same time, in times of scarcity of energy supply and high oil prices, providers of capital and technology have to compete for access to promising acreage.

However, in view of the high concentration of hydrocarbon reserves in a few countries, their depletion policy—especially when coordinated by a group like OPEC or the Gas Exporting Countries Forum—gives them potentially a strong influence on the supply function and acts as an instrument to maximize their revenue for the benefit of their population. The availability of energy (at affordable prices) has become crucial for economic development worldwide. Therefore the challenge is twofold: accounting for the interests of the totality of the world population, especially the poor, in the global governance of the energy sector; and creating generally applicable rules on the depletion of resources while dealing with the principle of sovereignty over natural resources.

Government Influence on Energy Demand

On the consumer side, the major determinant for energy consumption is the level and structure of economic activity of a country. In most countries, economic growth continues to be strongly correlated with the growth of energy, especially electricity, consumption. Energy demand depends on customers' decisions, which are dependent on income, preferences, and the competitiveness of the respective energy market.

However, the policies of consuming countries also have a decisive influence on both the level of energy demand and the energy mix. While the government cannot directly stipulate the consumption pattern (unlike its influence on the depletion path of natural resources), it has a variety of instruments to influence consumer decisions, such as norms and guidelines on energy efficiency, guidelines for use of clean energies, limits on pollution, emissions trading regimes, taxation and subsidies, and market regulation. Therefore targets on the level of energy consumption or a certain energy mix may be reached through an adequate mix of policy instruments, given a credible political will. The most prominent example is the policy to curb carbon dioxide emissions, which almost exclusively stem from burning fossil fuels. The overall CO_2 emission targets are increasingly defined on an international level via the UNFCCC and related mechanisms and then broken down to define the use of fossil fuels on a national level.

A major component of the overall CO_2 emissions of a country originates from its power sector. Its fuel mix, which is still strongly influenced by national givens and the resulting policy of national governments, largely defines the use of fossil fuels (mainly gas and coal) in the power sector. The remaining room for CO_2 emissions of a country (plus and minus the balance of emissions trading) can then be translated into an overall demand for carbon from hydrocarbons (gas and oil).

The above considerations illustrate the strong influence of energy-consuming countries on energy usage and fuel mix. Governments influence energy demand through CO_2 emission policies and policies for the power sector. CO_2 emission targets can be considered ambitious, and undercutting them is not likely except during major economic crises. These targets give a good indication of the medium-term development of energy demand and the energy mix of a given country, which energy-exporting countries may take as a basis for their depletion policy. Yet it is questionable whether or not producing countries are always aware of consumer countries' policies that determine medium- and long-term demand.

Conclusion

The restrictions imposed by the need to reduce carbon emissions are increasingly influencing energy demand and driving the deployment and development of energy-efficient technologies. Reducing carbon dioxide emissions is part of the global governance scheme by the UNFCCC. To allow for a smooth transformation of this scheme to the energy sector—while allowing for the energy supply necessary for development—the following seems to be necessary:

First and foremost, a free flow of energy, investment, and technology has to be fostered across borders by reducing as much as possible barriers to the trade of energy, the flow of investments, and the transfer of technology (this is to a large extent established by the WTO and the ECT).

Second, energy producers need to enhance transparency on the development of factors relevant for the depletion and export policy of producing countries. This would not conflict with sovereign depletion decisions but provide a better basis to market participants in making long-term decisions and help to avoid bottlenecks and price volatility.

Third, and as a flip side of the coin, consuming countries need to create transparency regarding their policies determining future demand development. This means that consumer countries need to enhance transparency on the way the global and national CO_2 emission targets are to be translated into national energy policy as well as policy for market development of the power sector as an indication of future demand of fossil fuels. Enhancing mutual transparency on factual supply and demand development and applicable policies would not interfere with the sovereignty of any country but would allow for better informed long-term decisions in the energy sector. Organizing that transparency would need the cooperation of all existing international institutions dealing directly or indirectly with energy.

Finally, it would be imperative to restrict—and in any case, to supervise—the flow of speculative money into the trading of energy commodities to avoid the resulting bidding up of energy prices beyond the fundamentals of supply and demand. Both elements would address the common interest shared by producing and consuming countries to reduce volatility, which might lead to developments that cannot be managed by market mechanisms.

PART TWO

Global Energy and Financial Markets

6

State-Backed Financing in Oil and Gas Projects

Amy Myers Jaffe and Ronald Soligo

A long process of structural change has been experienced in the international oil industry over the last several decades. Increasingly, control of oil resources has been returning to national governments through the stewardship of their national oil companies. National oil companies (NOCs) now command over 80 percent of the remaining global oil reserves and will overwhelmingly dominate world oil production and pricing in the coming decades. By comparison, Western international oil companies (IOCs), which dominated the world oil scene in the nineteenth and twentieth centuries, now control less than 10 percent of the world oil resources.

According to the respected industry journal *Petroleum Intelligence Weekly (PIW)*, of the top twenty oil companies worldwide in terms of breadth of assets, operations, and production, thirteen are NOCs or newly privatized NOCs. *PIW*'s oil company rankings show that Saudi Aramco, National Iranian Oil Company (NIOC), Petróleos de Venezuela, S.A. (PDVSA), China National Petroleum Corporation (CNPC), Mexico's PEMEX, Russia's Gazprom, Algeria's Sonatrach, Kuwait Petroleum Corporation, Brazil's Petrobras, Abu Dhabi National Oil Company, Russia's Lukoil, Malaysia's Petronas, and Nigerian National Petroleum Corporation are among the largest oil- and gas-producing companies in the world.[1]

1. "*PIW* Ranks the World's Top 50 Oil Companies," *Petroleum Intelligence Weekly*, December 3, 2007.

To be sure, NOCs are not a new institutional phenomenon. The first NOC was Direccion General de los Yacimientos Petroliferos Fiscales, a state oil board formed in Argentina in 1922 to prevent fuel shortages in the country. Other South American countries followed suit, but the most dramatic was the formation of the NOC PEMEX founded in Mexico in 1938 to take control of the country's national resources after a labor dispute pushed the Mexico government to expel foreign companies from the sector. In the 1960s and 1970s many countries either nationalized their energy assets or created new public sector energy companies.

The end of European colonialism and the rise of nationalist movements led to the nationalization of the oil reserves of such oil-producing countries as Saudi Arabia, Iraq, and Iran. Their aim was to regain control from foreign oil companies, which were not serving the national interests. NOCs were able to garner higher national revenue from the sale of the country's oil. Other NOCs were created in the aftermath of the 1956 and 1970s oil crises to help consuming governments like India, Japan, and Brazil protect their access to their fuel supply.

The pendulum swung back toward privatization, or at least partial privatization, of many of these firms over the past twenty years. But the beginning of the twenty-first century was marked by a return to resource nationalism and an empowering of NOCs, which is transforming international relations among major nations. The rise (or reemergence) of NOCs has large implications for the global economy and the governance system that regulates economic relations among nations.

NOCs have become the new ambassadors of international discourse, in some cases overshadowing foreign ministries. They are expected to control a greater proportion of future oil supplies over the next two decades, as oil and gas production in the mature producing regions of the Organization for Economic Cooperation and Development (OECD) continues on its natural geologic decline. The International Energy Agency projects that more than 90 percent of new hydrocarbon supplies will come mainly from the developing world in the next twenty years. By contrast, 40 percent of new production in the past three decades came from the industrialized West, with the majority of investment being made by IOCs.

The International Energy Agency projects that, over the next thirty years, US$5 trillion in new investments will be needed in the global oil sector to meet rising world demand for oil.[2] Despite these tremendous capital requirements, many governments continue to intervene in energy markets in a manner that is slowing or even discouraging this needed investment. Large undeveloped oil fields

2. International Energy Agency (2008), p. 323.

exist throughout the Persian Gulf, Latin America, Africa, and Russia, and there remain key areas such as Iraq's western desert that have yet to be explored fully. But the private sector firms in the best position to amass the capital required to make major risky and long-term investments in promising resources have been frequently denied access to many of these prolific and promising regions.

At the same time, Asian and Russian national oil companies have increasingly begun to compete for strategic resources in the Middle East, Africa, and Eurasia. These national oil companies have come to play a pivotal role in the international exploration and production business. Some NOCs have the benefit of state finance to give them an advantage in the global energy business. But generally speaking, in recent years governments have been siphoning oil revenue from their national oil companies to meet domestic requirements for socioeconomic welfare priorities or to meet budget deficits. This is especially true of the NOCs of oil-exporting countries, with their sizable economic rents.

Studies of national oil companies show that many governments use NOCs to achieve wider political and socioeconomic policy objectives. As Valerie Marcel and John Mitchell note in their book *Oil Titans,* "On the home front, national oil companies are often torn between national expectations that they should carry the flag and their own ambitions for commercial success, which might mean a degree of emancipation from the confines of the national agenda."[3] In a Baker Institute study Stacy Eller, Peter Hartley, and Kenneth Medlock conclude that noncommercial responsibilities can affect a firm's efficient use of revenues and that other goals, such as income redistribution and industrial development, often become equally important goals in the state firm's calculus of profit maximization.[4] The diffuse NOC objectives have implications for the financing of future NOC investments. The study notes that "domestically, these emerging national oil companies fulfill various important social and economic functions that compete for capital budgets that might otherwise be allocated to more commercial activities such as reserve replacement and oil production activities. These noncore, noncommercial obligations have imposed costs upon the NOC, and in some cases, dilute the incentive to maximize profits, hindering the NOC's ability to raise external capital and to compete at international standards."[5]

The tendency of oil-dependent governments to use oil revenues from national oil companies for other pressing national spending priorities has in many cases

3. Marcel and Mitchell (2006), p. 2.
4. Eller, Hartley, and Medlock (2007), p. 43.
5. Baker Institute (2007), p. 2.

hindered the firms from sustaining core operations. The list of NOCs with flat or declining oil production capacity is long and includes major resource holders such as Iran's NIOC, Mexico's PEMEX, Venezuela's PDVSA, and Russia's Gazprom. Many NOCs not only are having trouble retaining the necessary funds to increase their resource base and expand oil and gas production but are also facing production problems as older fields reach natural maturity and funds are not available either for enhanced oil recovery techniques in old fields or for drilling new fields. A good case in point is Venezuela, whose government shifted US$60 billion a year of PDVSA's budget to social welfare programs. Lower investments in oil field projects in Venezuela have translated into a 50 percent loss of production capacity (from 3.6 million barrels a day in 1998 to just over 2 million barrels a day in 2009). Mexico is another example: its lack of funding for new drilling and exploration has resulted in a 25 percent decline in output between 2006 and 2009 (from 3.68 million barrels a day to 2.72 million barrels a day).

The failure of certain governments to adequately finance resource development by their national oil companies has raised questions about global energy security and future oil industry governance. Can oil-consuming countries count on NOCs to make the necessary investments to meet the rise in demand? Will such investments be sufficient to counterbalance the sharp declines in supply being experienced across the globe as oil fields age?

This chapter focuses on possible sources of finance for NOC investments and on how to ensure that this financing is adequate to meet demand for oil in the future. We especially look at the role of international capital markets, at partial privatization, and at direct foreign investment. We consider the experiences of NOCs that have tapped international financial markets. Finally, we examine the operation of NOCs within the framework of the corporate governance literature, with its emphasis on the alignment of interests between principals and managers. This framework addresses the influence of private investors on the internal governance and transparency of NOCs.

Financing Exploration

The organization and operation of national oil companies vary according to the history, the domestic political circumstances, and the economic policy of the country. Generally speaking, oil-producing countries have two ways to finance oil and natural gas exploration and development, internal and external. That is, they can tap into their own cash flow or they can rely on external investors or lenders.

For many NOCs, the economic costs of finding, developing, and producing oil and gas are far below the prices at which these products are sold. The difference is a windfall gain, often referred to as an economic rent. The challenge for the NOC is, first, to separate the economic rent accruing from resource ownership from these costs and, second, to allocate this rent among stakeholders: the firm itself, the public treasury, labor (if it is unionized), consumers, and private shareholders (if any). Unfortunately, true economic costs, in particular the cost of capital, are not transparent, since investments by the government or the NOC itself are not arranged through a market transaction. Yet these investments do have an opportunity cost and should be included in assessing the economic costs of the NOC. In contrast, the cost of private equity capital (return to private shareholders) is determined in a market exchange and hence is explicit and transparent. If dividends or share price appreciation do not at least equal the risk-adjusted return on other comparable assets available to investors, the price of shares will fall and the cost of acquiring private capital in the future will rise.

In practice, the economic rent for a barrel of oil produced under a typical investment framework can be quite substantial. In a market where the price of oil averages $50 a barrel, the operating costs to the producer/investor are often as low as $2 a barrel, while exploration and capital recovery costs (including rate of return) could be similarly low, around $3 a barrel each, leaving overall costs at around $8 a barrel. This means that the economic rent from the $50 barrel is $42 or 84 percent. The cost of capital must be deducted from revenues before one calculates the economic rent. If the NOC has no private equity participation, the rent automatically belongs to the state. Often in these cases return on public investment in the firm is conflated with rent and treated by governments as revenue that can be extracted for its discretionary use.

If private investment is permitted, economic rent can be extracted through lease bonuses, royalties, corporate income taxes, and equity interest ownership. As a capital-intensive industry, the oil and gas sector is extremely sensitive to the cost of capital, which in turn is affected by investors' view of the political, technical, and economic risks of the local economy. A high-risk environment increases financing costs and thus decreases the economic rent to the state. For example, landlocked oil states in the Caspian Basin, whose geographic location increases the risks associated with oil resource development, have been forced to offer direct foreign investors a higher rate of return and greater stake in their oil fields than comparable oil producers in West Africa and Latin America, whose location is closer to end-user markets.

Self-Investment

One option for NOCs is to finance all of their oil exploration and development through NOC sales revenues or infusions of capital from other government revenues. Before the 2008 global financial crisis, this approach was gaining in popularity in many parts of the world as a resurgence of nationalism turned populations against foreign investment. Rising oil prices between 2002 and 2008 rendered this approach popular in Russia, Latin America, and the Middle East. Nationalists fervently want to protect the domestic patrimony from foreign exploitation and to retain the rents from resource exploitation for the nation and its citizens. These trends are increasingly evident in Bolivia and Russia. And although Venezuela, Nigeria, and Kazakhstan continue to host foreign direct investment, they have reduced the share of rents that accrue to foreign investors. Saudi Arabia, Mexico, and Kuwait maintain a policy of self-financing oil investments, and any adjustment in this policy would face strong domestic opposition.

A problem with a self-investment strategy for oil-producing countries is that it promotes dependence of the national economy on the oil sector. When a high proportion of government investment occurs in the oil sector, it tends to incentivize private capital and labor to focus on businesses and activities related to the oil sector, such as has taken place in Saudi Arabia and Kuwait. In this way, a self-investment strategy can thwart diversification of the economic base. In these cases, the NOC together with its domestic suppliers and subcontractors account for a large share of GDP and—as in all undiversified portfolios—increases the country's exposure to volatility in commodity prices. In addition, large inflows of oil revenue can create asset market and real estate bubbles and drive up the cost of production of tradable goods, which can further thwart the development of other industries. In these circumstances, imports squeeze out both domestic firms that can supply the economy as well as potential export-oriented businesses.[6]

It can be difficult for a country to determine how to maximize the benefits from the development of its natural resources and whether fully financing investment through government is the best use of national revenues. A nation has many worthy projects to consider for its national budget. In an ideal world, any investment in the oil industry would be compared with the economic return that can be gained from other, nonoil, opportunities. Investment in oil would then occur only if the return were higher than on those alternative investments. But this can be problematic for some developing economies. The advantage of continuing to

6. Karl (1998).

invest in an NOC is that returns are very high and immediate and that local people have been trained in the oil business and have acquired the skills necessary to manage and operate an oil firm. Comparable skills would have to be developed in other industries if governments were to pursue such investments. The learning curve can be steep and costly and therefore could discourage countries that already have developed hydrocarbon sectors, or that could have large hydrocarbon sectors, from developing new industries.

An alternative to investing in other sectors of the economy is to set up a sovereign development fund that invests in financial and other assets, often foreign assets. While this might be the most "efficient" or immediately profitable use of the financial resource, such a fund does not contribute directly to economic development because it does not create jobs and opportunities for the country's citizens in the way that investments in national enterprises would. So regardless of the economic arguments that long-term management of the public wealth should be focused on return to capital and diversification away from a resources portfolio, public support will most likely favor the operation of an NOC.

The issue is often framed in terms of what social purpose should be served by a country's natural resources. Who should participate in the resource rents? And when? The public may have different objectives from those of the administrators of the NOC or of the governing political elites. And, as Terry Lynn Karl points out, governments have difficulty resisting the demands of the population for a share of the resource wealth, especially in those countries where the resource wealth is significant relative to the rest of the economy: "Instead of economic efficiency or political learning, petrodollars are substituted for statecraft. Where this occurs, the capacity to resist demands is eroded, and relative insulation of policymakers is undermined. In effect, rulers lose the capacity to say no."[7]

In the 1980s and 1990s, social pressures developed in many oil-producing countries over the failure of governments to deliver adequate social welfare services and an equitable distribution of resource wealth. The result has been that many governments have increasingly reallocated revenue generated by the NOC for investments in such social service sectors as education, health, and infrastructure. Some governments have used NOC revenues to cover federal budget outlays or to repay foreign national debt. In other cases, NOC oil is sold at discounted rates or given away as aid to meet foreign policy goals. Saudi Arabia, for example, gave oil assistance to the Taliban during the Soviet invasion of Afghanistan. More recently Venezuela used part of its oil wealth to further its political objectives

7. Karl (1999), p. 37.

within the hemisphere. President Chavez has created Petro Caribe as a means of providing oil to members at a subsidized price.

Domestically, NOCs are also often asked to divert resources that might have been used for reinvestment in oil exploration and development to meet such non-commercial goals as income redistribution and national industrialization through fuel subsidies or other means.[8] This is the case in countries as diverse as China, Iran, Saudi Arabia, Nigeria, Indonesia, Venezuela, and Brazil. In fact most NOCs in major oil-producing countries provide subsidized fuel to both consumers and local industry.

Saudi Aramco, for example, provides natural gas for feedstock for the development of private domestic industries at prices that do not justify commercial development of its gas resources. This practice has discouraged the development of Saudi Arabia's natural gas resources and has resulted in distortions, wherein the kingdom uses highly valuable crude oil to generate electricity; whereas it could, instead, export that crude oil to the international market for a substantial profit. Adding to the distortions, the electricity is sold to Saudi businesses and citizens at nominal rates.

In Iran, to sustain the economic fortunes of the population and equitably share the country's oil wealth, NIOC sells gasoline at highly subsidized prices. Low gasoline prices have created soaring demand, but loss of revenues has meant that NIOC has had difficulty expanding to meet the rise in gasoline demand. Instead, Iran has had to import gasoline from international markets to meet domestic demand, at a substantial burden to the Iranian national budget.

NOCs also utilize local-content rules to promote local businesses by requiring their subcontractors and trading partners to buy goods produced in their home country, even though these may be more expensive than alternative sources.

Another characteristic that many NOCs share is overemployment, reflecting the confluence of the interests of politicians, who provide employment for votes, and the public, which sees jobs as a way to share the national patrimony. From the perspective of the public, the creation of jobs is a visible and tangible benefit; and although these jobs are a highly inefficient use of labor, they have the virtue of transferring income directly to the populace.

All of these policies can make it difficult for the NOC to amass the capital needed to replace its reserves and expand its oil production.[9] As mentioned above, Stacy Eller, Peter Hartley, and Kenneth Medlock find (in an empirical analysis

---

8. See Baker Institute (2007) for an extensive discussion of this trend. Its chapters cover the specifics of programs for fifteen NOCs.

9. Baker Institute (2007).

using a sample of eighty firms over a period of three years) that NOCs' noncommercial objectives tend to interfere with efficient production and maximum revenues. These outcomes have a negative effect on the ability of NOCs to replace their reserves and to expand production.[10]

While some of the social and other expenditures financed with NOC rents can enhance the productivity and growth of the economy and improve the lives of those on the bottom rungs of society, some are unproductive and even regressive in their impact. In many oil-producing countries, NOC revenues are siphoned off to support the consumption of middle- and upper-income groups. Fuel subsidies disproportionately benefit those who own automobiles, a group that does not tend to include the poor. Among the noncommercial objectives that political interests impose on OPEC NOCs, the subsidization of domestic fuel has been among the most debilitating. These subsidies are not only a direct drain on NOC revenues but also an indirect drain, since they promote domestic consumption and hence reduce foreign currency earnings from exports.

On a macroeconomic level, low petroleum prices stimulate growth in energy-intensive sectors and limit incentives for energy efficiency, which in high-population societies only exacerbates the budgetary problems of the NOC and the government. This problem is circular, since the subsidies leave fewer and fewer funds to reinvest in expanding oil production. At the extreme, the combination of rising oil demand and flagging domestic production ends in political and economic crises. The OPEC member Indonesia flipped from a net oil-exporting country to an oil-importing country in the last three years because of flagging oil production in aging oil fields combined with soaring demand driven by fuel subsidies. Those fuel subsidies, which by the late 1990s reached almost one quarter of the Indonesian government's entire federal budget, caused such massive economic dislocation for the Indonesian government that the longtime rule of President Suharto was ended.

Other major oil-producing countries, such as Iran, Mexico, and Algeria, face similar prospects: they could even become net oil importers in the years ahead, which would bring dire economic consequences. Iran is particularly exposed. With Iranian domestic demand for fuel skyrocketing, the state oil company, NIOC, has had to sell hard currency in order to import gasoline back into the country. The country's product import bill now runs in the billions of dollars, with NIOC predicting that gasoline subsidies will cost the industry US$15 billion to US$20 billion annually by the next decade. The subsidies, while extremely

10. Eller, Hartley, and Medlock (2007), p. 1.

helpful to middle-income Iranians, are becoming increasingly damaging to the Iranian treasury and have created a mounting deficit that even high oil prices have not been able to countermand.

Fuel subsidies in Mexico are much more modest. But the government has used PEMEX revenues to finance some 40 percent of its expenditures. This practice has allowed the government to avoid the politically difficult task of tax reform but has left PEMEX unable to finance sufficient exploration and development to prevent a rapid decline in its reserves and revenues. Predictably, as a result, Mexico is facing a crisis in public finance and, at a time of worldwide economic recession, a major decline in export of oil and, hence, export revenues.

As mentioned earlier, another problem with a self-investment strategy for oil-producing countries is that it tends to shift dependence of the national economy onto the oil sector. A high proportion of government investment in the oil sector tends to incentivize private capital and labor to focus on service businesses and activities that revolve around oil sector spending. This compounds the dependence of the economy on the international price of oil. In this way, a self-investment strategy prevents the diversification of the economic base and, unless proper institutional frameworks are put in place, promotes corruption. Thus noncommercial criteria become the basis for lucrative subcontracting with the state-run oil industry, as has been seen in Iran, Iraq, and Mexico. The NOC can also suffer from the negative effects of stop-and-start budgeting, which happens when oil prices fluctuate.

Ultimately, trade-offs are difficult to assess. It is particularly difficult to place a value on the services, such as education and health care, that are provided to the most disadvantaged and to compare that with the returns from investing NOC revenues in oil- and gas-related activities. However, oil revenues can be used for social welfare services without the state's controlling 100 percent of resource investment. It has been demonstrated in many oil-producing nations that investment in the oil and gas sectors can be left to the private sector, while the nation still derives economic rent through taxation. These governments are thus able to divert some resources to other needy sectors without hindering investment in the oil and gas sector.

Foreign Direct Investment

Given national budgetary pressures, even in light of nationalistic trends, most major oil-producing countries still permit foreign direct investment. This includes not only oil-producing countries within the OECD (Canada, Australia, Norway, and the United Kingdom, where exploration acreage leasing is common) but also developing countries such as Nigeria, Angola, Brazil, Abu Dhabi, Algeria, Kazakhstan, Azerbaijan, Indonesia, and Malaysia and to a lesser extent Iran and Venezuela. For developing countries with needs for large amounts of capital, foreign direct investment is one way that the country can increase total investment and enhance development prospects without sacrificing other government programs.

Private investors must be compensated for risk taking, so the distribution of revenues will reflect the allocation of risk between private investors and the government. The less risk the direct investor takes in undertaking exploration and development, the less the national government will have to share a portion of the economic rent. On the other hand, if the investor encounters a high level of risk, he will expect a commensurate share of the revenues. So for example in the case of Azerbaijan, where investors faced high geological risk, great distance from markets, and a lack of well-developed political institutions and governance, higher returns were required than in, for example, Abu Dhabi, which has more stable government institutions, an export infrastructure, and a forgiving and oil-rich geology.

Generally speaking, there are three kinds of foreign direct investment contracts: concession agreements, production-sharing agreements, and service contracts. Concession agreements are typically used in OECD countries, where title to the oil is not a national constitutional issue. Under a concession agreement the investor receives legal title to the oil and gas, while the state is shielded from all risk, collecting instead fixed royalties and taxes but leaving the investor with the windfall if oil prices rise significantly over the life of the investment. This kind of contract has been widely used in the United States, the United Kingdom, and Australia.

Production-sharing agreements typically include terms that allow the host government to take an increased share as production increases and to get a larger share over time as cumulative targets for revenues and volumes for the projects are reached. Thus typically under production-sharing agreements, the more profitable the venture, the higher the return will eventually be to the host government, but the government also shares in the risks of project costs and long-term oil prices along with the investor. Legal title to the oil and gas remains with the state, while the contractor receives the right to share in ongoing production. Many production-sharing agreements have provisions that allow the investor to recover his costs of exploration, development, and operations before profits are distributed.

Finally, some oil-producing countries favor service contracts in which investors are compensated for development and production through a direct fee. Such contracts were implemented successfully in Algeria and with mixed results in Colombia and Venezuela. Payment is typically linked to the volume of hydrocarbons produced or discovered, and the contract specifies a particular type and amount of work to be performed under a field development plan.

The government retains ownership and assumes all market and price risks. When development cost risk exposure is high, a "cost-plus" service contract is sometimes employed. Under this contracting structure, contractors or investors are given assurance that they will recover costs associated with implementing the service contract plus a fixed profit payment, typically linked to unit production performance.

In a twist on the service contract, Iran has offered buy-back service contracts, under which the investor or contractor provides all the finance for the project and in return receives a share of oil and gas production in a manner that provides a fixed rate of return. After the contractor or investor has recouped his costs and return, the operation of the field is fully transferred to the state. Again, as in all service contracts, the state retains legal title of the oil and gas.

Each type of contract has its disadvantages in terms the efficient exploitation of resources. A key downside to service contracts from the state's point of view is that the contractor or investor has no incentive to hold investment and operation costs down, and this can affect the state's rate of return from the project over time. On the other hand, production-sharing agreements provide disincentives for the efficient production of oil and gas because the firm bases its extraction decision on the marginal benefits and costs to itself, not the benefits to society or government. The share that must be paid to the government lowers the marginal benefit to the firm, and it will, as a result, produce less that the socially optimal amount. International oil companies tend to favor production-sharing agreements, which allow them to book hydrocarbon reserves on their balance sheets and thereby enhance the value of their corporate stock shares on public markets. However, these agreements are among the most controversial of the contract types and are increasingly being rejected by countries whose populations are skeptical of the benefits to foreign investment in the oil sector.

Initial Public Offerings and the International Capital Market

While it is possible for national oil companies to borrow money to finance exploration and development spending, this has not typically been the practice of most NOCs. Some countries, notably Mexico, have issued bonds from their NOCs, but the money raised was not used to cover or expand PEMEX's investment budget but rather to finance national spending. In recent years an increasing number of governments have viewed their NOCs as vehicles to raise international capital for a variety of purposes, including reducing foreign debt and supplementing national budgets. Rather than borrowing as a sovereign entity, these governments have been able to raise capital more cheaply by leveraging the intrinsic value of the assets of their NOCs.

A range of mechanisms have been used to cash in on capital by leveraging NOCs. As mentioned, Mexico simply issued bonds. But other countries have undertaken the direct sale of state-held assets or the sale of shares on domestic or international markets. Issuing the latter through initial public offerings (IPOs) has been a favored approach, with major state-run oil and natural gas companies in China, Russia, Norway, Brazil, and India offering equity shares on domestic and international financial markets. This strategy has been appealing to many emerging market countries because it has lowered their costs of borrowing while at the same time increasing the prestige and visibility of their national companies. But it is important to note that the motive for IPOs in most cases was not to raise capital for the NOC itself to engage in oil and gas exploration but rather was a mechanism for governments to raise additional resources for other expenditures. The notable exception is Norway's Statoil, whose share sales allowed the company to expand its international businesses.

When the NOC is wholly owned by the state, the amount of revenue that can be siphoned off by the government is ultimately limited by the current revenue stream of the NOC. But private investors are willing to pay a price for shares in the company that reflect the present discounted value of future revenue streams. In other words, by making an IPO the government can collect in the present some of the future revenues of the firm. In many cases a hybrid approach to selling equity is taken, with direct sales of shares to one or more strategic investors (often another international oil company or NOC) as well as offerings in public equity markets (table 6-1).

During the period 2002–07 when oil prices were rising, the global investment community was receptive to NOC shares, and indeed they experienced strong appreciation of share values even in comparison to the privately held, publicly traded international oil companies such as ExxonMobil, BP, and Shell. Share markets rewarded NOCs for their strong reserve position and also especially those NOCs that were well managed and expanding investments such as Petrobras and Statoil.

In the case of Norway's Statoil, the company has succeeded in increasing the value of the state's shares since the IPO, and some significant portion of this increase is not linked to higher oil prices according to analysis by Richard Gordon and Thomas Stenvoll in a Baker Institute case study on the corporation (figure 6-1).[11] Statoil management and the Norwegian government first considered a partial privatization of Statoil's shares in 1999, in an effort to improve competitiveness and raise capital for an expansion of the company's international activities

---

11. Gordon and Stenvoll (2007).

Table 6-1. *Equity Sales, National Oil Companies, Various Years*

National oil company	Equity sales
YPF	July 1993, IPO for 58.00% of company's equity
	January 1999, Repsol acquires 14.99% in secondary offering, government of Argentina retains 5.40% interest
	April 1999, Repsol tenders for all YPF shares
PetroChina, CNOOC, Sinopec	2000–01, IPO: international majors are largest purchasers, with BP purchasing 20% of PetroChina's shares; ExxonMobil, Shell, and BP purchasing 57% of Sinopec shares; Shell purchasing 20% of CNOOC shares
ONGC	2004, IPO of 10.0%, 8.3% going to institutional investors
ENI	1995–2001, five offerings of IPO shares
Statoil	June 2001, IPO via 49% issuance of new shares, 51% through sale of government's existing shares
Petron	February 1994, sale of 40% equity to Saudi Aramco
	September 1994, IPO for 20% of shares on the Philippine stock exchange
Lukoil	December 1995, places securities in the form of American depositary receipts
	2000, offers shares on London stock exchange
	2004, sells 7.9% of remaining government shares to ConocoPhillips
Rosneft	2006, IPO on London and Moscow stock exchanges

Source: Baker Institute (2007).

in the face of declining oil production and diminishing opportunities in the Norwegian North Sea.

On the back of political scandals involving huge cost overruns on two major projects—Mongstad oil refinery and Aasgard field development—political will was gathering behind a restructuring plan that would provide an increased return to capital. This change in philosophy mirrored gradual changes in domestic politics in the 1990s, as Norway moved away from Labour Party politics, which had favored national industrialization, toward new elites, who favored a more liberal, market-oriented economy.

Figure 6-1. *Share Price Performance of Oil at US$50 a Barrel, NOCs,*
WTI Spot, and Major Companies, 2002–07

Percent (October 2002 = 100)

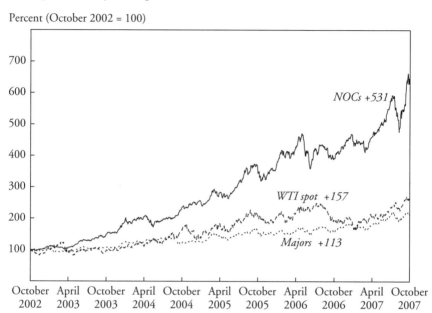

Source: Baker Institute (2007).

In the spring of 2000 the Labour Party presented a plan for Statoil to be partially privatized. The sale of Statoil shares in 2001 and subsequent trading on public exchanges as American Depositary Shares not only provided an influx of capital
but also established a clear, external valuation of the government's shareholdings
in Statoil. In the years after partial privatization, the company further reorganized
to enhance its profitability by consolidating and rationalizing its Norwegian holdings and expanding its international investments. It also expanded its natural gas
businesses and moved to expand its downstream operations to enhance the operational and financial benefits of vertical integration. During, and in the aftermath
of, its partial privatization, Statoil began to lose some of its national status, as its
monopolistic control of all pipeline infrastructure was stripped away in favor of
open access for all participants on equal terms.

Once partially privatized, Statoil's role in noncommercial activities such as foreign policy formation and national industrialization policy was reduced. Norway's
ascension to the European Economic Area, under which Norway gained access
to the Common Market, meant that the country was bound to follow common

competition directives. Statoil was no longer allowed to act as the controlling party to set natural gas prices and customers for all long-term sales of gas from Norway. The withering of Statoil's noncommercial national responsibilities, state-oriented status, and government interference in its operations after privatization contributed to the company's ability to focus on international activities and the restructuring that improved operations and profitability.

The disappearance of government interference in national oil company operations after privatization is not a given, and other NOCs have had differing experiences from those of Statoil. A good example of a firm whose foray into international capital markets has come with less favorable results is Russia's Rosneft, which moved to raise US$10 billion in 2006 through an initial public offering in London and Moscow (figure 6-2). The goal of the IPO was to pay back US$7.5 billion to four western banks, which had lent Rosneft the money for its purchase of a controlling stake in Russia's Gazprom. These shares, which represented about a 14 per-

Figure 6-2. *Rosneft and Statoil Share Prices, July 2006 to January 2009*[a]

US$

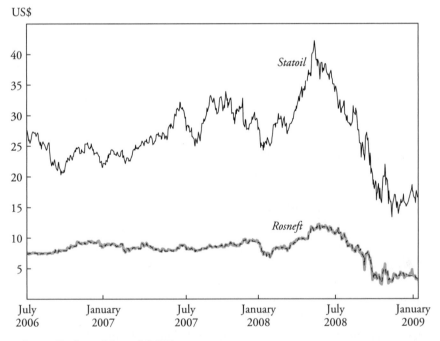

Source: Gordon and Stenvall (2007).
a. Rosneft is listed on the London Stock Exchange; Statoil is listed on the New York Stock Exchange.

cent stake in the company, traded initially at the value the company was seeking (in the range of US$7.55 a share). The IPO was helped by initial sales to other oil firms, including British Petroleum, China National Petroleum Corporation, and Malaysia's Petronas.[12] Those share purchasers were said to be seeking closer strategic alliances with Rosneft because of their interests in investing in Russia.

While the Rosneft IPO offering was successful, the offering sparked some controversy, with some European advisory firms and even the financier George Soros warning investors to stay away due to high political risk.[13] Rosneft share prices were volatile in 2008, falling to a low of US$2.11 a share in October 2008, before recovering to US$4.54 in March 2009. Rosneft had to seek assistance from the Russian government to avert a funding crisis and to restructure its US$20 billion debt. The price volatility in Rosneft's shares also partly reflects geopolitical risk associated with the impact of perceptions of Russia's foreign policy on the company's fortunes and its ability to pursue business opportunities.

Theory versus Practice

Studies published in the academic literature support the notion that the partial privatization of firm shares brings more efficiency to national oil company operations. The focus has traditionally been on the modern private corporation, termed by Alfred Chandler *managerial capitalism,* which separates ownership of the firm—the shareholders—from the professional managers who run it.[14] State-owned firms can also take this corporate form, when an independent board runs the firm as distinct from the case where the firm is run as a division within a government ministry. In practice the distinction can be blurred, as governments can interfere in the management of even corporatized firms and state-owned firms can subcontract work to private suppliers.

Until relatively recently the debate over the merit of private versus state-owned firms was mostly theoretical (and often polemical), since there were few data to test the theories. Now with the wider availability of data the number of empirical studies has increased, but there remains an important barrier to settling the issue with any finality. That barrier concerns the nature of the firm's objective. In the case of a private company, it is generally accepted that the firm's objective is (or should be) to maximize profits (the value of the firm for shareholders). For state-owned

---

12. Steven Mufson, "Russian Oil Firm IPO Ends Early," *Washington Post,* July 13, 2006, p. D5.

13. Roman Kupchinsky, "Russia: All Eyes on Rosneft ahead of Controversial IPO," Radio Free Europe (www.rferl.org/articleprintview/1068027.html).

14. Chandler (1990).

firms, this may not be the sole objective. We have already discussed many other objectives that have been assigned to state-owned forms. But there are others. For example, in the decades bracketing World War II the creation of many Canadian state-owned firms in rail, air, broadcasting, pipelines, and so on was to promote east-west trade and communication in a country in which natural economic forces favored a north-south flow. Because of the thin population density in the western part of the country, these industries were not profitable in a strictly business sense and hence would not have been undertaken by private capital.

Thus in many countries state-owned companies are created to forge a national identity and to foster national economic development. Nationalization is promoted precisely because private ownership did not fulfill these larger public goals. In the case of some undeveloped countries with weak public institutions, foreign resource owners or investors and domestic political elites exported the net revenues from the national resource production, thereby creating a dual economic structure with a small, wealthy enclave, leaving the rest of the country virtually untouched by resource development. This process is currently seen in several West African countries, including Angola and to some extent Nigeria. It occurs less in Latin America, but in the 1970s the process was behind the nationalization of the Chilean copper mines. Currently in Bolivia this phenomenon has caused a call on the part of the population for the nationalization of resources.

Nationalization, by transferring control to national interests, is seen by the public as the best means to redirect profits into sectors of the country that would most benefit lower- and middle-income groups. Political elites respond to these demands in order to maintain public support for their continued rule. In the best of circumstances there is a serious effort to evaluate investments and social programs and make choices that would, on a rational basis, further economic and social development. At the other extreme are populist leaders who see resource revenues as a means to blatantly buy political support. It is not easy to disentangle these motives, and indeed they may both exist at the same time. Public policy seldom reflects a single point of view. But these other objectives make comparisons with private firms difficult. NOCs are often called upon to provide employment and to subsidize their output—or even to meet obligations that lie outside their main line of business. In comparing the performance of state-owned and private firms one ideally would need to know what value to place on these noncommercial outputs. At best, one can calculate the difference in the firms' efficiency using traditional performance measures and view this difference as the cost of the other objectives.

The economic issue that arises in the large modern corporation, with its separation of ownership and control, was popularized in 1932 by Adolph Berle and

Gardiner Means.[15] They point out that firm managers, who may own relatively few shares of the company, and the majority of shareholders can have differing goals and objectives. Managers are tempted to operate the firm in ways that further their own interests and that do not maximize profits, even though that is the key objective of shareholders. This issue was further developed within the principal-agent paradigm introduced by C. M. Jensen and W. H. Meckling.[16]

In response to this principal-agent problem, institutional features of modern capitalism have emerged to constrain managerial behavior and to provide incentives to better align managerial and shareholder interests. These include monitoring requirements, such as financial reporting, that provide information to shareholders about managerial performance.[17] In some models of corporate governance, the performance of the share price is sufficient, since "the price set in the financial markets for a company's shares fully and efficiently reflects all the available information about the company and is thus the best measure of the net value of the firm."[18] Failure to maximize profits will be reflected in the share price of the firm, inviting other investors to assume control either by a proxy fight or by outright purchase or merger of the firm. The signal provided by the share price also works in the managerial labor market, where the manager's wages are determined in such a way as to ensure incentive compatibility. While this model is a simplification of reality—as all models must be—the market for corporate control does function this way.

Peter Hartley and Kenneth Medlock note that the principal-agent framework also can "be used to examine the likely behavior of government-controlled business enterprises."[19] They argue that, in the case of national oil companies, oil production and pricing decisions could be part of the "objective function of politicians" and that the political objectives of politicians overseeing the operations of the firm can take precedence over the maximization of shareholder wealth—where the shareholders are the government and, by extension, the general public. There is however no automatic mechanism to correct the principal-agent problem in the case of state-owned enterprises. By definition a government firm cannot be taken over by other investors. And since debt issued by national oil companies is ultimately guaranteed by the government, financial failure cannot send the firm into bankruptcy. Management can be replaced in cases where failure is clear, but because there is no market-determined price for the equity of

---

15. Berle and Means (1932).
16. Jensen and Meckling (1976).
17. Holmstrom (1979).
18. Blair (1995), p. 107.
19. Hartley and Medlock (2007), p. 16.

the firm, which is in essence the collective judgment of financial analysts and others of the manager's performance, it is difficult to know whether the firm is producing at its potential.

This theory of corporate governance as it applies to private firms depends on the precision with which markets can evaluate firm performance relative to the potential of the firm and the objectives and actions of investors. An alternative theory about the failure of corporate governance posits investor myopia, which results in investors' focus on the short-term performance of the firm at the expense of its long-term profitability. Investor orientation toward short-term price performance provides strong incentives for management to also focus on short-term performance. This tendency can be aggravated by compensation schemes that use stock options, thus providing a strong incentive for management to focus on raising share prices in the short term so that they can maximize and monetize their own personal compensation. This is a controversial theory, but the volatility of share prices lends credence to the idea that markets do not always set the appropriate value for a company's stock.

The same focus on the short run can also occur in the context of state-owned firms. "Politicians who do not care about the performance of the firm beyond their own term of office may be tempted to use the return to capital for other purposes even though it would leave insufficient funds to finance additional investments."[20] Such behavior can make sense for the managers of NOCs, who are often members of the governing elite and wish to maintain their power. Terry Lynn Karl remarks, "Such economically inefficient decision-making is not a miscalculation when viewed politically. Instead, it is an integral part of the calculation of rulers to retain their support."[21]

Another difference between privately owned firms with publicly traded shares and state-owned firms is that new investment by private firms will be reflected in higher share prices only if investors expect them to yield a positive net present value when discounted at the firm's cost of capital. Government-owned firms can borrow at the rate offered for government bonds. This rate is set not by perceptions of the economics of future investments but by a more complex set of variables related to the country's overall debt levels and political risk. Andrei Shleifer also finds that managers of state-run firms have less incentive to innovate or reduce costs than managers of private firms.[22] Indeed, government ownership can motivate managers to pursue nonfinancial objectives such as the well-being of the nation.[23]

20. Hartley and Medlock (2007), p. 18.
21. Karl (1999), pp. 31–48.
22. Shleifer (1998).
23. Aharoni (1981); Vernon (1979).

The empirical literature comparing private and state-owned firms shows that state firms are less profitable and more labor intensive than private firms. One of the earlier studies is by Kathryn DeWenter and Paul Malatesta, using data primarily from the more industrialized countries.[24] Among their conclusions is the fact that the return on sales of private firms is more than twice that of government firms. Similarly, they find a significant difference in return on equity. Labor intensity, as measured by employment per unit sales, shows that government firms have a higher level than private firms, although the differences are much smaller than in the case of profitability. The employment-to-assets ratio is also higher but is not statistically significant.

The authors also look at leverage, as measured by the ratio of total liabilities to assets, and find that state-owned firms have significantly higher ratios. This is consistent with the fact that a government firm can borrow at lower interest rates than private firms. It also suggests that the capital investment of government firms comes more through borrowing than through injections of capital from the government's budget. In contrast private firms acquire capital from both borrowing and selling shares.

The more interesting findings were obtained in studies that look at a time profile for these variables. DeWenter and Malatesta find that increases in profitability and declines in employment intensity and leverage occur *before* privatization and typically do not continue afterward. These results suggest that governments restructure their firms and improve profitability before privatization, possibly with an eye to increasing the attractiveness and price of the shares to be sold. It also suggests that government-owned firms are capable of operating with higher profit and less labor even without the structural benefits of privatization. However, without some mechanism to monitor firm behavior, such improvements might dissipate over time.

George Yarrow suggests that one reason for privatizing is to preserve these efficiency gains through market discipline.[25] It is possible, nonetheless, for a government to create an incentive structure for NOCs to sustain efficiency gains through public scrutiny by requiring firms to publish quarterly performance and annual reports (as required, for example, under the rules of the Securities and Exchange Commission of the United States) and by subjecting them to oversight by parliamentary or other government regulatory bodies.

One finding of the Baker Institute study on NOCs is that the structure of governance for an NOC can have significant impact on its abilities to "focus efficiently on its core businesses" and "greatly reduce the prevalence of corruption

24. DeWenter and Malatesta (2001).
25. Yarrow (1986).

and wasteful spending."[26] The study concludes that independent corporate boards
of directors "play a positive role in bringing transparency and performance measures into the oversight structure of NOCs such as Statoil, Saudi Aramco, and
CNOOC [China National Offshore Oil Corporation]."[27] The study also finds
that competition plays a strong role in promoting best practices.

This finding is supported by research conducted by Miranda Wainberg and
Michelle Foss at the University of Texas's Center for Energy Economics.[28] Their
study concludes that for commercialization goals, "upstream competition matters"
and that "the coordination and competition among commercial players often yields
the best results in activities that include many complicated decisions of a commercial and technical nature." The study also concludes that, in places where NOCs
compete or cooperate directly with foreign direct investors, "there was an initial
strong element of knowledge transfer from foreign oil companies and supply/
service companies."

Christian Wolf and Michael Pollitt apply a similar framework to oil companies,
using a database with twenty-two measures of firm performance.[29] Their conclusions are similar to those of DeWenter and Malatesta. Specifically, they find that
"over a seven-year period around the initial public offering, return on sales increases
by 3.6 percentage points, total output by 40%, capital expenditure by 47%, and
employment intensity drops by 35%." The study demonstrates that most of the
improvements in profitability and employment intensity begin to occur several
years before the sale of shares but taper off afterward. These gains occur despite the
fact that the government may still hold the majority of shares and hence operating
control. Significantly, Wolf and Pollitt do not find comparable efficiency gains with
subsequent share sales as governments reduce their stake in the firms.

Governance, Efficiency, and Transparency

From the perspective of the developed world, policy should facilitate the development of natural resources to ensure that supplies can grow with demand at fairly
stable prices. There is no doubt that at least some of the rapid increase in world
oil prices during the years 2005–08 is the result of insufficient investment in oil
producing capacity; much of that failure occurred in countries with dominant
NOCs. The concentration of large reserves by one national monopoly eliminates

26. Baker Institute (2007), p. 4.
27. Baker Institute (2007), p. 14.
28. Wainberg and Foss (2005); quotations on p. 30.
29. Wolf and Pollitt (2008); quotation on p. 36.

the possibility that local competition of firms will enhance the efficiency of all and promote an adequate pace of investment. From the perspective of the larger OPEC oil producers, one advantage of an oil monopoly is precisely that it can control the pace of investment and the expansion of capacity, thereby having some influence on price.

Over the past thirty years the policy of the United States and international organizations such as the International Monetary Fund and the World Bank has been to promote and encourage (or during periods of debt crises, even force) the privatization of state-owned firms in many developing countries and has had the effect of transforming many of these firms into more aggressive, commercially oriented global competitors.

The developed oil-importing countries also have an interest in promoting the efficient operation of NOCs, since more efficient firms are more likely to be able to finance and plan capacity expansion. Privatization, even partial privatization, has enhanced the performance of several NOCs, resulting in higher production. IPO shares, partial privatization, and even commercial bonds can bring NOCs into the monitoring systems of international financial markets, thereby improving transparency, accounting, and public reporting systems and corporate governance. Once shares are publicly traded, government interference in NOC activities will damage the value of the firm's shares and invite public criticism and exposure. To the extent that noncommercial objectives interfere with the firm's ability to meet core functions and commercial goals, related noncommercial practices will similarly weigh on the firm's market value. As in the case of Rosneft, concerns about the actions of the Russian government were reflected in the performance of Rosneft shares on the London Stock Exchange. Over time such problems could result in limiting access of the firm to international capital markets and in generating financial losses for the Russian government.

It can be argued that the institutional mechanisms of auditing, reporting, monitoring, and corporate governance, including a well-functioning independent board of directors, can discourage a diversion of rents to a favored political group and can build the constituency for long-term strategies that will ensure the firm's continued profitability and productivity. However, the benefits of at least the partial privatization of shareholding to produce greater efficiency are demonstrated empirically. Data suggest that government ownership reduces the ability of a firm to produce revenues for a given quantity of inputs.[30] In effect, accessing international capital markets forces NOCs to engage in more transparent accounting and financial record-keeping.

30. Eller, Hartley, and Medlock (2007), p. 31.

Conclusion

Given the importance of NOCs to world oil production, continued access of NOCs to international financial markets is an important element in improving governance and transparency and, thereby, operational efficiency. Especially in an environment in which oil prices are moderating, more resource-holding governments will want to tap IPOs as a means of raising capital for investment or to retire debt. If oil prices remain relatively low for a period of time, many oil-producing countries will be under greater pressure to generate revenues to maintain social investments and services to rapidly growing populations. Borrowing money will be costly, given the quantities involved and the perceived risk of government debt. Selling off part of the NOC will be seen as a politically palatable way of raising cash without sacrificing control over the country's patrimony.

Oil-consuming countries can also promote best practices for NOCs through existing and emerging bilateral and multilateral trade mechanisms, such as the World Trade Organization, the Energy Charter, the North American Free Trade Agreement, and other international architectures. These will be important elements in ensuring that there is sufficient investment to meet global demand in the years and decades ahead.

The World Trade Organization, while technically covering trade in energy goods, has not been tapped in any significant manner to structure international trade and investment in oil and natural gas.[31] The opportunity to make energy more central to international trade talks is better today than at any time in recent years, because the extreme price volatility of 2008 harmed the economies of both consumer and producer nations equally, highlighting the benefits to both sides of an improved international architecture for energy markets. While oil producers may have enjoyed rising state revenues from 2004 to mid-2008, the sudden collapse in oil prices in July 2008 and through early 2009 left state budgets and national economies of many oil-producing countries in crisis. So while producing countries might appear to have a short-term interest in unilateral pricing and investment policies, over the longer term it is clear that securing stable long-term revenues is preferable to the peaks and valleys seen in the last two decades. Russia's default on its sovereign debt during the oil price plunge in 1998 is but one example. The current financial problems of Venezuela and Iran are another.

An international architecture to promote an adequate and steady investment in oil and natural gas is sorely lacking in the existing financial and global economic

31. Goldthau and Witte (2009).

system. More consideration should be given to how to remedy this deficit. As discussed, functioning independent corporate boards of directors, greater reporting requirements, greater transparency for NOCs within their home regulatory frameworks, and expanded participation of NOCs in international capital markets will play a positive role in the oversight of NOCs. Such practices should be encouraged and supported by international institutions, nongovernmental organizations, and trading partners through an international architecture modeled along the lines of the European Energy Charter Treaty and other multinational trade agreements.

Trade agreements need to aim for not just fair competition within energy sectors but also adequate investment in upstream sectors. At present no major multinational trade policies address the prevalence of fuel subsidies in oil-producing countries and their debilitating effect on the ability of national oil companies to reinvest in new productive capabilities, nor is there any proposal for a multilateral agreement on cross investment that would guarantee removal (or even easing) of investment restrictions in many major oil-producing countries. As countries address the global financial crisis and increased market contagion among global commodities and economies, the cross investment in energy resources will become more relevant to the discussion. Large oil-consuming nations should insist that cross investment be on the agenda as part of an overall framework that keeps their markets open to global trade and investment in downstream energy businesses, nonoil commodities, financial services, and other goods.

International nongovernmental organizations should also open a dialogue with countries that have NOCs operating abroad and discuss how to institute corporate citizenship measures by all stakeholders in the international energy market. Current international corporate citizenship initiatives represent a major breakthrough in the creation of forums for discussion, the development of policies, and a review of practices to enhance human rights and sustainability. Statoil and Petrobras, for example, have been major contributors and participants in these forums, and their public statements and sustainability records indicate that they will remain corporate international citizens. In comparison, China National Petroleum Corporation, Oil and Natural Gas Corporation Limited, and PDVSA have largely been inactive.

References

Aharoni, Yair. 1981. "Performance Evaluation of State-Owned Enterprises: A Process Perspective." *Management Science* 27, no. 11.

Baker Institute. 2007. "Executive Summary." In Policy Report 35, *The Changing Role of National Oil Companies in International Energy Markets*. Houston.

Berle, Adolph A., Jr., and Gardiner C. Means. 1932. *The Modern Corporation and Private Property*. New York: Commerce Clearing House.

Blair, Margaret M. 1995. *Ownership and Control: Rethinking Corporate Governance for the Twenty-First Century*. Brookings.

Chandler, Alfred D., Jr. 1990. *Scale and Scope: The Dynamics of Industrial Capitalism*. Harvard University Press.

DeWenter, Kathryn L., and Paul H. Malatesta. 2001. "State-Owned and Privately Owned Firms: An Empirical Analysis of Profitability, Leverage, and Labor Intensity." *American Economic Review* 91, no. 1.

Eller, Stacy L., Peter Hartley, and Kenneth B. Medlock III. 2007. "Empirical Evidence of the Operational Efficiency of National Oil Companies." In Policy Report 35, *The Changing Role of National Oil Companies in International Energy Markets*. Houston: Baker Institute.

Goldthau, Andreas, and Jan Martin Witte. 2009. "Back to the Future or Forward to the Past? Strengthening Markets and Rules for Effective Global Energy Governance." *International Affairs* 85, no. 2.

Gordon, Richard, and Thomas Stenvoll. 2007. "Statoil: A Study in Political Entrepreneurship." In Policy Report 35, *The Changing Role of National Oil Companies in International Energy Markets*. Houston: Baker Institute.

Hartley, Peter, and Kenneth B. Medlock III. 2007. "A Model of the Operation and Development of a National Oil Company." In Policy Report 35, *The Changing Role of National Oil Companies in International Energy Markets*. Houston: Baker Institute.

Holmstrom, Bengt. 1979. "Moral Hazard and Observability." *RAND Journal of Economics* 10, no. 1.

International Energy Agency. 2008. *World Energy Outlook 2008*. Paris.

Jensen, C. M., and W. H. Meckling. 1976. "Theory of the Firm: Managerial Behavior, Agency Costs, and Ownership Structure." *Journal of Financial Economics* 3, no. 4.

Karl, Terry Lynn. 1998. "The Paradox of Plenty: Oil Booms and Petro-States." *Studies in International Political Economy* 26. University of California at Berkeley.

———. 1999. "The Perils of the Petro-State: Reflections on the Paradox of Plenty." *Journal of International Affairs* 53, no. 1.

Marcel, Valerie, and John V. Mitchell. 2006. *Oil Titans: National Oil Companies in the Middle East*. Brookings.

Shleifer, Andrei. 1998. "State versus Private Ownership." *Journal of Economic Perspectives* 12, no. 4.

Vernon, Raymond. 1979. "The International Aspects of State-Owned Enterprises." *Journal of International Business Studies* 10, no. 3.

Wainberg, Miranda Ferrell, and Michelle Michot Foss. 2005. "Commercial Frameworks for National Oil Companies." Working Paper. Center for Energy Economics, University of Texas at Austin.

Wolf, Christian, and Michael G. Pollitt. 2008. "Privatizing National Oil Companies: Assessing the Impact on Firm Performance." Cambridge Judge Business Working Paper 02/2008. Cambridge University.

Yarrow, George. 1986. "Privatization in Theory and Practice." *Economic Policy* 1, no. 2.

7

How Do Emerging Carbon Markets Influence Energy Sector Investments?

William Blyth

This book is concerned with the energy security and governance challenges associated with meeting an increasing demand for energy from an expanding global population. While there is no lack of hydrocarbons on the planet, the extent to which these can be used is constrained by, among other things, the capacity of the atmosphere to absorb carbon emissions without dangerously altering the world's climate. Globally, the energy sector contributes almost 60 percent of the world's annual greenhouse gas emissions, making it impossible to disentangle questions of energy policy from questions of climate policy.

The total value of the world's energy consumption is equivalent to almost US$3 trillion a year, or around 7 percent of global GDP. Reducing emissions from this energy consumption could cost at least as much as the fuels themselves. The latest *World Energy Outlook* from the International Energy Agency (IEA) estimates that, to contribute to meeting a 450 parts-per-million concentration, a cap-and-trade scheme in OECD countries would result in a carbon price of US$180 a tonne of CO_2, whereas meeting a 550 ppm concentration target by 2030 would result in a carbon price of US$90 a tonne of CO_2.[1] Table 7-1 shows

1. International Energy Agency (2008), p. 47.

Table 7-1. *Forecast of Coal, Oil, and Gas Prices in 2030, with and without Additional Carbon Price*[a]
US$

Fuel	Dollar price without additional carbon price	Dollar price with additional carbon price of US$90	Dollar price with additional carbon price of US$180
Coal per ton	64	215	430
Oil per barrel	63	40	80
Gas per thermal unit	0.86	0.53	1.06

Source: European Commission (2008).
a. These forecasts are adapted from the PRIMES model and expressed in barrels of oil equivalent of US$63 for oil, US$47.6 for gas, and US$14.9 for coal. Carbon prices are converted to physical and thermal quantities using standard thermal conversion rates and IPCC emission factors.

how these carbon prices translate into an additional cost for using fossil fuels and how these compare to price forecasts for 2030 in a recent EU modeling exercise.

Clearly, the introduction of such price signals should have a significant effect on energy sector investment decisions. However, these carbon prices have to be created through policy mechanisms, since there is no "natural" value to saving CO_2 at the point of emission. The task is, therefore, to set up governance structures for the regulation of greenhouse gas emissions that are equivalent in scale and value to the structures governing energy markets. Governance structures for energy trade have developed over many decades, since energy has been an important driver of international relations for much of the past century. Although they are far from problem free, nevertheless, these governance structures have emerged with relatively clear principles of national resource allocation and strong foundations for international trade, since the commodity being traded is tangible. By comparison, governance structures for climate change are still embryonic, the commodity to be traded far more nebulous, and the underlying principles of resource allocation far from resolved. Tackling climate change needs a new multinational approach to assigning emissions rights and abatement responsibilities and will require international collaboration on an unprecedented scale.

The main platform for building such an agreement is the UN Framework Convention on Climate Change (UNFCCC). Agreed on in 1992 and adopted by almost every country on the planet, the UNFCCC commits countries to "common but differentiated responsibilities" for taking action to avoid "dangerous anthropogenic interference with the climate system." This framework convention defines general principles but not concrete steps. A significant amount of detail has since been added, with the Kyoto Protocol in 1997 defining quantitative reduction targets for industrialized countries, the Marrakech Accords in 2001 defining rules for the international trade of carbon credits, and the 2007 Bali Action Plan defining terms for the negotiation of a successor to Kyoto. However, the difficult issues remain to be resolved: agreeing on the levels of abatement required to avoid dangerous interference and defining precisely what is meant by common but differentiated responsibilities.

Frustrated by the slow process of multilateral negotiations involving 190 countries, the United States championed a parallel process starting in 2007, the Major Economies Meeting on Energy Security and Climate Change, which was designed to provide more focused discussions on abatement among the fifteen or twenty countries responsible for around 95 percent of global CO_2 emissions. The logistics of negotiating in such a group are more straightforward than in larger groups; however, the politics has proven no less thorny. Difficulty has arisen from the perceived lack of neutrality of talks championed by the United States and the possibility that the process could weaken the main negotiating tracks that have been established in the UN process. In practice, the meeting has not become the forum where a breakthrough deal on climate change will be done. It has instead, together with the climate discussions under the G-8 process, contributed to the lesser but still worthy goal of building trust and mutual understanding among major parties as a prelude to more formal negotiations within the UNFCCC process, and this role is likely to continue to be needed in the future.

If and when a global climate change deal is struck, a huge challenge will remain in delivering the required changes to the energy infrastructure. International agreements will have to be ratified and then translated into domestic policy mechanisms, which will in turn translate into a change in investment decisions by individuals and companies. The international agreements will have to be strong enough to overcome the difficult domestic politics that politicians will inevitably face when they come to implement costly policy measures in their own jurisdictions. And the domestic policies will have to be sufficiently robust to overcome not only the financial barriers to new technology but also the commercial risks associated with a wholesale shift away from doing business as usual.

Climate Change: The Underlying Challenges

The basic challenge that climate change policy has to tackle is to direct investment flows toward low-emitting technologies. This task is made more complex by the presence of fundamental uncertainties in the science and economics of climate change. These uncertainties together with other barriers introduce limitations on the effectiveness of carbon pricing as a policy tool and present risk to investment decisionmakers.

The Science and Economics of Climate Change

The arithmetic of climate change in its simplified form is straightforward.[2] At current emission levels, humans emit around thirty gigatonnes of CO_2 a year, mostly from the combustion of oil, gas, and coal, with total emissions of all greenhouse gases measuring around fifty gigatonnes of CO_2 equivalent. Assuming that the removal of greenhouse gases from the atmosphere due to natural sinks continues at its current rate, these emissions still result in an increase in atmospheric CO_2 concentration of 2 parts per million a year. The current concentration of carbon dioxide is 380 ppm CO_2 (around 425 ppm CO_2 equivalent, including other greenhouse gases).[3] This is up from a level of 280 ppm before industrialization and exceeds by far the natural range over the past 650,000 years of 180–300 ppm.

There is no general agreement over what level of greenhouse gas concentration increase could be considered safe, but a doubling of CO_2 emissions relative to preindustrial times is often used as a benchmark for scientific studies on the sensitivity of the climate system. The *Stern Review* suggests that somewhere between a doubling of greenhouse gas concentrations (450 ppm CO_2 equivalent) and an upper level of 550 ppm CO_2 equivalent would be a suitable range to consider for policy purposes.[4] At current rates, therefore, the lower limit will be exceeded in around a decade and the upper limit in around six decades. Other studies recommend limits outside this range. For example, to limit warming to less than two degrees Celsius, a position adopted by the European Union, the World Wildlife Fund estimates that concentrations would need to be brought down to 400 ppm of CO_2 equivalent.[5] On the other hand, cost-benefit analysis carried out by William Nordhaus arrives at a recommended abatement level of only 10–15 percent below unconstrained emissions levels, a path that would lead to an increase in carbon in the atmosphere of approximately three times preindustrial levels by the end of the twenty-first century.[6]

---

2. Broecker (2007), p. 1371.
3. CO_2e is shorthand for the concentration of all greenhouse gases converted to a CO_2 equivalent, that is, the amount of CO_2 that would be required to produce the same amount of warming as the actual concentration of the gas concerned. Key non-CO_2 gases include methane, nitrous oxide, SF6, CFCs, and HFCs. These other gases add around 50–100 ppm CO_2e depending on assumptions about their relative emission levels. Because their actual volumes emitted are relatively low compared to CO_2, they can often be abated at relatively low cost.
4. Stern (2007).
5. European Council (2004); World Wildlife Fund (2007).
6. Nordhaus (1992), p. 1315.

CARBON MARKETS AND ENERGY SECTOR INVESTMENT 137

Various features of climate change make it different from other environmental problems and frustrate attempts to arrive at a truly objective economic analysis of how the problem should be tackled. The first feature is that greenhouse gases accumulate in the atmosphere as they are emitted, and once they are there they take centuries to be removed. Current emissions are therefore essentially irreversible.[7] The physical risks we face are also nonlinear, such that the prospect of nasty surprises increases with concentration level and with the rate at which the concentration levels are increased, a concern that has been exacerbated following evidence of previous abrupt changes in the earth's geological history.[8] Policymaking therefore becomes a problem of decisionmaking under uncertainty. If we learn over time that climate change is less damaging than originally anticipated, early action will turn out to have been wasted. But if we learn over time that climate change is more damaging than originally anticipated, because the accumulation of greenhouse gases in the atmosphere is irreversible, it will be too late to reverse the process.[9] Not only the impacts but also the costs of mitigating climate change are highly uncertain. The review of the literature in the *Stern Review* puts the range between −1 percent and 4 percent of global GDP to achieve the suggested range of 450–550 ppm, a quite significant difference between upper and lower bounds.

The second feature is the long-term nature of the problem. The atmosphere warms slowly because of the thermal inertia of the oceans, creating a lag of many decades between increases in greenhouse gas concentrations in the atmosphere and temperature increases. There is then an even greater lag of hundreds to thousands of years between the temperature increase and some of the most damaging impacts, such as the melting of ice leading to sea-level rise. These lags mean that high-emission and low-emission scenarios produced quite similar damages over the course of this century. The worst of the climate change damages under the high-emission scenario are expected to occur a century from now and continue to worsen during the twenty-second century. Accounting for such long-term intergenerational effects raises difficult economic and ethical issues.[10]

7. Various technical options are being researched for removing CO_2 from ambient air (see Broecker, 2007, p. 1371), but none of these have been technically proven, and the costs are highly uncertain at this stage. In any case, even at full scale, it is hard to see that these technologies could remove greenhouse CO_2 from the atmosphere at a significantly higher rate than we are currently emitting, meaning that any reductions in emissions would still take many decades.

8. Schneider (2004); Alley and others (2003), p. 2005.

9. For a review of the economics of decisionmaking under uncertainty, see Ingham and Ulph (2005); Heal and Kristroem (2002).

10. See for example Schelling (1995).

These first two features of climate change make decisionmaking complex, even if there was an idealized single decisionmaker who could act optimally on behalf of the planet. The third feature makes decisionmaking even more complex. Although climate change is a global phenomenon, the physical and economic impacts vary considerably by region. The most affected regions are also likely to be the poorest, partly because they are often located in areas already climatically challenging and partly because poverty tends to reduce adaptive capacity.[11] These tend not to be the countries responsible for the emissions of greenhouse gases, so that the incentives of different countries to tackle the problem are not well aligned. These features of irreversibility, uncertainty, and differentiated impacts all have important consequences for the politics of reaching a solution to climate change.

Carbon Pricing: Theory and Limitations

In a perfect world, climate mitigation policy would be straightforward. A single global carbon price could be established (either through a tax or a cap-and-trade scheme) that incentivized emission reductions by raising the cost of high-emitting technologies relative to the cost of low-emitting technologies. In principle, these additional costs would be factored into companies' operating and investment decisions, creating an incentive to switch between existing technologies or to bring forward new low-carbon technologies. Emission reductions would occur from the cheapest sources first, with costs rising over time until emissions are brought close enough to zero to be absorbed by the natural sinks. To avoid emissions "leaking" from this constraint, the scheme would have to cover virtually all sources of anthropogenic greenhouse gas emissions on the planet.

In 1974 Martin Weitzman discussed the pros and cons of taxes or tradable permits, concluding that in the case of climate change there is a case for preferring taxes.[12] However, the politics of raising taxes is difficult, especially in an international context. Emissions trading has achieved more traction because the problem of stranded assets of incumbent emitters can be solved by giving away free permits, thus sweetening the pill of paying for emissions. Most of the discussion of carbon markets in this chapter assumes that trading schemes will continue to be the way forward for carbon pricing schemes, although several of the conclusions also apply to attempts to develop a common international taxation scheme.

However, real-world problems limit the effectiveness of carbon pricing. Perhaps most fundamental is the difficulty of creating a sufficiently stable regulatory

11. Intergovernmental Panel on Climate Change (2007).
12. Weitzman (1974).

regime that allows emission reductions to be bankable assets against which companies could finance the necessary investments. Related to this are significant political difficulties associated with reaching international agreement on harmonized rules either for taxes or for trading schemes, due to the possible large transfers of wealth between companies and between countries and to the associated difficulties of agreeing on how revenues from such taxes or trading schemes should be allocated and spent.

Even if these regulatory difficulties could be overcome, however, another important limitation to carbon pricing is that it will tend to underdeliver investment in research and development of technologies that are currently far from commercial viability. This is because companies cannot guarantee to be able to appropriate all the knowledge gained through research and development (R & D) for themselves. Knut Rosendahl shows that optimal tax rates should be differentiated to reflect the capacity for learning; they will therefore not necessarily be the same across all sources, contrary to the standard assumption of environmental economics.[13] In addition, the problem of time inconsistency makes it difficult for policymakers to credibly guarantee high future prices to justify current expenditure on R & D in new technologies, and there is evidence that, in the presence of multiple market externalities, multiple policy measures may perform better than single policy measures.[14]

Nevertheless, carbon pricing is an essential component of the policy mix, supplementing technology-specific support policies.[15] Technology policy can be seen as putting solutions on the shelf, with carbon pricing required in order to take solutions off the shelf. The *Stern Review,* for example, recommends a combination of carbon pricing, technology-specific policy support (such as R & D), and information programs. However, policymakers need to be careful to ensure that such policy packages are well coordinated. Pushing too fast down a technology-specific path will tend to undermine carbon prices, reducing the effectiveness of investment signals under a cap-and-trade scheme.[16]

Uncertainty over the required rate of abatement and the irreversibility of major investments in energy infrastructure mean that mitigation policy is a problem of decisionmaking under uncertainty. The price signal created by carbon trading schemes is therefore subject to risks that may inhibit the effectiveness of this mechanism as a basis for investment decisionmaking.

13. Rosendahl (2004). See also Richels and Blanford (2008); Otto and others (2008).
14. See for example Helm and others (2003).
15. Fischer (2008).
16. Blyth (2008).

Uncertainty about Investment Decisions

Carbon differs substantially from the other tradable commodities that feed into companies' investment decisions. This is partly because the drivers of the carbon price tend to be more diverse than in most commodity markets. Perhaps more important, this is also because of the political nature of the decisions that ultimately determine the supply of the commodity being traded. In the context of an emissions trading scheme, for example, these political decisions will be manifested as price risks in the carbon market. Such risks raise the cost of capital for investment and therefore create an additional barrier to a transition to a low-carbon energy system.

Policy uncertainty creates an uncertain outcome in the cash flow of projects that companies consider for investment. Companies may have the option to wait until the policy uncertainty is resolved; by waiting, they may be able to avoid the worst outcomes by tailoring investment decisions to policy developments. On the other hand, by waiting they forgo income. The value of waiting therefore has to be balanced against the opportunity cost of waiting. This balance will be tipped in favor of immediate investment if the expected project revenues are sufficiently high. The greater the level of policy uncertainty, the higher the expected profit has to be to justify immediate investment; uncertainty therefore effectively creates an additional risk premium, which must be covered by the expected returns from the project.

For fossil fuel generation, these risks are significantly dampened in markets where the cost of carbon will be passed through to the price of electricity. In markets with regulated electricity prices, companies would aim to cover the additional compliance costs through a renegotiated rate. Such a rate rise could in principle accurately reflect the increase in costs for the company, although there would still be some residual risk that an appropriate rate increase might not be allowed by the regulator.

In competitively priced markets, the passing on of carbon costs to the price of electricity would occur for the marginal plant in the system. For coal- and gas-fired generation, the carbon price would therefore increase both revenues and the cost of generation, so that the project's profitability would be relatively insensitive to carbon price shocks. Analysis of energy supply investments carried out by the International Energy Agency indicates that electricity prices would rise modestly as a result.[17] Electricity price rises on the order of 5–10 percent would be expected

17. International Energy Agency (2007a).

if regulatory intervention occurred every five to ten years and could be more than this if there were an investment hiatus and capacity shortage close to the time of an expected regulatory intervention.

Some technologies are more vulnerable than others to these risks, and thus regulatory risk can affect technology choice. A notable and somewhat counterintuitive conclusion is that low-carbon, high-capital-intensive technologies, such as nuclear power and renewables, may be particularly vulnerable to uncertainty in climate change policy.[18] These technologies would benefit from a pass-through of carbon costs from fossil fuel generating plants to the price of electricity, but variations in carbon price would therefore feed directly through to variations in plant profitability. Regulatory risk is calculated to raise the threshold for nuclear investment by between 3 percent and 33 percent of capital costs, depending on the timing of uncertain regulatory events and the rate at which CO_2 costs are passed through to electricity costs.

Investment in carbon capture and storage (CCS), too, is affected by various risks. This technology removes 85 percent or more of the CO_2 from the combustion plant, transports it in pipelines, and then pumps it down into a geological site for long-term storage. From the perspective of the CO_2 emitter, the key risks associated with this relatively new technology are uncertainty over the costs of the CO_2 separation equipment, over the performance and security of the storage site, and over how much the avoidance of emissions will be worth in terms of the reduced cost of emitting CO_2. If coal plants are built in a suitable way and at a suitable location, CCS can be relatively easily retrofitted at a later date. CCS therefore provides coal plants with a good hedge against uncertain future CO_2 prices. The existence of CCS as a future retrofit option therefore makes current investment in coal look attractive, although there are still significant technical and cost risks associated with CCS that have not been fully proven at scale, creating a policy dilemma regarding the licensing of new, unabated coal plants.[19]

Certainly, without some other kind of policy support, CCS will not be implemented until carbon prices are significantly higher than they are today. Estimates of the breakeven price of carbon required to pay back the additional capital and operating costs of CCS vary but are typically in the region of US$35 a tonne of CO_2, once the technology is fully proven, with early plants costing considerably more than this. However, taking account of policy uncertainty adds significantly

18. Blyth and others (2007).
19. Lockwood (2008).

to the price that would be required to make the technology fully commercially viable (the price at which a company would choose to invest under normal market conditions). The 2008 IEA study estimates that the breakeven price of carbon would have to rise to around 15–40 percent above this breakeven level depending on the timing of policy decisions.[20] These calculations reinforce the general intuition that an uncertain policy environment makes investment in low-carbon technologies risky and therefore expensive. In essence, uncertainty raises the cost of tackling climate change.

What Are the Rules? A Review of Existing Frameworks for Carbon Markets

Carbon markets are at an embryonic, and therefore arguably most uncertain, stage of development. Regional schemes such as the EU Emissions Trading Scheme (EU-ETS) have proven the concept at scale. Nevertheless, nations are still far from an idealized world of a single global carbon price. This chapter argues that the emergence of an effective global carbon market will require both top-down actions to negotiate and define terms for engagement of the international community in climate change mitigation and in the bottom-up development of many different regional schemes. These can subsequently be strengthened and eventually linked to the top-down rules. This section provides the basis for this argument by reviewing experiences to date of building the rules through both top-down negotiations and bottom-up regulations (as illustrated to date mainly by the EU-ETS).

The Political Economy of International Climate Negotiations

Although some progress has been made since 1992 on the details of an international policy framework, the political problems remain difficult. Climate negotiations have been likened to the prisoner's dilemma in game theory.[21] Each country has an incentive to allow other countries to take on the burden of emission reductions, since it will then get a free-ride benefit from these reductions without having to make the costly emission reductions itself.

This perspective has led to a strong demand among many OECD countries, and particularly the United States, that any future deal will have to include all major economies in order to avoid competitive distortions. Such concerns around competitiveness have been widely discussed, and although some studies suggest

20. International Energy Agency (2008).
21. Barrett (2002).

they may be overblown, they are politically sensitive enough to create a significant obstacle to progress.[22] At the time of writing, draft legislation is being considered by the U.S. Congress that, among other things, puts an economywide cap on U.S. emissions of greenhouse gases.[23] To address domestic competitiveness concerns, the draft bill includes a provision for a "border adjustment" program. Under that program, foreign manufacturers and importers would be required to pay for and hold special allowances to cover the carbon contained in U.S.-bound products. Such measures clearly help politically with the passing of such unilateral legislation, despite doubts about the effectiveness and desirability of these measures in broader economic terms.[24]

Equally entrenched, however, is an opposing perspective. Developed nations have benefited from a century or two of industrial development dependent largely on fossil fuels, and developing countries argue that they should not be denied the same opportunity. Not only that, but responsibility for the greenhouse gases already emitted to the atmosphere lies largely with countries that industrialized in the previous century, while the damages from these emissions will be borne disproportionately in poorer countries. Equity considerations and liability for historical emissions have never been well defined or explicitly recognized in the UNFCCC or the Kyoto Protocol, and these questions still burden the negotiations.[25] For example, the Kyoto Protocol includes adaptation funds intended to provide a flow of money from emitters to those most in need of help in adapting to the effects of climate change. It also includes mechanisms to encourage the transfer of low-carbon technologies to developing countries. However, so far developed countries have not lived up to their commitments to these funds and mechanisms.

These political considerations have a strong influence on the prospects and likely future direction of UNFCCC negotiations. The UNFCCC is a framework treaty, setting out key principles and broad definitions of responsibilities. Nearly every country has been able to agree to these principles and definitions. However, the difficulty has been to go beyond the general to the specific. Although negotiators agreed at Bali at the end of 2007 on a new deadline of 2009 to come up with a post-Kyoto deal for the period beyond 2013, the negotiations are proceeding at a snail's pace.

Multinational forums outside the UNFCCC have failed to provide a breakthrough to the prisoner's dilemma. The Major Economies Meeting championed

22. Reinaud (2008); Carbon Trust (2009).
23. The draft Waxman-Markey bill is entitled "American Clean Energy and Security Act of 2009."
24. McKibbin and Wilcoxen (2008).
25. See Baer and others (2000); Mueller (2002).

by President George W. Bush led to three high-level meetings involving state leaders of the world's major economies, representing a high proportion of global emissions. Although there seemed to be hopes from the U.S. administration that this meeting might provide the necessary breakthrough, other countries were more cautious. Apart from the obvious risk of making a deal on nonneutral ground, developing countries in particular had concerns about divorcing the climate abatement deal from the adaptation deal. Although the countries at the meeting account for the great majority of greenhouse gas emissions, climate impacts will be felt by all countries. Ultimately this inequity will restrict the value of a deal made by emitters only. Regardless, those involved in the meeting noted that the level of trust among parties did build over the series of meetings, and in this sense the process has probably made a positive contribution toward ultimate delivery of a deal within the formal UNFCCC process.

The other major multinational forum for climate change is the G-8. Climate change has regularly been on the agenda of these meetings since 2005, when the United Kingdom hosted the meeting at Gleneagles. This resulted in the Gleneagles Action Plan, which has largely involved commissioning additional analysis by the International Energy Agency of various policy options. Subsequent G-8 meetings have focused on a shared vision of the scale of the problem, culminating in an agreement in July 2008 by G-8 leaders "to share with all Parties to the UNFCCC the vision of, and together with them to consider and adopt in the UNFCCC negotiations, the goal of achieving at least 50 percent reduction of global emissions by 2050."[26] This statement was strengthened in the 2009 G-8 communiqué to recognize the need to keep global temperature rises to below two degrees Celsius and to "support a goal of developed countries reducing emissions of greenhouse gases in aggregate by 80% or more by 2050."[27] However, this does not yet constitute an agreement on how the burden of effort of achieving the 50 percent reductions is to be divided between the G-8 countries and the rest of the world. This is the contentious part of the problem, and tellingly this vision was endorsed in the G-8 statement rather than the G-8 + G-5 statement, suggesting that major developing countries are not willing to endorse this kind of target without an understanding of the associated liabilities. Clearly, these additional multinational processes can play a role in building political consensus, but the UNFCCC remains the only credible institution where a formal deal can be made.

26. G-8 Summit Leaders' Declaration. Hokkaido Toyako, July 8, 2008
27. G-8 Leaders' Declaration, "Responsible Leadership for a Sustainable Future," L'Aquila Summit, Italy July 2009.

International Carbon Markets

The term *international emissions trading* is somewhat ambiguous. In its original form it applied to the trading of so-called assigned amount units, the official country-level units in which targets under the 1997 Kyoto Protocol were defined. The Kyoto Protocol defined a list of developed countries (so-called Annex B countries), which were to bring their emissions in the period 2008–12 down to, on average, 5 percent below their emissions levels in 1990. This kind of direct trading between governments has not materialized in practice, having become caught up in arguments about the environmental integrity of trading in the presence of so-called hot air—assigned amount units that were granted to former USSR countries in excess of their likely requirements following the severe reduction in emissions from those countries during the 1990s.[28]

What is usually understood by *international emissions trading* is the trade of international certificates generated under the clean development mechanism (CDM), defined by the Kyoto Protocol, together with a subsequent set of rules called the Marrakech Accords. Under this mechanism, annex I countries could finance low-carbon projects in developing countries and claim credit for the resulting certified emission reductions against their own reduction commitments. The Kyoto Protocol defined a third set of internationally tradable permits, namely emission reduction units, which could be generated under a similar project-based mechanism called joint implementation, which allows for projects to be funded jointly by annex I countries. This mechanism has so far been less than successful in generating international trade.

Under the CDM buyers tend to be either annex I governments, which use the credits against their Kyoto commitments, or individual companies, which use them against their liabilities within a company-level emissions trading scheme (for example, the EU-ETS). The volume of CDM credits traded tripled between 2006 and 2008 (from 550 million in 2006, 800 million in 2007, and 1,500 million in 2008), with average value of credits in 2008 of US$22.[29] The bulk of primary CDM credits (80 percent) are bought for compliance purposes from EU countries. Because of this, the price of CDM credits is largely driven by the price of allowances in the EU-ETS. Japanese companies are the other significant buyers, using the credits against their targets under the Keidanren Voluntary Action Plan.[30] Selling is dominated by China, representing 84 percent of transacted volumes in 2008.

28. International Energy Agency (2001).
29. World Bank (2009).
30. Japan Business Federation (2008).

Emission reductions under the CDM are calculated on a project-by-project basis and measure the difference between actual emissions and the emissions that would have occurred in the absence of the project. The process for verifying these project-based emission reductions is complex because of the need to establish a credible counterfactual baseline for what the emissions would have been without the project. Project developers have to develop a methodology for calculating these emission reductions, a methodology that is vetted by a special CDM methodology panel. Although necessary to prevent gaming of the system, this oversight process is laborious and creates a cost penalty, particularly for smaller projects.

At around 1 percent of global emissions, the quantity of emission reductions generated under the CDM market is nowhere near the scale required to meet the environmental challenge. The 2009 World Bank report highlights a number of problems that need to be addressed in order to streamline the system and improve its performance. Ultimately, a system that relies on a project-by-project definition of counterfactual baselines may be structurally unable to cope with the demands placed on it. One of the difficulties is balancing the many competing expectations of the CDM. Some view the CDM as a key bargaining chip in the international negotiations and therefore support the maximum possible use of this instrument in order to show commitment for the principle of financial transfers to developing countries. Others want to reduce the quantity of credits used in developed countries to ensure that they do not dilute the effort to transform their own energy systems. Still others worry about whether CDM credits represent real emission reductions (or other social benefits) and want to restrict the mechanism to a smaller volume of higher-quality credits.

Countries have given themselves until the end of 2009 to negotiate a successor to the Kyoto Protocol, which expires in 2013. An important element of these negotiations concerns the future of the CDM. Suggestions include sectoral or programmatic approaches in which the baseline is defined at a much broader scale (such as by economic sector), so that whole classes of investments could be classified as producing additional emission reductions, reducing the administrative burden of proof.[31] Defining the terms under which international credits can be generated will have a major influence on international carbon markets.

A crucial element is the role of credits generated from avoided deforestation. Deforestation currently accounts for an equivalent of around 25 percent of annual global greenhouse gas emissions; avoiding this is urgent and could be relatively

---

31. International Energy Agency (2007b).

cheap.[32] Savings of 1,500 million tonnes of CO_2 are estimated to be economically achievable at a cost of less than US$20 a tonne.[33] Some suggest that carbon markets could provide the required financing to save forests that would otherwise disappear or be degraded. However, significant problems arise in such areas as developing procedures for monitoring and verifying actions, governance issues around transfer of wealth, and treatment of sustainable development issues around forestry other than carbon emissions.[34] There is also a question about the ability of the international carbon market to absorb a high volume of potentially low-cost credits.

These questions about international credits will be important in international negotiations and are intimately linked with the international architecture of any future climate agreement. Questions about the demand for credits are subject to both national and international policy developments. The next section looks in more detail at the case of the EU-ETS, which so far has provided the key test case for international emissions trading mechanisms.

Regional Carbon Markets: The EU-ETS

Experience in international emissions trading is dominated by the EU-ETS, with traded volumes in 2008 of 3,100 million tonnes of CO_2, worth US$93 billion compared to total global trading figures of 4,800 million tonnes of CO_2, worth US$126 billion.[35] Not only is it the largest market, but it also provides the key driver of prices for CDM credits, which dominate the remainder of international trade (1,500 million tonnes of CO_2, worth US$33 billion) and is therefore the major influence on experiences of carbon markets to date.

The design of the EU-ETS is somewhat particular to governance structures in Europe, but the scheme also displays several classical features of emissions trading schemes, and as the largest and most mature carbon market in the world, it provides a model for a global carbon market. The EU-ETS currently covers annual emissions of around 2,000 million tonnes of CO_2 from large stationary combustion sources of more than fifty megawatts of thermal energy. This includes most of the industrial sector (including refineries), all of the power-generation sector, and the offshore energy sector. Each company in the scheme is required to keep sufficient allowances in an electronic registry account to cover every tonne of CO_2 it emits each year. If a company fails to hold sufficient allowances to cover its

32. Stern (2007)
33. Smith and others (2008).
34. Streck and others (2008).
35. World Bank (2009).

independently verified annual emissions, it pays a fine of EUR 100 a tonne of CO_2 and then has to cover the shortfall in the subsequent year.

In the first two phases of the scheme, companies were given a large proportion of their required allowances free of charge. New entrants to the scheme (such as newly built plants) have also been allocated free allowances, despite the lack of economic justification on the grounds of stranded capital. Companies can sell any surplus allowances, and any shortfall must be purchased from the carbon market. Third-party traders and brokers are also allowed to trade, and the market comprises a mixture of over-the-counter trades and carbon exchanges. Considering the high degree of free allocation, liquidity in the first two phases has been relatively good. It should become significantly better if proposals to move to predominantly auctioning of allowances in the third phase of the scheme are realized.

An important feature driving the price of the EU allowances so far has been the rules concerning banking and borrowing of allowances. The scheme does not allow borrowing of allowances from future periods to be used in the current trading period. In the first phase of the scheme (2005–07), no banking of allowances from this period into the subsequent 2008–12 period was allowed either. This meant that surplus allowances left over at the end of 2007 were essentially worthless, and the price of carbon dropped to zero. From now on, banking of allowances from one trading period to another is allowed, so that we should not see a repeat of the price collapse that occurred in phase 1 as long as there is an expectation of scarcity of allowances in the long run. Borrowing is still not allowed, so in principle the spiking of the carbon price at the end of a trading period is still possible. In practice, companies will probably hedge against this risk by abating or purchasing more allowances than necessary and banking these surplus allowances to create a safety net.

The day-to-day behavior of the allowance price in phase 1, before the price collapse, was linked to the marginal cost of switching from existing coal-fired to gas-fired power generation. As the gas-coal price differential increases, the price of carbon required to incentivize this switch also rises, and vice versa. In the longer run, as the generation mix in the EU finds a new equilibrium factoring in the existence of a carbon price, and taking account of the retirement of significant amounts of coal in Europe as a result of the EU Large Combustion Plant Directive, other abatement options will come into the equation.[36] Already, in phase 2,

---

36. This directive aims to control sulfur emissions by requiring a coal plant either to fit desulfurization equipment by 2015 or to close, a more likely option for older plants for which retrofitting would not be cost effective.

carbon prices show signs of responding to other factors than simply the gas price. For a time, carbon prices seemed to be based on expectations of the future cost of CCS.[37] But these prices then fell, together with the price of many other commodities, in response to the financial crisis. Carbon prices then reached around EUR 8 a tonne, the floor of CDM credits set by the Chinese government. Since then prices have been steadily rising, again in response to the overall shortage of many of the main power generators in Europe. This behavior illustrates the diverse range of drivers that can affect the carbon price in an emissions trading scheme that covers a broad range of economic sectors.

The design of the EU-ETS was reviewed in 2008 as part of a proposed package of measures designed to achieve the EU's stated goals on climate and energy security for 2020. The more straightforward changes for the period 2012–20 include the following: the addition of new emissions sources (aviation; petrochemicals, including key sources of nitrous oxide; and aluminum, including emissions of petrofluorocarbons); a rise in the emissions threshold for entering the scheme so as to reduce the burden on smaller enterprises; inclusion of carbon capture and storage; and improvements to monitoring, reporting, and verification procedures.

More contentiously, the scheme will have much more auctioning of allowances after 2013. The original proposals required full auctioning for the electricity sector from 2013 onward and a progressive increase in auctioning for other energy sources, to reach almost 100 percent by 2020. In theory, auctioning should remove competitive distortions among member states, since all companies would have equal access to allowances at the same price. Although full auctioning is accepted by most economists as the most efficient method of allocation, the politics was nevertheless difficult to overcome. Auctioning requirements were loosened for sectors deemed to be exposed to international carbon leakage, and complicated exceptions were made for coal-intensive Eastern European countries, allowing them to phase in full auctioning between 2013 and 2020.[38]

Also significant is the question of the use of auction revenues, which could be in the range of EUR 30–60 billion a year, depending on the carbon price. Eighty-eight percent of all auctioned allowances are distributed among member states in

37. Deutsche Bank (2008).
38. These countries are required to submit a national plan and report annually to the commission to show that they are investing in the modernization of their electricity sectors at a level "equivalent, to the extent possible, to the market value of the free allocation." See Directive of the European Parliament and of the Council amending Directive 2003/87/EC so as to improve and extend the greenhouse gas emission allowance trading scheme of the Community, 2008/0013(COD).

proportion to their share of EU emissions, while the remaining 12 percent are distributed preferentially to the new member states. Another contentious issue during the negotiations between the commission and member states was the extent to which these revenues should be earmarked for predefined climate-related projects or for projects outside of the EU. The earmarking of auction revenues was increased from the 20 percent suggested in the original proposals to 50 percent in the final adopted text.

As a mandatory regulatory instrument, the EU-ETS is likely to be very stable. What is less certain is the ambition level of the cap. The EU and national governments have conflicting priorities in this regard. On the one hand, predictability and transparency in policymaking processes are important to investors, suggesting the need for target setting to be specifically focused on the needs of the EU carbon market.[39] On the other hand, the same national governments are involved in international negotiations in which political and gaming considerations are predominant. In this context it may make sense to set targets that are contingent on the actions of others in order to prevent commitments from getting too far out of line with economic partners. In any case, parties to a negotiation need to have flexibility in what they are able to offer, otherwise there is no negotiation. Given how far apart the major parties to the UNFCCC currently are, the degree of flexibility required to reach common ground is large, and the prospect of regulatory certainty in such a situation is low.

Regional trading schemes implemented elsewhere provide useful lessons. The Regional Greenhouse Gas Initiative agreed to by ten northeastern U.S. states is a mandatory carbon trading scheme covering power sector installations. The majority of allowances in the scheme are obtained through quarterly auctions, which started in the summer 2008. The scheme was intended to have modest initial reductions in order to minimize economic disruption, and the clearing price so far has been low (US$3 a tonne of CO_2). One of the problems that a regional scheme like this faces is the difficulty of scaling up to more ambitious levels of reduction when neighboring states do not face the same mandatory caps. For example, Pennsylvania is an observer rather than a participant in the scheme, so that companies there can provide electricity into the grid of the other states without incurring the emissions charges.

Another U.S. example is the Chicago Climate Exchange, which provides a trading platform for voluntary emission reduction credits. These credits measure

39. Gross and others (2007).

reductions relative to voluntary (but legally binding) commitments undertaken by participating firms. While being valuable in building institutional capacity for managing trading schemes, the carbon price is typically below US$3, a level that makes almost no difference to carbon abatement. These trading schemes may be superseded if the Waxman-Markey energy bill, being considered by the U.S. Congress, is passed.

Building the Rules: Prospects and Challenges

How are carbon markets likely to evolve, given the uncertainty over the architecture of future agreements? There is a top-down scenario and a bottom-up scenario for achieving a more global coverage of carbon markets. Under a top-down scenario, an agreement is reached in the UNFCCC to set targets and timetables for a cap on greenhouse gas emissions. This scenario is effectively an extension of the Kyoto Protocol approach and would represent the most direct route to a global carbon market. Targets might be set at the global level or perhaps would only cover certain regions; but they would at least cover a substantial fraction of global greenhouse gas emissions. The deal would need to allocate emissions caps regionally and, through successive rounds of subnegotiations, ultimately to the individual country level. These subnegotiations would have to deal with all the issues around the fairness of allocation and competitiveness, and therein lies both the strength and the weakness of this approach. If it were possible to satisfactorily address all these competitiveness concerns in one centralized negotiation, then the way would certainly be cleared for an effective and reliable regulatory regime to underpin a global carbon market. On the other hand, the political difficulty associated with arriving at a fair allocation of emission rights is precisely what makes achieving such an outcome unlikely in the near future.

In the bottom-up scenario countries and regions would unilaterally implement an emission cap-and-trade scheme within their own territories. Such an approach might be taken, for example, as a result of popular pressure, or as a response to expected future requirements under a centralized negotiating process, or as an attempt to show leadership and influence other countries in the centralized negotiation. It is much easier for a single regulatory body to enact such legislation, as is illustrated by the EU-ETS and schemes in the United States, Australia, and New Zealand.

In a bottom-up scenario it may be relatively easy for countries to set up independent emissions trading schemes, but then the development of a global carbon market rests on linking these schemes together to allow companies to trade emissions permits. At this point there would be many technical issues to address to determine whether or not two trading schemes were compatible enough to allow for cross-border trading of emission rights.[40] Differences in design would complicate the linking of trading schemes and would probably limit trading among them. The single most important issue, however, is the mutual recognition of emissions rights as a tradable commodity between two countries that are considering linking their emissions trading schemes. For this to happen, both countries need to agree that the overall cap set for the scheme in their respective countries reflects a fair balance of effort, and they must both have trust in the monitoring, reporting, and verification procedures of the other regime. This need not mean that the carbon price in both schemes has to be the same. Indeed, the efficiency benefit of linking two emissions trading schemes is greatest when the prices are dissimilar.[41]

For this bottom-up scenario to result in significant global emission reductions, the incentive for other countries to follow suit and set their own emissions caps needs to be engineered. One possible mechanism (as included in recently proposed U.S. cap-and-trade bills) is to use border tax adjustments to account for differing production costs associated with operating in a carbon-constrained economy, although the benefits of such a mechanism have been questioned. Warwick McKibbin and Peter Wilcoxen, for example, find that "the benefits produced by border adjustments would be too small to justify their administrative complexity or their deleterious effects on international trade and the potentially damaging consequences for the robustness of the global trading system."[42]

The most promising way forward seems to be to combine both top-down and bottom-up approaches to developing climate policy in general and carbon markets in particular. The EU climate policy position again makes an interesting case study in this regard. Historically, the EU went down the route of developing a company-level emissions trading scheme in response to the fact that it needed a mechanism to ensure that it could meet its Kyoto commitment. The cap set for EU industry directly reflects the structure of the Kyoto deal; if the Kyoto Protocol had a different structure, it is likely that the EU scheme would also look dif-

40. Blyth and Bosi (2004).
41. This leads to a rather paradoxical situation: although the efficiency benefits of linking are highest when the price levels are very disparate, such a disparity in prices is likely to be taken as a sign that the distribution of allowances between the two schemes is in fact not fair. If prices in the two schemes are equal, this may be judged to be fair, but linking would produce little in the way of efficiency gains.
42. McKibbin and Wilcoxen (2008), p. 4.

ferent. Now that the EU has implemented the EU-ETS, it is one of the strongest proponents in the international negotiations of continuing with a similar structure of cap setting.

The EU is attempting to persuade other countries to follow suit by offering a contingent target. In a recent paper setting out its negotiating position for the Copenhagen meeting in 2009, the European Commission reiterated the position it adopted in 2007 in that its unilateral target of a 20 percent emission reduction by 2020 will rise to a substantially more ambitious 30 percent if other major economies take on similar commitments in the UNFCCC process (making the direction of internal EU policy quite uncertain in the meantime).[43] This contingent offer is clearly focused on the politics of international negotiations and could carry some weight as a negotiating strategy—but only if there is a set of domestic policies in place that makes delivery of the 30 percent reduction a credible offer. So far, internal wrangling by member state leaders over the 20 percent target makes the 30 percent target look like a rather empty promise.

Other countries are in any case less formally committed to such a structure of cap setting. The United States, having rejected the Kyoto Protocol, does not have a place in the negotiation of the next commitment period beyond 2013. Instead, it is pursuing a successor under the more general banner of the UNFCCC negotiations. This has led to a split negotiating track since the Bali round of negotiations in 2007, which for the time being is dividing effort and slowing progress. Resolving this split, and bringing all parties to a common position to find an overall architecture for a future agreement, will be an important goal for negotiations in the Copenhagen round in 2009.

The U.S. position appears to be changing significantly under the Obama administration, but the new president will still have to carry the U.S. Congress with him. This means that a climate deal will need to involve other major developing countries. In this regard, the United States and China will become dominant players in finding a solution, not only because they are the two highest emitting countries but also because of their economic and political influence globally. Several different architectures are possible for reaching an agreement, and they mostly fall into one of the following general categories:

—A targets and timetables approach, with evolving emissions targets based on a formula that reflects differentiated responsibilities for developed and developing countries, political realities (in the form of limits on the maximum cost that

43. European Commission (2009).

countries are asked to bear), and long-term equity considerations (in the form of a gradual progression toward equal per capita targets).

—A set of harmonized domestic policies, together with a portfolio of international agreements that separately address various sectors and emission sources as well as such key issues as technology R & D, deforestation, and adaptation.

—A system of harmonized national taxes on greenhouse gases, in which all countries impose the same level of tax and keep resulting revenues. Equity concerns would be addressed by side payments or other assistance from developed to developing countries.

—A system of national or regional cap-and-trade programs that are linked, either directly (in the sense that allowances from either program are valid for compliance in the other program) or indirectly, through an emission reduction credit program like the existing clean development mechanism (CDM).[44]

Each approach requires both national and international commitment and coordination but places a different emphasis on top-down versus bottom-up policy action. In each case, achieving an effective environmental outcome requires that issues of burden sharing, technology development and transfer, future of the CDM, and deforestation are all addressed. The next year or two is a crucial time, during which decisions will be taken that will shape how these agreements are framed; what underpins them all is the extent to which there is the political ambition to make deep cuts in greenhouse gas emissions.

In terms of specific emissions trading schemes, the EU-ETS seems likely to continue on its current basis, the key uncertainty being the level of the cap. Other major developments could well include the introduction of a federal cap-and-trade scheme in the United States. Several draft bills have been put to Congress over the past few years, the most recent being the Waxman-Markey bill, which would establish a mandatory emissions trading scheme with much wider coverage than the EU-ETS, since emissions from every sector of the economy, including transport and domestic heating, will be counted. The proposed cap would lead to a decline in emissions below 2005 levels by 3 percent in 2012, 20 percent in 2020, 42 percent in 2030, and 83 percent in 2050. This long-term cap is highly significant in terms of scheme design.

While the short duration of the caps in the EU-ETS reduces the effectiveness of the signal for long-term investment, it does have the advantage of allowing caps to

44. Aldy and Stavins (2008).

be adjusted in response to changing circumstances.[45] Setting caps over a fifty-year period, on the other hand, creates the risk that prices will diverge very significantly from expectations. To limit the associated political risks, proposals for U.S. schemes tend to include measures such as price caps, which have not been considered necessary for the EU scheme to date. Cost containment, together with resolving what measures might be required to protect competitiveness and reduce leakage, is likely to be the key defining feature of the development of a U.S. scheme. Australia proposes to start its emissions trading scheme in 2010. The proposed scheme is mandatory, covering 75 percent of emissions, including stationary energy sources, transport, and industrial processes. The scheme aims for a 60 percent reduction by 2050 but allows flexibility by setting medium-term targets within gateways, or predefined ranges, with only the short-term caps being firm.

Experiences of trading schemes so far suggest that, in order to create an effective carbon price signal, national and regional cap-and-trade schemes need to be mandatory, with caps that are binding (that is, tighter than a business-as-usual method), able to manage leakage of emissions to sources outside the scheme, and able to manage expectations about future caps and prices.

Conclusions

Fundamentally, the problem facing policymakers is to set up institutional infrastructure for regulating greenhouse gas emissions that is equivalent in scale and value to that for energy markets. Achieving this quickly enough to be environmentally effective is a challenge.

Carbon pricing is likely to be an important element of the policy approach to regulating greenhouse gas emissions, but significant hurdles stand in the way. The toughest problem is the politics of agreeing to the necessary comprehensive binding treaty. The history of international climate change negotiations so far shows the difficulty of moving beyond the generalized 1992 framework treaty of the UNFCCC to agree on the more specific and quantified responsibilities inherent in the 1997 Kyoto Protocol. The Kyoto Protocol aims to take a harmonized global approach, consistent with the global trading scheme idea. Although the emissions caps specified in the protocol only applied to developed countries, the assumption was that other countries would join at some later date in a way that was left for future negotiations. However, the approach was more or less derailed by the

---

45. Ellerman and Buchner (2007).

rejection of the treaty by the United States. Despite the fact that a replacement for the Kyoto Protocol is supposed to be negotiated in 2009, at the time of writing it was still not clear whether a new agreement will attempt a continuation of this top-down approach or whether it will emerge as a patchwork of measures.

The other important limitation to carbon pricing is its inability to stimulate investment in demonstration technologies, which are far from commercial viability. This is because companies cannot guarantee being able to appropriate all the knowledge gained through R & D for themselves and because the problem of time inconsistency makes it difficult to guarantee future prices to justify current expenditure on R & D. Policy solutions to reducing greenhouse gas emissions are therefore more likely to be differentiated by individual country circumstances than a simple global analysis of the problem might suggest. Technology-focused policies are likely to be needed that can help put new technologies on the shelf, with price-based policies helping to get those technologies off the shelf.

The key to overcoming this impasse will be to combine a bottom-up development of robust national climate policies with an international treaty that provides top-down control of the environmental outcomes of the various national programs, together with some kind of enforcement mechanism. Neither the top-down or bottom-up approaches will be sufficient on their own. Without clear and achievable implementation plans for delivering emission reductions, internationally agreed emission reduction targets will lack credibility, and countries will be either unwilling or unable to negotiate stringent targets in good faith. On the other hand, without wider international agreement, domestic policy will founder on concerns of fairness and international competitiveness. Breaking out of this chicken-and-egg situation requires pursuing robust domestic and international policy solutions simultaneously, across all aspects of climate change policy, including R & D; technology transfer; institutional infrastructure for monitoring, reporting, and verifying emissions; markets for energy services; and the transformation of product markets.

Specifically in terms of carbon markets, the bottom-up process entails developing a patchwork of country-level or regional markets, which converge sufficiently over time in terms of their design to allow trading among them. This convergence could be facilitated by top-down mechanisms that are agreed upon through central UNFCCC negotiations. An important example is the trade in international emissions credits—currently through the CDM. The future design of the CDM (or its replacement) and the treatment of credits from reduced deforestation in the post–Kyoto Agreement will have important consequences for the operation of country-level trading schemes. Likewise, the design of country-level trading schemes will have important effects on the demand for these international credits, illustrating the symbiosis between the two levels. Centralized negotiations under the UNFCCC framework will also help to reach an agreement on mutually acceptable caps, which will facilitate the linking of domestic schemes.

This kind of iteration between domestic action and central coordination risks a slower start to emission reductions than might be envisaged under a single, centralized negotiation that tries to achieve everything in one go. On the other hand, it would have the advantage of building trust among the parties, the lack of which currently makes the passage of a single, all-encompassing international treaty seem such a remote possibility. Building this trust and capacity for domestic action can also be helped by keeping climate change on the agendas of such international forums as the G-8 and the Major Economies Meeting on Energy Security and Climate Change.

This all adds up to a situation in which investors relying on a carbon price face considerable policy risk in the short to medium term but in which carbon prices will nevertheless play a significant role in framing overall climate policy by steering investment decisions in the direction of a transition to a low-carbon energy system. Policymakers should aim to reduce policy risk as far as possible by aligning domestic policy targets with their international negotiating positions, by being clear about contingency plans for responding to international policy developments, and by managing interactions between technology-focused policies and price-based policies. Key issues affecting carbon markets that need to be resolved in the next year or two of international negotiations relate to the supply of international emission reduction credits, notably from the CDM and from reduced deforestation. The process by which these mechanisms will operate, and particularly the volume of credits that will be generated, are significant risk factors for the carbon market that need to be resolved. Also essential will be developing the capacity for monitoring, reporting, and verifying greenhouse gas emissions, since these procedures underpin the robustness of any carbon pricing mechanism and are a prerequisite for the expansion of carbon markets or carbon taxes to a wider range of countries.

The direction of travel in terms of climate policy now seems clear: national governments will surely come to an agreement in time over the terms on which they are prepared to collaborate to address climate change and over the design of the governance structures for implementation of these terms. The speed of travel—and therefore the implications for company-level decisionmaking in the short to medium term and the environmental effectiveness of the solution—is much less clear.

References

Aldy, Joseph, and Robert N. Stavins. 2008. "Designing the Post-Kyoto Climate Regime: Lessons from the Harvard Project on International Climate Agreements." Belfer Center for Science and International Affairs, Harvard University Kennedy School.

Alley, Richard B., and others. 2003. "Abrupt Climate Change." *Science* 299 (March).

Baer, Paul, and others. 2000. "Equity and Greenhouse Gas Responsibility." *Science* 289 (September).

Barrett, Scott. 2002. *Environment and Statecraft.* Oxford University Press.

Blyth, William. 2008. "Making Sense of the EU Climate Package." In *Energy and Environment Program.* London: Chatham House.

Blyth, William, and Martina Bosi. 2004. "Linking Non-EU Domestic Emissions Trading Schemes with the EU Emissions Trading Scheme." Paris: OECD/IEA.

Blyth, William, and others. 2007. "Investment Risks under Uncertain Climate Change Policy." *Energy Policy* 35, no. 11.

Broecker, Wallace S. 2007. "Climate Change: CO_2 Arithmetic." *Science* 315 (March).

Carbon Trust. 2009. *EU ETS Impacts on Profitability and Trade 2008.* London.

Deutsche Bank. 2008. "Carbon Emissions: It Takes CO_2 to Contango." London.

Directorate General for Energy and Transport. 2008. *European Energy and Transport: Trends to 2030.* Brussels: European Commission.

Ellerman, Denny, and Barbara Buchner. 2007. "The European Union Emissions Trading Scheme: Origins, Allocation, and Early Results." *Review of Environmental Economics and Policy* 1, no. 1.

European Commission. 2009. "Towards a Comprehensive Climate Change Agreement in Copenhagen." Brussels.

European Council. 2004. *Proceedings, Spring European Council.* Document 7631/04 (annex).

Fischer, Carolyn. 2008. "Emissions Pricing, Spillovers, and Public Investment in Environmentally Friendly Technologies." *Energy Economics* 30, no. 2.

Gross, Robert, and others. 2007. *Investment in Electricity Generation: The Role of Costs, Incentives and Risks.* London: U.K. Energy Research Centre.

Heal, Geoffrey, and Bengt Kristroem. 2002. "Uncertainty and Climate Change." *Environmental and Resource Economics* 22, no. 1–2.

Helm, Dieter, and others. 2003. "Credible Carbon Policy." *Oxford Review of Economic Policy* 19, no. 3.

Ingham, Alan, and Alistair Ulph. 2005. "Uncertainty and Climate-Change Policy." In *Climate-Change Policy,* edited by D. Helm. Oxford University Press.

Intergovernmental Panel on Climate Change. 2007. *Climate Change 2007: Synthesis Report, Summary for Policy Makers.* Geneva.

International Energy Agency. 2001. *International Emissions Trading: From Concept to Reality.* Paris.

———. 2006. *World Energy Outlook.* Paris.

———. 2007a. *Climate Policy Uncertainty and Investment Risk.* Paris.

———. 2007b. *Sectoral Approaches to Greenhouse Gas Mitigation.* Paris.

———. 2008. *World Energy Outlook.* Paris.

Japan Business Federation. 2008. *Results of the Fiscal 2007 Follow-up to the Keidanren Voluntary Action Plan on the Environment.* Tokyo (www.keidanren.or.jp/english/policy/2007/089.pdf).

Lockwood, Matthew. 2008. *After the Coal Rush: Assessing Policy Options for Coal-Fired Electricity Generation.* London.

McKibbin, Warwick J., and Peter J. Wilcoxen. 2008. "The Economic and Environmental Effects of Border Tax Adjustments for Climate Policy." In *Climate Change, Trade, and Competitiveness: Is a Collision Inevitable?* Brookings.

Mueller, Benito. 2002. *Equity in Climate Change: The Great Divide.* Institute of Energy Studies, Oxford University.

Nordhaus, William D. 1992. "An Optimal Transition Path for Controlling Greenhouse Gases." *Science* 258.

Otto, Vincent M., and others. 2008. "Directed Technical Change and Differentiation of Climate Policy." *Energy Economics* 30, no. 6.

Reinaud, Julia. 2008. *Climate Policy and Carbon Leakage: Impacts of the European Emissions Trading Scheme on Aluminium.* Paris: International Energy Agency.

Richels, Richard G., and Geoffrey J. Blanford. 2008. "The Value of Technological Advance in Decarbonising the U.S. Economy." *Energy Economics* 30 (6):2930–2946.

Rosendahl, Knut Einar. 2004. "Cost-Effective Environmental Policy: Implications of Induced Technological Change." *Journal of Environmental Economics and Management* 48:1099–1121.

Schelling, Thomas C. 1995. "Intergenerational Discounting." *Energy Policy* 23:395.

Schneider, Stephen H. 2004. "Abrupt Non-Linear Climate Change, Irreversibility and Surprise." *Global Environmental Change* 14:245–258.

Smith, Pete, and others. 2008. "Greenhouse Gas Mitigation in Agriculture." *Philosophical Transactions of the Royal Society* 363 (1492):789–813.

Stern, Nicholas. 2007. *The Economics of Climate Change: The Stern Review.* Cambridge University Press.

Streck, Charlotte, and others. 2008. "Climate Change and Forestry: An Introduction." In *Climate Change and Forests: Emerging Policy and Market Opportunities,* edited by C. Streck and others. Brookings.

Weitzman, Martin L. 1974. "Prices vs. Quantities." *Review of Economic Studies* 41 (4):477–491.

World Bank. 2009. *State and Trends of the Carbon Market 2009.* Washington, D.C.

World Wildlife Fund. 2007. *Climate Solutions: WWF's Vision for 2050* (www.wwf.org.uk/filelibrary/pdf/climatesolutionreport.pdf).

8

Financing the Future: Investments in Alternative Sources of Energy

Hillard Huntington and Christine Jojarth

The confluence of technological breakthroughs, exploding oil prices, and political concerns about energy dependence and climate change has made alternative energy an attractive investment choice. New investments in this sector recorded more than a sevenfold increase between 2004 and 2008, and the market capitalization of clean technology companies more than doubled during this same period. However, this trio of technological, economic, and political investment drivers has been severely hit by the financial crisis into which the world plunged in the fall of 2008.

The credit crunch is drying up the financial flows into research and development, threatening to slow the pace of technological progress of the past few years. The collapse of the price of fossil fuels has (at least temporarily) slashed the hoped-for cost advantage of alternative energy and undermined the economic logic of green investments.[1] The future of renewable energy hinges therefore more than ever on politics. But even this third investment driver stands on weaker grounds today than in the first half of 2008. Public concern over high

---

1. Lindsay Riddell, "Clean-Tech Firms Buck IPO Trend," *Sacramento Business Journal,* July 11, 2008. We use the terms *green investments* and *clean investments* as shorthand for investments in energy efficiency and alternative sources of energy (excluding nuclear and hydroelectric).

oil prices has lost much of its salience now that conditions have—at least temporarily—turned from a sellers' to a buyers' market. To avoid a repetition of the boom and bust cycle that renewable energy investments experienced in the aftermath of the oil shocks of the 1970s, governments must resist the temptation to drop their promotion from government agendas. Instead, governments need to step up their efforts not only to sustain but even to increase clean technology investments if renewables are to play their (indispensable) role in tackling climate change.

In this chapter we shed light on the ups and downs of investments in renewable energy by exploring separately each of the three investment drivers: technology, economics, and politics. We show how each of these drivers has been affected by the global economic turmoil and argue that decisive political action is of greater necessity than ever to compensate for the investment obstacles created by tightening credit markets and plummeting oil prices. We argue that strong government action in support of renewables can be justified on the grounds both of the negative spillover effects of dependence on fossil fuels and of the positive knowledge externalities associated with investments in the research and development of alternative energy. In the conclusion, we summarize the key requirements that policies need to meet to ensure the effective deployment of renewable energy technologies at the lowest possible cost.

Investment Drivers

Recent growth in alternative energy investments has been meteoric. Between 2002 and 2008 world green investments grew on average by more than 60 percent a year, resulting in an increase from US$7 billion to US$119 billion. This massive expansion can be attributed to technological, economic, and political drivers that throughout this period worked to increase the attractiveness of renewables. Each of these three drivers has its own particular role to play. The technological sphere provides the innovations that drive down the costs of renewables and expands their applicability. The economic sphere finances investments in research, development, and deployment (RD & D) and the successful commercialization of innovation. The political sphere sets the incentives (and removes disincentives) for innovation and investments. In the following, we show how these three drivers are interconnected, how they have been severely shaken by the current financial crisis, and how future progress will rely to an even greater extent on government support for reinforcing the incentives required for this transformation.

Technology

Clean technology investments have been boosted by recent progress in core technology and manufacturing processes in alternative energy.[2] This has helped to erode the price differences between conventional and renewable energy to the point where a number of renewable energy technologies—in particular biofuels, wind, and solar—have become, or are close to becoming, commercially viable under realistic oil price scenarios.

Conventional biofuels can already be produced competitively under climatic conditions favorable to the cultivation of high-yield crops, in particular sugarcane. At production costs of US$0.87 a gallon in 2006, Brazil's sugarcane-based ethanol was 15–40 percent cheaper than gasoline, even without subsidies.[3] Advanced biofuels, which rely on lignocellulosic technology, present even greater potential.[4] This technology could reduce production costs to as little as US$0.6 a gallon in some parts of the world.[5] Biofuels' enormous potential is mirrored by the massive expansion of investments in this technology: between 2004 and 2008 global biofuel investments grew from US$1.3 billion to US$16.9 billion, resulting in the second-highest growth rate among all new clean technology investments (figure 8-1).

Among the renewable sources of electricity, utility-scale wind power is closest to reaching grid parity. Greater reliability and a 100-fold increase in turbine size have dramatically slashed wind energy costs by 80 percent and more over the past twenty years.[6] The cost of one kilowatt hour of wind-generated electricity has fallen from US$0.3 in 1980 to just US$0.06 today; it can cost as low as US$0.04 in very favorable areas.[7] Large-scale wind farms (fifty megawatts and larger) are now cost competitive in class 6 wind power densities.[8] (This level of wind power density is found in Alaska, Hawaii, and the northern Great Plains in the United States; Denmark, the Netherlands, and Scotland in Europe.) These advances have helped to make wind the most prominent nonhydroelectric form of renewable

2. Pernick and Wilder (2007).
3. Assis, Elstrodt, and Silva (2007), p. 37; Pernick and Wilder (2007).
4. This technology offers an advantage over conventional biofuels in that it does not rely on food crops and uses instead cheaper feedstock, such as wastepaper, wood waste, pulp sludge, grass straw, and algae.
5. Caesar, Riese, and Seitz (2007).
6. Capacity has changed from 25 kilowatt hours in the early 1980s to 2,500 kilowatt hours today. European Wind Energy Association (2009).
7. See European Wind Energy Association (2009); Pernick and Wilder (2007).
8. Swisher, Real de Azua, and Clendenin (2001).

Figure 8-1. *New Investments in Renewable Energy, by Technology, Billions of US$, 2004 and 2008*[a]

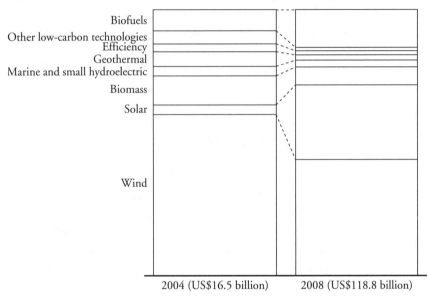

Source: UN Environmental Program (2009).

a. New investments refer to those made by venture capital and private equity firms in clean technology start-up companies; by public markets in publicly quoted companies; and by a company's internal balance sheet, debt, or equity finance in renewable energy projects. It excludes small-scale projects and research, development, and deployment activities. If these two categories were included, new investments in clean technology would have been US$156 billion in 2008.

electricity, accounting for more than half (57 percent) of all such renewable electricity produced in 2006 among the nations of the Organization for Economic Cooperation and Development.[9] It is also the technology that commands by far the greatest share of clean investments (43.5 percent in 2008), albeit its share was considerably squeezed by the more rapid expansion of investments in solar and biofuel technology (figure 8-1).

Solar power has a still longer way to go to become cost competitive with conventional grid power. It is therefore not surprising that solar remains marginal in terms of global electricity output (total electricity from nonhydroelectric renewable sources was 1.6 percent in 2006).[10] However, solar (both photovoltaic and thermal) offers considerably greater prospects of low-cost electricity than wind

9. International Energy Agency (2008b).
10. International Energy Agency (2008c).

power. Economies of scale allow for an approximate 20 percent cost reduction with each doubling in manufacturing capacity.[11] Technological innovations are driving costs even lower. By allowing for the production of thinner wafers—silicon currently accounts for at least a third of the total manufactured cost of a typical solar module—and higher efficiency, a further 60 percent drop in system costs is considered achievable by 2016.[12] Under this scenario, at least ten regions with strong sunlight are projected to reach grid parity by 2020, with the price of a kilowatt hour of unsubsidized solar electricity falling from US$0.30 to US$0.12 or even to less than US$0.10.[13]

Other sources estimate that grid parity may be achieved by around 2012.[14] Partly thanks to these innovations, solar showed the highest growth rates in 2008 among green investments, expanding from US$0.6 billion in 2004 to US$33.5 billion in 2008.[15] Also, solar power production expanded more rapidly than electricity from other renewable sources, growing on average by more than a third each year between 2000 and 2006.[16] These spectacular growth figures should, however, not distract from the fact that solar photovoltaic and concentrating solar power accounted for less than 2 percent of all renewable nonhydroelectric power produced in the OECD in 2006.[17]

These advances in renewable technologies reflect the commitment of governments and the corporate sector to invest in clean technology RD & D.[18] But although these investments more than doubled between 2004 and 2008, they—and by extension the pace of technological progress—face an uncertain future.[19] Corporate RD & D budgets are being slashed as debt financing becomes considerably harder to obtain, venture capitalists become increasingly risk averse, and the commercial viability of many renewable energy technologies is undermined by the fundamental uncertainties regarding the future price of oil.

Economics

The most direct cause of the growth in renewable energy investments has undoubtedly been the exploding price of fossil fuels. With oil prices above

11. Lorenz and Seitz (2008); Pernick and Wilder (2007), p. 308.
12. Swanson (2007).
13. Lorenz, Pinner, and Seitz (2008).
14. Marsh (2008).
15. UN Environmental Program (2009).
16. International Energy Agency (2008b).
17. International Energy Agency (2008b).
18. Standard and Poor's.
19. UN Environmental Program (2009).

US$100 a barrel and credible sources predicting oil prices to reach US$200 in the near future, a number of green technologies reached or were close to reaching cost parity.[20] Consequently, investments in both start-ups and established companies focused on benefiting from this new opportunity for high returns.

A number of high-profile venture capital firms (such as Kleiner Perkins Caufield and Byers and Khosla Ventures) made clean technology one of their most important portfolios, boosting venture capital and private equity investments in renewable energy from US$0.6 billion in 2002 to US$13.5 billion in 2008.[21] They bet on clean technology becoming the next revolution, similar to the one triggered by the arrival of the Internet, offering potentially "the largest economic opportunity of the 21st century," according to the venture capital veteran John Doerr.[22]

At least until recently, this strategy seemed to work. Clean technology companies recorded strong interest in their initial public offerings (IPOs), attracting more than US$13 billion in the record year 2007 (up from US$0.1 billion in 2002) and accounted for one in five new listings on NASDAQ in the first half of 2008.[23] However, the dramatic reversal of energy prices in the fall of 2008 undermined the economic logic behind renewable energy investments, at least in the short term.[24] As a result, the wave of clean technology IPOs has come close to a standstill, and the market capitalization of these companies has collapsed more dramatically than the economy as a whole.[25] The leading index in this segment—the WilderHill clean energy index—lost 78 percent of its peak value, compared

20. Goldman Sachs Global Markets Institute (2007); U.S. Energy Information Administration (2009a).

21. UN Environmental Program (2009).

22. Doerr is quoted in LaMonica (2006). See also Pernick and Wilder (2007). Regarding comparison to the Internet, one has to keep in mind that the green energy revolution differs significantly in terms of the magnitude of investment capital it required, the much longer duration of the initial public offering stage, and the extent to which regulation presents a make-or-break factor in the commercial success of these enterprises.

23. UN Environmental Program (2009); Lindsay Riddell, "Clean-Tech Firms Buck IPO Trend," *Sacramento Business Journal,* July 11, 2008. Riddell (2008); Cleantech Group, "Clean Technology Venture Investment Reaches Record $8.4 billion," press release, January 6, 2009 (http://cleantech .com/about/pressreleases/010609.cfm).

24. The rapid depletion of existing oil fields and the technological challenges posed by new fields will result in a structural floor for the price of oil that is significantly higher than the US$40 a barrel recorded in early 2009. International Energy Agency (2008c); Jojarth (2008).

25. The number of IPOs of renewable energy companies and the money they managed to raise shrank by almost 60 percent between 2007 and 2008, despite the a strong start in 2008. UN Environmental Program (2009).

Figure 8-2. *Standard and Poor's and Wilderhill Clean Energy Indexes, July 6 of Year, 2004–08*

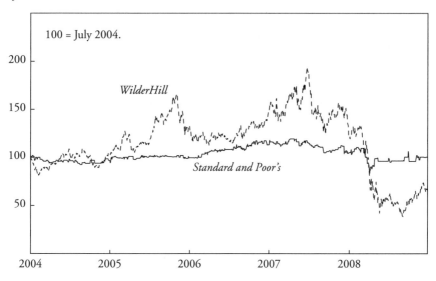

Source: UN Environmental Program (2009).

to the 52 percent loss of Standard and Poor's 500 index (figure 8-2). A number of clean technology companies had to declare bankruptcy, and more are to follow as the industry goes through a period of consolidation. Most severely hit is the ethanol industry, where for instance the market leader Verasun had to file for chapter 11 bankruptcy in November 2008. Also the solar industry faces difficult times. Prices for solar panels are tumbling amid growing overcapacity, dragging along share prices of industry leaders such as Germany's Q-Cells and China's Suntech Power, which lost over 60 percent.

This development demonstrates dramatically the limits of what markets can do to promote renewable energy. The high volatility of oil prices on which the commercial viability of renewables depends makes it difficult for markets to provide the long-term capital necessary for the development and—in particular the deployment—of alternative sources of energy. The proper working of markets is further complicated by the fact that the pricing of fossil fuels—the main competitor of renewables—is not fully market based but distorted by a range of political factors, including the oil cartel OPEC, fuel taxes, and fuel subsidies. Furthermore, electricity generated from renewable sources needs to be integrated with the highly regulated and politically sensitive electricity market. The way this market is regulated in most countries undermines the incentives for private actors to make the massive investments needed to update transmission lines so they can cope with the intermittent electricity supply from renewables and the remote location of many good generation sites (offshore wind, solar arrays in deserts).

In recognition of the challenges that renewables face and of the negative externalities associated with heavy dependence on fossil fuels, policymakers have devised measures to promote alternative sources of energy, ranging from grants and subsidies of various kinds (such as RD & D grants, feed-in tariffs, and tax breaks) to mandated standards (renewable energy portfolio standards, caps on carbon emissions). Now that private RD & D funding is drying up and the falling oil price undermines the commercial logic for investing in alternative energy, renewables will have to rely on political support more than ever.

Politics

Two main themes propelled green energy onto the policy agendas of countries around the world: energy security and climate change. U.S. President Barack Obama summarized this twin energy crisis when he warned in his inaugural address that "each day brings further evidence that the ways we use energy strengthen our adversaries and threaten our planet."[26] In this section we show how policies launched in response to energy security and climate change concerns overlap but also diverge from each other in the way they affect renewables. We argue that the latter provide a stronger argument for advocating political support for green energy investments.

ENERGY SECURITY

Energy security resembles a Rorschach test, offering itself to a wide range of interpretations and political agendas. Two partly interrelated and overarching concerns can be discerned; one relates to the risk of supply disruptions and their adverse impact on the price of oil and the other to the national security implications arising from dependence on petroleum-exporting regimes with adverse norms and values. For instance, a panel of oil market and geopolitical experts found that there is an 80 percent chance that a geopolitical, military, or terrorist event could remove at least two million barrels a day of petroleum supplies at some point over the next ten years.[27] But even if the major oil-exporting countries were all perfectly

---

26. See www.whitehouse.gov/blog/inaugural-address.
27. Beccue and Huntington (2005).

reliable suppliers, oil-importing nations would still feel uneasy about the national security implications of transferring billions of dollars to countries that are hostile to the Western way of life and that harbor terrorists.[28]

Against this background, energy importers have introduced or are currently debating a number of policies to increase their energy security by reducing their dependence on conventional oil supplies (United States) or on Russian natural gas (Western Europe). A thoughtful strategy for achieving energy security would include diversifying a country's mix of imports or reducing its level of imports, but it is unlikely to aim for full energy independence from all imports, which would remain both too costly and too elusive in the foreseeable future. The promotion of renewables and energy efficiency are two policy options available to achieve the goal of diversifying and reducing imports.

Energy dependence on foreign oil can also be lessened through policies that boost domestic production of energy from conventional sources, such as nuclear and—more problematic—coal. In addition to being relatively cheap, coal is abundant in many oil-importing countries. For instance, U.S. coal reserves could supply 225 years' worth of energy at today's level of use, and China has enough coal to sustain its rapid economic growth for a century or more.[29] Also, a number of oil importers—most notably the United States—are seeking to increase domestic production of oil and gas by promoting research into the recovery of unconventional oil and gas resources (oil shale, tight gas), providing companies with incentives to invest in domestic exploration and production and—most controversial—granting access to areas with fragile ecosystems, including Alaska's Arctic National Wildlife Refuge.

Although alternative sources of energy can indeed help reduce the dependence on imports of conventional hydrocarbons, energy security is often an imperfect platform for promoting government support for renewables. The argument's power is further weakened by the fact that the political salience of energy security is highly correlated with the price of oil. Many citizens equate energy security with lower petroleum prices and lobby their government the hardest when the price of oil is high, only to drop their political pressure as soon as the oil price falls below their pain level. Furthermore, low petroleum prices mean that less money is transferred to prop up authoritarian, anti-Western regimes, thus reducing the national security risk posed by a heavy reliance on foreign oil. As seen in the aftermath of

28. OPEC's net export revenues in 2008 were close to US$1 trillion. U.S. Energy Information Administration (2009a).

29. Peter Fairley, "China's Coal Future," *Technology Review,* January 4, 2007.

the oil shocks in the 1970s, policy initiatives that rely on the energy security argument reinforce the detrimental effect that oil price volatility has on renewable energy investments.

CLIMATE CHANGE

Climate change provides a more powerful and reliable argument for promoting long-term investments in alternative energy and the best hope that the boom and bust cycle of renewables experienced in the past will not be repeated. In contrast to the energy security argument, safeguarding the global climate requires significantly larger cuts in the consumption of hydrocarbons, and the need for these reductions is, at least in theory, independent of the origin (foreign versus domestic) and price of fossil fuels.

The International Energy Agency (IEA) estimates that, to achieve the greenhouse gas reduction target that the Intergovernmental Panel on Climate Change (IPCC) calls for (at least a 50 percent reduction between 2000 and 2050), the share of renewables in global electricity production would have to more than double by 2050.[30] Also, the mix of renewables would have to change dramatically both with respect to the status quo and the business-as-usual scenario. Based on certain assumptions about the potential of the various clean energy technologies, the IEA presents a scenario analysis that sees the current dominance of hydroelectric power being challenged by both wind and solar.[31] While electricity production from hydropower is assumed to expand modestly both in absolute terms and relative to the business-as-usual scenario, electricity from both wind and solar would have to grow aggressively during the period covered by the scenario analysis (2005–50).[32] In particular, electricity production from solar would have to record a 160-fold increase compared to the 2005 baseline, which is almost thirty times more than solar would produce without supporting policies that are climate change oriented. Under the 50 percent reduction scenario, wind and solar would reach parity with hydroelectric power, each

---

30. International Energy Agency (2008a) also analyzes other technologies—including nuclear and carbon capture and sequestration—that will have to be deployed in order to reach the stipulated CO_2 emission reduction target.

31. Hydroelectric power accounted for 88 percent of total renewable energy production in 2006. International Energy Agency (2008c).

32. The IEA calculates an 80 percent increase of hydroelectric energy between 2005 and 2050, 15 percent higher than the corresponding value under the business-as-usual scenario. International Energy Agency (2008a).

Figure 8-3. *Global Electricity Production, by Technology, Terawatt Hours a Year,*
2005 and 2050, Two Scenarios[a]

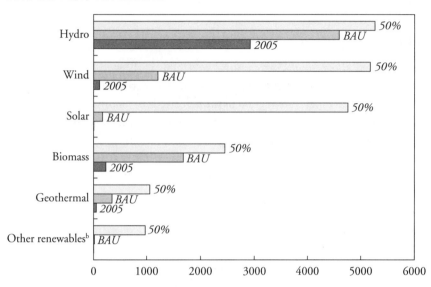

Source: International Energy Agency (2008a).

a. The two scenarios for 2050 production are a 50 percent reduction in hydroelectric power (labeled 50%) and the business-as-usual scenario (labeled BAU).

b. Tidal and hydrogen.

accounting for roughly a quarter of total renewable electricity output.[33] The remaining quarter of renewable energy production in 2050 will be generated from biomass, geothermal, and other types of renewable energy—namely tidal and hydrogen (figure 8-3).

To achieve this massive expansion of green power generation beyond the business-as-usual scenario, the IEA estimates that more than US$5 trillion in additional investments would have to be mobilized between 2005 and 2050.[34] These investment sums will never be deployed without supporting policies, which take into account the importance of the negative environmental spillover effects

33. Precise percentages are 26.7 percent for hydroelectric, 26.3 percent for wind, and 24.2 percent for solar.

34. To make this number comparable with the figures about clean energy investments provided by the UN Environmental Program, we are excluding investments in hydroelectric power.

of fossil fuel consumption and the difficulties companies face in appropriating the full benefits of their R & D investments.

Expanding Renewable Investments

As discussed above, replacing carbon-based fuels with energy from renewable sources will require consistent investments and supporting incentives over half a dozen or more decades. A reduction in the perceived risk of investments in renewables is thereby essential. A first imperative for governments is not only to quickly restore trust in financial markets through new institutions and regulations that are better at managing risks in uncertain economies but also to institute macroeconomic policies that will prevent a sudden escalation in interest rates and inflation. However, an efficient and stable financial market is not the only requirement for the successful transition to a greener energy future. Equally important are policies that address risks specific to the energy sector, both economic (high volatility in fossil fuel and greenhouse gas prices) and non-economic (limited grid access, poor social acceptance, and long and bureaucratic authorization procedures).

This section explores these issues through the prism of two externalities that need to be internalized through appropriate, complementary policies: the costs of greenhouse gas emissions and the benefits of investments in research and development of renewables. Only if these costs and benefits are fully internalized can financial markets realize the full potential of renewables.[35]

Climate Change Policies

The two basic approaches to internalize the environmental costs of greenhouse gas emissions are a cap-and-trade system and a carbon tax. After much controversy, the drafters of the Kyoto Protocol to the United Nations Framework Convention on Climate Change of 1997 decided in favor of the former policy option. Under this cap-and-trade regime, developed nations—so-called annex I countries—cap the emissions of their industries at some level but allow them to sell excess allowances to groups and sectors that find it more expensive to abate emissions.

This flexibility mechanism should ensure that emission reductions are achieved at the lowest possible cost by letting the price of carbon direct green investments toward the technologies that offer the cheapest reduction in greenhouse gas. How-

---

35. The difficulties of developing consistent policies to rectify a global or pooled externality are not discussed here. See Nordhaus (2008) for a good and recent discussion.

Figure 8-4. *Carbon Credit Price, June 2007 to January 2009*

Euros per ton CO_2

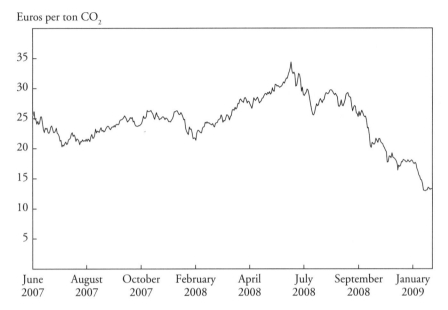

Source: European Climate Exchange, 2009 (www.ecx.eu).

ever, under its current design this cap-and-trade system is prone to result in a highly volatile price for carbon credits. Since its launch in 2005, the world's largest bourse for carbon credits, the European Climate Exchange, recorded carbon prices over EUR30 (about US$38) a tonne in July 2008, only to see this price collapse by 65 percent to just over EUR10 (about US$13) half a year later (figure 8-4).

This high volatility poses a serious problem for investments in renewables, as sales of the freed-up carbon credits can be indispensable to ensuring that green investments pay. In addition to the volatility problem, the price of carbon tends to correlate with the price of oil.[36] This means that at the very moment renewable investments lose in value because the cost advantage of their main competitor

36. This correlation results from the fact that the price of both oil and carbon credits reacts strongly to inaccurate economic growth forecasts. When oil companies overestimate future growth they end up with surpluses, which drive down the price of oil. Similarly, when governments overestimate future growth they allocate more emission allowances than companies need because they reduce production in response to lower consumer demand.

(fossil fuels) has further increased, they also generate smaller revenues from sales in carbon credits. This high correlation between the price of oil and carbon credits reinforces the boom-and-bust nature of renewable investments and accentuates the risks associated with this investment. Moreover, the allocation of emission allowances has so far been too generous, resulting in a carbon price that remains substantially below the US$500 price per ton that the IEA calculated would be needed to reach the IPCC targets for greenhouse gas concentrations.[37]

These problems have led a number of prominent voices, such as the former U.S. vice president Al Gore, to favor a direct carbon tax over a cap-and-trade system. Although taxes have some limitations as well, they offer an important advantage in that they tend to ensure greater predictability in the price that industries will have to pay for their carbon emissions and thus in the savings they can generate from investing in renewables.[38]

In addition to the all-encompassing cap-and-trade scheme, countries are also pursuing their carbon mitigation objectives through a number of more sector-specific policies, ranging from financial incentives to mandatory quotas. For instance, the United States grants domestic biofuel producers cheap federal financing and tax credits of US$0.51 a gallon, while the EU Energy Taxation Directive of 2003 allows member states to grant tax reductions and exemptions in favor of renewable fuels under certain conditions.[39] Generous feed-in tariffs guaranteed for a sufficiently long period have been the principal motor behind the widespread deployment of electricity from renewable sources in Germany, Spain, and other European countries. Also, six U.S. states are currently providing this type of financial incentive.[40] An alternative approach is the imposition of so-called renewable portfolio standards, which define a minimum share of electricity to be generated from renewable sources.

At the time of writing, twenty-seven U.S. states had introduced binding standards, and three had voluntary standards. Among the most ambitious states are California (20 percent minimum share by 2010), New York (24 percent by 2013),

37. International Energy Agency (2008a) and Parry (2007) provide clear and balanced perspectives on both policy options. See also Nordhaus (2007).

38. The volatility of carbon prices can also be contained under a cap-and-trade scheme by allowing firms to bank unused permits and through so-called safety valve provisions, which ensure that carbon prices do not exceed a certain threshold. Parry (2007).

39. David Rotman, "The Price of Biofuels," *Technology Review,* January 5, 2008. Rotman (2008); see also OECD (2008), p. 26. It provides data on targets for renewable energy and fuels in 2010 for selected countries.

40. As of summer 2008, these are California, Hawaii, Illinois, Michigan, Minnesota, and Rhode Island.

and Illinois, Minnesota, and Oregon (all 25 percent by 2025). The EU has also spelled out a similar target, with 20 percent of all energy to be derived from renewable sources by 2020. Some member states have set themselves even more aggressive targets, with Sweden (49 percent by 2020) taking the lead, followed by Latvia (42 percent), Finland (38 percent), Austria (34 percent), and Portugal (31 percent). Similar mandates have also been adopted to promote biofuels. The U.S. Energy Independence and Security Act of 2007, effective since January 1, 2009, includes a renewable fuels standard, which stipulates that by 2020 at least 36 billion gallons of renewable fuel (usually ethanol) need to be blended into conventional gasoline, and the EU's Biofuel Directive of 2003 (Directive 2003/30/EC) spells out the nonmandatory target of replacing 5.75 percent of diesel and gasoline with biofuels by 2010.[41]

These policies have unquestionably led to a remarkable boost in the deployment of renewables around the globe. However, the global increase in renewables (including hydropower) fell behind the even faster growth in conventional energy, and the extent to which countries have realized their renewable energy potentials remains very uneven.[42] One reason for the internationally uneven deployment of renewables results is that the second-largest greenhouse gas emitter, the United States, has not ratified the Kyoto Protocol. Another reason is that the protocol imposes binding reduction or stabilization targets only on developed nations. Thus China, the world's largest emitter of CO_2, is not bound by the Kyoto Protocol.

These unequal commitments result in greenhouse gas reductions well short of the recommendations of the IPCC not only because a number of important emitters are let off the hook but also because annex I countries were reluctant to commit to more aggressive reduction targets. They fear that their industries might no longer be competitive internationally if they have to pay for their carbon emissions while their competitors in China and the United States can continue to emit for free. Also, partial participation in a climate change regime threatens to undermine its effectiveness because emissions reduced in some countries can leak back through the system if production shifts from the country imposing the restriction

41. The full text of this directive is available at http://ec.europa.eu/energy/res/legislation/doc/biofuels/en_final.pdf.

42. Russia has so far barely tapped into its vast potentials for alternative energy, in particular in biomass. See Resch and others (2008). But Germany currently boasts the world's largest installed wind power and solar photovoltaic capacity, despite having relatively low solar radiation and few places with good wind resources. International Energy Agency (2007); Global Wind Energy Council (2007).

to a nation outside the regime. Further, the public goods nature of this problem gives rise to free riders: countries that benefit from the efforts of other nations without restricting their own emissions.

One option to prevent carbon leakage and a loss of competitiveness among companies in countries with restrictions on greenhouse gas emissions is the imposition of carbon tariffs on imports from countries that have not committed to emission reductions. Such a tariff is currently being discussed in the European Union and the United States.[43] Even though the legality—and in particular the compatibility with the World Trade Organization—of such a trade measure is controversial, a number of proposals have been made for antileakage measures that are compatible with existing international obligations.[44]

Policies that seek to positively promote the deployment of renewables through financial incentives in the form of a carbon price and various subsidies need to be complemented by policies that remove the numerous obstacles that still exist. Among the obstacles are the subsidies that many developing countries—and in particular oil producers—grant to the domestic consumption of fossil fuels, which make renewables uncompetitive even under the most favorable environmental conditions.[45] In the West, the inadequacy of the existing electric grid in accommodating these new sources of energy poses one of the most important barriers to the expansion of renewables.

As mentioned above, many good sites for the production of renewable energy are far from population centers, with no—or only low-capacity—transmission lines connecting the two. Construction of new lines is held back not only by the enormous capital investments required but also by the unfavorable tax treatment such investments face and by the lengthy and uncertain authorization procedures and regulation required.[46] Furthermore, utilities have to have a backup production capacity that can respond quickly to fluctuations in supply and demand, advanced information technology providing real-time data on energy usage (smart meters), and such innovative technology as decentralized car batteries to cover peak demand. These challenges cannot efficiently be met by the imposition of car-

43. The Lieberman-Warner bill, or America's Climate Security Act of 2008, contained provisions aimed at protecting American industries against unfair advantages of competitors that operate without a carbon fee. Although this bill did not pass, it seems most likely that similar provisions will be included in future U.S. climate protection bills.

44. See for example World Bank (2007); Weber and Peters (2009).

45. Many oil-producing countries are in regions of the world with the highest solar radiation.

46. Metcalf (2009); Joskow (2008); "Tree-Huggers versus Nerds," *The Economist*, February 12, 2009.

bon fees and mandated quotas. They also require the removal of non-economic barriers and the promotion of investments in updating the electric grid.

Research and Development Policies

To ensure that global targets for the reduction of greenhouse gas are reached at the lowest possible cost, investments in the research and development of cheaper renewable technologies are of paramount importance. An appropriate price for carbon through a cap-and-trade system or a carbon tax incentivizes investors to shift their funds into energy sources that enable society to reduce climate warming. However, a carbon price by itself will not guarantee adequate investments in RD & D because of the externalities associated with such activities.[47] Even if carbon prices are sufficiently high to reflect climate change damages, firms may not invest sufficiently in RD & D because they fear that other firms will adopt these same measures and eliminate the profits from the initial investment. Governments have an important role to play in overcoming this type of market failure.[48] When designing technology, governments need to recognize that RD & D activities related to renewable energy are incredibly diverse. They range from the most basic research all the way to redefining the final product to making it acceptable to the purchaser. The demands on the innovator change as one moves along this continuum.

Some of the most promising options are those that facilitate opportunities for saving on carbon and other greenhouse gases. These options require an RD & D strategy that fosters open research that can be communicated and disseminated quickly, broadly, and liberally. Avoiding unnecessary duplication and building on past successes are key. The benefits of this type of research usually far exceed the private return from these investments, because there are limited opportunities to restrict access to these fundamental discoveries. For this reason, governments often provide public funds directly to universities or other nonprofit research institutions for RD & D related to renewables. In the past such funding has unfortunately often tracked the price of oil: it increased during the late 1970s and early 1980s in response to the oil shocks, was then cut by two-thirds, and remained low until the onset of the price hike at the turn of this century (figure 8-5).

At the other end of the continuum are the business and legal endeavors in which proprietary rules dominate. Openness is not as critical to these businesses

---

47. Nelson 1959; Arrow (1962).
48. Grübler, Nakicenovic, and Nordhaus (2002).

Figure 8-5. *Research, Development, and Deployment Expenditures and Oil Price per Barrel, 2007 US$, 1974–2007*

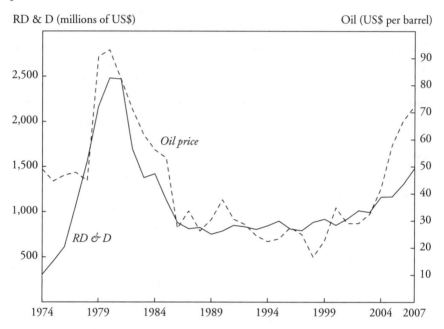

Source: Figures from International Energy Agency and British Petroleum.

because they focus on specific products or markets. Without patents, licenses, and other government restrictions on copying the original innovation, the investor would quickly lose any incentive to undertake the RD & D. Government's role in this area is to provide enough rules to protect the original RD & D investment without stifling future research along similar lines. Mistrust in other governments' willingness or ability to protect the intellectual property rights of foreign firms has therefore been a major stumbling block in the transfer of clean technologies from developed to developing nations, called for by the Kyoto Protocol.

To ensure favorable conditions for research and development of renewables, governments must operate effectively in both the open science and the proprietary regimes.[49] These regimes complement each other, and their success depends upon the other one flourishing. Governments need to understand the complementari-

49. Aghion, David, and Foray (2007).

ties between the two arenas and that the rules governing these very different activities may also be quite different. Any particular innovation may begin in the basic and open science paradigm, be transformed into applied research, and end up being adjusted to meet consumers' particular needs.

Unlike the Manhattan Project for developing the atomic bomb during World War II or the Apollo program for space exploration begun in 1961, technologies for mitigating climate change require a policy framework that fosters open competition.[50] A wide range of renewable energy technologies exists and is currently being developed, each offering its own advantages and disadvantages. Governments are therefore well advised not to adopt policies that require them to pick a "winner" among different technological options or that lock in a certain technology or set of technologies, as they may preclude other, more promising, options. To the greatest extent possible, governments should design a system that is flexible enough to respond to clean technology breakthroughs. This is particularly important given the fact that energy infrastructure is notoriously slow to change. Committing to certain technologies and infrastructure is likely to dominate energy decisions for at least the next half century.

Conclusion

Replacing carbon-based fuels with energy-efficient improvements and renewable energy sources will be a long-run process, requiring consistent investment and financial incentives over half a dozen or more decades. Oil price and carbon fee volatility, combined with unstable economic conditions, weaken these incentives significantly and deter critical investments. An efficiently operating financial market is a necessary but not sufficient condition for ensuring this transition. This chapter describes the numerous policies and conditions that must hold if financial markets are to operate effectively. We posit five requirements for improving the current energy governance.

First, governments must quickly restore efficient financial markets, including new institutions and regulations for managing risks in uncertain economies.

Second, the world community must make a long-term and concerted effort to strengthen the role of prices in governing decisions about energy production, transmission, and use. Specific examples include expanding the role of prices in electricity planning and distribution to enable the sector to introduce new and

---

50. Yang and Oppenheimer (2007).

promising technologies. Also, market-based end-use prices are badly needed in many developing economies.

Third, carbon and other greenhouse gas fees must be stable so that investors can plan their investments over several decades. Current emissions-trading schemes are oriented toward meeting given environmental targets, but they produce enormous investment uncertainty through extreme carbon price volatility.

Fourth, climate change policy must be coordinated with trade and other economic policies. In seeking open and free trade, the World Trade Organization also recognizes that countries may restrict trade where important global externalities (health and conservation) are violated. These rulings may allow an opening for trade policies that also facilitate climate change protection, because nonsignatory countries can be punished for their failure to cooperate.

Finally, countries must expand research and development policies in the aggregate and allow the combination of energy prices and greenhouse gas fees to shift R & D toward climate protection. With this expanded research base and proper incentives, the world can aggressively finance the new investments and technologies that are needed for more stable climatic conditions. Human capital investments will be particularly valuable in transferring the new technologies to rapidly growing economies at various stages of the development process.

References

Aghion, Philippe, Paul A. David, and Dominique Foray. 2007. "Science, Technology, and Innovation for Economic Growth: Toward Linking Policy Research and Practice in 'STIG Systems.' " Discussion Paper 06-039. Institute for Economic Policy Research, Stanford University.

Arrow, K. J. 1962. "Economic Welfare and the Allocation of Resources for Inventions." In *The Rate and Direction of Inventive Activity: Economic and Social Factors,* edited by R. R. Nelson. Princeton University Press.

Assis, Vincente, Hans-Peter Elstrodt, and Claudio F. C. Silva. 2007. "Positioning Brazil for Biofuels Success." *McKinsey Quarterly* 2 (March, special ed.).

Beccue, Phillip, and Hillard G. Huntington. 2005. "Oil Disruption Risk Assessment." Special Report 8. Energy Modeling Forum, Stanford University.

Caesar, William K., Jens Riese, and Thomas Seitz. 2007. "Betting on Biofuels." *McKinsey Quarterly* 2 (May).

European Wind Energy Association. 2009. *Wind Energy: The Facts.* Brussels.

Global Wind Energy Council. 2007. *Global Wind 2007 Report.* Brussels.

Goldman Sachs Global Markets Institute. 2007. "Alternative Energy: A Global Survey." New York.

Grübler, Arnulf, Nebojsa Nakicenovic, and William D. Nordhaus. 2002. *Technological Change and the Environment.* Washington: Resources for the Future.

International Energy Agency. 2007. *Trends in Photovoltaic Applications.* Paris.

————. 2008a. *Energy Technology Perspectives*. Paris.

————. 2008b. *Renewables Information 2008*. Paris.

————. 2008c. *World Energy Outlook*. Paris.

Jojarth, Christine. 2008. "The End of Easy Oil: Estimating Average Production Costs for Oil Fields around the World." Program on Energy and Sustainable Development, Stanford University.

Joskow, Paul. 2008. "Challenges for Creating a Comprehensive National Electricity Policy." Washington: Technology Policy Institute.

Lorenz, Peter, Dickon Pinner, and Thomas Seitz. 2008. "The Economics of Solar Power." *McKinsey Quarterly* (June).

Metcalf, Gilbert E. 2009. "Taxing Energy in the United States: Which Fuels Does the Tax Code Favor?" Report 4. Energy Policy and the Environment, Manhattan Institute for Policy Research.

Nelson, R. R. 1959. "The Simple Economics of Basic Scientific Research." *Journal of Political Economy* 67.

Nordhaus, William D. 2007. "To Tax or Not to Tax? Alternative Approaches to Slowing Global Warming." *Review of Environmental Economics and Policy* 1, no. 1.

————. 2008. *A Question of Balance: Economic Modeling of Global Warming*. Yale University Press.

Parry, Ian. 2007. *Should We Abandon Cap-and-Trade in Favor of a CO_2 Tax?* Washington: Resources for the Future.

Pernick, Ron, and Clint Wilder. 2007. *The Cleantech Revolution: The Next Big Growth and Investment Opportunity*. New York: Collins.

Resch, Gustav, and others. 2008. "Potentials and Prospects for Renewable Energies at Global Scale." *Energy Policy* 36.

Swanson, Richard. 2007. "Solar Power: A Path to Grid Parity?" Paper prepared for MIT Energy Conference.

Swisher, R., C. Real de Azua, and J. Clendenin. 2001. "Strong Winds on the Horizon: Wind Power Comes of Age." *Proceedings of the IEEE* 89, no. 12.

UN Environmental Program. 2009. *Global Trends in Sustainable Energy Investments 2009: Analysis of Trends and Issues in the Financing of Renewable Energy and Energy Efficiency*.

Weber, Christopher L., and Glen P. Peters. 2009. "Climate Change Policy and International Trade: Policy Considerations in the U.S." *Energy Policy* 37.

World Bank. 2007. *International Trade and Climate Change: Economic, Legal, and Institutional*. Washington.

Yang, Chi-Jen, and Michael Oppenheimer. 2007. "A 'Manhattan Project' for Climate Change?" *Climatic Change* 80.

9

A New Green Deal and the Future of Global Energy: A Policy Perspective

Joseph A. Stanislaw

It took just over a year to scramble the already complex calculus of local and global energy governance beyond recognition.

That was then: in October 2007 Al Gore shares the Nobel Peace Prize; shortly thereafter, concern over climate change reaches fever pitch as the Intergovernmental Panel on Climate Change (which shared the Nobel with Gore) issues a damning report on global warming. By summer 2008, oil hits US$147 a barrel, and gasoline in the United States hurtles to more than US$4 a gallon. Energy producers are kings of the game. Venture capital and private equity flow into green technology start-ups at record rates. The media rhapsodizes about "going green," and consumers flock to energy-saving, environment-friendly products. Meanwhile, resource nationalists flex their muscles from Latin America to the Niger Delta and all the way north through Siberia to the Arctic Circle.

Just a year later the energy world had been upended: As quickly as you can say "subprime mortgage," most previous assumptions have been upended. The price of oil has vacillated wildly, going as low as US$35, and gasoline has followed suit. Despite this, the United States experienced the biggest year-over-year decrease in miles driven (see chapter 8, this volume). Consumers are too worried about losing their jobs in the Great Recession to pay much heed to climate change. Investment in all forms of energy, including alternative and renewable technologies, dried up due to the traumatized credit and equity markets, as well as concerns about the future of demand. And the resource nationalists—focused simply on staying in power in the face of dwindling oil revenues—mostly shrunk from the world stage.

Intuitively, with governments and world leaders absorbed by economic survival, the challenge of reworking our approach to global energy governance does not seem like a top priority. Climate change certainly has not fallen off the agenda, thanks in great measure to President Obama's elevation of energy and environment issues; yet the economic crisis no doubt has downgraded climate change's place on the global agenda and sapped public attention from it. The steep fall in energy prices, meanwhile, echoes the early 1980s, when green ventures died quickly on the vine. As Hillard Huntington and Christine Jojarth vividly illustrate in chapter 8, these vicissitudes underscore the limits of the market in leading us to and through an energy (r)evolution; without firm government guidance, investors and the markets cannot reconcile short-term tribulations with long-term goals. Political recognition of the damage done by volatile energy prices was evident at the G-20 summit in autumn 2008 when leaders put commodity price stabilization at the top of their agenda.

This economic crisis, in fact, marks an ideal moment to move the energy agenda forward for at least three reasons.

First, as governments seek to wrestle with the crisis, the state is taking the dominant role in stimulating and directing economies—a powerful Keynesian position from which to shape patterns of research, investment, education, and consumer spending. As long as governments do not overreach—channeling market forces, rather than choosing winners—this could help jump-start a green recovery and pave the way to a new clean economic development model.

Second, the extreme volatility in energy prices has humbled both producers and consumers, leveling the playing field and making them more likely to consider new approaches to energy governance. As long as the pursuit of a global climate change deal does not collapse into recriminations and polarization, the conditions are ripe for generational progress on this front. Political leadership, in this context, will be crucial.

Third, individuals, even though absorbed by personal hardship, are as willing as ever to contribute collectively to solving urgent challenges; in fact, financial difficulties mean that they are looking for every possible means of conserving energy.

And one final reason: the failure to address energy security and climate change, as President Obama underscored in his first major address to the U.S. Congress, could lead us further into economic catastrophe. Meanwhile, certain critical risks remain constant and thus serve as an impetus for reform. One such risk is that a purist focus on "green" energy will take our focus off of what really matters—*clean* energy. Traditional fossil fuels, which constitute the greatest current source of energy and are the backbone of our economy, also can be clean. Put another way: the future is *clean* energy, not green energy; all forms of energy, if carbon can be removed from them, can and should be allowed to compete on a level playing field.

"A Crisis Is a Terrible Thing to Waste": The Green New Deal

Stanford economist Paul Romer is said to have quipped, back in 2004, that "a crisis is a terrible thing to waste." Whether this crisis is wasted will depend on how wisely and under what conditions trillions of dollars in stimulus funds are disbursed. But it is clear that the present confluence of forces—if managed nimbly—will allow us to tackle the twin challenges of energy security and climate change.

Yet the current opportunity, if mishandled, could be the precursor to the next energy crisis. The trauma inflicted on investors and the market by the spike and subsequent collapse in energy prices could cripple investment and lead to low supplies in the next three to four years, thus prompting a new spike in prices. It is critical to avoid such an unvirtuous cycle.

From the vantage point of energy transformation, the stimulus funds are a windfall that not only could lead to a green recovery in China, the United States, and elsewhere but also could help create the conditions for a global deal on climate change. The scale of investments in energy efficiency and alternative energy that countries need to make in order to meet emissions targets might have been out of reach before the economic crisis. Now they are more readily at hand. The economic crisis also fortuitously reverses the order in which a global compact on climate change would be made. Emissions targets can be tackled as part of a Green New Deal, whose primary goal is to create jobs locally and to kick-start economies. Before the crisis, political leaders would have had to first negotiate a successor treaty to Kyoto and, only then, seek to persuade their publics that the investments needed to meet emissions targets were necessary.

The other force that has emerged with precision timing is the administration of Barack Obama, which with one fell swoop has reversed the two trademarks of the Bush administration's policy that have hindered energy reform: skepticism about climate change and aversion to multilateralism. Obama seems to recognize that, just at the moment that America's role as global financial leader has been put in jeopardy, another opportunity has arisen: for America to become the global leader on energy and climate change.

"In the twenty-first century," Obama said shortly before his inauguration, "we know that the future of our economy and national security is inextricably linked with one challenge: energy."

Obama's choice of a powerful energy and environment team—and the creation of a new position of White House coordinator for energy and climate—left little doubt that this critical clutch of issues is now at the center of American policy. Perhaps his most notable appointment was one of the most outspoken American voices on climate change, Stephen Chu, as energy secretary.

Obama wasted no time in translating commitment into new policy priorities as epitomized by his goal to create the world's leading "clean-energy economy." In his first week, Obama directed federal regulators to move swiftly on an application by California and thirteen other states to set strict automobile emission and fuel-efficiency standards—moving the fuel-efficiency standard from the current twenty-seven miles per gallon to thirty-five miles per gallon by 2016—a request denied by the Bush administration. These new standards were formalized by the Obama administration just four months later, on May 19.

Also at the outset of his term, Obama persuaded Congress to pass an unprecedented economic stimulus bill—one of whose principal goals was to spark a "second industrial revolution." He said: "After decades of dragging our feet, this plan will finally spark creation of a clean energy industry that will create hundreds of thousands of jobs over the next few years." Before the stimulus bill, the federal government budget for energy research was the same, adjusted for inflation, as it was in 1968: about US$3 billion. And, quickly following in the footsteps of the stimulus package, the two key energy bills were introduced and debated in the U.S. Congress. These bills aim to take the Obama energy and climate change commitment to the next step, setting the stage for comprehensive national energy and climate change policies. However, the bills omit important elements of a robust clean-energy strategy by failing to emphasize carbon-removal from fossil fuels (except coal) and to support the potential of clean oil and clean natural gas (they do pay heed to clean coal). Nonetheless, a broad framework has been created that can be adjusted in the future.

The stimulus bill constitutes the most momentous shift in American energy priorities in decades—even though it came before the unveiling of the Obama administration's energy plan. The bill allocates tens of billions of dollars in spending and tax breaks that aim to double the amount of electricity produced from renewable sources in just three years. It also earmarks billions of dollars for a smart grid investment program. "Today, the electricity we use is carried along a grid of lines and wires that dates back to Thomas Edison—a grid that can't support the demands of clean energy," Obama said in signing the stimulus bill. "This means we're using nineteenth- and twentieth-century technologies to battle twenty-first-century problems, like climate change and energy security." The investments in a smart grid symbolize a broader effort to transform outmoded, energy-wasting industrial processes into ones suitable for a green economy. This is the true underpinning of the second industrial revolution.

Meanwhile, the Department of Energy's responsibility will dramatically increase under the stimulus plan, which more than doubled its budget, allocating US$40 billion over two years for a range of clean energy grants. At the same time, the Office of Energy Efficiency and Renewable Energy, which received US$1.7 billion in 2008, was given an additional US$18 billion over two years. But to a large degree, much of the energy security agenda will reside with the State Department. The challenge of energy policymaking is that it is generally decentralized within the federal government, with responsibilities shared among agencies, and with some resting in individual states. This has implications for the effectiveness and swiftness of policymaking.

Similar pro-employment Green New Deal packages have been advanced in China, Japan, the United Kingdom, and elsewhere. They are equally relevant to developing economies in terms of jobs, fighting poverty, and creating new opportunities at a time of increasingly uncertain commodity prices and exports. The trillions of dollars that have been mobilized to address current woes, together with the trillions of investors' dollars waiting in the wings, represent an opportunity that was unthinkable a short while ago.

The next stage, now, is not just to develop a strategy for a global Green New Deal, but to encourage a clean-development economic model that allows all energy forms to compete to be clean.

The Global Energy Bargain: One Thing Leads to Another

If recovery and restructuring at the national level will take exquisite skill, designing new global deals on energy and climate change is an even more complex Gordian knot, as Will Blyth rightly points out in chapter 7. The economic crisis can be a globalizing event, with energy and climate change as a unifier; or it can be a polarizing one, with protectionism as the outcome—and the downfall. The linchpin for success will be designing an approach to multilateral cooperation on energy security and climate change that is built around the idea of mutual interdependence and a clean-development future.

On the international stage, too, the Obama administration has shown early signs of its willingness to demonstrate muscular leadership. Secretary of State

Hillary Clinton chose China as her first official visit, seeking consensus with Beijing on reconciling the need for a coordinated economic stimulus, on the one hand, and for a global climate treaty, on the other. Together, the United States and China share many similarities. They account for about 40 percent of all greenhouse gas emissions: the United States generates 50 percent of its electricity from coal and China a staggering 80 percent. In fact, China surpasses America as the world's largest greenhouse gas emitter.

Pressure was intense on negotiators to craft a post-Kyoto pact by the time of the Copenhagen summit in December 2009. But even before the economic crisis, it would have been foolhardy to assume that the all-in-one approach implied by a post-Kyoto treaty is the best way forward. In fact, abiding by such a goal could lead to the worst of all worlds. It would place tremendous pressure on relations already strained by the global financial crisis, while also leading to climate targets that could prove unrealistic—thus undermining the legitimacy of the entire process. What is needed at the international level is a framework agreement that outlines the key ingredients to tackle climate change but leaves the binding, treaty-like elements for future negotiations. Such a framework should include targets to reduce carbon emissions; commitments to emissions-trading systems or carbon pricing; commitments to new and renewable energy forms, and to conservation and efficiency; and commitments to develop transparent systems to monitor these objectives.

The march to a new global treaty will continue in earnest, of course. But at the same time, as Blyth argues, we should be investing heavily in a bottom-up approach—one that focuses on bilateral, regional, and sector-specific agreements. Targets could be set by region; differentiated approaches could allow one region to learn best practices from another. Taken together, these can redefine the governance of energy markets and the battle against climate change; they also can provide a safety net, or a halfway house, in case a global pact falls short in any way. If such agreements are to emerge, then at their core must be the notion of mutual interdependence—wherein producer and consumer nations, developed and developing countries, come to understand that they need each other equally.

Regional and cross-regional gatherings have been occurring alongside the Copenhagen process. The recently convened Major Economies Meeting on Energy Security and Climate Change is a cross-regional grouping of the seventeen largest economies. These will informally discuss frameworks and approaches related to Copenhagen. Similarly, the G-77—the developing nations' forum led by China—is a grouping to frame the position of the emerging nations.

The regional approach is exemplified by the European Union, which has made exceptional progress in reducing emissions, while achieving relatively high economic growth. The fifteen member states that were part of the EU at the time Kyoto was ratified reduced their emissions of greenhouse gases by 2.2 percent below 1990 levels by 2006; over the same period, their economies grew by almost 40 percent. The EU also agreed in 2008 to a comprehensive package of climate and energy legislation that will allow it to further reduce greenhouse gas emissions by 20 percent by 2020 (relative to 1990 levels).

Making progress at the regional level also raises the stakes for other parties in global negotiations. Indeed, the EU, while it was negotiating its 20 percent by 2020 deal last year, built in a conditional sweetener as an incentive for other countries to agree on a post-Kyoto pact. Specifically, the EU has pledged to seek a 30 percent cut in its emissions if other developed countries make comparable efforts. One thing, as they say, leads to another.

One of the linchpins for a climate treaty, meanwhile, is the eventual creation of a global carbon market and a carbon price that will drive investment behavior changes. Here again, though, the advantages of regionalism and incrementalism are evident. If a global carbon market is to emerge, it will have to be built on regional progress. The EU has taken the lead with its Emissions Trading Scheme— a qualified success, despite the plunging price of carbon. Now, President Obama in his 2010 budget has proposed that the United States develop an ambitious, nationwide carbon-trading scheme that potentially would generate more than US$600 billion in a decade and reduce 2005-level emissions by 14 percent by 2020 and by 83 percent by 2050. The next step would be to negotiate a transatlantic carbon trading system—which, given the commitment of both the EU and the Obama administration to address climate change, should be a viable goal. Eventually, a single market among all OECD countries would be cobbled together. Such a market might also underpin another crucial aspect of the global energy governance challenge—establishing mechanisms to finance the mitigation and technology transfer efforts at the heart of a global compact. Yet any new energy governance architecture must have as part of its core mission not just climate change, but also energy security and other key aspects of energy management, such as the need to stabilize energy markets so that price swings are nowhere near as extreme—as destructive—as we have recently experienced.

Energy today remains stuck in the world of twentieth-century governance, relying on institutions like the International Energy Agency (IEA), OPEC, and the Energy Charter Treaty. A new architecture is needed for the twenty-first century and is beginning to evolve in the context of mutual interdependence. Major progress is being made, for instance, in specific sectors, especially in the realm of alternative and renewable energy. Proof of this came in early 2009, when the founding conference of the International Renewable Energy Agency (IRENA) was held in Bonn. Seventy-five countries signed up to create an organization dedicated to promoting a rapid transition toward the widespread and sustainable use of renewable energy on a global scale. IRENA will help countries build regulatory frameworks, effective financial mechanisms, and state-of-the-art technological expertise to tap renewable sources of energy. Importantly, IRENA will be based in the United Arab Emirates, the heartland of fossil fuels—underscoring the stake that *all* countries have in creating clean energy. But IRENA is just one piece of a reformed global energy framework. A "total energy" architecture, built around the notion of mutual interdependence, must be established—in part through the redesign of existing institutions.

The IEA, with its limited representation and twentieth-century structures, was founded to address oil shortages and was extended into other areas when other organizations failed to do so. With the advent of institutions like IRENA, a more rational overall architecture is evolving. The IEA will remain relevant in the realms of oil and energy policy; in fact, IRENA and other international efforts can learn from the effectiveness of the IEA's approach to country targets and action plans. Yet for the IEA to maintain its power, it needs to welcome the major new consumer nations, especially China and India, and redefine the collective interests of its members.

Yet while the IEA can work to coordinate consumer nations, thus providing an essential balance to OPEC, and IRENA can help guide the development of renewable energy forms, fostering mutual interdependence will require additional institutions. One such entity could be the International Energy Forum (IEF) in Riyadh, which facilitates mutual exchange between producers and consumers. It could develop into a clearinghouse of crucial information, such as production levels, which already is the subject of its Joint Oil Data Initiative. By offering transparent data and tracking energy market developments, the IEF would allow all stakeholders to plan their energy needs with far greater security much further into the future.

There is a role for the G-20 to play as well. In almost every case, at the global and regional levels, leadership by the developed world will be necessary to achieve real and sustainable progress. This translates, inevitably, into American leadership. It is a challenge Barack Obama has said he is prepared to confront. "Few challenges facing America—and the world—are more urgent than combating climate change," he said shortly after his election. "My presidency will mark a new chapter in America's leadership on climate change." He later added: "Clean energy development must be a central focus in our relationships with major countries in Europe and Asia." The world can only hope that conditions allow him to follow through on this vision.

In short, as Blyth compellingly writes, neither the top-down nor the bottom-up approach will be sufficient on its own. "Without clear and achievable implementation plans for delivering emission reductions, internationally agreed emission reduction targets will lack credibility, and countries will be either unwilling or unable to negotiate stringent targets in good faith. On the other hand, without wider international agreement, domestic policy will founder on concerns of fairness and international competitiveness."

Blyth also offers a viable solution: "Breaking out of this chicken-and-egg situation requires pursuing robust domestic and international policy solutions simultaneously, across all aspects of climate change policy, including R&D; technology transfer; institutional infrastructures for monitoring, reporting, and verifying emissions; markets for energy services; and the transformation of product markets."

Finally, it is worth underscoring again that the global economic crisis also has abetted a bottom-up approach. A year ago, it would have been inconceivable to think that the United States would have found hundreds of billions of dollars to promote energy efficiency and alternative energy initiatives. Yet the need for an economic jolt led directly to this in the stimulus bill passed by Congress last February. And energy investments also constitute a major part of stimulus efforts in countries around the world, from Australia to China to the European Union.

Grass Roots Are Green, But "Clean" Is the New Gold

Perhaps the linchpin to energy and climate change success in these deeply politicized times will be the stance of individual consumers and voters. Here, too, the signs are positive.

The convergence of concerns about climate change and energy security over the past three years has allowed the world to move past the tipping point of awareness to the transformative stage of action. Individuals around the world now feel that it is up to them to help save the world from environmental catastrophe. They are busily screwing in fluorescent light bulbs, buying hybrid cars that run on cleaner energy, and "greening" their homes. Many consumers are even tracking their personal emissions on websites like mycarbonfootprint.eu and buying carbon offsets through programs like the Conservation Fund's Go Zero program.

Ordinary people, in short, understand that they are the warriors in this battle and that every individual can be an agent of change. Big oil was the protagonist of the twentieth century; individuals are the stars of the twenty-first. Consumers understand that reduced demand is potentially the largest source of supply. It is their drive toward efficiency—enabled by end-use technologies that sip rather than chug energy—that must be at the heart of the new energy era. The economic crisis offers them even greater incentive to act—and the crisis-era policies of the United States, the EU, and other countries must reinforce these incentives in order to accelerate their actions.

Perhaps the most encouraging characteristic of this environmental and energy revolution is that it is led by a broad-based, grassroots, global movement of the most unlikely bedfellows: conservatives and liberals, rich and poor, young and old. It has succeeded in driving personal, political, and corporate behavior despite the apparent entrenched apathy of establishments. Among the most fervent clean-energy crusaders are the young: 38 percent of teens say they are "concerned" about the environment, and 15 percent describe themselves as "hard core" environmentalists. This bottom-up dynamic will have to be sustained if the world is to move past the current awareness stage to the forging of a clean-energy world. Complacency must be kept at bay.

These are still the early days of a monumental, multigenerational global challenge. Yet for the first time in history nearly every country on earth—led by the grassroots activism of millions of individuals—is working toward the same goal. And even more heartening, despite the large government stimulus packages, they seem inclined to use the market as the principal means of achieving this goal.

PART THREE

Short-Term Supply Management and Long-Term Energy Cooperation

10

Consumer Country Energy Cooperation: The International Energy Agency and the Global Energy Order

Wilfrid L. Kohl

N ew consumers such as China and India change the global energy landscape in a number of ways. Most prominently, these newcomers are treated as mere competitors over global resources, challenging the dominant position of the well-established Western consumer bloc. Yet the rise of China and India, along with other emerging economies, also has important implications for the architecture of global energy regarding consumer-consumer cooperation. Cooperation among consuming nations is key to buffering the risks stemming from the volatile oil market and to combat climate change. Hence it is appropriate to assess the impact the newcomers have on existing forms of cooperation and to examine how these need to adjust to ensure their effectiveness.

This chapter reviews consumer country energy cooperation with particular attention to the role of the International Energy Agency (IEA). It begins with an overview of the present structure and functions of the IEA and other international forums and their roles in international energy security and in responding to climate change, a more recent and equally important energy problem. I analyze the

The author would like to thank Ambassador William Ramsay, until recently the deputy executive director of the International Energy Agency, and other IEA staff for meeting with him in September 2008 while he was researching this chapter. He is also grateful for helpful comments from an anonymous reviewer.

role of the new consumers on the world energy scene (especially China and India), how they are affecting global energy security and climate, and question whether, in the future, the IEA might broaden its membership to include these countries. I also examine the role of the IEA in developing technology strategies to mitigate climate change, as the world faces the challenge of altering its energy use and moving toward a lower carbon future. I conclude by reviewing options to enhance consumer country cooperation in these fields, identifying areas where the architecture of global energy needs to be strengthened.

International Forums for Energy Cooperation among Consumer Countries

The most prominent forum for energy cooperation among consumer nations certainly is the IEA, an international organization designed particularly to address energy issues. In addition to the IEA, a number of forums have emerged that deal with energy and climate and, in that, deserve further examination. These include the European Union, a supranational organization comprising major oil-consuming nations and the bulk of OECD oil producers; the G-8, a forum comprising most of the world's largest consumers but also including Russia as a major non-OECD producer; the various groups representing the global climate change regime; and the World Bank, an international donor organization with a mandate to improve energy efficiency and to accelerate investments in clean energy, mainly in consuming nations in the developing world.

International Energy Agency

Established in November 1974 in response to the first OPEC oil embargo, the International Energy Agency is an intergovernmental organization attached to the OECD in Paris. It initially consisted of eighteen industrialized countries; by 2008 its membership had expanded to twenty-eight countries. IEA members must also be members of the OECD. The IEA has a governing board that meets periodically; the board is made up of senior energy officials from member countries. The IEA also has a secretariat, which is led by an executive director; the current executive director is Nobuo Tanaka of Japan. According to the International Energy Program (IEP), its founding document, the IEA's objectives are to establish and maintain a system of emergency oil sharing to cope with future oil supply disruptions; to promote rational energy policies in a global context; to operate a permanent information system on the world oil market; to improve the world's energy supply and demand structure by developing alternative energy sources and increasing energy efficiency; to promote international collaboration on energy technology; and to assist in the integration of energy and environmental policies.[1]

Today the IEA summarizes its purposes as the promotion of energy security, environmental protection (especially within the context of climate change), economic growth through stable energy supplies and free markets, and global engagement, including engagement with nonmember countries.[2] IEA members agree to nine shared goals, including free and open markets, undistorted energy prices, free and open trade, improved energy efficiency, environmental sustainability, and energy technology research and development.[3]

The core of the IEA is its emergency oil crisis management system, the one area in which the IEA has international authority. As prescribed in the IEP, members must agree to maintain oil stocks equivalent to ninety days of imports (based on the previous year), plus a system of demand restraint. Under the original IEP the somewhat cumbersome sharing system was to be triggered when the secretariat, acting alone or at the request of one or more member governments, made a finding that the daily rate of oil supplies had been reduced by at least 7 percent, either for the group as a whole or for one or more member countries. IEA member countries were expected to implement the measures prescribed under the IEP within fifteen days, unless the governing board reversed the finding. The formal emergency sharing system has never been used.

In 1979 the IEA adopted the Coordinated Emergency Response Mechanism (CERM), a more rapid and flexible response to an actual or imminent oil supply disruption; the mechanism emphasizes early release of stocks. The Initial Contingency Response Plan allows the executive director to consult with member countries and decide on actions within twenty-four hours of a market interruption. Countries can formally consider options of stock release (public or industry stocks) and demand restraint and, if available, surge production and fuel switching. The U.S. preference has always been for coordinated stock drawdown, which can serve to offset all or most of the shortfall created by a market disruption. This also helps to dampen a surge in oil prices. Country contributions are generally proportional to their share in total IEA oil consumption. A combination of measures, mostly stock draw, was used in the IEA action to release 60 million barrels of oil

1. Agreement on an International Energy Program, as amended in September 2008 (www.iea.org/about/docs/IEP.pdf).

2. See www.iea.org/about/docs/IEP.pdf.

3. See www.iea.org/about/sharedgoals.htm.

into the market following Hurricane Katrina in September 2005. The CERM was also used in a coordinated stock release by the United States, Germany, and Japan at the start of the first Gulf War in January 1991.[4]

The IEA holds periodic exercises to test emergency oil sharing and stock drawdown procedures. Monthly checks are also performed on stock levels. Every few years there are peer reviews of the emergency preparedness of IEA member countries. The IEA also offers training on emergency preparedness to nonmember countries. In addition, the secretariat, with its staff of energy experts, collects and analyzes data on energy markets and makes global energy projections based on various scenarios. The most widely known of its many publications are the *Oil Market Report,* published monthly, and the annual *World Energy Outlook.* These publications have become authoritative sources in the energy field. The IEA also organizes high-level workshops to explore new topics.

Its normative activities include policy recommendations to member governments regarding, for example, available technologies to reduce greenhouse gas emissions as requested by the G-8; and periodic evaluations, led by peer reviewers, of member country energy policies. Operational activities include technical missions to third countries, upon request, to give advice and assistance. The IEA also brings together industry and government experts to work on particular research and development projects.

As an intergovernmental organization, the IEA has limited authority in rule creation and enforcement. Outside of the rules for emergency oil crisis management, where it does supervise member country implementation, the IEA cannot force its members (which are sovereign governments) to adopt policies. It can only make recommendations. The additional function that it can occasionally perform is the issuance of "report cards" on country behavior, a very useful action that could be expanded.

In recent years the IEA, through its annual *World Energy Outlook,* has called attention to the threat of climate change and the unsustainable path of the world's energy consumption, dominated by fossil fuels. The IEA has proposed alternative energy scenarios to reduce greenhouse gas emissions. The *World Energy Outlook 2008* contains a detailed analysis of energy and climate policy and makes proposals for a post-2012 climate regime based on scenarios of CO_2 emissions reductions to 550 or 450 parts per million.

4. International Energy Agency (2007b).

The European Union

The European Union (EU) is both an intergovernmental and a supranational organization. It currently has twenty-seven member countries, with a combined population of 500 million. The EU currently is the second-largest oil consumer (2007); it also comprises some of the world's most important OECD oil producers. Its institutional bodies include a Council of Ministers, composed of representatives of national governments, and a European parliament, which is directly elected. Together these bodies can take legally binding decisions, which can be enforced by the European Court of Justice. The EU evolved out of earlier treaties creating the European Coal and Steel Community (1952), the European Economic Community (1957), and the Euratom Treaty (also 1957). The European Commission is the executive body of the EU, with powers of proposing and implementing legislation.

There is no specific article on energy in current EU treaties. Most existing energy legislation has been developed since the mid-1990s under competition policy, with the purpose of creating functioning liberalized internal markets in electricity and natural gas. Considerable progress has been made in these two sectors, but more remains to be done. The Lisbon Treaty (still to be ratified by all member states) contains a strong basis for a common energy policy. Meanwhile, in January 2007 the commission proposed, and the council agreed to, an integrated energy and climate change package with the objectives of reducing greenhouse gas emissions by 20 percent below 1990 levels by 2020, of raising the share of renewable energy to 20 percent by the same year, and of increasing biofuels in transportation to a 10 percent share. Members have also agreed to reduce energy demand by 20 percent relative to its projected amount by 2020. The main instruments to achieve these goals are energy policy and the EU Emissions Trading Scheme (EU-ETS). A legislative package published in January 2008, which sets national targets for member countries in order to meet the new objectives, was approved by the European Parliament in December 2008.[5]

Member states still retain sovereignty over their national energy mix and their indigenous energy resources. They also bring their separate political and social models to the organization of the energy sector. So far they have been reluctant to give up this sovereignty. One result has been difficulty in agreeing to a common

5. European Commission (2007). See also Van der Linde (2007); Europa, "Climate Change: Commission Welcomes Final Adoption of Europe's Climate and Energy Package," December 17, 2008 (http://europa.eu).

EU external energy security policy and in speaking with one voice. This has been most noticeable in the natural gas sector: the EU is heavily dependent on imports from Russia, yet member states have different views on how to respond to recent reductions in gas supplies following Russia's conflicts with Ukraine.

However, member states appear willing to accept national targets on energy efficiency and renewable energies, and in general the EU has done well at integrating energy and climate goals in its 20/20 by 2020 program and in establishing the ETS. It has set a bold example for the world. The challenge will be in monitoring and enforcing implementation of its policies. At this writing the European Commission has made proposals for a global pact on climate change at the Copenhagen meeting in December 2009, including a reduction in greenhouse gas emissions by developed countries to 30 percent below 1990 levels in 2020, while developing countries (except the poorest ones) should limit growth in their collective emissions to 15–30 percent below business-as-usual levels by 2020. Other proposals call for an OECD-wide carbon market by 2015, linking the ETS with comparable cap-and-trade systems, and for additional investment in developing countries.[6] The council has yet to respond to these proposals. The EU has a budget for energy technology research and development and expects to use it under its new Strategic Energy Technology Plan to encourage new technologies, including carbon capture and storage, to enable a shift to a lower carbon economy.[7]

EU members are required to hold emergency oil stocks covering ninety days of consumption in the form of petroleum products. However, most EU countries are also members of the IEA crisis management system, which has broader acceptance. In the case of a disruption in supply, and an IEA authorized stock drawdown, the EU Oil Supply Group would consult and authorize reduction in European stocks below ninety days of consumption. In 2007 an effort began to review the EU system in order to make it more compatible with the IEA emergency stockholding system.

The Global Climate Change Regime

For most industrialized countries, the problem of rising emissions of greenhouse gases is fundamentally an energy problem rooted in human combustion of fossil fuels. Given an overall contribution of oil to primary energy demand of more than

6. Europa, "Climate Change: Commission Sets Out Proposals for Global Pact on Climate Change at Copenhagen," January 28, 2009 (http://europa.eu). See also European Commission (2009).

7. European Commission (2009).

a third, many industrialized countries also regard climate change policies as an important way to reduce oil demand. As such, brief mention is made here of the components of the evolving global climate change regime.

The 1992 UN Framework Convention on Climate Change (UNFCCC) set the objective of "stabilizing greenhouse gas concentrations in the atmosphere at a level that would prevent dangerous anthropogenic interference with the climate system." The Kyoto Protocol of December 1997 established a system of binding but differentiated emissions reduction targets for industrial countries, which on average agreed to reduce their emissions 5.2 percent below 1990 levels by 2008–12. Developing countries were exempt from obligations. The protocol entered into force in 2005. As of 2008 it had been ratified by 183 countries. The United States and several other countries declined to participate. Instead, the Bush administration called for voluntary measures to reduce the greenhouse gas intensity of the U.S. economy. In September 2007 it convened the Major Economies Meeting on Energy Security and Climate Change (including major developing countries) to discuss the setting of a long-term goal for reducing global greenhouse gas emissions but with each nation designing its own strategy.

Meanwhile, the Intergovernmental Panel on Climate Change (IPCC), a body of some 2,500 scientists from around the world, has issued periodic assessment reports presenting evidence that most of the warming of the earth over the last fifty years is attributable to human activities. The Fourth Assessment Report, issued in 2007, stated that the warming of the climate system is unequivocal and that the effects are already visible in increased air and ocean temperatures, higher average sea level, and reduced snow and ice. The projection is that, without changes in human behavior, the global climate could warm by as much as six degrees Celsius by 2100.[8]

Meeting in Bali in December 2007, the parties to the UNFCCC set a framework for future negotiations on long-term emissions cuts post-Kyoto. The goal is to create a new treaty at a meeting in Copenhagen at the end of 2009, to take effect in 2012. A preparatory meeting was held in Poznan, Poland, in December 2008. Meanwhile, there is growing consensus in the United States on the need for national measures to reduce greenhouse gas emissions, which would seem to provide a foundation for action by the Obama administration. It will be challenging to put in place a national plan, plus a position on a new international agreement, in the short time before the Copenhagen meeting in December 2009. The responsibility lies with the main consuming nations, their ability to cooperate (potentially

8. Intergovernmental Panel on Climate Change (2007).

under the leadership of the United States), and their capacity to accommodate the legitimate interests of newly emerging consumers.

The G-8 Summit Process

Since 1975 the heads of state or government of the industrial democracies have been meeting annually to deal with major economic and political issues facing their countries and the world. Six countries met at Rambouillet, France, at the request of French President Valery Giscard d'Estaing in November 1975 (France, the United States, Britain, Germany, Japan, and Italy). Canada joined the 1976 summit and the European Community the London summit of 1977. After 1991 Russia participated in postsummit dialogues with the G-7. Russia gained full participation in 1998, in what became the G-8. The summit process has traditionally dealt with macroeconomic policy issues, international trade, and relations with developing countries. East-West economic relations, energy, and terrorism have also been on the agenda, as have, at times, political security issues. The G-7 first focused on energy issues and reduction of oil imports at the Bonn summit of 1978, the 1979 Tokyo summit, and the Venice summit of 1980.[9]

The G-7 and G-8 summits provide an important opportunity for busy leaders to meet and discuss complex international issues and to establish personal relationships, which can help them respond to and manage international crises. Moreover, the summits focus the attention of domestic bureaucracies and provide them with direction. Supporting ministerial meetings throughout the year continue the work through agendas set forth at the summits. Within governments there is usually a high-level official, frequently referred to as a sherpa, who is tasked with coordinating summit preparation and implementation.[10]

Recent G-8 summits have devoted considerable attention to energy and climate change. This began with the July 2005 Gleneagles summit, chaired by Prime Minister Tony Blair. That summit issued the detailed Plan of Action on Climate Change, Clean Energy, and Sustainable Development, with the purpose of reducing greenhouse gas emissions and moving toward a low-carbon economy. Its goal is to develop markets for clean energy technologies, increase their availability in developing countries, and help vulnerable communities adapt to the impact of climate change. Leaders of Brazil, China, India, Mexico, and South Africa and heads of relevant international organizations were invited to join the discussions. The

9. Kohl (1983).
10. For more background, see the G-8 Information Center, University of Toronto (www.g8.utoronto.ca).

IEA was specifically asked to advise on alternative energy scenarios and strategies aimed at a clean, clever, and competitive energy future, and the World Bank was asked to take a leadership role in creating a new framework for investment and financing clean energy and development.

The July 2006 G-8 summit in St. Petersburg concluded with an extensive statement on global energy security. In June 2007, at the summit at Heiligendamm, chaired by Chancellor Angela Merkel of Germany, the G-8 agreed on the need for urgent and concerted action on climate change to achieve a post-2012 and post-Kyoto agreement that included all major emitting countries based on the principle of common but differentiated responsibilities and capabilities. At the July 2008 meeting in Hokkaido, Japan, the leaders of the G-8 endorsed the goal of cutting greenhouse gas emissions in half by 2050. They were less specific about short- and midterm goals but offered considerable financing and technology transfer to other countries. The Outreach Five (China, India, South Africa, Mexico, and Brazil) agreed to take appropriate measures to control their own carbon emissions. The IEA's twenty-five recommendations on energy efficiency were received by the G-8, which promised implementation. Meanwhile, the IEA was asked to develop a road map for innovative technologies and to cooperate on carbon capture and storage.

It should be noted that G-8 members are not all purely energy-consuming countries. The group is an eclectic mix and includes six energy consumers/importers and two exporters of oil and gas (Russia and Canada). This mix can lead to divergent views on energy. On the whole, however, the G-8 summit process has been useful in getting country leaders to agree on broad goals to move forward on energy and climate. The G-8 can also assign tasks to international organizations on pressing issues and can help create and build international regimes. Compliance by governments with summit declarations, however, is mixed and depends largely on the extent of monitoring and the will of individual sovereign countries. There is no formal method of enforcing decisions.

World Bank

The World Bank provides loans to assist low-income and middle-income countries in reducing poverty and increasing economic growth. These countries develop strategies to reach these goals in various sectors, including universal education, infrastructure (roads, water, sanitation), health care, energy, and governance. In 2007 about 7 percent of country lending was focused on energy and mining. Recently, the bank has been developing new strategies to deal with climate change. The G-8 Gleneagles summit in 2005 asked the World Bank to produce a road map

for accelerating investments in clean energy for the developing world, in cooperation with other financial organizations.

The result is the Clean Energy Investment Framework (CEIF), which identifies the scale of investments needed to increase access to energy, especially in sub-
Saharan Africa; to accelerate the transition to a low-carbon economy; and to adapt
to climate variability and change. Two climate investment funds were approved
in July 2008 as a collaborative effort among the multilateral development banks
and countries. Donor countries subsequently made pledges exceeding US$6 bil-
lion to these funds over a three-year period. This financing is in addition to existing official development assistance. The two funds are the Clean Technology
Fund, designed to accelerate cost-effective mitigation of greenhouse gas emissions
to move toward a lower carbon growth path; and the Strategic Climate Fund, with
targeted programs to provide financing for new approaches, with the potential for
scaling up outcomes. The Clean Technology Fund will be a pilot program for climate resilience.

Meanwhile, the World Bank's Strategic Framework for Development and Climate Change is at an advanced stage of discussion. The framework is based on the
principle that developing countries and the poorest communities are likely to suffer the most from climate change, which will increase the costs of development
and threaten to reverse development gains.[11]

The New Consumers and Other Major Players in the World Oil Market: Share of Global Demand, Impact on Energy Security, Climate, and the IEA

As the IEA itself has observed, energy consumption outside its member countries
now is responsible for most of the growth in global energy demand.[12] With a combined population of more than 2.5 billion people and rapid economic growth,
China and India are becoming leading energy consumers. The IEA projects that
together they will account for 45 percent of the increase in world energy demand
by 2030.

Although both countries rely heavily on indigenous coal resources, they are also
dependent on oil and, increasingly, on oil imports. The *World Energy Outlook
2007* forecasts that global oil demand will increase from 84.5 million barrels a day
(mbd) in 2006 to 116.3 mbd in 2030. About 42 percent of this increase will come

11. World Bank (2008).
12. International Energy Agency (2007b).

from China and India. The IEA estimates that China's net oil imports will grow from 3. 5 mbd in 2006 to 13.1 mbd in 2030 and that India's net imports will rise from 1.9 mbd in 2006 to 6 mbd in 2030. These increased oil flows, mostly from the Middle East, will add urgency to the need for increased supply and to the risks of oil tanker shipments through sometimes vulnerable transport routes (such as the Strait of Malacca). There is also the question of how to include new consumers in the IEA's system of emergency stock drawdown in order to enhance its ability to offset a market disruption and to prevent free riding.

Simultaneously, India and China are projected to increase their coal use substantially in the immediate future, and both countries have already become coal importers. The rise in coal use, mainly for power generation, will mean increases in CO_2 emissions. China overtook the United States in 2007 as the largest CO_2 emitter, and India is projected to become the third-largest world CO_2 emitter by 2015.

Responding to increased oil consumption and imports, the IEA has adopted an informal outreach strategy to encourage emergency oil stock building in China and India and the development of emergency response measures that might eventually be compatible with the IEA. At the same time, India and China, though not IEA members, have been involved in energy technology implementation agreements.

China and India Emergency Stocks

As noted earlier, a requirement for IEA membership is that a country hold emergency oil stocks (public or private) equivalent to ninety days of net imports for the previous year. What is the state of Chinese and Indian emergency stocks?

Undoubtedly moved by its growing oil imports, China announced in 2003 that it would establish a strategic petroleum reserve. Construction began in 2004 at four sites. When completed, these facilities are expected to have the capacity for 102 million barrels, which is equal to thirty-seven days of China's net oil imports in 2005 (China's oil imports will, however, increase in the future). The process of filling these sites has begun. The National Oil Reserve Office has been established within the National Development and Reform Commission (NDRC) to oversee the development of these strategic oil reserves, with each reserve site being operated by one of the national oil companies (Sinopec, Sinochem, PetroChina). In 2007 these reserves amounted to an estimated 15–22 million barrels of oil. This amount was projected to expand by 2010 to around 88 million barrels. Meanwhile, the government is planning second and third phases of storage facilities, including the use of underground caverns, for a total capacity of more than 500 million barrels. The long-term goal is to have reserve stocks equivalent to ninety days of net imports by 2020. Oil companies are constructing their own commercial storage facilities in various locations.[13] In the future the Chinese government may require its oil industry to hold a certain level of emergency oil stocks, which could also be counted toward the IEA's obligation of ninety days of net imports.

India began planning in 2004 for a strategic oil reserve at three locations. Construction of rock caverns was expected to start at the end of 2007, to be completed by 2010, after which fill will begin. This first phase would yield reserves roughly equivalent to twenty days of net imports, based on 2005 levels. However, India's oil consumption and imports will continue to rise. After a second phase, yet to be scheduled, the goal is to create reserves of about 110 million barrels. Indian storage facilities are being managed by the Indian Strategic Petroleum Reserves Limited, an agency owned by the Oil Industry Development Board. These facilities are in addition to existing facilities storing crude oil and products belonging to oil companies. To have net import coverage of forty-five days, India would probably need a reserve of around 276 million barrels by 2030, according to the IEA reference scenario in the *World Energy Outlook 2007*. The Integrated Energy Policy of 2006 states that India strives for a total coverage of ninety days of net imports and that it anticipates cooperative actions with the reserves of other countries, such as IEA member countries, to improve their effectiveness.[14]

The IEA and China

Informal cooperation between China and the IEA began in 1996, when the IEA and the predecessor of the NDRC signed a memorandum of policy understanding in the field of energy. In 2001 the IEA and the Ministry of Science and Technology signed the Framework for Energy Technology Cooperation. Numerous exchanges, joint conferences and workshops, studies, and energy technology cooperation activities ensued. High-level Chinese officials have occasionally attended IEA ministerial meetings. Since 1996 the IEA has had a regular communication and exchange with the Chinese National Bureau of Statistics, and in 2006 the IEA trained Chinese oil statisticians to assist in establishing China's emergency oil data system. A three-year program of cooperation began in 2007.

In the area of emergency preparedness, Chinese delegates participated in IEA workshops and seminars in 2001 and 2002. This was followed by Chinese expert

13. International Energy Agency (2007b).
14. International Energy Agency (2007b).

participation in a 2004 IEA emergency response exercise in Paris, followed by a joint workshop on oil security in Beijing in 2006. The IEA maintains a dialogue with NDRC on strategic oil reserves, and has regular communication with China's national oil companies.[15]

China's largest coal producer, Shenhua, joined the IEA Coal Industry Advisory Board (CIAB) in 2007. In May 2008 the CIAB held a conference in China on clean coal technology and policy. The IEA has published a joint study, *Developing China's Natural Gas Markets 2002*, and another study on *China's Power Sector Reforms in 2006.* Chinese delegates have attended meetings of the IEA Renewable Energy Working Party, and an assessment of China's renewable energy markets has been included in IEA global renewable assessments.

Contacts on energy efficiency go back to a workshop in 1996 held by the IEA with the Committee on Environment and Natural Resources of the National People's Congress, followed by another workshop on standards and labels in 2001 with the State Economic and Trade Commission. China has ambitious plans to improve energy efficiency, and Chinese delegates participated in IEA workshops on energy indicators and industrial energy efficiency in 2006 and 2007.

With regard to energy technologies, China is a contracting party in three IEA implementing agreements on energy technology research and development programs: hydropower, fusion materials, and multiphase flow. China is also a sponsor in the IEA Clean Coal Centre. Under the Gleneagles Plan of Action, the IEA seeks to expand China's participation in implementing agreements via the Networks of Expertise in Energy Technologies (NEET) initiative.

The *World Energy Outlook* has regularly included chapters on China; the 2007 edition focuses on China and India. The IEA is advising China on short- and long-term energy forecasting, energy modeling, and energy indicators. A workshop on the application of IEA's energy indicators to China's energy efficiency program was held in Beijing in March 2008. Moreover, the IEA and China are discussing collaboration in tracking greenhouse gas emissions and related issues under the Gleneagles Plan of Action.

Various parts of the IEA are now working in or with China, and there are several staff missions each month. Under its new executive director, Nobuo Tanaka, in office since fall 2007, the IEA has declared its intention to broaden China's participation in the work of the IEA, with an eventual goal of seeking China's membership. China (as well as India and Russia) were invited and sent high-level representatives to an IEA ministerial meeting in October 2009. The IEA has

15. International Energy Agency (2008e).

set up an Office of Global Dialogue and currently has a senior staff person in charge of China programs. IEA staff receive frequent invitations to speak at events in China.

The IEA and India

India's cooperation with the IEA is almost as extensive as China's. It began a little later, in 1998, when a declaration of cooperation was signed. Since then an annual high-level policy dialogue has occurred between senior Indian officials and the leadership of the IEA.

IEA-India cooperation covers all energy sectors and involves several energy-related ministries. It also includes public sector companies, the private sector, universities, and industry. In the first several years cooperation was focused mainly on bringing IEA expertise to India through workshops and seminars. More recently, cooperation is a two-way exchange of information, expertise, knowledge, and lessons learned. Recent joint activities focused on electric power, energy efficiency, technology collaboration, clean coal technology, and energy security. In 2008 the IEA organized three joint workshops in India, and Indian experts participated in a number of meetings at IEA headquarters and elsewhere.[16]

On energy statistics, regular workshops and training sessions have been held for Indian policymakers and statisticians, and India has joined as a participant in the multinational Joint Oil Data Initiative. On oil emergency preparedness, Indian officials have attended a number of IEA seminars and workshops since 2000. A joint IEA-India workshop on issues surrounding strategic oil stocks was held in New Delhi in 2004, and Indian experts participated in emergency response simulation exercises in Paris in 2004 and 2008. The IEA maintains a regular dialogue with the Ministry of Petroleum and Natural Gas on strategic oil reserves.

On coal, the Coal Industry Advisory Board of the IEA published *Coal in the Energy Supply of India* in 2002. The IEA, jointly with the World Coal Institute, organized the 2006 workshop, Coal for Sustainable Energy: Clean Development and Climate Change, in New Delhi. On natural gas, the IEA published *Potential for Gas Fired Power Supply in India* in 2006. On electricity, the IEA in 2002 released the study *Electricity in India: Power for the Millions*. An earlier workshop was held in New Delhi in 2001 on policies to accelerate renewable energy markets development.

In the area of energy efficiency, workshops were held in India in 2004 and 2006. Indian delegates participated in a 2006 workshop at the IEA on energy indi-

16. International Energy Agency (2008f).

cators and industrial energy efficiency. Under the Gleneagles Plan of Action, the IEA and India are discussing collaborative activities on energy efficiency. With regard to energy technology, India has joined two IEA implementing agreements (greenhouse gases and demand-side management) and has expressed interest in joining agreements on renewables and clean energy technologies. India is a sponsor of the IEA Clean Coal Centre.

The IEA has paid special attention to India as well as China in recent editions of *World Energy Outlook,* particularly in 2007, when there was a major focus on these two countries. The IEA continues to seek opportunities for cooperation on specific topics related to Indian electricity and gas market reform and on improvement in India's energy statistics.

Other Major Emerging Economies: Consumers and Producers

Brazil is a leading energy producer and consumer in Latin America and an important G-8+5 country. With a population of 196 million, it, is the fifth-largest country in the world. Brazil's GDP of US$1.8 trillion ranks ninth in the world; it is the second-largest non-OECD economy after China. It is an important oil producer (but not a member of OPEC). In 2007 Brazil produced 2.28 million barrels a day of oil. Production was predicted to increase to 2.41 million a day in 2008. It is likely that the country will become a net oil exporter in 2009.[17] Most of Brazil's oil production is in the offshore Campos and Santos basins on the country's southeast coast. The recently announced discovery of oil in the Tupi field, a subsalt zone deep beneath the ocean floor, is potentially the largest oil discovery since the Kashagan field in Kazakhstan, though it will be difficult to develop. While Petrobras, the state-owned oil company, dominates oil production, the country's oil and gas sectors have been otherwise deregulated. Brazil is also one of the world's largest ethanol producers and exporters, and more than half of all cars in the country are flex-fuel vehicles. Brazil's electricity supply is dominated by hydroelectric generation.

South Africa is a middle-income emerging market with abundant natural resources. It has a GDP of US$467.8 billion and a per capita income of US$9,700. It is Africa's largest economy and until recently was growing at 4.5 percent a year. Its energy source is primarily coal, which supplies 88 percent of primary energy and 90 percent of electric power generation. The country also has an important synthetic fuels industry, which is based on a coal-to-liquids system. Oil and gas resources are small, and the country must import about 66 percent of its crude oil.

17. Energy Information Administration (2008a).

Its electric utility, Eskom, is one of the largest in the world and supplies two-thirds of the electricity on the African continent. However, aging power plants and rapid demand growth have recently produced a shortfall in power supply. Eskom has two nuclear power plants and is constructing the first in a new generation of high-temperature gas-cooled nuclear reactors.[18]

Mexico is a free market economy with a mixture of modern and antiquated industry and agriculture. It has a population of 110 million and a GDP of US$1.35 trillion. It is the sixth-largest oil producer in the world, with an average production of 3.71 million barrels a day. It is also a large exporter. Most of its production comes from the giant offshore Cantarell field. However, Mexican oil production is declining. The state oil company, PEMEX, dominates the industry, and foreign oil companies are not allowed to participate. However, due to large financial obligations to the government, PEMEX lacks sufficient funds to invest in new exploration and production. Mexico is not a member of OPEC, although it has cooperated with OPEC several times in the past to raise oil prices. Mexico has joined the OECD but is not a member of the IEA. It does not want to sign the International Energy Program and commit itself to obligations under the old oil-sharing system, even though the system has since been revised informally. Moreover, Mexico has a mostly state-run energy sector, not open to competition and foreign investment, and would therefore be subject to criticism by IEA members.

Russia is a major energy producer and consumer. It has a population of 140 million people and a GDP of US$2 trillion. In 2007 it was the second-largest oil producer, at 9.8 millions of barrels a day of crude oil and other liquids. It exports around 7.0 million barrels a day of crude oil and oil products. Russia also holds the world's largest reserves of natural gas; in 2006 it was the world's largest gas producer (23.2 trillion cubic feet) and exporter (6.6 trillion cubic feet). Most Russian gas is produced by Gazprom, a large state-controlled company. Since 2000 the Russian economy has seen strong economic expansion (until the 2008 financial crisis), with GDP growing by about 8 percent in 2007. In the same year, the oil and gas sector generated more than 60 percent of Russia's export revenues. Russia has for several decades been a reliable supplier of oil and natural gas to Europe. However, recent interruptions of gas exports to Ukraine and Europe have called Russia's supply into question.

IEA relations with Russia date back to 1994, when a memorandum of understanding was signed providing for information exchange, roundtables, and visits.

18. Energy Information Administration (2008b).

The IEA published major reviews of the Russian energy sector in 1995 and 2002. The Russian energy minister has also on occasion been invited to attend IEA ministerial meetings, and he attended the meeting in October 2009.

More recently, however, in early 2006 and again in early 2009, the interruption of gas supplies to Ukraine raised questions about the security of the Russian gas supply for Europe. The IEA has expressed concerns about the adequacy of Gazprom's investments in upstream gas and whether these investments will keep pace with the growing demand for gas. The IEA has also called for more transparent and fair third-party access to gas transmission systems and for more competition. With regard to oil, the IEA has noted a lack of stability in Russia's investment regime and the trend toward nationalization in the oil sector at a time when Russian oil production has leveled off. The IEA has called for fiscal, legal, and regulatory reform in Russia and more transparency of information.[19]

Russia had been on a fast track for admission to the OECD but has not submitted the requisite memorandum. In light of the above IEA concerns about the Russian energy sector, plus the political tensions caused by Russia's 2008 invasion of Georgia, it is unlikely that Russia will be a candidate for admission to the IEA in the near future. There is also speculation that Russia, as a large world producer, might prefer to stay separate from the IEA, acting instead as a middleman between OPEC and major world consumers; other speculation is that Russia might prefer to join OPEC.

Confronting Global Climate Change: The Role of the IEA in Energy Efficiency and Technology Policy

At their July 2005 summit in Gleneagles G-8 leaders adopted the Plan of Action on Climate Change, Clean Energy, and Sustainable Development. Energy efficiency is a major focus of the plan. However, a number of other topics are also included. The G-8 asked the IEA to play a major role in delivering the Plan of Action. While the IEA had done previous analysis on climate change and policy responses, this assignment greatly expanded the IEA's efforts. In what has become known as the Gleneagles program, in the following three years the IEA focused on six broad areas:

—Alternative energy scenarios and strategies
—Energy efficiency in buildings, appliances, transport, and industry

19. Tanaka (2008).

212 WILFRID L. KOHL

—Cleaner fossil fuels
—Carbon capture and storage
—Renewable energy
—Enhanced international cooperation.

The principal resulting studies and policy recommendations of the IEA's work over the last three years are summarized below.[20]

Alternative energy scenarios have been explored by the IEA in the *World Energy Outlook* and in two editions of *Energy Technology Perspectives: Scenarios and Strategies to 2050* (2006 and 2008). Some general conclusions are that, without a change in current policies, the world could be on a path to more than doubling energy-related CO_2 emissions by 2050. China and India will be responsible for large increments in future CO_2 emissions, so they and other non-IEA members need to be involved in any future climate regime. To achieve a stabilization at 450 parts per million, consistent with the smallest increase (2.4 degrees Celsius) in the IPCC scenarios, energy-related CO_2 emissions need to peak in 2012 and then fall considerably below today's levels by 2030. This would require an energy technology revolution with substantial costs.

As the IEA observes, "Emissions savings come from improved efficiency in fossil fuel use in industry, buildings and transport, switching to nuclear power and renewables, and the widespread deployment of CCS in power generation and industry. Exceptionally strong and immediate policy action, on an unprecedented scale, would be essential for this to happen. The costs of this transition would be very substantial in the energy sector."[21] The 2008 edition of *Energy Technology Perspectives* includes an initial road map for the deployment of seventeen key energy technologies that will be necessary if this scenario is to be realized. Governments will need to adopt a range of regulatory and market-based policies to promote CO_2 reductions in all sectors. More road map studies are planned.

Energy efficiency is a focal point of the Gleneagles Plan of Action, and the IEA has developed some twenty-five policy recommendations across seven priority areas for presentation at subsequent G-8 summits. The priority areas are cross-sectoral activities, buildings, appliances, lighting, transport, industry, and power utilities. The IEA contends that global implementation of its recommendations could save about 8.2 gigatons of CO_2 a year by 2030, which is the equivalent of one-fifth of the global reference scenario energy-related CO_2 emissions in 2030.

20. International Energy Agency (2008c).
21. International Energy Agency (2008c), p. 9.

Each recommendation is designed to save a large amount of energy at low cost, to address market imperfections or barriers, to fill a gap in existing policy, and to receive a high degree of international consensus.[22]

A weakness in the G-8 process is the implementation of policy recommendations. The IEA in late 2007 and early 2008 conducted a preliminary assessment of progress in implementing its recommendations, and this progress report was presented to the 2008 Hokkaido summit. The progress report shows mixed results. "In the case of several of the IEA recommendations, many countries have established a range of pertinent measures. Yet, in most instances, these measures could be updated or further strengthened, and the scope of their applications broadened. This applies notably to the recommendations on new and existing buildings, and to those on minimum energy performance and standby power requirements for appliances."[23] The IEA also notes that, in several areas, countries have introduced voluntary standards rather than the preferred mandatory standards.

Energy indicators are an important tool for analyzing energy efficiency trends and potentials. The IEA is attempting to assist and internationalize the use of such indicators by developing transparent and consistent international databases and methodologies and by collaborating with other international organizations in four areas of concern: cleaner fossil fuels, carbon capture and storage, renewable energy markets and policies, and international cooperation networks for research and development.

CLEANER FOSSIL FUELS. The IEA is giving priority to enhancing coal power plant efficiency, which could significantly reduce CO_2 emissions. On a global basis, coal-fired plant efficiency averages about 28 percent. IEA studies under the G-8 Gleneagles program suggest that all new coal-fired power plants be state-of-the-art supercritical or ultrasupercritical units with no less than 40 percent efficiency. Consideration should also be given to integrated gasification combined cycle plants as they become commercially available, since they promise higher efficiencies and a more concentrated exit stream of CO_2 susceptible to capture and storage. The IEA also recommends that all coal-fired units below 300 megawatts, using subcritical technology and aged twenty-five years, be gradually replaced by larger units using supercritical or ultrasupercritical technology. Some older plants should be retrofitted with newer technology, or they should replaced if they have

22. International Energy Agency (2008d).
23. International Energy Agency (2008c), p. 16.

efficiencies under 30 percent. If implemented, such a program could reduce CO_2 emissions up to 1.7 gigatonnes a year and result in a reduction in coal consumption. More international cooperation is needed to diffuse advanced coal technologies in developing countries.

CARBON CAPTURE AND STORAGE. This technology will become essential in the power and industrial sectors. To demonstrate the technology and deploy it by 2020, the G-8 must organize at least twenty fully integrated industrial-scale projects by 2010. Government incentives could help bridge the financial gap. After 2015 all new fossil fuel generation should include carbon capture and storage in order to meet 450 parts per million global CO_2 stabilization. To reach this goal, a price on carbon will be needed, along with appropriate legal and regulatory frameworks. Any developer of new fossil fuel power stations should plan to include the possibility of retrofit with carbon capture and storage. Another priority should be to include the technology spelled out in the clean development mechanism. The IEA has published a more detailed study of international approaches to the development and commercialization of the technology, including capture technologies, CO_2 transport and storage, and financial, legal, and regulatory issues.[24]

RENEWABLE ENERGY MARKETS AND POLICIES. To reduce CO_2 emissions to 450 parts per million, the IEA argues that renewables could contribute almost 4 gigatonnes a year to reductions by 2030. Thus far only a few countries have implemented effective support policies for renewables, but there is much potential for improvement. Renewable policy design should include the following five actions: remove non-economic barriers, address social acceptance issues, design a predictable and transparent investment framework, introduce transitional incentives, and consider cost effectiveness and system reliability in relation to overall energy. "The main objective of policies is to bring a portfolio of renewable energy technologies into the mainstream in an evolved market, i.e. to lead the smooth transition from the current system, in which many renewables need subsidies, to a future fully competitive level playing field taking into account carbon prices and other external costs of energy technologies."[25] Governments are urged to implement effective support mechanisms. Other recommendations are made regarding renewable energy heating and cooling and grid integration of renewables.[26]

INTERNATIONAL COOPERATION NETWORKS FOR RESEARCH AND DEVELOPMENT. Since 1975 the IEA has served as a catalyst for energy technology research and

24. International Energy Agency (2008a).
25. International Energy Agency (2008c), p. 42.
26. International Energy Agency (2008b).

development projects involving two or more countries and other international organizations or private sector participants. In 2007 there were forty-one collaborative projects based on as many implementing agreements, with several thousand participants from seventy-two countries. The IEA does not provide financing for these projects: unlike the European Commission, the IEA does not have a budget for research and development. Instead, it identifies areas of common interest, provides legal advice and support, and reports on progress and results of collaborative activities via the IEA website, publications, and other materials. Activities are overseen by the IEA Committee on Energy Research and Technology. Current projects include work on fossil fuels, renewable energies and hydrogen, end use (buildings, electricity, industry, transport), fusion power, and cross-sectional activities. Nuclear fission is not included because the OECD has a separate Nuclear Energy Agency.

Countries involved in these initiatives need not be IEA members. Financing is on a cost-sharing basis, a task-sharing basis, or a combination of the two. While most implementing agreements focus on research and design, some focus on demonstration and deployment. Non-IEA participants tend to focus on renewable energy technologies, whereas IEA members focus more on end-use technologies.[27]

As the share of OECD countries in global energy demand and CO_2 emissions has fallen below 50 percent, the IEA has realized the importance of involving non-IEA members, and especially the large emerging economies, in IEA activities. The recent IEA NEET initiative seeks to expand participation of all major energy consumer nations in IEA energy technology collaboration. The focus here is on the Plus 5 countries (Brazil, China, India, South Africa, and Mexico). Launched in 2006, the NEET initiative organizes workshops for representatives of countries participating in IEA implementing agreements and working parties to discuss developing and deploying clean, efficient energy technologies.

The response to this outreach effort has been very favorable. In 2007 NEET workshops were held in South Africa, China, and Brazil. Following these workshops, the countries involved expressed interest in joining IEA technology implementing agreements. These outreach activities encourage important non-IEA consumer countries to join the IEA technology network, which helps to spread clean technology expertise. The IEA is also taking steps to strengthen its interaction with industry regarding the kind of incentives and market conditions it requires for the development and deployment of lower carbon technologies. A roundtable of chief technology officers from more than thirty major companies

27. International Energy Agency (2007a).

was held at the IEA in January 2008 to discuss the technology outlook and the need for international collaboration.[28]

Conclusions and Policy Recommendations

What follows from this analysis for consumer country cooperation? One conclusion is that organizations involved with consumer country cooperation in energy and climate vary regarding enforcement mechanisms. The IEA has evolved as an intergovernmental organization with distinct authority over its members in the area of emergency oil crisis management and with a high-quality staff engaged in data collection and policy analysis on energy markets. It has contributed substantially to world oil market stability. More recently it has undertaken studies of technology responses to climate change. It also has an energy research and development cooperation mechanism. The organization has gained an international reputation for its technical expertise and nonideological approach. The IEA has the advantage of global industrialized country membership and is reaching out to involve the new consumer countries in its activities.

In contrast, the European Union is by definition a regional organization with some supranational powers in sectors where it has authority and can reach agreement on legislation, through the Council of Ministers and the European Parliament. It so far lacks a mandate for a common energy policy but has been developing common policies toward achieving a liberalized internal energy market. It is establishing an ambitious and commendable common policy on energy and climate change. It has a research and development budget, which it uses on a matching basis to promote investments in clean energy technologies. There is inevitably some overlap with the IEA on oil emergency preparedness and energy research and development, but the IEA has the advantage of a more global membership, including the United States, Canada, Australia, and Japan. The EU could do more to promote security in the area of natural gas, including storage, market interconnections, and a common external gas security policy vis-à-vis Russia, on which it is heavily dependent. The Russia-Ukraine-EU gas crisis and interruptions of gas supply in early 2009 demonstrate how vulnerable the EU is.

The G-8 annual summits fulfill a different function. They are first and foremost useful in bringing high-level attention to energy and climate policies and goals and the need for cooperation. The G-8 is now increasingly involving the Plus

28. International Energy Agency (2008c).

5 economies (Brazil, China, India, Mexico, South Africa) in parallel meetings, which is a positive development. Frequently, the G-8 assigns implementation tasks to the IEA or the World Bank. The latter specializes in development assistance and is nurturing a new program to finance technology responses to climate change. A question that might be asked is whether the World Bank has sufficient expertise to engage in capacity building on energy technology or whether more cooperation is needed with the IEA, which has access to a large amount of this expertise but does not normally engage in large-scale capacity building.

The Conference of the Parties to the UN Framework Convention on Climate Change is the negotiating body on future climate agreements, as guided by the scientific advisory body, the IPCC. The conference currently faces the daunting challenge of achieving a post-Kyoto climate agreement at its scheduled meeting in Copenhagen in December 2009. This will be difficult even if the Obama administration advances a more cooperative U.S. role.

In all, there is no question that the new global energy order must take greater account of the new consumer countries, such as China and India, which are expanding their energy consumption at a rapid rate and are having a great impact on world energy demand. Despite the fact that some forums of cooperation may include the newcomers (such as the emerging format of the G-20), the IEA is set to remain the most important platform to deal with the most pressing issues and risks among consumer nations. The IEA is conscious of this need and has been developing informal relations with China and India over the past decade or more. Both countries have been given the status of special observers at IEA committee meetings. They have also participated in particular activities aimed at involving their countries in emergency preparedness, energy efficiency, energy technology development, clean coal technologies, and energy statistics. The IEA itself has recently reorganized and now has a Directorate for Global Energy Dialogue, with the goal of continuing outreach to China, India, and other nonmember countries. But is this enough to ensure effective future consumer-consumer cooperation?

Nobuo Tanaka, the current IEA executive director, has stated his intention to expand these outreach activities to facilitate China's and India's eventually becoming members of the IEA. Both countries were invited and sent high-level representatives to an IEA ministerial meeting in October 2009. The question of China's and India's membership was discussed at an IEA ministerial meeting in March 2008, but a decision was postponed. Neither country is pressing for early membership, although indications are that China may be ready to discuss the question earlier than India. Currently, both countries seem content to expand their informal cooperation with the IEA. Thus far the United States has been the most active member country to support Chinese and Indian membership, with Japan being the most cautious.[29]

What would it take for both countries to become members? The current requirements for IEA membership are OECD membership; the obligation to hold emergency stocks (government-owned or privately owned) equivalent to ninety days of net imports and to coordinate their use with the IEA; agreement to the IEA shared goals; and data transparency, such as the stock data and other energy data implied in the shared goals. The requirement of OECD membership (traditionally reserved for market democracies) is perhaps a more difficult hurdle for China than for India, given that India is a functioning democracy. Removal of this requirement would require a decision by the OECD Council based on a new political consensus forged by the member governments. The OECD itself involves nonmember countries in many of its activities. In May 2007 it offered "enhanced engagement with a view to possible membership to Brazil, China, India, Indonesia and South Africa."[30]

The ninety-day emergency stock obligation will be difficult for both China and India to achieve in the near term. China has begun construction of storage capacity for a strategic reserve that would reach the necessary volume in the next ten or fifteen years. The first phase may produce a fill level of 88 million barrels by 2010 (equivalent to thirty-two days of net oil imports in 2005, but the number of days will decrease as imports increase). The ninety days' worth of net imports could be reached sooner if the government required its oil industry to hold emergency stocks, a requirement the Chinese government is believed to be considering. India decided in 2004 to construct stockpiling facilities up to 100 million barrels. The first phase will have a combined capacity of 37 million barrels (equivalent to twenty days of net oil imports in 2005; the second phase will be announced later). The Integrated Energy Policy 2006 recommends an ultimate reserve of ninety days of net oil imports. Counting commercial stocks could make it easier to reach the ninety-day requirement, but so far there is no stockholding obligation on the oil industry in India.

The IEA's shared goals could be another stumbling block to Chinese and Indian membership. The goals include commitments to collective international action to respond to energy emergencies, which would require China or India to

---

29. Snow (2009).

30. Organization for Economic Cooperation and Development, "OECD Invites Five Countries to Membership Talks, Offers Enhanced Engagement to Other Big Players," press release, May 16, 2007.

give up some sovereignty over use of their strategic petroleum reserves. The shared goals also include commitments to environmental sustainability, the clean and efficient use of fossil fuels, energy efficiency, undistorted energy prices, and international energy cooperation. Data transparency would also be a problem, since China does not release data on current oil stocks. If there are reasons to accelerate China's and India's membership in the IEA, perhaps to enhance the agency's credibility, it might be useful for the organization to consider an associate member status for such countries. IEA outreach also includes the important Plus 5 countries, making a special associate membership an important step. Such a membership would have to carry with it a commitment to provide data on stocks and to coordinate with the IEA on emergency measures.

Overall, expanding IEA membership would strengthen international energy security by including new consumers in its emergency stock release system. Broader membership would also promote the building of stocks, free markets, and data transparency. It could also assist in IEA efforts to combat climate change by involving new consumers in the adoption of cleaner energy technologies. (The IEA's weighted voting formula, based on 1974 oil consumption, is overdue for revision. If China or India were to join the IEA, and if the voting formula were revised, they would receive large voting shares based on their oil consumption. But since the IEA usually makes decisions by consensus, not by weighted votes, it is hard to assess how critical the voting formula is.)

Energy efficiency is encouraged by twenty-five recommendations in IEA's Gleneagles program developed for and approved by the G-8. Implementation, however, proceeds slowly. A progress report was given privately to the G-8 members in Hokkaido, Japan, in 2008. The idea of scorecards by country is currently under discussion. Such scorecards, if made public on a regular basis, could exert pressure on countries to implement the recommendations. In the area of energy technologies to mitigate climate change, the IEA, in its 2008 publication of *Energy Technology Perspectives,* lays out road maps for seventeen technologies. However, more work needs to be done. The agency needs to continue its efforts to share best practices, and it could do more in assisting technology transfer and capacity building, especially in the Plus 5 countries, perhaps together with the World Bank.

The IEA has demonstrated that it is adapting to the new challenges of a globalized energy world and is cooperating with the new consumers on energy security and responses to climate change. Eventually, after further convergence, this should lead to expanding the membership in the agency so that it continues to be the primary venue for consumer country energy cooperation in an adjusted system of global energy governance in the twenty-first century.

References

Energy Information Administration. 2008a. "Brazil." In *Country Analysis Briefs*. U.S. Department of Energy.

——. 2008b. "South Africa." In *Country Analysis Briefs*. U.S. Department of Energy.

European Commission. 2007. "An Energy Policy for Europe." Communication from the Commission to the European Council and the European Parliament, January 10, 2007. Brussels.

European Commission. 2009. "Towards a Comprehensive Climate Change Agreement in Copenhagen." Communication from the Commission to the European Council and the European Parliament, January 28, 2009. Brussels.

——. 2009. "Investing in the Development of Low Carbon Technologies." Communication from the Commission. October 7.

Intergovernmental Panel on Climate Change. 2007. "Summary for Policymakers." In *Climate Change 2007: The Physical Science Basis*. Contribution of Working Group I to the Fourth Assessment Report of the Intergovernmental Panel on Climate Change. Geneva.

International Energy Agency. 2007a. *Energy Technology at the Cutting Edge*. Paris.

——. 2007b. *Oil Supply Security: Emergency Response of IEA Countries*. Paris.

——. 2008a. *CO₂ Capture and Storage: A Key Carbon Abatement Option*. Paris.

——. 2008b. *Deploying Renewables: Principles for Effective Policies*. Paris.

——. 2008c. *Towards a Sustainable Energy Future: IEA Programme of Work on Climate Change, Clean Energy, and Sustainable Development*. Paris.

——. 2008d. "Energy Efficiency Policy Recommendations." In *Support of the G-8 Plan of Action*. Paris.

——. 2008e. "Highlights of IEA-China Activities." Internal working document, Jonathon Sinton.

——. 2008f. "Highlights of IEA-India Activities." Internal working document, Dagmar Graczyk.

Kohl, Wilfrid. 1983. "International Institutions for Energy Management." Energy Paper 7. London: Policy Studies Institute.

Snow, Nick. 2009. "Clinton: Energy Security a Major US Foreign Policy Element." *Oil and Gas Journal* 107, no. 9.

Tanaka, Nobuo. 2008. "Increasing Mutual Dependence and Global Energy Security: The Importance of the IEA-Russia Energy Dialogue." Paper prepared for International Energy Week, October 22, 2008, Moscow.

Van der Linde, Coby. 2007. "External Energy Policy: Old Fears and New Dilemmas in a Larger Union." In *Fragmented Power: Europe and the Global Economy*, edited by A. Sapir. Brussels: Bruegel.

World Bank. 2008. *Strategic Framework for Development and Climate Change*. Washington.

11

The Evolving Role of LNG in the Gas Market

Dick de Jong, Coby van der Linde, and Tom Smeenk

The global energy scene is changing rapidly. Producing countries are tightening their grip on the development of their resources, emerging (and other) economies are taking a direct political interest in securing supplies, politics and business are increasingly integrated in international energy deals, and energy is on the political agenda of every government. Compounding this, prices of energy skyrocketed over the four years leading up to August 2008. As a result more gas resources became economical to develop, creating more supply potential than before.

However, the severe crisis in international financial markets and national banking systems is now changing this outlook. Prices have come down, and this, combined with the current decline in economic activity, is likely to affect the timing of investment decisions on new pipeline and liquefied natural gas (LNG) projects. The impact on national economies on energy demand, and on the relative position of gas in the energy market could be considerable. At the same time, some consuming countries are also reviewing the environmental effect of their energy policies and the security of their energy supply. Any change in these policies could affect the place of gas in the energy mix. These developments are still unfolding; it is difficult to say at this stage in what ways and to what extent the position of natural gas will change.

Nevertheless, some expect further globalization of the gas business, with different market structures, more fragmented value chains, more flexibility in supplies to markets, and shorter term contracts. In this respect, LNG is regarded as the major potential game changer. Indeed the LNG business model has been changing over recent years into one of greater flexibility, promising producers higher rewards, albeit in return for higher risks. More recently the perspective of high rewards in a market hungry for supplies has changed radically, at least for the next few years. A global crisis, lower oil and gas prices, and reduced demand have created a new business environment. Whether the changing business model will progress into a new way of doing business depends on a number of factors:

—The risk appetite of LNG suppliers to continue to develop their resources on the basis of the new business models in the current situation of lower or volatile energy prices.

—The ability and willingness of the markets, particularly European and to a lesser extent Asian LNG buyers, to accept and manage the supply risks associated with this new business model.

—The preparedness of producing and consuming governments to distance themselves from LNG transactions.

This chapter examines developments in the global gas market, the main markets for natural gas and the position of LNG in these markets (particularly Europe), and higher risks in the LNG business and risk management mechanisms for mitigating short-term supply disruption.

Developments in the Global Gas Market

The following reviews general developments in the global supply and demand balance in natural gas, assessing current trends in still regionalized markets in the United States, Asia, and Europe. The tendency of governments to enhance state control in the gas industry and the potential of the Gas Exporting Countries Forum (GECF) for producer countries to coordinate their policies are also examined.

Global Supply and Demand: From Feast to Famine?

While demand for energy has grown globally, leading to competition for new supplies among gas markets, world gas reserves are sufficient to satisfy gas demand—including the expected increase in demand for LNG—for the foreseeable future. The bigger issue, however, is not the availability of reserves but

the pace of and potential for development. In recent years, the global development effort, both in pipeline gas and LNG, did not in this respect keep pace
with demand prospects.

In recent years rising gas prices have had a considerable effect on the LNG business. First and foremost, hitherto stranded gas resources became economical candidates for new LNG projects, leading to a greater variety of potential LNG
suppliers. In addition, LNG suppliers became bolder in their approach to risk,
entering into more flexible and shorter term business transactions. However, new
developments have been slow to reach their final investment decisions not just for
LNG but also for pipeline gas. These projects have virtually ground to a halt, in
view of lower gas prices and sagging demand. During the forthcoming years LNG
may even glut the global market, as new capacity starts production at a time of
economic slowdown and reduced demand for imports in the U.S. market. This
surplus may create a sense of comfort, but it may be short-lived.

Regional Markets Remaining Regional?

The question is whether by 2015 there will be enough new capacity of pipeline
gas and LNG to meet demand in the three main regional gas markets: the U.S.
market, the Asian market, and the European market.

THE U.S. MARKET

The U.S. market is characterized as deep, liquid, and based on short-term
trade. For a long time the North American market was self-sufficient, but after
the year 2000 domestic supplies started to fall, and U.S. demand was increasingly difficult to satisfy. In 2007 the United States imported roughly 20 percent
of gas supply (figure 11-1). Most came from Canada via pipeline (106.9 billion
cubic meters). The rest was LNG (20.1 billion cubic meters).

The U.S. market does not employ the business model of long-term contracts
between buyers and sellers, the staple of the Asian and European markets. Rather,
it offers a market in which any volume of gas can be sold at the prevailing spot
price. For example, when incremental supplies from Canada were no longer available, U.S. gas prices rose to levels not found anywhere else; as a result, LNG suppliers began to find their way to the U.S. market on the strength of the gas prices
at that time, particularly because existing LNG terminal capacity could be
demothballed to access this increasingly attractive market.

In the past LNG was the only option for new supplies until higher gas prices
and fiscal incentives stimulated unconventional gas development, such as in the
Barnett Shale in Texas, which is already contributing 6 percent to total production

Figure 11-1. *Gas Supply to Three Regional Markets, by Type and Supply, 2007*[a]

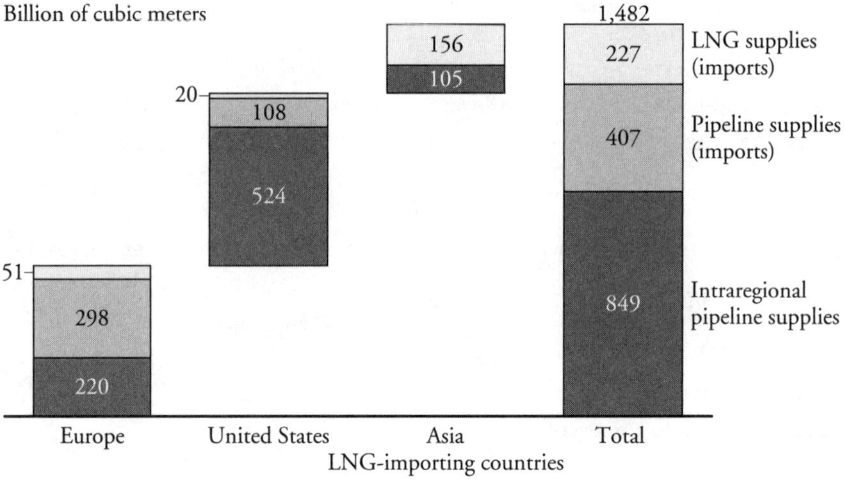

Billion of cubic meters

LNG-importing countries

Source: Authors' analysis, based on International Energy Agency (2008a).
a. Totals may not add up due to rounding.

in the lower forty-eight states.[1] As a result of the ongoing economic downturn and the success of unconventional gas production, however, prices are lower in the U.S. market than in most other markets. Nevertheless, in view of its depth and liquidity, this market remains a major outlet for possible LNG surpluses. Gas prices in this market will be set essentially by competition between LNG and unconventional gas production in the years to come.

ASIAN MARKETS

Gas consumption in the Asian markets was around 420 billion cubic meters in 2007.[2] While a few large producing countries in Southeast Asia (for example, Indonesia and Malaysia) are self-sufficient in gas supplies, others, such as China and India, which were self-sufficient until the turn of the century, now need to import gas. China is looking for reliable supplies available through long-term contracts, so as to establish a robust supply base. India, on the other hand, has thus far relied more on short-term and flexible trade.

1. International Energy Agency (2008b), p. 292.
2. Asia is defined as all Asian countries excluding Turkey, and the Asian countries in the Middle East and in the Commonwealth of Independent States.

In contrast to markets in Europe and the United States, Asian LNG-importing countries are not interconnected with gas pipelines from outside the region (although the potential exists), rendering LNG the only source of their gas imports (see figure 11-1). The share of LNG in the total gas consumption in Asian LNG-importing countries is 60 percent.[3] Given this import dependence, the main Asian markets can be expected to stick with traditional long-term contracts (despite the availability of short-term supplies).

EUROPEAN MARKETS

European energy markets are undergoing major restructuring, enforced by directives aimed at lowering the barriers to entry, enhancing competition, and integrating national markets into a single European gas market.[4]

Europe relies mainly on pipeline gas, importing roughly 85 percent of its needs via pipeline from three main suppliers: Norway (which in 2007 supplied 88 billion cubic meters of gas to the United Kingdom and northwest continental Europe); Algeria (which in 2007 supplied 27 billion cubic meters of pipeline gas to the Iberian peninsula and Italy); and Russia (which in 2007 supplied 156 billion cubic meters of gas to northern, central, and southern Europe).[5] While LNG, mainly from Algeria and Nigeria, has made a contribution to the European gas supply for some time (representing 9 percent of total gas consumption), LNG accounts for only 15 percent of gas imports. However, this share is growing (figure 11-1).

Both pipeline gas and LNG are supplied mainly through long-term contracts, with prices indexed to oil products. Yet European markets are changing, driven by the goal of the European Union to create an internal market and to facilitate spot markets. (The U.K. market, with its self-sufficiency in the 1990s, led the way in this respect.) These spot markets operate alongside the traditional LNG and pipeline gas market; consequently, Europe is faced with a hybrid pricing structure: spot prices for a small proportion of its wholesale market and oil-indexed prices for the rest. While pipeline gas will continue to form the backbone of gas supplies to Europe, there is a greater interest in LNG than before, and European market players have joined the trade in short-term LNG.

---

3. LNG-importing countries are Japan, South Korea, Taiwan, India, and China.

4. Europe and the European gas market include EU member states, Balkan non-EU member states, Norway, Switzerland, and Turkey. They exclude countries of the Commonwealth of Independent States. See also figure 11-3.

5. Clingendael International Energy Programme (2008).

Government Control of the Gas Industry

Recent changes in the geopolitical and geoeconomic balance of power have affected the conditions under which gas (and oil) will be produced and traded in the foreseeable future, both globally but especially in Europe and Asia.

The thinking in the 1990s—that international oil and gas markets would be increasingly free of government involvement and management and that governments would limit their role to market regulator and tax collector—has evaporated in recent years. Instead, governments in producing countries are asserting control and management over their energy resources and economic rents through (majority) ownership. Consumer governments are also increasing their control over their energy sectors again, despite the liberalization and privatization processes of the 1990s. They are regulating markets within the constraints of their public interests (environmental effects and supply security), and they are subsidizing new energy sources and taxing the energy sector, thus limiting the space for competitive forces to work.[6] At the heart of all government intervention in the energy sector is the distribution of risks and benefits throughout the energy resource value chain in the short and long term; these policies are often termed security of supply and security of demand.

The explanation for the more interventionist energy policies can be found in a paradigm shift in international oil and gas markets, from a long period of ample supplies, during which production capacities grew faster than demand, to world oil and gas markets that were, until autumn 2008, much tighter. In these years demand grew much faster than supply, and overcapacity in the oil and gas industries disappeared, reducing flexibility in the value chain. In the gas market the excitement over the increasing availability of LNG—with the unlocking of the substantial but previously stranded reserves of the Middle East—quickly dampened when it became clear that demand would outpace supply and that the much-heralded flexibility to supply markets would remain limited for some time to come.[7] However, in the next few years gas demand will be affected by the economic crisis and the success of unconventional gas production in the United States; supply will be affected by the deferring of investments.

In energy, the long lead times between discovery and production, the capital intensity of certain parts of the value chain, the inflexibility of transportation (particularly in gas and coal), the dedicated investment requirements, and the large

---

6. In the EU, the European Commission is also attempting to break up the value chain by ownership unbundling. Conversely, a large number of EU member states oppose unbundling.

7. Dutch Energy Council (2005), p. 54.

economic rents create market imperfections along the value chain and in the various submarkets. These imperfections create significant risks for market players. Moreover, the impact of these investments on national economies and supply security remains considerable in both producing and consuming countries. Consequently, the role of government is crucial in a market-based system, in a mixed economic system, and in a state-oriented economic system. In all of these systems, governments go beyond their role as regulator, market model designer, or even prime owner of energy assets.

Governments also play a vital role in shaping the investment climate, which is important for the very capital-intense energy industry. Governments are also responsible not only for macroeconomic and monetary stability but also, as owners of the subsurface, for issuing permits to explore, produce, transport, transit, and distribute energy. They also have a role as tax collector, laying claim to both profits and the large economic rents from energy resources. In addition, public interests such as the environment and security of supply are matters best addressed through government policies.

It is therefore unthinkable that government would not be involved in the energy sector or that it would allow the industry to be governed by market behavior or self-regulation. The potential benefits from capturing economic rents, the impact on the balance of trade (and payments), and the social and political stakes are simply too high for any government to leave the industry to self-regulate. At the same time, the value chains in energy are often not limited to a single jurisdiction, which not only complicates the choice of regulatory regime but also may thwart capturing the full benefits from the energy sector. Multiple jurisdictions even make public benefits, such as security of supply and protection of the environment, harder to obtain. It is in this sphere that security of supply, transit, and demand may introduce strategic political interests into the decisionmaking.

GECF: Risk Management by Producing Countries?

The members of the Gas Exporting Countries Forum (GECF) represent a very large part of world gas reserves (more than 70 percent) and are responsible for around 45 percent of total world production and around 90 percent of global LNG trade.[8] The initial assessment that the cartelization of the gas market would be difficult is being challenged by recent developments in the market behavior of the main suppliers.[9] A certain coordination of investments and orientation in specific

8. British Petroleum (2008).
9. Hadouche (2006).

markets can be imagined. Producer governments are reconsidering their export strategies and are beginning to focus on supply management as a means of ensuring value protection for their resources. They also prioritize the use of gas for growth in their domestic economies. Moreover, they control most world reserves of oil and gas through their national oil companies.

Both pipeline gas and LNG are capital intense and expensive businesses. Producing countries may want to protect their investments by not oversizing their industry and coordinating capacity extensions in order to realize better returns on invested capital. The strength of the organization will be proven when the international gas market weakens, prices fall below their competitive value, and the members feel compelled to intervene in the market.

LNG Markets

The emergence of a few significant LNG suppliers, such as Qatar, has contributed to the making of a truly global gas market. The business models in LNG and piped gas are changing, and this changing nature of the business is likely to affect the European gas market, which is characterized by long-term supply and purchase agreements.

LNG Expansion: From the Atlantic Basin to World Markets

The size of the LNG market increased between 1996 and 2006 by almost 8 percent a year (in 2006 global LNG demand was more than 200 billion cubic meters), with Japan, Europe, and South Korea the most significant markets for LNG.[10] Higher gas prices have produced more candidates for LNG production in locations with gas reserves, locations hitherto considered stranded, particularly those in the Middle East. Consequently, more LNG projects have been announced and more LNG has been offered to international gas markets. Therefore LNG is expected to account for an increasing share of the international gas trade.

LNG is an attractive alternative to pipeline gas, as it offers supply diversity and few transit complications. These attributes have created a strong interest in LNG by markets in Europe. Furthermore, LNG markets are developing in not only the United States and South America but also in the fast-growing developing economies of China and India. On the supply side, traditional LNG suppliers—

10. Clingendael International Energy Programme (2008).

Indonesia, Australia, Malaysia, Algeria—have been joined by other countries with major gas resources, such as Qatar (which displaced Indonesia as the biggest LNG exporter in 2006), Nigeria, Egypt, and Equatorial Guinea.

The globalization of LNG trade developed in two distinct stages and did not begin until after 2000. Initially, LNG trade was concentrated in the Atlantic Basin and the Asia-Pacific Basin; the connection between these two regional markets is a recent development. There were instances of other business transactions, at times leading to much-quoted examples of movements of LNG cargoes around the world, but these were essentially one-off deals. In the Atlantic Basin, with the developing appetite of the U.S. market for LNG, arbitrage grew. Only a few years ago, U.S. gas prices rose to levels not found anywhere else. This led initially to the diversion of LNG cargoes destined for European markets; subsequently, new LNG supplies were earmarked for but not committed to the U.S. market. While U.S. gas prices have fallen due to the development of unconventional gas, and more recently also due to the economic downturn, it is likely that much of this gas will now find its way to European markets until such time as U.S. prices make the market attractive for suppliers.

The emergence of Qatar as the most significant LNG supplier has made the gas market global, as mentioned. Qatar's geographic position makes it possible to supply both the European and the Asian markets at similar costs, while the U.S. market is also within competitive reach (figure 11-2). Both European and Asian markets are interested in acquiring LNG from Qatar, while Qatar producers also are interested in preserving the option to supply the U.S. market.

Yet the pace and potential of LNG development has been slowed by limited human and material resources for project construction, by the increasing complexity of LNG projects, and by geopolitical factors. A sellers' market for new LNG developments has been the result. Under various business-as-usual scenarios, the sellers' market is likely to come back. Ironically, the shorter-term outlook for LNG is one of abundance. Many large LNG projects (such as those in Qatar and Nigeria) are coming onstream in 2009–10, with much of them falling into the category of flexible LNG and mostly earmarked for Europe and the United States. However, U.S. demand for gas imports has dropped as a result of the surge in development of unconventional gas. In addition, in both the United States and Europe the recession has started to make an impact on demand. Some of the new flexible LNG has already been diverted to Asian markets, a region also showing less appetite for the product in the light of the economic slowdown. Hence, flexible LNG is likely to become a truly global commodity, looking for markets where it can realize the best netback value.

Figure 11-2. *Atlantic and Asia-Pacific LNG Trading Basins*[a]

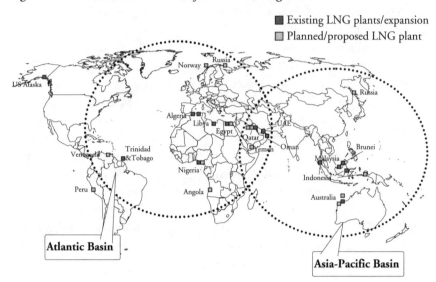

■ Existing LNG plants/expansion
☐ Planned/proposed LNG plant

Source: Based on Wood MacKenzie, unpublished data.
a. Figure does not include all (planned) LNG plants.

New LNG Business Models but Not (Yet) a Global LNG Market

The market is not the only part of the industry that is changing; business models for the gas business (both LNG and pipeline) are also experiencing major changes. The traditional model was based on long-term contracts between producers and buyers in Asia and Europe. A number of LNG producers—notably those aiming for the liberalized markets of the Atlantic Basin—moved away from this model. They were driven mainly by arbitrage opportunities, the opening of the U.S. market for LNG, high gas prices, and a sellers' market.

To realize the value of arbitrage opportunities, LNG producers moved to business models offering more flexibility of supply. However, the financing and in many cases the corporate structures of LNG ventures generally require the security of long-term offtake contracts. The high gas prices of recent years allowed LNG producers to finance investments in new production with far less than the total capacity locked into long-term supply contracts. Also, to create a bridge between the need for security through long-term offtake contracts and the prospects of greater gains from flexible supplies, financially strong producers bought (their own production) LNG under long-term contracts in order to dispose of it as they saw fit, either in the form of LNG to buyers under short- or medium-term contracts or by taking the LNG to a (liberalized) market, regasifying it, and selling it in the markets. The Qatargas/ExxonMobil development of two trains of LNG, 7.8 million tonnes a year each and earmarked for the U.K. market, is an example of self-contracting by producers. It was announced as the world's first fully integrated value chain LNG venture. Another new phenomenon is the third-party aggregator, which acquires a portfolio of LNG, purchased under long-term contracts from different sources and sold at different terms in a variety of markets.

The downside of the new business models are higher risks related to both revenue and volume. The change from a sellers' market to a buyers' market may make short-term and spot gas prices less attractive than those realized under long-term contracts. It may even prove difficult to place LNG in traditional markets. For these reasons, self-contracting producers and aggregators often develop at least one haven of last resort for their LNG, in the form of regasification capacity with access to a liquid market. In many cases this lies in the United States, the most liquid market, with the most capacity to absorb surplus LNG even in an oversupplied global market, albeit at potentially very low gas prices.

The consequences of self-contracting and other forms of flexible LNG are considerable not only for producers but also for markets. To realize the potential of arbitrage, producers need regasification capacity in different markets and need sufficient shipping capacity to reach all markets that can be included in their arbitration portfolio. In addition, without long-term supply contracts for flexible gas, producers need to have the physical capacity to sell gas directly in markets of their choice: shipping capacity capable of reaching any market and access to regasification terminals in different markets. This is likely to lead to chronic surpluses in shipping and regasification capacity.

Until recently it was widely expected that the percentage of flexible LNG in the market as a whole would rise. In the tight market for LNG of the past few years, the downside risks were considered to be relatively small. However, current international economic problems and the resulting low spot prices for gas in the main liberalized markets could increase these risks substantially and could (maybe temporarily) raise the appetite of producers for traditional long-term commitments with market parties. Estimates of flexible LNG trade in the Atlantic Basin have been 40 percent of total trade. That was before the economic downturn. The share of flexible LNG in the Asian market was expected to be considerably lower, as its markets remain focused on long-term supply agreements (with some spot purchases on the side). It is too early to judge whether the higher costs of creating flexibility are justified by higher income for producers over a period of time. The fall in U.S. and European spot prices has certainly changed estimates.

Meanwhile, as long as the lion's share of LNG continues to be sold under long-term contracts, a truly global LNG market will not develop (that is, if such a market is characterized by liquidity and short-term trade).

Effect of New Business Models on Regional Markets

Growing volumes of flexible LNG will come into production over the next few years. This LNG will respond mainly to price signals, although politics and customer relations could also play a role in its final destination.[11]

The U.S. market expects its purchase of LNG to vary, depending on price. LNG is a marginal U.S. source and a price taker in this market. Flexible LNG will enhance available LNG at times of high demand. Due to the development of shale gas in the United States (stepped up before the economic crisis), the import needs of the U.S. gas market have been substantially reduced. U.S. gas prices (Henry Hub) are now the lowest of the three regional markets.[12] Shale gas production could be large, but its cost would also be large. The long-term outlook for the United States is that shale gas and LNG will be in competition with each other.

Asian markets, with only few pipeline import alternatives, rely nearly fully on LNG for their gas supply. Long-term contracts remain the basis of business between buyers and sellers. While this region offered the highest spot prices for LNG in 2008, in the current economic climate the conclusion of new long-term contracts is slowing down, with China the only remaining interested buyer. However, since the Asian market has significant potential for economic growth and corresponding growth in demand for energy, following the recovery of the global economy, this market may well be a significant buyer of Middle Eastern LNG (even though LNG must compete with possible pipeline imports and indigenous production).

European markets have been most affected by the new business models and the global competition for LNG. For quite a few years Europe's markets have been

---

11. Pipeline suppliers to the European market, notably those from Russia, Norway, and Algeria, also appear to add flexible supplies. These are supplies not committed to their markets by means of long-term contracts and are in their supply portfolio for Europe for purposes of direct marketing and sales in the wholesale spot market. For Gazprom, another driver may be the need to maintain more optionality in its supply position, given the potential domestic demand (even though it has recently fallen markedly).

12. See Energy Information Administration (2008). Under the influence of high prices, U.S. gas production in 2008 was up 9 percent, mainly due to unconventional gas and deep offshore gas, which more than compensated for falling production in the shallow part of the Gulf of Mexico. International Energy Agency (2008), p. 292.

unable to secure new supplies of LNG under long-term contracts. First U.S. gas prices worked as a magnet to new LNG production, then the demand of the Asian market attracted the attention of LNG producers in the Middle East and Asia. Moreover, LNG producers required the physical availability of LNG regasification terminals as a precondition for doing business. As a result, interested European LNG buyers have been making speculative investments in regasification capacity without having acquired the necessary LNG supplies. These investments create more financial exposure for this market. The ability of Europe to acquire LNG under long-term contracts, thereby preserving security of supply, has been affected.

Europe and Global Competition for LNG

Its complex supply portfolio of indigenous gas production, pipeline gas, and LNG imports, and an unfinished institutional framework, makes Europe an interesting case for discussion. Its outlook for gas demand and supply is more uncertain than ever. Making forecasts would be a risky business today and could create a false impression of factual insights on future developments. There are in fact very few certainties left for Europe.

First, while it is broadly assumed that there will be growth in European gas demand, the amount of growth is highly uncertain (even a prolonged period of static demand is not entirely unthinkable). Second, although Europe will need to import more gas than it does today,[13] given the recession it is uncertain when that will be, where the gas will be coming from, and at what prices. Last, business models of gas suppliers have been changing, which will affect security of supply. It is therefore prudent to measure future challenges against different perspectives on the attractiveness of LNG for Europe, and vice versa. We particularly focus on challenges that will stem from tight supply conditions, as it is probable that these will return after the current LNG glut.

Outlook for European Supply

European demand for gas relies on substantial imports through pipelines from Norway, Algeria, and Russia (figure 11-3). With increasing import dependency, the need for more diversified gas flows (pipeline and LNG) will also grow. New possibilities are being explored and encouraged to increase existing supplies and to complement them with supplies from Central Asia and the

13. Commission of the European Communities (2007).

Figure 11-3. *Gas Pipelines and Supplies to Europe, 2007*

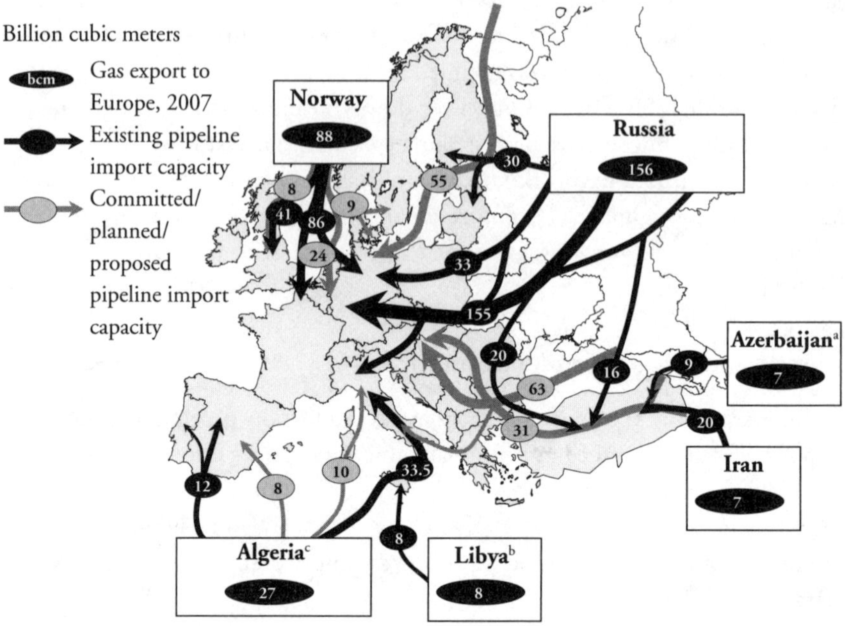

Billion cubic meters

- **bcm** Gas export to Europe, 2007
- ➤ Existing pipeline import capacity
- ➤ Committed/ planned/ proposed pipeline import capacity

Norway **88**

Russia **156**

30

55

8

9

41

86

24

33

155

20

63

16

9

31

Azerbaijan[a] **7**

20

Iran **7**

12

8

10

33.5

8

Algeria[c] **27**

Libya[b] **8**

Source: Clingendael International Energy Programme (2008); authors' adaptations.
Note: Converted to European bcm (billion cubic meters).
 a. Azerbaijan data are from 2006; the contract is not solid. The South Caucasus pipeline could be extended to 16 billion cubic meters a year in 2012.
 b. Libya's greenstream could be increased to 11 billion cubic meters a year.
 c. Algeria's total excluded LNG supply to Europe.

Middle East. When East Siberian reserves are developed, pipeline supplies and LNG both will have a role to play. Europe's greater import dependence will affect the mechanisms of supply risk management in a changing LNG and pipeline market.

Even though Europe is geographically well positioned for new (pipeline) supplies, surrounded as it is by the majority of global gas reserves, not many major supply developments ongoing in producing countries (other than Russia) are earmarked for Europe's markets (figure 11-3). To be sure, logistically and geographically, Russia is the most obvious supplier for Europe's growing gas demand. But realizing more supplies from this country other than those already committed is not a foregone conclusion. Russia and other possible pipeline suppliers to Europe are also looking to diversify their export markets, notably the fast-growing developing economies in Asia. Although the global economic downturn could delay some of these projects, gas pipeline producers want to diversify: Russia has announced pipeline projects that connect the inland basin in East Siberia with South Korea and Northeast China. Turkmenistan is constructing a pipeline system to China and has proposed a pipeline project from its gas fields to Pakistan and India. Iran has proposed plans for exporting gas to this region as well.

In this light, and in view of the commercial and political objective of the markets to diversify its supply sources, European stakeholders have given much attention to LNG and the role that it could play in supplying European markets. As mentioned above, about 15 percent of European gas imports consist of LNG, while 85 percent is imported through pipelines. The share of LNG is, however, growing, and new supplies are expected. The volume of LNG is unevenly distributed, however, as are suppliers. With the expansion of regasification capacity in the northwest European market, the share of LNG may also rise in this region. However, Europe will be in competition with the rest of the world for any additional LNG supplies.

The question of increasingly diversified imported gas flows has not only geo-economic dimensions but also geopolitical ones, because the role of government in the gas sector is significant. International long-term business-to-business contracts, including LNG contracts, require a substantial contribution from government-to-government relations. While many importing countries have privatized the gas sector, exporting countries' governments have increasingly taken a direct interest in their gas export business. The quest of consuming markets to attract diversified gas flows cannot be separated from the framework of the dominating political and economic order of the producing country; it becomes the context in which these gas flows are realized.[14]

The current economic crisis will also affect the development of the European gas market, particularly in the electric power segment of the market. It is likely that certain investment plans will be delayed or scrapped as the demand outlook remains uncertain. At least temporarily, the competitive position of gas in this segment of the market, with its lower capital costs and shorter lead times for new generating capacity compared to other fossil fuels, might be strengthened. In addition, the large rescue operation by national governments of their financial sectors may reduce stimulation of the market for sustainable energy.

---

14. Clingendael International Energy Programme (2004); Van der Linde (2005); Hoogeveen and Perlot (2005).

Yet declining economic activity might also reduce demand for energy in general and also negatively affect demand for gas. Many large investment projects in producing countries that were about to gather pace could be reexamined. These include projects to unlock the vast reserves in Shtokman and Yamal and pipeline projects like Nabucco and South Stream. What is certain is that a period of expansionary growth has come to an end and that earlier predictions about demand levels and prices will be pushed into the future. Whether the current economic downswing is strong enough and long enough to produce a prolonged switch from a sellers' to a buyers' market is unclear, because ownership at the upstream part of the value chain allows for more production management than before. Much will also depend on how growth of gas demand in the fast-growth markets of Asia will be affected by the economic downturn.

Attractiveness of LNG for Europe

The attractiveness of LNG for Europe lies mainly in LNG's potential to add diversity and thus security to supply. Traditional long-term supply contracts with European buyers already offer diversification and security of supply, but flexible LNG could improve security of supply by helping to accommodate seasonal shortages. Thus LNG could make a positive, but for flexible LNG uncertain, contribution to security of supply.

Conversely, there is a risk that the European market will rely on flexible LNG to make up for seasonal and other shortages at the expense of further investments in underground storage. This could lead to a reduction in Europe's short-term supply security. Therefore, since Europe cannot count on flexible LNG to be available to provide gas security, it is recommended that Europe make sure that there are no avoidable barriers to the development of underground storage, which will be a more secure and probably more cost-effective way of creating the necessary flexibility in the market. Further analysis is needed to establish the relationship between the costs and opportunities for LNG to contribute in a secure manner to flexibility and the use of underground storage.

Even though flexible LNG may reduce the effect of a disruption of pipeline gas supply, it is important to realize that LNG can also suffer supply disruptions and is in certain aspects more vulnerable to geopolitical tension than pipeline gas. Provided that regasification and shipping capacity are available, flexible LNG can alleviate the effect of disruptions or higher winter demand in Europe but at a price topping other markets and provided there are no other political obstacles. Given increasing global competition for LNG, there will be no certainty that short-term LNG will be available when needed.

In today's market there is no clear optimal balance between LNG and pipeline gas. Instead, given the current dynamics of the market, Europe should be aiming at being the attractive outlet for both pipeline gas and LNG. Pipeline supplies should continue to form the basis of Europe's gas supply, while LNG offers a prospect of new supplies and supply diversification. Flexible LNG can also make a contribution to short-term supply security but not one that the market can count on.

Attractiveness of Europe for LNG Producers

In a sellers' market producers will be looking closely at Europe's attractiveness as a consumer market, compared to Asia and North America. Continued regulatory uncertainties in the European market may undermine efforts to attract long-term LNG supplies. Furthermore, relatively tight regulation hinders buyers in their negotiations with suppliers, as it reduces the flexibility necessary to develop win-win opportunities.

Price uncertainty is another issue. For buyers in the Continental market, a major long-term LNG contract with other than oil-related price indexes creates significant price exposure in a market dominated by oil-indexed prices. LNG producers have a choice of markets and of prices. Given the current price setting of (mainly pipeline) gas in Europe and price levels for long-term LNG in Asia, it is not certain that Europe will be able to out-compete Asia-Pacific buyers on price in a sellers' market.

The uncertainty of future European demand for gas further compromises Europe's attractiveness. Growth will be determined by many factors, whose eventual effect is hard to establish. These uncertainties are felt not just with regard to Europe but universally, albeit to different extents. For Europe, demand uncertainty is compounded by the strong position of Gazprom as a supplier of gas and by questions regarding future incremental pipeline supplies to Europe. Producers of LNG, looking for security of demand, will not draw much comfort from the European outlook unless they are protected by long-term contracts with strong buyers.

The EU as a whole is politically not a transaction partner for governments of producing countries. Instead, bilateral, country-by-country deals secure long-term LNG supplies (and government-to-government relations underpin business-to-business relations). Furthermore, European market players are traditionally active in scouting for new supplies and in creating the conditions for new supplies. These initiatives should be useful in a sellers' market. However, European markets face similar competition from Asian markets, which have also shown their ability to secure supplies in this manner. Moreover, LNG regasification terminal capacity is currently expanding, confirming the appetite of European markets for LNG. However, if new LNG flows fail to enter European markets, the regasification expansion would imply a cost burden to market players. A slowdown in the construction of new regasification capacity can be expected as an investor's response to new market circumstances.

Europe and the LNG Bubble

A surge of new LNG production will become available in 2009–10. Some commitments for this LNG were made in 2005–06, at the time of high gas prices and high demand, but much of this gas is flexible. It was widely expected at the time that most of this LNG would find its way to the United States. In fact U.S. demand is lower than anticipated, resulting from the success of unconventional production.

After 2006 very few new LNG projects were brought to a final investment decision. The lack of new investment in LNG is a matter of concern. The situation is compounded by reduced demand in all main gas markets. Spot prices have nosedived in the liberalized markets. LNG under contracts to markets will still find its way to buyers in these markets (although these buyers may well use contractual flexibility to minimize their commitment). This situation leaves flexible LNG virtually stranded, looking for markets. Prices for flexible LNG could be very low indeed, in any case below prices for gas under long-term contracts to Europe and Asia. Europe may well seek to benefit from this glut in LNG and the overcapacity of its regasification terminals: where demand permits, European buyers may reduce their contractual minimums and purchase flexible LNG instead.

Scenarios for 2015

Nine LNG scenarios for European markets in 2015 arise from combining three demand scenarios and three supply scenarios for pipeline gas (figure 11-4) and the utilization factor of regasification terminals in Europe (figure 11-5). The scenarios are based on the assumption that the LNG glut will have been absorbed by 2015. With the additional premise that LNG will balance European supply and demand after pipeline gas has found its way to the market, the contribution of LNG to European markets could vary considerably, from around the current supply to levels well above the capacity of LNG regasification terminals. The scenarios also suggest that LNG demand of around 100 billion cubic meters could probably be accommodated under manageable pricing and supply conditions and would offer European markets a reasonable balance between pipeline gas and

Figure 11-4. *Call on LNG Imports, Nine Scenarios of European Pipeline Gas Demand and Supply, 2015*

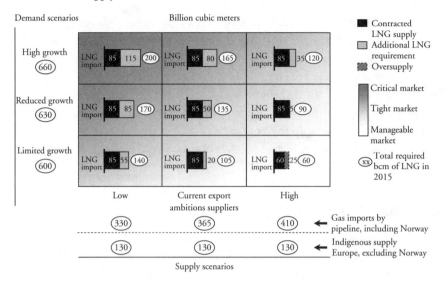

Source: Clingendael International Energy Programme (2008); updated in February 2009 by the authors.

Figure 11-5. *Utilization Factor of Regasification Terminals in Europe, Nine Scenarios of European Pipeline Gas Demand and Supply, 2015*[a]

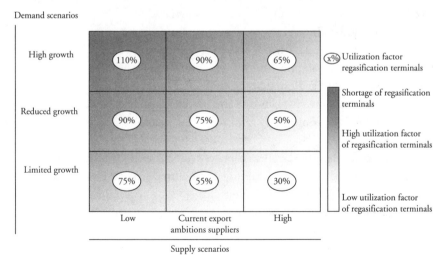

Source: Clingendael International Energy Programme (2008); updated in February 2009 by the authors.
a. Regasification capacity in 2015 assumed to be 185 billion cubic meters.

LNG. However, European demand for LNG, combined with strong demand for LNG from other regions, could total well above global LNG production capacity. In the latter situation, high demand for LNG in Europe could lead not only to higher spot prices for LNG but also to higher than current prices for both pipeline gas and LNG under long-term contracts in Europe.

Current contracted LNG supplies to Europe are in the order of 85 billion cubic meters a year. It should be noted, however, that some of these supplies are flexible LNG, notably self-contracted supplies from Qatar to the United Kingdom; or they contain elements of flexibility, which means they can still be diverted to other markets.

Spreading the Risks in LNG Investments

The risk future in LNG looks very different from the past and involves security of supply and security of demand. In this light it is not surprising that governments of many producing and consuming countries are taking more interest in and control over gas supplies.

Producers and Producing Countries

Producing governments may be facing a dilemma. While many of them are inclined to seal commercial supply transactions with a government-to-government understanding, this can only be achieved through traditional long-term contracts from a producing country to a particular market. Flexible LNG does not fit that model. In a global environment with major price differentials between regions, as has been the case in recent years, producer governments may not want to miss opportunities to acquire the highest possible rent for their resource. But to achieve that, producing governments have to accept that flexible LNG may switch from one market to another in order to realize a higher value for the commodity and, therefore, cannot be committed to one customer.

The choice for these governments lies between repeated short-term value optimization through destination flexibility and political destination management. Value optimization through arbitration thus comes at a cost for producers (and producing governments) of less or no government-to-government support for the major investments associated with LNG projects. It also comes at higher costs, particularly the need to own regasification and shipping capacity in the various markets, more than would be necessary in a single long-term transaction with one buyer.

A lower risk variation on the theme of self-contracting is for a producer to sell to one buyer under a long-term agreement, which allows for occasional selling of cargoes to third parties offering higher value. This generally requires the consent of both parties to the long-term contract and is constructed to create win-win conditions for both.

A further consequence of flexible LNG (and pipeline gas), notably the type based on self-contracting by producers, is that owning the capacity to land LNG on the beach of a market may not be enough for a producer to realize the full value of the commodity, particularly at times of a buyers' market or in a market with limited liquidity. In such a market the producer also needs to understand the market to be able to secure the full rent for his gas. Therefore, increasingly LNG (and pipeline gas) producers are taking positions in markets to allow them to dispose of their gas at a satisfactory value.

Consumer Markets

The three major consumer markets for gas are Asian markets, the U.S. market, and European markets. The LNG industry is here explored from their perspectives.

ASIAN MARKETS

Given their strong dependence on LNG supplies for their energy economies, the main Asian markets are likely to continue to look for firm long-term LNG supply commitments from their suppliers, although they were greatly helped by the existence of flexible LNG at times of shortages, such as when nuclear power stations were out of operation in Japan. In the sellers' market up to the autumn of 2008 producers have been able to dictate their terms, and some flexibility may have crept into some contracts. However, as long as Asian buyers can manage to acquire LNG on traditional terms, supply risks for their markets will not change significantly, and the risk profiles of the business will not materially change.

THE U.S. MARKET

The supply risks for the U.S. market will be positively affected by the new LNG business models. There are hardly any long-term supply contracts with U.S. buyers. Given the structure of this market, it is helped by the availability of flexible LNG, which will find a way to the United States when its prices make this attractive. Virtually all regasification capacity in the United States is owned by (potential) LNG suppliers. As long there is sufficient LNG landing capacity, and as long as most of this regasification terminal capacity is in the hands of suppliers, the higher supply costs (of potentially underutilized regasification capacity) will be to suppliers and not to consumers.

EUROPEAN MARKETS

In recent years Europe has experienced difficulties acquiring LNG under long-term contracts. The attractiveness of LNG for European markets lies mainly in its potential to add diversity of supply. Long-term contracts contribute to long-term security of gas supply. Flexible LNG could improve short-term security of supply if it is available to accommodate seasonal shortages. But for flexible LNG, European markets may be in competition with other markets. Their structures and price levels may not allow them to outbid other markets for the marginal LNG at times of high global demand. Thus LNG could make a positive (but for flexible LNG, uncertain) contribution to security of supply, both for the long and short term.

Also in Europe it is not only LNG suppliers that have invested in regasification terminal capacity but also buyers and potential buyers (wholesale gas companies and distributors). Some of these investments have been speculative: LNG supplies were not secured at the time of the commitment. Also it is generally expected that in Europe in the medium to longer term the LNG regasification capacity will be underutilized. This has raised the cost of doing business for these gas market players, while the contribution to their security of supply remains uncertain. This uncertainty confirms the need to ensure that pipeline supplies remain secured for European markets and the need to evaluate other options to enhance supply security for Europe.

Gas Supply Risk Management for Europe

The EU member states have always been comfortable with the arrangements in the International Energy Agency (IEA) for oil security and crisis management, due to the limited political and strategic role of the EU in securing oil flows but also due to the intergovernmental character of this cooperation. The coalition on oil crisis management has been a great benefit to EU countries. Although the benefits of the IEA go undisputed, the U.S. policy in Iraq guaranteeing oil flows in the future did create unease among European countries and led them to shore up their national or regional efforts. The call for one voice in external European energy affairs exemplifies this position.

The IEA does not have competency in the field of gas, nor is there a crisis mechanism at this level. The EU security mechanism (2004 directive, possibly replaced when a recent regulation proposal is adopted) is just a first step for this group of countries. The gas sector is vulnerable to disruptions. In addition, gas security of supply is mainly an EU member-state issue, perhaps explaining the bilateral nature of many of the new long-term supply contracts involving both governments and companies.[15] For most EU member states, diversification of gas supplies is an important instrument, as it enhances both security and, in many cases, competitiveness. For a small group of European countries, LNG makes a valuable contribution in this respect.

The answer to enhancing security of supply in these markets may not always lie in diversification of supply, accommodating other gas supplies in markets where they would otherwise be uncompetitive (as is done in Spain, where competitive LNG supplies offer alternatives to Algerian gas supplies). Instead, the lack of diversified gas supplies may be more economically dealt with by diversifying the energy mix and enhancing regional cooperation on energy with neighboring states, allowing these countries to tap into their neighbors' fuel mix distribution or tying their gas markets to the interests of other parts of the European gas market.

Based on the successful strategy of economic integration, European companies could integrate their activities along the value chain with upstream companies, and vice versa. The idea behind this strategy is that—with intertwined economic or energy interests, or interdependency—both producers and consumers have a vested interest in maintaining good economic relations. At the same time, such ventures work toward securing additional supply and demand between producers and consumers.

In the case of Russia and Europe, such interdependency is an important disciplining force. For smaller countries or for markets dependent on Russian supplies, becoming part of the larger Europe-Russia relationship can provide them with the security that a bilateral relationship cannot. When alternative gas flows are not a commercial option to reduce gas dependency on the one dominant supplier, mixing economic interests within the infrastructure and in markets with other upstream and downstream players could reduce exposure to risk or abuse of market power. The competition policy of European markets, and particularly their measures against the abuse of market power, can discipline the market behavior of the players in that part of the internal market, while a crisis mechanism could increase those countries' safety.

The recent expansion of the LNG sector in European markets and the prospect of more LNG penetrating the market could offer the prospect of diversifying gas flows, but this impact should not be overstated. LNG flows have their own

15. Van der Linde (2005, 2008).

rigidities, and competition for LNG, particularly in a tight supply market, could reduce the impact on Europe's pipeline flows. Moreover, Russia and other traditional suppliers are preparing new strategies to defend their market share.

Conclusion

Higher prices and the new sources of LNG supply, particularly from the Middle East, have created a global environment for the LNG industry. New models, particularly flexible LNG, are contributing further to the globalization of the LNG business. Whether this trend will continue depends largely on whether this new way of conducting business continues. It will be tested during the coming years, in the face of lower margins, lower spot prices (than under long-term contracts), uncertain demand, and stricter financing requirements. (Conversely, the LNG glut may also put pressure on the conditions of existing and new long-term contracts, notably gas prices.)

From the geopolitical perspective, the outlook also depends on the role of producing governments: whether they exercise control over the development of their resources and their destination and whether they are able to carry the risks associated with this model. Risks of doing business have risen for those producers that self-contract their supplies. One of the consequences is that they will be taking positions in the markets to control the full value chain and to acquire the fullest rent for their commodity.

Based on the netback pricing mechanisms in Europe's long-term pipeline supplies, European gas prices have been lower than those of Asia, which relies nearly completely on LNG. While this benefits the European consumer, it does not help the European position as a potential outlet for LNG under long-term contracts in a competitive global market. Over the short term there will be oversupply and uncertainty. Thereafter, the sellers' market of the last five years may well return. In such a market there will be global competition for gas among the three world market regions. This implies the need to refocus European policies from the internal market to the external market. The current internal market design is of value in a buyers' market with an abundance of supply. In a sellers' market a successful energy policy depends on obtaining competitive supplies from outside Europe.[16]

Price competition in the gas market takes place for the most part in the international market. Designers of the European gas market should take this into account, because while focusing on redesigning internal market dynamics, they

---

16. The EU has commissioned a feasibility study on the acquisition of gas from the Caspian region.

may inadvertently drive up prices for consumers. Flexible LNG could play a role in alleviating shortages in Europe and lowering peak spot prices, but its availability is uncertain. While the U.S. gas market is the market of last resort at times of surpluses of LNG, in a tight LNG market the U.S. and Asian markets may well outcompete Europe for available LNG. Acquiring LNG under long-term contracts should continue to be an important objective of European markets. A structured dialogue on gas between producing countries and European markets could make a significant contribution to lowering barriers to entry.

Given its geographical position, Europe is essentially a market for pipeline gas. In the future, new possibilities should be explored and encouraged so as to complement this supply with pipeline gas from Central Asia and LNG from the Middle East. The importance of pipeline gas also has consequences for Europe's external energy policy. Recent difficulties with Russia and the differences of opinion among EU member states on how to manage this relationship affect all links in the gas value chain. Investments along the gas value chain can be delayed if the current uncertainties are not resolved, including those about transit risks. Although LNG certainly cannot cover the possible large volumes of imports Europe needs in the next decades, a stable relationship with gas-exporting countries, in which the needs for security of supply and demand are met, can contribute greatly to Europe's competitive position.

References

British Petroleum. 2008. *Statistical Review of World Energy.* London.
Clingendael International Energy Programme. 2004. *Study on Energy Supply and Geopolitics.* Final Report, TREN/C1-06-2002. The Hague: Clingendael Institute.
———. 2008. *The Gas Supply Outlook for Europe. The Roles of Pipeline Gas and LNG.* The Hague: Clingendael Institute.
Commission of the European Communities. 2007. *EU Energy Policy Data, SEC.* Brussels.
Dutch Energy Council. 2005. *Gas for Tomorrow.* The Hague.
Energy Information Administration. 2008. "Is U.S. Gas Production Increasing?" U.S. Department of Energy.
Hadouche, Hadi. 2006. "The Gas Exporting Countries Forum: Is It Really a Gas OPEC in the Making?" NG 13. Oxford Institute for Energy Studies.
Hoogeveen, F., and W. Perlot. 2005. *Tomorrow's Mores: The International System, Geopolitical Changes, and Energy.* The Hague: Clingendael Institute.
International Energy Agency. 2008a. *Natural Gas Information 2008.* Paris
———. 2008b. *World Energy Outlook.* Paris.
Van der Linde, Coby. 2005. "Energy in a Changing World." The Hague: Clingendael Institute.
———. 2008. "Turning a Weakness into a Strength: A Smart External Energy Policy for Europe." The Hague: Clingendael Institute.

12

The International Energy Forum and the Mitigation of Oil Market Risks

Enno Harks

O il and gas markets are once again at the forefront of international attention and home politics. The years of oil prices racing to hitherto unknown levels—close to US$150 a barrel, which would have been called a crisis in former times—signaled to some the end of cheap oil and to others the end of oil itself. Since then the implosion of oil prices in the wake of financial turmoil has brought consumers some relief but has also raised some fundamental questions: What exactly happened to the oil market? More important, where were the tools to remedy signs of irrational volatility? What policies—if any—would have been feasible? And how can the sector (and its captive customers) avoid repetition of its boom-and-bust history?

Notwithstanding alarmist reviews in the press, most symptoms are quite normal in market-based environments, especially in resource commodities: some degree of price volatility, concern over sustainability of production levels, cobweb investment cycles, and so on. However, oil is at the center of the world's energy supply (ranking first, being some 35 percent of the world's primary energy supply); it is the

The author would like to thank the many energy experts and unnamed referees from the IEA, the IEF, Chatham House, CSIS, and business who commented on drafts of this chapter. He especially thanks William Ramsay, former deputy director of the IEA (now at ifri.org), Simon Stoddart of the IEF, and Mark Finley of BP.

source for the world's transportation sector and thus a strategic commodity. Actual and perceived supply disruptions present a political and macroeconomic threat: the sheer relevance of oil in current economies means that price volatility cannot be easily disregarded in policymaking. Further, the global oil market exhibits some rather odd characteristics even beyond the fact that the price is usually being targeted by cartel policy. Some of these aspects are inbuilt challenges to the world economy and are thus relevant for producers and consumers alike. Moreover, some of the recent developments can be addressed effectively only by a coordinated global community of policymakers, be it institutional or informal.

The Need for a Global Energy Policy

Global energy policy has stayed surprisingly uninstitutionalized. Even though national or regional policies can mostly be dismissed as ineffective facing global oil markets, a coordinated international energy policy or a global institution or organization for energy has failed to materialize. Oil (and to some extent natural gas) had a history of nondialogue and perceived antagonistic interests for much of the last century, causing them to be a vacuum in international organizations.

The World Trade Organization (WTO) and its predecessor, the General Agreement on Tariffs and Trade (GATT), have tacitly circumvented the mention of oil and gas, based on a gentlemen's agreement among the founding fathers of GATT.[1] Consequently, WTO rules (with minor exceptions concerning recent claims on particular forms of product trades) do not apply to oil or gas and their trade. The International Energy Agency (IEA) has become a highly respected international energy body over the last decades, but its global reach is hampered by two facts: first, it represents the consumer side of the global energy balance only and excludes the world's largest producers of oil and gas.[2] And second, membership is restricted to OECD countries, excluding the rapidly emerging (Asian) consumers.[3] The European Union, as an international organization with an extraordinarily high degree of policy authority, has enacted far-reaching energy policy regulation; however, its reach is regional by definition. Last but not least, the UN is a truly global institution, but in fact competence for energy policy has never been transferred to it, and therefore it does not act.

---

1. Schorkopf (2007).
2. The IEA exceptions are Norway and Canada, which are net exporters.
3. BP (2008).

New Players

In recent years the world oil market has been characterized by the arrival of massive new oil and gas consumers, mostly Asian. Institutions like the IEA have not been able to accommodate the newcomers, as these institutions are rooted in the past and are not equipped to adapt to a new dynamic. Consequently, the IEA as a consumers' body is facing a declining weight in the market; its member countries represented 75 percent of global oil demand in 1970; it was a mere 57 percent in 2008. China's share rose from 1 percent to almost 10 percent over the same period. The IEA itself predicts that its members' share will fall below 50 percent before 2015.[4] IEA demand-side policy obviously will suffer, as will the IEA's core emergency response mechanism of stock releases.

This development was paralleled by a reemergence of national oil companies (NOCs). Mostly based in non-IEA countries, NOCs' size, production capacity, capability, and especially their reserves have been noted by market analysts with some surprise. The notion of a new set of Seven Sisters was easily framed.[5]

Western institutions have not kept pace with either development. If they are to keep their weight and influence in the markets they will have to devise new frameworks that will accommodate these emerging players.

Low Level of Information

The oil market is a truly global market, highly integrated across industry players, spot markets, nations, and continents. Hundreds of thousands of movements of oil are carried out every day, with millions of corresponding trades on the upstream and the downstream sides of the market.

However, there is a remarkably low level of information about the market in the real world. While the market for crude oil, its refineries, and associated products involves all 200 countries in the world, only 30 of them—the members of the IEA—provide timely data on the state of their oil markets.[6] All other information is based on estimations, which in most cases are educated guesses by bankers, industry traders, or journalists. While references to oil markets and the ubiquitous Brent and West Texas Intermediate marker prices are omnipresent on

---

4. International Energy Agency, *World Energy Outlook* (2008), p. 93.

5. Carola Hoyos, "The New Seven Sisters: Oil and Gas Giants Dwarf Western Rivals," *Financial Times*, March 11, 2007.

6. The IEA has twenty-eight member countries; however, all thirty OECD countries agree to data submissions.

newswires, the information cited is often based on such guesswork—an example of why visibility should not be mistaken for transparency.

IEA members have signed a legally binding international agreement making data submission compulsory. Consequently, high-quality and timely information is available on the state of their oil markets (production, consumption, imports, exports, and stocks). Information about the rest of the market is, in contrast, difficult to pin down. It is difficult if not impossible to get hold of even the most basic data, including information about oil production and exports from Saudi Arabia, demand and stocks from China, and stock levels in India. An inquiry in these countries usually confronts one of two problems: either the information is classified (is considered of military or strategic national interest) or it is unavailable even to the central ministry itself.

Furthermore, information gathering is a painstaking and expensive occupation and unveils the unfortunate characteristics of a public good, namely that individual data collection only marginally improves transparency in the global market; and if everybody else collects data, the free-rider position of the non-collector is optimal. As a consequence, traders deal with the information they have, accurate or not, and quickly revise positions when new or other information becomes available. The prime consequence of this is price volatility, which by itself fosters a public perception that some kind of speculation must be at work.

Price Volatility

Unfortunately, recent years have been characterized not only by historically high oil prices but also by increases in price volatility. Annual price variations moved from a band (price spread) of around US$5 a barrel throughout the 1990s to some US$100 a barrel in 2008, and the standard deviation of daily prices versus preceding months increased tremendously (figure 12-1). Intraday price spreads also exceeded all expectations, with variations easily exceeding US$10 a barrel within just a few trading hours. While the mainstream media were happy to marvel at the resilience of the booming world economy to high oil prices during 2008, perhaps the real story lay in the long-term impact of extreme volatility and the mechanisms that allowed the phenomenon to flourish for so long.

Several factors were responsible for the structural volatility increase in recent years: the shrinking level of market information, the erosion of spare production capacity, tensions in the Middle East with the invasion of Iraq and the nuclear concerns over Iran, and last but not least, the massive influx of financial investors on the oil spot and paper markets.

Figure 12-1. *Oil Price Volatility and Absolute Price Spreads, 1992–2008*[a]

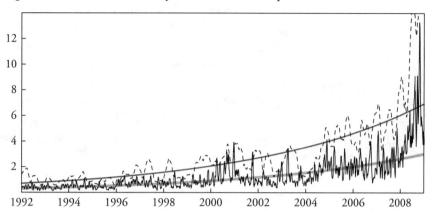

US$ barrel[b]

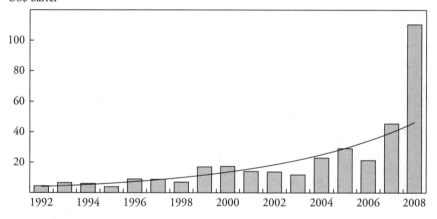

Source: www.plats.com; BP.
a. Oil price volatility measured as the standard deviation of daily Brent prices to moving average of trailing 1 and 6 months periods.
b. Maximum annual price difference, Brent's daily closings.

These last do not participate in the physical oil industry (thus the term *non-commercials*) but have discovered the oil market as an investment vehicle.[7] Their arrival was further propelled by the fact that commodity exchanges around the

7. While in the past the oil market was regarded as a hedge against stock markets (which used to move in the opposite direction), the new millennium has shown concurrent upward trends in both equity and oil price, with the oil market offering great returns with an ever-increasing price.

world decided to move to electronic trading systems and to grant access to trading over the Internet. This was first and prominently done by the London ICE, which abandoned floor trading in April 2005. The ICE was followed by NYMEX, which reduced its floor trading hours.[8] Trading in oil futures was thus facilitated, with the result that the paper market for oil soared to several hundred billion U.S. dollars.[9] Much obvious blame-gaming ensued, as both OPEC producers and consumer governments attempted to quantify and justify the influence exerted by these new players (often dismissed as speculators).[10] However, whether much of the price or volatility increase can really be blamed on these financial investors has never been finally proven.

Fundamentally, price volatility is of concern, as it inflicts macroeconomic costs on both consumers and producers. This is due to the fact that volatility alters the system of relative prices to which market participants have to adjust, causing macroeconomic transition costs. For consumer nations it means costly changes in their consumption patterns, as different factor costs may change the optimal investment portfolio (for industrial users), or new, energy-efficient capital goods need to be bought (by individuals). For producer nations it means that oil-dependent state budgets have unpredictable revenues and are bound to bounce between surpluses and deficits, causing the damaging effect of procyclical fiscal policy. Another key consideration is the uncertainty that volatility brings into investment planning, thus delaying upstream projects—a fact that itself may increase volatility. From a purely macroeconomic point of view, volatility is thus worse than a high (but stable) oil price, which would ultimately be absorbed by the system.[11]

Spare Capacity and Supply Security

Spare capacity is a rather peculiar concept: production capacity is built (platforms are constructed and bore holes drilled) only to be left idle.[12] Neither in economic

8. Evidence is emerging that this in itself has increased oil price volatility. Liao, Lee, and Suen (2008).

9. Index funds investments in commodities are estimated to have risen from US$13 billion to US$260 billion between 2003 and 2008. "Double, Double, Oil and Trouble," *The Economist*, May 28, 2008.

10. See for example the OPEC bulletin of March 2008 (www.opec.org/library/OPEC%20 Bulletin/2008/pdf/OB03_042008.pdf); and the U.S. Senate investigation into this matter (http://levin.senate.gov/newsroom/supporting/2006/PSI.gasandoilspec.062606.pdf).

11. For macroeconomic studies on oil price changes, see Ferderer (1996).

12. Spare production capacity is usually defined as capacity that can be brought onstream within thirty days and remain sustainable for at least ninety days. International Energy Agency, *Oil Market Report, Annual Supplement* (2008).

Figure 12-2. *Spare Capacity in Oil Production, 1971–2008*

Percent of world population

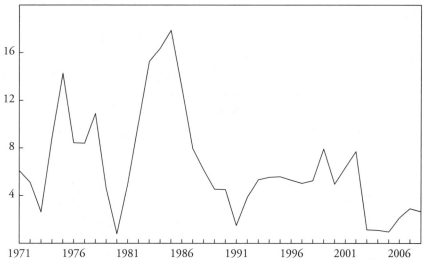

Source: International Energy Agency, *Oil Market Report* (2002–08); Stevens (2008); author's estimates.

theory nor in the real world does such capacity exist in most commodity markets, since it contradicts a shareholder value approach. The oil market is the one exception: OPEC countries do hold such spare capacity as a result of historic investment decisions compounded with cartel production quota and oil price targets (figure 12-2).

Spare production capacity in the oil market has proven to be the most important single asset for the world's supply security. Every time a supply disruption has occurred, the shortfall was covered by ramping up production from spare fields. Examples include the following supply disruptions: in Venezuela during the strikes in December 2002 to January 2003 (the third-biggest oil producer basically stopped producing); during the invasion of Iraq in March 2003 (the fourth-biggest oil producer was disrupted for several months); and during the Iraqi invasion of Kuwait in 1990. The response to each of these disruptions was to call on spare capacity. Consequently, the main tool for consumers' oil supply security is in the hands of and paid for by producer countries, quite a peculiar political situation.

At the same time, traders know the relevance of spare capacity: its magnitude is widely reported and its ability to respond to physical supply disruption widely accepted. Market psychology factors a so-called risk premium into the oil price, a premium dependent on traders' perception of the volume and availability of spare capacity. The extreme lows of spare capacity between 2003 and 2008 made a substantive risk premium probable and go some way toward explaining increased volatility.

Unfortunately for security of supply, spare capacity has been disappearing in recent years. The reasons for this include the Asian demand boom, the supply disruptions of the Venezuelan strike in December 2002, and the invasion of Iraq in March 2003, compounded by producer country reluctance to invest in the face of repeated political calls for a move to alternative fuels. The world has become aware of the dilemma of calling for spare capacity and for fossil (oil) demand reductions at the same time.

The beginning of a global recession in fall 2008 changed the above equation. The market is now faced with the prospect of spare capacity of around 7 million to 8 million barrels a day.[13] On the face of it, the world is where it wants to be, but it arrived here by default, not design. The risk is that if comfort turns into complacency and the issue of spare capacity is not an ongoing topic of discussion between producers and consumers, the next cyclical upturn will erase the cushion once again.

Oil Production and the Western Plateau

The so-called end of oil has been part of the public debate since petroleum was first produced in the nineteenth century. This debate was prominently reignited in recent years, with a focus on the imminence of peak oil.[14] However, most market observers do not believe in the mirage of geological peak oil but are concerned more about the above-ground factors of oil production. Oil production growth is mainly dependent on upstream investment, the attraction of capital, access to acreage, optimal extraction paths in oil-rich nations, and political stability.

While the fact that physical oil will not easily run out may be taken as comforting, a close look at market realities makes clear that most remaining conventional oil reserves are concentrated in a few countries in OPEC and the former Soviet Union. To look at it another way: oil supply outside the countries of OPEC and the countries of the former Soviet Union is reaching its plateau, even when one

13. This level was predicted by Daniel Yergin, chairman of CERA, in a 2008 report. It is quoted here from Energy Intelligence Group, "What's New around the World?" *Petroleum Intelligence Weekly*, January 5, 2009.

14. Peak oil is considered to be a point after which oil production will decline. For more information and background on this theory, see its most important propagator, the Association of Peak Oil (www.peakoil.net/publications/peer-reviewed-articles).

Table 12-1. *World Oil Production to 2030*
Millions of barrels a day

World Energy Outlook 2008	2007	2030
Former Soviet Union and OPEC	48.8	69.5
Rest of world[a]	35.5	36.9
Total	84.3	106.4
World Energy Outlook 2002	*2000*	*2030*
Former Soviet Union and OPEC	36.8	79.8
Rest of world	37.1	30.3
Nonconventional	1.1	9.9
Total	75.0	120.0

Source: International Energy Agency, *World Energy Outlook* (2002, p. 96; 2008, p. 103).
a. Rest-of-world production now includes both nonconventional fuels and biofuels.

includes optimistic scenarios for biofuels and nonconventional supplies. The IEA has been projecting this plateau for a number of years (table 12-1), however, without drawing too much attention to it.

With oil production plateauing in consumer regions—and unlike in the 1970s, with no new North Sea to be found—to avoid a supply crunch producers and consumers must enter into constructive discussions either about access to resources or (if more appropriate) about IOC and NOC investment plans.

Beyond the Cobweb

Economic theory suggests that commodities for which production capacity follows investment decisions with a (considerable) time lag have a tendency to show boom-bust investment cycles. This reflects the fact that investment decisions are based on the supply, demand, and price experiences of the past. Textbooks call this phenomenon the cobweb, of which resource commodities (copper, wheat, nickel, and so on) are excellent examples, as they have considerable time lags in production and huge swings in prices.

Oil markets share many of these characteristics: the time lag for an upstream project usually takes eight to ten years from planning to commercial oil, and thus investors must make hard calls on their price expectations one decade down the road.[15] This time lag makes oil prices all the more volatile, as even small extensions of capacity are nearly impossible in the short term (a price elasticity of

15. Costs are enormous; in 2008 they mostly ranged from US$20 billion to US$30 billion for production capacity of half a million barrels a day. International Energy Agency, *World Energy Outlook* (2008), p. 312.

production close to zero): hence, again, the paramount relevance of timely and sufficient upstream investment in oil markets.[16]

Recent history is exemplified by misplaced projections and expectations. A good example of this is the fact that no investment planning predicted the oil demand boom of emerging Asia during 2003–08, which fueled a historic seven-fold price increase through inelastic supply.[17] And no one, obviously, saw the crash coming. The financial crisis and global recession in the second half of 2008 put investments in a difficult position, so that it is no surprise that projected capital expenditures on upstream projects are being curtailed or that capital expenditure plans for 2009 were slashed industrywide. While this may seem appropriate and unavoidable in current times, this behavior bears a risk for future supply and demand balances, as low investment now may mean another round of price spikes a few years down the road.[18] Transparency among producer and consumer nations about investment planning of market participants is therefore crucial.

A Global Response: The International Energy Forum

Many of the problems intrinsic to the oil market stem from the fact that it is a global market, and thus policymaking needs a global response. No institutions or organizations can make this global response because those that exist have no real clout or are burdened by preconceptions of allegiance and thus lack the nec-essary trust.

However, the emergence of the International Energy Forum (IEF) can rightly be called a successful change of course. This forum was first convened in the wake of the 1991 Gulf War, when the need for international cooperation on the global oil market once again came into sharp focus. A conference to include the world's top producers and consumers of oil and gas was called at the ministerial level and has been meeting biennially ever since. Today, conferences are preceded by a busi-ness forum for senior executives of leading companies in the oil and gas sector and related industries.[19] Discussions are still informal, and the agenda does not follow a formal procedure.

16. See the excellent analysis by Stevens (2008).

17. Low investment is also a consequence of a decade of extremely low oil prices, down peaking as recently as 1998 to below US$10 a barrel Brent.

18. For warnings about such a supply crunch, see International Energy Agency, *World Energy Outlook* (2008), p. 303.

19. In the May 2008 meeting in Rome, some fifty ministers, thirteen international organizations, and more than thirty top industry executives joined discussions.

In 2003, following an initiative by Crown Prince Abdullah of Saudi Arabia (motivated by the painful experiences of the 1998 oil price collapse), the IEF was organizationally strengthened by the inauguration of a permanent secretariat in Riyadh. The secretariat facilitates continuity of the dialogue between the regular biennial meetings, structuring the debate and coordinating topic proposals.

While organizationally still in its infancy, the IEF is unique in its convening power. Participation in the forum is open to all countries (its executive board currently counts Russia, China, and India among its members). All major oil market nations have been participating in the discussions in recent years. The otherwise usual dichotomy between IEA and OPEC members does not exist, and any issue can be brought forward.

The fact that the IEF was not set up as a full-fledged international organization bound by treaty, and thus has no binding decision authority, could easily be criticized. But it was intentionally set up below the level of an international organization, as it was clear that it would have been difficult to gather the support of all players behind a binding agreement and that important out-of-the-box discussions would have been difficult. It is, finally, this very lack of organizational structure that has proven to be the true strength of the IEF: the dialogue has initiated the end of producer-consumer antagonism, and the informality allows all issues to be discussed. Consequently, the goal of IEF meetings has not been to reach formal decisions but rather to foster a mutual understanding of oil market issues, usually summarized in a statement by the host.

Recent Meetings and Milestones

In 2008, after witnessing the turbulence in the oil market and prices moving into hitherto uncharted territory, the producer-consumer dialogue moved to center stage in order to find causes and remedies for the unhealthy market development. Three IEF meetings followed, starting off with the regular biennial ministerial meeting in Rome.

ROME, APRIL 2008

The agenda for the IEF April meeting in Rome was structured around four main issues: sustainability, affordability and price volatility, deliverability and investments, and availability.[20] However, the price of oil had reached US$110 a barrel just a few days before, and so the price level and its cause were the central (and somewhat thorny) issues of the meeting.

20. Hulst (2008).

Unfortunately, though, producers and consumers were far from reaching a consensus on why the price had risen and even further from any decision on a plan of action. Consumers blamed the price rise on tight supplies (that is, on the producers), while producers mainly blamed it on speculation (mostly rooted on trading floors in consumer nations) and on minor causes like the collapse of the U.S. dollar and tight refineries. The finger-pointing, obviously, was not yielding any tangible solution. As one former OPEC minister put it: "It [the price] brings the parties together, but it also shows how they differ."[21]

JEDDAH, JUNE 2008

Apparently, with a booming world economy, the collective sense of urgency was not yet high enough. That changed just two months later, when Brent passed US$135 a barrel and Saudi Arabia urgently convened an IEF meeting in Jeddah.[22] The price of oil was now so high that even skeptics had to acknowledge the threat of severe macroeconomic impacts and long-lasting demand destruction. Protests about fuel prices, food prices, and shortages raised international pressure to extremes.

As a result, Saudi Arabia, the biggest oil producer and most influential OPEC member, steered the discussion toward production capacity and upstream investment. It then made the surprise announcement of a detailed capacity extension plan to raise the ceiling on its national oil production to 15 million barrels a day. This announcement, admittedly conditioned upon signs that the market would need such capacities, was welcomed by the consumers and added to the general sentiment that the debate had taken a more long-term and constructive view about oil market challenges.

The sense of producers and consumers being in the same boat was palpable in Jeddah, so much that it was possible to find enough common ground to issue a joint statement. Saudi Arabia, the host of the meeting, and the secretariats of the IEA, the IEF, and OPEC mention hitherto thorny issues: the importance of spare capacity for the stability of the market, the need for regulation of financial markets (and their investors in the oil market), a call for IEA-OPEC "immediate collaboration" on a shared oil market analysis, and even the promotion of energy

21. Cited in Schaik (2008).
22. Strictly speaking, the Jeddah meeting and the following London meeting were not IEF meetings. However, they were direct sequels of the producer-consumer dialogue within the forum, and participants were mostly identical.

efficiency.[23] Such a statement would not have been thought possible before Jeddah, and it was a huge step toward the realization of urgency and also trust in the dialogue.

LONDON, DECEMBER 2008

At the time of the third meeting, in London in December, the price of a barrel of oil had collapsed to US$39, the financial crisis had caused bankruptcy throughout the world, oil demand had plummeted, and the impact of the downturn on investment and thus midterm supply was looking disastrous. Again, a sense of urgency made participants agree to take the forum idea one step further, and it was agreed that a high-level expert group would be formed to make proposals for strengthening the institutional architecture of the IEF.[24]

The results and recommendations of this group are to be presented to the next IEF ministerial meeting, which is to be hosted in Mexico in 2010 (with co-hosts Germany and Kuwait). Judging from past experience in setting up organizations with perceived antagonistic parties, expectations ought not to be set too high. However, the current turmoil in financial markets, the economic havoc it has brought, and the hard-earned lessons of oil price volatility may spur common interest in an institutionalized global oil market framework.

Market Transparency

Currently, the most tangible outcome of cooperation in the IEF structure has been the Joint Oil Data Initiative (JODI).[25] This initiative, which was transferred to the IEF secretariat in 2003, aims to tackle the problem of lack of transparency in the oil market. Seven international organizations, coordinated by the IEF, are collaborating to collect data from their member countries (which are responsible for 90 percent of world oil supply and demand). The data themselves are limited, but they are up to date (due to monthly submissions) and contain information that does not exist elsewhere. The data have been made public (on a website) in order to get critical appraisal and to prove their accuracy to the industry and trade community.

---

23. See Al-Attiyah and Bin Hamad, "Ultimate Goal Is Full Transparency of Agendas 2008" (www2.iefs.org.sa/Ministers/Pages/UltimateGoalisFullTransparencyofAgendas.aspx).
24. The chairman's final report mentions that meeting participants called the formation of this group "a matter of urgency" (www.meti.go.jp/english/press/data/pdf/081219EnergyMeeting.pdf).
25. Joint Oil Data Initiative (2008).

Notwithstanding technical problems with data quality and comparability, JODI is the first publication to shed light on the otherwise dark side of the oil market—and is a huge success in itself. It will take time for the market to appraise the data, but this initiative may become an authoritative part of market information. Thus the volatility caused by absence of information is bound to diminish, and the Joint Oil Data Initiative may prove to be a major step toward lowering the macroeconomic cost of the oil market for both consumers and producers.

The Way Forward: Recommendations

The structural challenges the oil market confronts today requires a global policy response. Specifically, what could be changed in order to arrive at an appropriate policy response to the risks of market exuberance or crisis-like disruptions? Three actions are recommended: to recognize the paramount role of investment, to increase transparency, and to supply infrastructure

The Role of Investment

While the boom and busts since 1998 should be proof enough that a balance between supply and demand is difficult to attain, the current global recession puts even more brakes on investment decisions. Several factors contribute to this very difficult environment:

—The oil price collapse makes the future range of oil prices uncertain.

—The slumping world GDP in 2009 leaves future recovery unclear in timing and size.

—The price elasticity of demand has surprised analysts. U.S. demand reduction, for example, was more than a million barrels a day in 2008.

—The credit freeze adds yet another dimension and is compounded by squeezed cash flows due to the sharp decline in oil prices.

A structured dialogue is necessary, a dialogue revolving around several fundamental aspects: harmonize the understanding and view of the market future, increase transparency on investment plans, frankly debate depletion paths, and stimulate spare capacity.

HARMONIZE MARKET UNDERSTANDING AND REDUCE MIDTERM VOLATILITY

One measure to reduce the boom-bust swings in the oil market is to engage all relevant producers and consumers in a constructive and intensive discussion about their respective mid- to long-term market projections. If producers and consumers seek a mutual understanding of one another's perspectives, supply and demand in future market conditions can be more easily anticipated and thus balanced. Investment needs appear more obvious, and the understandable need for supply security and demand security could be met.

The importance of such an approach is recognized by IEF participants.[26] However, achieving this is by no means an easy task. Any balancing of supply and demand intrinsically means raising the thorny issue of price. Nevertheless, recent years and months have witnessed booms and busts that have been extraordinarily harmful to both producers and consumers, and the 2008 meetings show that a mutual understanding of detrimental price and volatility levels does exist.

TRANSPARENCY ON INVESTMENT PLANS

Investment planning by market participants is fundamental to future market development. From a microperspective, an investor must make a judgment as to how much investment is being made by the rest of the market and as to when that oil is coming to the market compared to the date when first oil from his own project is expected. From a macroeconomic perspective, producers and consumers need knowledge about current investment planning if they are to discuss future market developments.

In this respect, the IEF London meeting brought an interesting idea to the table: to collect investment planning information from participating countries (in fact from international and national oil companies) via a questionnaire, the results of which would be published.[27] While the intention is commendable, realizing it will not be easy: it will demand relatively high accuracy (the marginal barrel sets the price) and also that companies reveal relatively sensitive information. But the push is in the right direction.

OPEN DEBATE ON DEPLETION PATHS

The oil market's most peculiar aspect is that, unlike most other commodity markets, long-term global resource depletion does not follow textbook optimization based on market conditions only.[28] Rather, the resource base is divided into

---

26. Hulst (2008).
27. "UK Chair's Report," London Energy Meeting, 2008 (www.meti.go.jp/english/press/data/pdf/081219EnergyMeeting.pdf).
28. Oil does not follow Hotelling's model of resource depletion over time. The best example is the counterintuitive fact that the most expensive oils get extracted first and not last (when depletion would force increasing marginal cost ventures).

nations, each of which legitimately follows its own optimal (or sometimes legacy) depletion path.[29] The sum of these paths may not coincide with what would be a global optimum. The result is a price that is higher than it would be in the hypothetical scenario of a totally open market. This basic thought makes clear that national depletion policies have in fact been the crucial driver for market fundamentals over the last decades.[30]

The same relevance is currently accruing to the consumption paths of consumer nations. Although they have for decades depended on oil prices and economic growth, consumption paths have recently moved away from this trend: most OECD consumer nations are vocally and sometimes effectively gearing national policies toward reduction of oil consumption, independent of its price level, as concerns about climate change rise.

Hence both fundamentals of the oil market balance—consumption paths and depletion paths—will in fact be decided upon in the political realm. Consumers need supply security, producers need demand security (or otherwise they have no incentive to invest in needed production capacity). Scenarios need to be developed for a common approach to this two-sided issue; common ground needs to be found. Alarmist warnings or criticisms are of no help. Technologies for combating climate change will certainly allow continuing use of hydrocarbons. Depletion paths will be altered, but it is to be hoped that this will be done with the help of a better understanding of the consumer side of the equation. This is one of the IEF's most difficult but important agenda items.

Stimulate Spare Capacity

Spare capacity has proven to be the prime tool for energy security over the last decades. It nearly vanished between 2003 and 2008 only to reemerge with the recent recession. A more rational approach is needed, one that concerns not only the comfort zone of sufficient capacity but more important the peculiar fact that producer nations alone are effectively holding the safety cushion of the entire oil market. This lopsided balance merits a structured discussion on how producer

---

29. Depletion paths may depend on social, political, or institutional factors (of the state or the NOC); on parameters of national economic size and system setup; and on interest rate, price expectations, and time preference.

30. The issue of access to reserves does, in fact, lose its traction. From a global perspective on the market, the real question is not who gets access to the reserves but whether whoever has access to these reserves optimizes his depletion path according to market conditions or according to other considerations (political, social, developmental, curse avoidance, and so on).

(OPEC) nations can be incentivized to hold spare capacity. Unfortunately, self-interest does not seem to work.[31]

Out-of-the-box thinking and debate among producers and consumers might yield results. One such unconventional line of thought is the proposal to incentivize OPEC nations by giving spare capacity first priority over stock release by consumers during a supply disruption.[32] That would allow producers to shave off the price peaks and thus reap the maximum benefit for amortizing their capacity investments. One major uncertainty hampering producer investment is that the business case for spare capacity is severely weakened by the existence of consumer nations' emergency stocks.

However probable or politically possible this proposal may seem (it would entail making producer countries sit with consumer nations during IEA decision-making on emergency responses), it is an example of the way that further dialogue about spare capacity may bring results. It should be borne in mind that producers and consumers formulated a common call for comfortable levels of spare capacity for the first time at the Jeddah summit.

Transparency

Two ways to increase transparency are to improve and extend JODI and to address the problem of data inconsistency and lack of comparability across organizations.

JOINT OIL DATA INITIATIVE

As mentioned, JODI is an important tangible result of IEF cooperation. Unfortunately, though, the initiative has suffered difficulties with data collection, especially on some of its crucial data points like industry oil stocks. IEA countries publish such data on government and industry stockholdings on a monthly, some even on a weekly, basis. However, in many relevant countries information on oil stocks is considered a matter of national security (as they are of strategic importance for military planning). And bureaucracies tend to be slow (giving the data a mere historical value) or to prohibit declassification outright. Oil stocks, clearly

---

31. Some debate revolves around the question of whether spare capacity is a rational business for OPEC countries. That is, has it generated huge gains when releases occur during disruptions and price spikes? The answer is in doubt. What is apparent is that, if it were true over the lifetime of an investment, then spare capacity would exist under market conditions (that is, in non-OPEC countries), and it does not.

32. Stevens (2008).

the most market-moving information, is still unavailable for many countries. (They are a sort of thermometer, taking the temperature of the national oil market.) Further cooperation and information sharing may bring results as well as the funding and training of national statistical administrations and capacity building of local staff.

In addition, current data collection is restricted to oil. However, the emergence of a global natural gas market will make collection of information on liquified natural gas (LNG) shipments, trade, and production equally important. Again, as the IEF is the only forum in the world with the membership of all major producers and consumers, it is perfectly suited to extend its vision to the natural gas market. Much of the analysis of this chapter will, rather sooner than later, be relevant to the gas market. Today most transnational natural gas trades are done via pipelines, but projections see the share of LNG in world natural gas trade rise to 70 percent by 2030.[33]

DATA CONSISTENCY, COMPREHENSION, AND COMPARABILITY

By the same token, producers and consumers ought to sit down together and arrive at an understanding about differences in methodology and data. A barrel is not always a barrel in IEA and OPEC publications. Consequently, future scenarios of market development are difficult to compare. While much of the basic number work has improved considerably with JODI data, more work needs to be done. It seems especially important to take the next step and work out the differences in approach between the *World Energy Outlook* (IEA) and the *World Oil Outlook* (OPEC). This will require discussions about nonpublished methodologies and may not yield identical projections; however, it will clarify the differences and increase an understanding (instead of mistrust) of incompatible projections. As this endeavor demands some tricky number crunching, no improvements will be achieved in the short run. But understanding the global energy landscape's representation in data should be at the core of cooperation.

Supply Security and Infrastructure

Maybe the most important point of concern and risk is the huge and increasing portion of world oil that needs to transit the Strait of Hormuz. Some 17 million barrels a day pass through this strait, an amount projected to increase to more than

---

33. International Energy Agency, *World Energy Outlook* (2008), p. 121.

24 million barrels a day by 2030.[34] This being roughly a third of total interregional oil trade, the world's supply security hinges upon uninterrupted flows through the Strait of Hormuz. This strait, however, is known among energy and military experts as the ultimate world choke point: shipping lanes are just three kilometers wide, disputed islands lie in the midst of the strait, basically no alternative routes exist, the sheer size of the oil has no alternative sources, and geopolitical tensions have existed in the Middle East for a century.[35]

Producers and consumers at the IEF should address the possibility of creating alternative export routes. One such alternative currently operating is the East-West pipeline through Saudi Arabia, running from Abqaiq on the Persian Gulf to the port of Yanbu on the Red Sea. This pipeline has a capacity of 5 million barrels a day.[36]

Installing and maintaining alternative or spare infrastructure involves costs of significant scale, but at the same time their benefit accrues to all participants in the market.[37] It seems that a discussion of security-sensitive infrastructure is a perfect example of a public good that could be at the heart of consumer-producer cooperation within the IEF dialogue. It is true that at the end of the day financing will be a heated discussion topic. However, infrastructure that increases supply security (and traders' tranquility) is insurance for all, independent of where the pipelines will ultimately be lying.

Outlook

The current state of the oil market makes any predictions about as reliable as those from a crystal ball. Admittedly the main risk to a significant improvement of the institutional setup and the agenda setting of the IEF stems, perversely, from an oil price implosion. History tells us that consumer nations tend to forget about the oil market and its pending economic dangers and tend to revert to their prior

---

34. International Energy Agency, *World Energy Outlook* (2008), p. 106. This number, although huge, is a rather conservative estimate compared to prior IEA projections; see International Energy Agency, *World Energy Outlook* (2004), p. 119.

35. For more information on choke points, see Lehman Brothers (2008).

36. There are other routes for oil exports circumventing Hormuz (such as the TAP through Saudi Arabia and Iraq's export pipes through Turkey and Saudi Arabia), but they all operate under difficulties or are actually mothballed.

37. The East-West pipeline currently operates at only half its capacity, as international loadings off Yanbu are immaterial (low demand due to longer shipping times to Asian consumers), a fact that increases its total lifetime costs. Harks (2007).

low-price mentality and consumption patterns. At the same time, producers are suffering hard times, with OPEC refocusing on itself and aiming toward strengthening cartel policy. Consumers and producers could again become oblivious of the need for mid- to long-term cooperation, and the perception of a crisis would vanish at least from the consumer nations' view. Short-termism would reduce most impetus for institutional reform.

That would be the flawed way forward. But that need not be; and the price collapse to below US$40 a barrel has (such is the current impression) made consumers and producers even more aware of a need to cooperate on the fundamentals of the oil market. The IEA (and also the IEF) have been warning that the price implosion may bring investment delays, which in turn may simply delay the coming oil crunch.[38]

Viewing the IEF as an organizational setup, it is hard not to see the progress achieved in recent years. Dialogue is maturing on content and organization, largely witnessed by its recent branching out into substantive topic events covering much of the current international energy topics.[39] Events in 2008—consecutive meetings in Rome, Jeddah, and London—show how well producers and consumers understand that they are in the same boat. Further, data collection has improved, and the extension of JODI toward collecting annual gas data (not monthly; however, it's a start) is planned to begin sometime soon. Most important in all this activity, the IEF has managed to keep its reputation as a truly neutral broker, with developing oil producers and industrial energy consumers trusting in its work.

True, when it comes down to details the idea of cooperation needs regular reinforcement. That is, both sides will need self-interested incentives for any future commitment. Events in 2008 with their market exuberance made that rather easy; however, the future is not quite that certain. Other incentives may be, for example, long-term transparency of the market balance and consistently understanding one another's data and methodology. The inclusion of spare capacity in the stock draw mechanism is one example of a dialogue yielding results even on thorny financing issues.

38. International Energy Agency, *Oil Market Report* (2008), p. 104.
39. Among others there have been an International Energy Forum–International Gas Union in November 2008, an International Energy Forum–IFP Technology Forum in December 2008, and an IOC-NOC forum hosted by the International Energy Forum and the government of Kuwait in March 2009 (www.iefs.org.sa).

Signs sent by the last London IEF meeting were highly encouraging. Participating countries were daunted by the recession taking shape, and a sense of urgency for cooperation prevailed. The most significant sign was the agreement that an examination of the institutional architecture of the energy dialogue in the IEF was necessary. A high-level steering group (consisting of Saudi Arabia, the United Kingdom, Algeria, France, Germany, Japan, Kuwait, Mexico, Qatar, and the United States) was established to select an "expert group" that will hopefully make institutional proposals to propel cooperation a necessary step ahead.

No real alternative is at hand: it is good news that producers and consumers speak to each other on mostly good terms in a mutually beneficial manner. And no alternative institution or forum encompassing all necessary actors is in sight or of any pragmatic probability. The IEF secretariat is an excellent first step and should be fostered, not undermined, by concurrent proposals.

References

British Petroleum. 2008. *BP Statistical Review.* London.
Ferderer, J. P. 1996. "Oil Price Volatility and U.S. Macroeconomic Activity: A Solution to the Asymmetry Puzzle." *Journal of Macroeconomics* 18.
Harks, Enno. 2007. "Der globale Ölmarkt." Berlin: Stiftung Wissenschaft und Politik.
Hulst, Noé van. 2008. "Key Messages from the 11th IEF in Rome, 20–22 April 2008." *Middle East Economic Survey* 51, no. 21.
International Energy Agency. Selected years. *World Energy Outlook.* Paris.
———. Selected years. *Oil Market Report.*
Joint Oil Data Initiative. 2008. "JODI Questionnaire."
Lehman Brothers. 2008. "Global Oil Choke Points." New York
Liao, Huei-Chu, Yi-Huey Lee, and Yu-Bo Suen. 2008. "Electronic Trading System and Returns Volatility in the Oil Futures Market." *Energy Economics* 30, no. 5.
Schaik, John van. 2008. "Deep Divide." New York: Energy Compass.
Schorkopf, Frank. 2007. "Energie als Thema des Welthandelsrechts." In *Die Sicherung der Energieversorgung auf globalisierten Märkten,* edited by S. Leible, M. Lippert, and C. Walter. Tübingen: Mohr Siebeck.
Stevens, Paul. 2008. *The Coming Oil Supply Crunch.* Chatham, N.J.: Chatham House.

13

The Future of Producer-Consumer Cooperation: A Policy Perspective

Albert Bressand

The picture of the relations between energy-consuming and energy-producing countries that emerges from chapters 10, 11, and 12 is a contrasted one. On the one hand, a policy agenda of global cooperation on energy matters has begun to take shape, albeit still timidly. As documented by Dick de Jong, Coby van der Linde, and Tom Smeenk (chapter 11), consumers and producers have overcome their bipolar view of the past and now recognize a number of common challenges, at least as far as oil markets are concerned. The institutional structure supporting this emerging policy dialogue is strengthening, in a low-key yet significant way, whether under the aegis of the International Energy Forum (IEF) or in the form of a dialogue between the resource-rich national oil and gas companies (NOCs) and international oil and gas companies (IOCs).[1]

As partial as it is, this dialogue, as well as the many business links between NOCs and IOCs, has fostered many forms of cooperation. Governments cooperate on essential themes like data collection and market transparency, and IOCs and NOCs are now joining forces to meet new challenges, as BP and the China

---

1. An NOC forum has been convened by the energy consultancy PFC Energy for several years now. In March 2009 the IEF organized a dialogue between NOCs and IOCs in Kuwait.

National Petroleum Corporation(CNPC) did when they became the only companies to accept the tough conditions of the first 2009 Iraqi auction.[2]

Yet new players have emerged that are not properly integrated into the present institutional structure. While Russia has reassumed its century-old role of prominent energy exporter, Russia and its Eurasian partners have failed to live up to the spirit of the 1994 Energy Charter Treaty, as illustrated by conflicts over existing and proposed transit routes for Russian and Central Asian gas exports. Liquefied natural gas (LNG) still accounts for a small share of total gas imports, and as shown by de Jong, van der Linde, and Smeenk, the hopes for a liquid and purely business-driven global gas market are bound to materialize only slowly.

Meanwhile, India and China are developing their own resources with a clear, even if incomplete, national preference and are currently not integrated into the existing institutional setup in a manner consistent with their huge share (more than 40 percent) of the expected increase in oil demand by 2030.[3] In the Andean countries, the policies of Hugo Chávez's Venezuelan administration and the echoes they find in Bolivia and Ecuador put investors—including Brazil's state-controlled Petrobras—in a challenging position, with some producer countries even opting out of arbitrage procedures that investors find essential in order to limit the discretionary power of host governments when national courts are not seen as independent.

Drawing on the three previous chapters as well as on personal work, this chapter presents an integrated view on how market and government forces shape relations in oil and gas, identifying three policy arenas that call for attention. This chapter then considers how enhanced cooperation between producers and consumers of oil and gas resources can take relations beyond today's combination of market-based relations and zero-sum game approaches to disputes over contracts and resource development. Two approaches to producer-consumer cooperation are identified and applied to each of the three policy arenas to create two contrasted scenarios.

Before looking at the agenda for cooperation between producers and consumers, an agenda that we see as structured around the three policy arenas described below, let us highlight what are the two different approaches that could inspire enhanced cooperation. The first approach to cooperation considered here would aim to provide an institutional framework to bring oil and gas relations into the

---

2. "BP, China Win Right to Develop Iraq's Rumalia Oil Field" (www.iraqoilforum.com).

3. This would amount to 43 percent, in the mainstream scenario of the IEA. International Energy Agency (2008), p. 77.

marketcentric framework that applies to most other sectors of the global economy. The cornerstone of this approach would be the inclusion of energy trade and energy investment in an adapted World Trade Organization (WTO) framework along the lines suggested in other work by Andreas Goldthau and Jan Martin Witte.[4]

In contrast, and in close synergy with the emerging institutional and policy apparatus taking shape in the climate change mitigation field, the second approach would acknowledge the growing role of sovereign objectives in energy policymaking and the fact that, as explained below, consumer countries increasingly bring their own disruptive influence to bear on energy markets (disruptive from the standpoint of oil and gas producers by comparison to purely market-based approaches). Under this second approach to cooperation, producer-consumer cooperation would concentrate on creating an institutional basis for market-friendly global governance of hydrocarbon resources in which governments have a role reflecting the current importance of sovereign objectives. It would do so with a view of protecting the long-term interests of producer and consumer countries, giving each group a better understanding of the objectives of the other. In order to see how these two different approaches would be applied, one should distinguish between the various types of issues calling for attention.

Three Policy Arenas for Cooperation

Forty years of bumpy consumer-producer interactions since the first oil shock and the abrupt end of the "concessions" age have generated a complex agenda in which three policy arenas—three layers of policy interactions—can be distinguished. These arenas deal respectively with

—Protection against natural or politically inspired interruptions in oil and gas supplies (hereafter short-term supply risks)
—The promotion of long-term investment in resources development
—The increasing role of governments in influencing energy-resources depletion and consumption paths.

Short-Term Supply Risks

Half-hearted negotiations toward a New International Economic Order (NIEO) notwithstanding, the first policy arena took shape in the 1970s around consumer-

4. Goldthau and Witte (2009).

only policies to deal with short-term disruption of oil supply that might result from politically motivated embargos or from war in the Middle East.[5] As Wilfrid Kohl discusses in chapter 10, Western oil-importing countries that make up the International Energy Agency (IEA) have put in place a thoroughly integrated and fairly effective set of instruments, which were tested during the Gulf War and Hurricane Katrina and have largely alleviated initial concerns over supply shocks. Ongoing developments in this first policy arena are of an incremental nature, as IEA members endeavor to enlist the participation of China and India in IEA crisis management schemes and to perfect the doctrine guiding strategic reserves usage.

More striking, extending this crisis-management capacity to cover potential disruptions in natural gas imports has become a growing concern for European Union member states. While unlikely to lead to the equivalent of a gas OPEC, saber rattling on the part of major gas producers within the Gas Exporting Countries Forum (GECF) makes traditional supply security considerations more acute, as do Gazprom's sometimes hectic efforts to enter into "strategic alliances" with whatever producer the EU may turn to in search of gas import diversification.[6] As a result, a new set of EU policies is supporting a multibillion-euro program of interconnection of national gas grids, expansion of natural gas storage, and diversification of gas supply sources, notably in the form of LNG.

These policies are being conducted in the tradition of the Trans-European Network (TEN) programs, which have greatly contributed to the modernization and interconnection of Mediterranean member countries. Although they are likely to foster convergence of views and policies as well as a more resilient EU posture on matters of gas imports, these efforts do not receive much attention: it is easier to blame the EU for lacking an external energy policy than to observe how such a policy can only be the next step in the integration road, which began with the decision to make energy policy a community competence, a decision made only ten years ago at the European Summit in 2000. Adding an external dimension to what was initially an internal market policy will be a key aspect of the tighter foreign policy integration made possible by the Lisbon Treaty as it enters into force.[7]

---

5. Gas supplies from the Soviet Union were also a source of concern and a bone of contention between the United States and Europe during the cold war and détente periods.

6. Hadi Hallouche, "The Gas Exporting Countries Forum: Is It Really a Gas OPEC in the Making?" (www.oxfordenergy.org/pdfs/ng13.pdf). For a description of Gazprom initiatives in Algeria, Libya, and Nigeria and over the Trans-Sahara gas pipeline, see Bressand (2009).

7. For an analysis of EU energy policies and the way forward, see Albert Bressand, "European Integration and the Eurasian Energy Challenge," paper prepared for the Hamburg Global Public Policy Institute conference, December 2009, forthcoming.

Long-Term Investment Risks

The second policy arena is about the level of investment needed to develop oil and gas resources in ways that satisfy the IEA's call for "economic growth through stable energy supplies and free markets."[8] While some countries are tempted to go after such objectives under the banner of energy independence, the need for massive investments to develop energy sources far away from the consuming areas makes clear that interdependence is the name of the game, with opportunistic behavior a permanent risk and cooperation between producers and consumers an essential tool to keep it in check.

As discussed by Wilfred Kohl, in chapter 10, a first component in this cooperative agenda is the search for greater transparency of data regarding potential reserves in key OPEC countries. While few in the industry consider Matthew Simmons's bestseller *Twilight in the Desert* a properly researched work, the full size of Saudi oil reserves—and for that matter the size of Iraqi oil and gas reserves and of Turkmen gas reserves, to take the most visible examples—is still uncertain, albeit larger than existing figures, which are based on partial exploration only.[9]

The long-term investment challenge, however, is not just about the existence of reserves but also about the capacity and willingness of major resources–holding (MRH) countries to develop their resources at a pace and in a contractual environment that leaves room for market logic. Meeting this challenge requires dealing with obstacles both at the country level and at the level of the global energy system. At the country level, NOC relations with IOCs are critical in achieving an efficient division of labor, as are the contractual terms of access to upstream "acreage" for IOCs. One of the most important issues in this respect is what form of risk taking and what type of remuneration are available to IOCs and to those NOCs that have become international investors (like Statoil, Petrobras, Sinopec, and Gazprom). While some MRH countries (like Saudi Arabia, Kuwait, and Mexico) are fundamentally closed to IOC investment, a number of countries (including Iraq, in spite of six years of U.S. military and legal presence) accept IOCs only within various forms of enhanced service contract, which Western companies perceive as inappropriate for fostering the massive risk taking associated with upstream projects. The companies' reasoning is based not just on the resulting lower remuneration but also on the lack of fit with the entrepreneurial and highly capitalistic nature of such projects and on the impossibility to book

8. See www.iea.org/about/sharedgoals.htm.
9. Simmons (2005).

reserves on their balance sheets if they are not remunerated with some rights over the production.[10]

As for obstacles common to all countries, the negative impact of oil price volatility on investment is of growing importance in assessing and assuming long-term investment risks, by MRH countries and investors alike. Moreover, price volatility triggers opportunistic behaviors on the part of whoever has the temporary advantage, to the long-term detriment of both parties to the contract.

Sovereign Objectives Influencing Production and Consumption Strategies

As the previous chapters discuss, a third policy arena is emerging as a result of the growing role that governments are now assuming in setting the framework for energy relations. A major transformation is under way, well captured in the warning by de Jong, van der Linde, and Smeenk in their chapter: "The thinking in the 1990s— that international oil and gas markets would be increasingly free of government involvement and management and that governments would limit their role to market regulator and tax collector—has evaporated in recent years." Labeling such changes *resource nationalism* obscures more than it reveals, notably as it overlooks two considerations. First, producers express demands and follow development strategies that can be perfectly rational and in their best interest even if they embody an optimization perspective different from those of international investors and consumers. Second, consumer countries' governments are beginning to exercise an influence over the supply and demand balance, which implies higher levels of government intervention and adds significant levels of uncertainty and risk for producers.

Regarding the first consideration, producers like Saudi Arabia and Russia see the development of their resources from a long-term perspective, which does not coincide with the market optimum as it would be defined from the standpoint of international investors and consumers. Keeping production levels low enough to keep proven reserves unchanged or slowly decreasing is clearly assessed to be in the long-term interest of the Kingdom and of the ruling dynasty.[11] Russian

10. In addition to absolute returns, remuneration in the exclusive form of rights over production is one of the three essential tests that companies must meet in order to be able to book reserves on their balance sheet under IASC and SEC rules. Chinese NOCs have shown less reluctance to embrace service contracts. For a discussion of these issues, see Bressand (2009), pp. 178–80, on the developments on the Shtokman gas field and the contractual agreement put in place between Gazprom, Total, and Statoil.

11. Saudi Arabia continues to add to its "proven reserves" as exploration proceeds and recovery techniques improve. For a discussion of long-term trends in production levels, proven reserves, and potential reserves in the Kingdom of Saudi Arabia, see Nansen G. Saleri, "Dawn in the Desert" (www.energytribune.com/articles.cfm?aid=627).

energy experts and policymakers, meanwhile, are concerned that the timing and pace at which the fields considered strategic could be developed will reflect company-level arbitrage rather than Russia's best interest. A similar trend among the major natural gas producers in the GECF is observed by de Jong, van der Linde, and Smeenk: "Producer governments are reconsidering their export strategies and are beginning to focus on supply management as a means of ensuring value protection for their resources. They also prioritize the use of gas for growth in their domestic economies."

Meanwhile, a second reason that *resource nationalism* captures only a fraction of the transformation under way is that consumer countries follow energy security policies, such as the promotion of domestic biofuels and wind energy, and policies intended to reduce emissions of greenhouse gases, which amount to economic subsidies in favor of specific energy sources and of investments in energy efficiency. As they are increasingly "regulating markets within the constraints of their public interests" (chapter 11), they pursue changes in their "energy mix" through policy mandates and through a set of prices different from those that would emerge from pure market interactions.

What resources are developed in the EU, the United States, and China—that is, oil, natural gas, coal, biofuels, offshore wind farms, nuclear, and new generations of technology—is determined by a hybrid process that sees governments picking the winners and tilting the playing field in ways that would have been described in industrial policy terms when that concept was still acceptable. Policy mandates of the 20/20 type (that is, cutting greenhouse gas emissions by 20 percent and producing 20 percent of energy from renewable sources by 2020), feed-in tariffs that guarantee purchase prices for alternative electricity well above market prices, and massive subsidies across the value chain are reshaping fuel choices in the power generation and transport sectors. Such is the case notably with the EU Energy and Climate package of December 2008 and with U.S. legislation currently under discussion.[12]

As a result, a third consideration for producer-consumer cooperation should be Enno Harks's observation, chapter 12, that "both fundamentals of the oil market balance—consumption paths and depletion paths—will in fact be decided upon in the political realm." While producers also create important distortions in their own energy consumption—witness the huge energy and water subsidies that are exacerbating demand for oil in countries like Iran and those in the Gulf. Energy taxes and, increasingly, carbon taxes (levied by consumer countries'

---

12. European Commission (2007).

governments) and carbon market prices (set by consumer countries' institutions) play a major role in promoting fuel substitution and energy efficiency. One can denounce all such interference or, on the contrary, look at them as producing public goods like climate change mitigation and long-term security in a carbon-constrained world. This debate and value judgments aside, it is clear that the global energy system is now subject to a hybrid form of governance. The latter, and its sophisticated relation to market regulation, can be understood, for example, in reference to the cap-and-trade institutional model now in place for carbon emissions in Europe and under discussion globally.[13] Market mechanisms play an essential role in such schemes—indeed a new trillion-dollar market in carbon sink assets has been created—but they do so around rules of the game and within quantitative limits that are set by governments and not by the market itself.

Two Contrasted Approaches to Cooperation

Producer-consumer cooperation can play a major role in overcoming the drawbacks of, and in developing opportunities in, all three policy arenas reviewed above: supply-crisis prevention and management, long-term energy investment promotion, and coordinated energy development and usage. What form such cooperation can take and through what institutional framework it can be achieved are questions that raise a paradox.

The paradox is this. Compared to previous decades, the role of the market has increased through a combination of, first, "a liquid and competitive global market for oil," second, the role now assumed by the futures market in oil price formation based in New York and London, and, third, the radical transformation of the EU gas industry triggered by three waves of liberalization Directives.[14] Yet at the same time the role of governments in setting the long-term parameters has become far more central than most economists could have anticipated. The tight control that MRH countries exercise over access to upstream acreage and over the pace of resource depletion is only half of the transformed picture. The picture also includes increasingly effective interventions reminiscent of industrial policy on the part of some of the most powerful consumer countries' governments. These policies stem not only from security concerns, which have less of an impact than U.S. election-time rhetoric might suggest and that proper cooperation might assuage.

13. Ellerman and Joskow (2008).
14. See Goldthau and Witte (2009), pp. 375–77; Mabro (2005).

They also stem from objectives and institutions aiming to support various forms of energy production and to remodel the energy mix that fuels economic growth. How to deal with this paradox is a defining question in any view of producer-consumer relations. Articulating the policy options clearly is an essential antidote to the conceptual confusion generated by loose denunciations of "energy nationalism."[15] Contrary to some claims, more market does not necessarily mean less government. Instead, the two can operate together (as can be seen from the way President George W. Bush's promarket administration presided over two major military expeditions, Keynesian deficits, and the Sarbanes-Oxley Act, which provides for the jailing of CEOs and CFOs in breach of their financial reporting obligations). Modern governments can actually intervene through the market and not just in its stead, thus making hybrid forms of governance a sustainable part of advanced market economies, intent on both dealing with market failures and meeting societal objectives.[16] Hence two approaches could inspire producer-consumer cooperation.

First Approach: Return to the Market

The first approach is for producers and consumers to put in place an institutional framework that establishes the primacy of market logic in dealing with all three policy arenas. This cannot be done, however, by wishing away the sovereign objectives of governments, as these objectives are deeply embedded in society's expectations and, in the case of climate, in the mitigation of risks identified as critical by the world's scientific community. An essential part of this first approach is therefore to systematize the internalization of objectives that are not spontaneously served by the market and to put in place institutions and cooperative processes that make the pursuit of these interests transparent.

Andreas Goldthau and Jan Martin Witte provide a comprehensive description of the institutional reforms that could apply this market-centric approach to global energy governance.[17] Departing from the zero-sum game associated with the narrow view of energy security, they describe how a fully marketcentric energy system could emerge. Two recommendations come together in their proposal:

—Incremental policies to develop efforts already under way, from enhanced data transparency to accommodation of China and India in a revamped IEA.

---

15. I personally seldom meet nationalists, although I am quite often in the company of patriots.

16. *The Shell Global Scenarios to 2025* describes in detail how forces of market incentives, government regulation or coercion, and forces of communities can interact, with two of the forces gaining in importance and the third one expressing itself through one or the other. Bressand (2005).

17. Goldthau and Witte (2009).

—Radical change in the form of WTO rules to ensure fair competition within the energy sector, including with respect to access by international investors to producer countries' upstream resources. This would put an end to energy exceptionalism and provide conditions conducive to an optimal investment path.

Second Approach: Enhanced International Energy Governance

The second approach builds on the increasing role of governments in influencing energy consumption and the rate of depletion of producers' resources. In this respect, it is worth reflecting on Enno Harks's understatement in chapter 12 of this book—that "the global oil market exhibits some rather odd characteristics." Recent developments in Eurasia, the Andes region, and the Gulf make clear indeed that, in the blunter words of Ed Morse, "Energy is a unique exception to the rules that govern most sectors of the world economy."[18] While this role of governments may appear a thing of the past, the brief review of consumer countries' policies here suggests that this role is finding a new life as part of efforts to promote technology change and a transition toward a low-carbon, global economy.

With this approach, consumers acknowledge that sovereign objectives, including those related to climate change, have a major impact on energy markets and they engage producers in a policy dialogue. To do so constructively, consumers need to step back and look at the world energy scene through the eyes of producers. Such insight would disclose two major threats to producers: oil price volatility and the transition toward a low-carbon economy that may no longer be based on oil. Cooperation on these two threats will be essential in providing win-win opportunities.

Two Scenarios for Producer-Consumer Cooperation Spanning the Three Policy Arenas

Each of the approaches described above would lead to producer-consumer cooperation but with quite different results in terms of policy. Let us therefore compare how the return-to-market and the enhanced energy governance options would transform producer-consumer cooperation in each of the three policy arenas.

Short-Term Security of Supply under the Two Scenarios

Under each of the two scenarios, even if in a different manner, the benefits of cooperation would materialize most easily with regard to policies to mitigate or

18. Edward Morse, "Energy Breaks the Economic Rules" (www.sais-jhu.edu/pressroom/publications/saisphere/2005/morse.html).

avoid short-term supply disruptions. In a return-to-market world, the extension of the IEA instruments to China and India and the deployment of similar instruments for Europe's gas supplies would provide a buffer against political interference in oil and gas markets. A road map for these important policy enhancements regarding oil supply security is presented by Wilfrid Kohl, in chapter 10. As shown by Kohl, these security-driven efforts can be accompanied by an array of cooperative policies that bring to light the win-win dimension, policies like the IEA Networks of Expertise in Energy Technologies initiative (NEET), and the efforts to promote technological innovation and initiatives in the G-8 and at the World Bank. While more radical steps could be taken, they would not be essential to this first scenario.

In an enhanced energy governance world, by contrast, the consumer-only nature of IEA processes would be an impediment to in-depth cooperation. The direct participation of producers in energy security would be sought through a combined approach to OPEC's spare capacities and to consumer-held strategic reserves. Enno Harks points to one of the ways in which this could be done: "to incentivize OPEC nations by giving spare capacity first priority over stock release by consumers during a supply disruption." Observing that this would allow producers to shave off the price peaks and thus reap the maximum "benefit" for amortizing capacity investments, he suggests that this could be achieved by "making producer countries sit with consumer nations during IEA decisionmaking on emergency responses." An alternative approach, consistent with the two other policy arenas under this scenario, would be to move the crisis-response capacity—at least the overall coordination capacity—from the IEA to the IEF in Riyadh.

Promotion of Long-Term Energy Investment under the Two Scenarios

Under both scenarios, transparency would be an essential tool in support of freer and better informed energy investment. As discussed by Harks, the Joint Oil Data Initiative (JODI) as currently conducted by the IEF would be reinforced through exchanges of data among companies, as was proposed at the 2008 IEF meeting in London. But transparency could also be promoted through proactive encouragement to standardize resources evaluation for major oil and gas fields in underexplored MRH countries. Funds could be made available, for instance, to certify major unassessed reserves, as Turkmenistan did in 2008 for its Osman–South Yolotan field with the help of the specialized UK-based consultancy Gaffney, Cline and Associates.[19]

19. Bressand (2009), p. 153.

Developing common criteria for booking reserves by international investors under International Accounting Standards (IAS) and modernizing the criteria of the U.S. Securities and Exchange Commission by opening the spectrum of eligible rights-sharing arrangements could improve the comprehensiveness and quality of energy reserves data. These developments would also help MRH countries and IOCs reconcile producer countries' preference for service contracts with the need of IOCs to be remunerated in ways that enable them to book reserves—which implies being remunerated in proportion to the value of the production that their huge capital expenses make possible if and when successfully deployed.

The second policy arena would be the most trying one for a return-to-market scenario, as it implies going well beyond the transparency measures common to the two scenarios. Placing national oil and gas resources under WTO supervision would imply a far more open and sophisticated view of sovereignty than most nations have. As it becomes a net gas exporter, thanks to the development of shale gas, the United States itself may not be overly exhilarated at the prospect of accepting some droit de regard over "North American destinations only" clauses in gas pipeline agreements or compatibility of its offshore drilling bans with a regime of open access to hydrocarbon resources that looks natural from a U.S. standpoint in other parts of the world.

Nevertheless, the program presented by Goldthau and Witte includes a number of low-hanging fruits, such as applying commonsense market rules and trade discipline to vastly inefficient biofuels programs like the U.S. corn-based ethanol program. Addressing these issues first could build trust in support of a gradual application of WTO rules to other aspects of energy trade and investment. In addition, as the two authors observe, a long-lasting buyers' market in oil and gas (a prospect that large-scale exploitation of previously unexploitable shale gas may reinforce) would provide an opportunity to "convince producing nations that an institutional environment favouring an effective allocation of capital and investment is more likely to generate stable and reliable revenues than a situation in which price hikes result from inelastic supply and an overstretch in oil and gas infrastructure."[20]

In an enhanced energy governance world, by contrast, the WTO would not assume a similar role, and sui generis institutions would be developed to balance producer and consumer interests. The starting point may not be the investment rules themselves—where each MRH country's idiosyncrasies are

20. Goldthau and Witte (2009), p. 388.

immense, as the cases of Mexico, Iraq, and Nigeria illustrate—but may reside instead in bold approaches to deal with global impediments to energy investment. In particular, "the thorny issue of price," to which Enno Harks draws attention in chapter 12, may become the testing ground for a quantum leap in producer-consumer cooperation.[21]

Inspiration in this respect may be sought from ideas put forward by Robert Mabro, the founder of Oxford Energy and one of the most respected observers of the energy scene. The starting point in Mabro's proposal is that oil price formation has little to do with an oil price cartel but rather centers on the trading strategies of participants in oil futures markets. He writes,

> Since OPEC does not fix the oil price but is always very concerned about its level and movements it can only attempt to steer their course by sending signals to the futures markets where reference prices are determined. . . . The only signal it can use is the decision to reduce production quotas. Markets can receive the signal and act upon it or simply ignore it and indulge in skepticism.[22]

Some of the largest participants in futures markets are producer countries, such as Mexico, that aim to hedge their future production in order to reduce uncertainty regarding their budgetary resources. But financial trading houses are also key players in these markets, and their trading decisions reflect arbitrage among asset classes at least as much as considerations of oil supply and demand. While Enno Harks leaves open the role that financial players end up playing in setting prices in these futures markets, market participants such as Ed Morse—formerly chief energy economist of Lehman Brothers and now with Louis Commodities—would support Robert Mabro's view that financial sectors do indeed play a major role and that arbitrage among financial asset classes may at times weigh more than energy balance considerations in their trading decisions.[23]

Against this background, Mabro's proposal is to adopt a central bank model, whereby a committee of respected economists and practitioners sets the price of

---

21. For a description of six groups of MRH countries and the different approaches they take to exploiting their resources, and for in-depth analysis of Saudi Arabia, Kuwait, and Mexico, see Bressand (2009), pp. 142–53.

22. Robert Mabro, "OPEC, the Futures Oil Markets, and the Price of Oil" (www.robertmabro. co.uk).

23. Author's conversations with persons quoted. See also Mabro (2005).

the even more essential commodity called money. In his view, producer and consumer countries should jointly appoint a group of "wise men" charged with identifying the price (or a large enough "price band") for oil prices that would stimulate long-term investment and be fair to producers and consumers. Keeping oil prices within an agreed band would require the equivalent of controls over money supply at the disposal of central bankers.

Consistent with the description of the first policy arena in this scenario, Mabro's view is that consumer and producer countries would cooperate to keep prices at the desired levels when faced with short-term disruptions by drawing on commercial and strategic inventories in the hands of consumers as well as on spare production capacities in the hands of producers. While such a view may appear outlandish, elements of a de facto cooperation of that type exists between the United States and Saudi Arabia. The impression producer countries have—that final prices are influenced by consumer countries' governments—can only grow, as policy mandates and feed-in tariffs transform the energy mix and as cap-and-trade mechanisms embed carbon prices in energy prices. In such conditions, an institutionalized dialogue on oil price formation of the type put forward by Robert Mabro may be far less radical than it seems.

Other developments under way in the global economy would also increase the attractiveness of the Mabro proposal. The world has just witnessed a major institutional transformation in the form of carbon cap-and-trade markets and of associated carbon instruments, such as the Clean Development Mechanism (CDM) that have created, or will create, assets potentially worth trillions of dollars and that already result in large cross-border financial transfers. Seen in this context, the role of the wise men suggested by Robert Mabro would be similar to that of the Nobel Prize–winning Intergovernmental Panel on Climate Change (IPCC), which, as discussed by Kohl, issues "periodic assessment reports" related to the nature and extent of the climate change risk, with experts and governments drawing implications in terms of which carbon prices are consistent with IPCC objectives. From a global governance perspective, and subject to a still-raging policy debate, the international community has taken a major step forward with the fact-finding and debate-framing role it has now ascribed to this eminent community of scientists led by Rajendra K. Pachauri. In the enhanced energy governance scenario, taking a similar step regarding the long-term availability of energy resources and the economic conditions for their optimal development would be seen as a natural follow-up and complement.

Sovereign Approaches to Production and Consumption under the Two Scenarios

The third policy arena also presents opportunities that would be harnessed in both scenarios. A case in point is international cooperation to accelerate technology development in support of energy efficiency and a low-carbon economy. Initiatives like the World Bank's Clean Energy Investment Framework, which identifies the scale of investments needed to increase access to energy especially in sub-Saharan Africa (Enno Harks), would develop further, probably in a decentralized manner and in synergy with various carbon market instruments.

This policy arena, however, is also one in which producers and consumers may elect to confront what Qatar's Energy Minister Al-Attiyah refers to as the "joint planning of the global energy balance."[24] The reason to do so would not be a taste for Soviet-style planning but, as described above, a realization that governments, notably in leading consumer countries, are now actively influencing the energy mix. Some form of collective oversight involving all parties would have more than one benefit, at a time when these consumer countries' governments seem to be mesmerized by "20 by 20" or "30 by 30" headline-making objectives and mandates. Indeed, providing oil producers with some visibility and influence in the transition out of the oilcentric economy—a transition illustrated by the number of electric vehicles on the drawing boards—would make producer-consumer cooperation an essential part of twenty-first-century international governance.

Success in establishing a climate framework for the post-Kyoto, post-2012 period is most certainly a sine qua non condition for the bolder step considered under this scenario. An agreed, universal institutional framework in which to seek the reduction of carbon emissions would establish the legitimacy of looking at resources—the atmosphere's sink capacity as well as the underground carbon-heavy reservoirs of hydrocarbons—as the common resources of mankind. This would be in line with, again, a more sophisticated view of what sovereignty really is: control over one's nation's actual fate; and what it is not: a magic wand to keep interdependence at bay.

Conclusion

Altogether, under each of the two scenarios sketched here, the role of energy producer-consumer cooperation can be a major component of international

24. H. E. Abdulla Bin Hamad Al-Attiyah, "Ultimate Goal Is Full Transparency of Agendas" (www2.iefs.org.sa/ministers/pages/ultimategoalisfulltransparencyofagendas.aspx).

governance for a planet confronted simultaneously with new levels of economic abundance and with scarcity of environmental and natural resources. The three policy arenas identified above offer a map by which to assess the consistency of the various aspects of the proposed producer-consumer cooperation and to chart institutional and policy developments commensurate with the present transformation in the world's energy, trade, and climate system. This can be done under each of the two contrasting policy approaches that we have outlined, one centered on the application of the full market logic to the world of energy, the other based on a balance between market forces and intergovernmental cooperation to reduce the likelihood of misunderstanding and conflict.

Which of the above cooperative scenarios, if any, materializes will depend on which set of interests coalesce around the policy options described. As observed by Douglass North, institutions do not emerge spontaneously to create and nurture the market but reflect the interests of those players in a position to put them in place.[25] How energy-producing and -importing countries define their immediate and long-term interests—and how they relate them to other aspects of the international security agenda and climate negotiations—will be the defining variables.

References

Bressand, Albert. 2009. "Foreign Direct Investment in the Oil and Gas Sector: Recent Trends and Strategic Drivers." *Yearbook on Investment Law and Policy,* edited by Karl Sauvant. Oxford University Press.

———, ed. 2005. *The Shell Global Scenarios to 2025.* Washington: Royal Dutch/Shell and Peterson Institute for International Economics.

Ellerman, Danny, and Paul Joskow. 2008. "The European Union Emissions Trading System in Perspective." Arlington, Va.: Pew Center on Global Climate Change.

European Commission. 2007. "An Energy Policy for Europe: Communication from the Commission to the European Council and the European Parliament." Brussels.

Goldthau, Andreas, and Jan Martin Witte. 2009. "Back to the Future; or, Forward to the Past? Strengthening Markets and Rules for Effective Global Energy Governance." *International Affairs* 85, no. 2.

International Energy Agency. 2008. *World Energy Outlook.* Paris.

Mabro, Robert. 2005. "The International Oil Price Regime: Origins, Rationale, and Assessment." *Journal of Energy Literature* 11, no. 1.

North, Douglass. 1990. *Institutions, Institutional Change, and Economic Performance: Political Economy of Institutions and Decisions.* Cambridge University Press.

Simmons, Matthew R. 2005. *Twilight in the Desert: The Coming Saudi Oil Shock and the World Economy.* New York: John Wiley and Sons.

25. North (1990).

PART FOUR

Emerging Issues
and Outlook

14

The Good/Bad Nexus in Global Energy Governance

Thorsten Benner and Ricardo Soares de Oliveira
with Frederic Kalinke

Traditionally, global energy governance has been a value-blind enterprise dominated by crude realpolitik concerns. For energy-importing governments in the industrialized world only two variables mattered: the price and the security of supply of the lifelines of industrial civilization, especially oil. Likewise, oil-exporting countries (which are mainly in the developing world) put a premium on price as well as continuous and long-term rent generation through exports. International energy companies were powerful intermediaries; they cared about maximizing access to hydrocarbons and about their own profits. International financial institutions, both private banks and public institutions such as the World Bank, cared solely about a project's narrow economic viability when making investment decisions on the huge capital needs of oil extraction ventures. The broader political, environmental, and development impact on oil-rich countries was not a concern.

In short, with profits and geopolitics being the main guiding concerns, the key actors and institutions in global energy governance were value blind with regard to the broader societal implications of the hydrocarbons business. *Good* and *bad* mattered only as far as the basic honoring of contracts was concerned. For example,

The authors would like to thank Björn Conrad, Alexandra Gillies, Max Hummel, Nicholas Shaxson, and Jan Martin Witte for valuable comments on drafts of this chapter.

during the cold war the major consuming nations were certainly worried about the danger that the assets of Western multinationals might be nationalized.

This situation has changed dramatically over the past ten years due to the rise of good governance as a concern in global energy matters. In their 2007 Heiligendamm summit statement, the G-8 countries affirmed:

It is in our common global interest that resource wealth be used responsibly so as to help reduce poverty, prevent conflicts and improve the sustainability of resource production and supply. We firmly agree that significant and lasting progress in this area can only be achieved on the basis of transparency and good governance. Against this background, we support increased transparency with regard both to the extractive sector and the subsequent trade and financial flows.[1]

To put these words into action and "foster transparency with regard to resource-induced payment flows" in practice, the G-8 vowed to "support good governance and anti-corruption initiatives, such as the Extractive Industries Transparency Initiative (EITI)."[2] This was a dramatic shift: within just a decade, good governance and transparency, rhetorically at least, made its way to the top of the global energy governance agenda. The G-8 took to supporting institutional answers such as the EITI. What explains the rise of the good governance agenda? What is the record in terms of implementing reform initiatives promoting the good in global energy governance? What are the prospects for the good governance agenda?

This chapter tackles these questions in three steps. The first part analyzes the context and the drivers of the rise of good governance. The second part reviews the record of good governance reform initiatives, focusing on voluntary transparency initiatives, chiefly EITI, and reviewing its performance in crucial cases (Nigeria and Azerbaijan). It also analyzes other institutional experiments, such as the Chad-Cameroon pipeline and the EITI++. The third part discusses the prospects for the role of the good in global energy governance. It argues that good governance is far from being anchored into the rules of the game of global energy governance due to the lack of political will on the part of Western political powers to mainstream the agenda into the financial system, the lack of coverage (that excludes major producers such as Saudi Arabia and Russia), and the lack of inter-

1. G-8 (2007).
2. G-8 (2007).

est on the part of such new consumers as India and China, which never subscribed to the good resource governance reform agenda in the first place.

The Rise of the Good/Bad Nexus in Energy Governance

The paradox of plenty is not exactly a recent revelation. Reviewing the experience of the rise in oil prices after the founding of OPEC in the 1970s, economists have held that "paradoxically, despite the prospects of wealth and opportunity that accompany the discovery and extraction of oil and other natural resources, such endowments all too often impede rather than further balanced and sustainable development."[3] For a long time, however, the discussion focused on the economic dimensions and origins of this phenomenon. Two economic mechanisms stand out: currency appreciation due to resource revenues and its negative effects on the competitive position of other industries (the so-called Dutch disease); and the negative effects of the fluctuation in oil prices.

The political and societal origins and dimensions of the paradox of plenty rarely came into relief.[4] Juan Pablo Pérez Alfonso, the Venezuelan oil minister who cofounded OPEC, complained as early as 1975: "I call petroleum the devil's excrement. It brings trouble. . . . Look at this *locura*—waste, corruption, consumption, our public services falling apart. And debt, debt we shall have for years."[5] However, such observations were mostly inconsequential. Certainly the pathologies associated with energy governance have a long history, and it was hard not to notice them. But under the dominant realpolitik approach they were ignored and did not factor into high politics. Here matters of hard energy security, such as security of supply and good relations with energy producers as well as the core business concerns with price and profits, were paramount.

From the mid-1990s onward, all of a sudden the perverse outcomes of oil extraction in developing countries came into the policymaker's and the broader public's spotlight. A number of developments contributed to this.

First, policy research identified bad governance as a driver behind the dismal development outcomes in resource-rich countries. Academics and policy centers (such as the World Bank) conducted further research on the links between natural resource exports and "development." Broad research showed an inverse connection between mineral resource endowment and broad-based development.

---

3. Humphreys, Sachs, and Stiglitz (2007), p. 1.
4. Karl (1997).
5. Quoted in "Oil and Development," *The Economist,* May 22, 2003, p. 78.

Indeed, research suggested that oil- and mineral-rich states in the developing world were more likely to suffer from heightened political competition, lack of provision of basic public goods, corruption, and civil war than non-resource-rich states and were also more likely to be poorer.[6]

In this context, of particular importance is the work of the Extractive Industries Review, an independent commission convened by the World Bank: the review acknowledged that the extractive industries had failed to alleviate poverty in much of the developing world and had frequently brought about disruption to the environment and local communities.[7] Often these important findings were presented under the label "resource curse." This is a crude misnomer, since the term *curse* suggests a quasi-automatic correlation between the presence of petroleum and dismal development outcomes. Furthermore, the examples of the United Kingdom and Norway, both major oil exporters, demonstrate otherwise. The U.K. and Norway did not magically or accidentally escape the spell of the resource curse. Rather, they had institutions in place and made political decisions on how to use the revenues responsibly. This shows that the resource curse is not an unavoidable fact of life, nor is it a chiefly economic phenomenon. It is mainly a "political/institutional phenomenon."[8] In other words, it is a question of governance, a realization that has taken a while to sink in among policymakers and the public.

A related observation is that the dismal development outcomes are due to a linkage between international and domestic factors (both of which make up global energy governance arrangements). This means that the global "institutions shaped by multinational oil companies, their host governments, and foreign lenders" *and* the elites and institutions powering the producer states and the public and private oil companies of producers are jointly responsible for the perverse development outcomes. This nexus continued to be "an inconvenient reality that is often not addressed."[9] Once the resource curse was reframed in terms of a political-institutional challenge—of moving from bad to good governance—remedies were easier to identify.

Second, the diagnosis of bad resource governance ties in with the broader good governance agenda, which put institutions at the heart of development efforts after the disappointment with narrow Washington consensus policies: "Public sector institutions are the black holes of economic reforms. In most countries they absorb

---

6. Collier and Hoeffler (2004); Ross (2001).
7. The six-volume review is available at www.eireview.org (June 2009).
8. Karl (2007), p. 257.
9. Karl (2007), p. 257.

efforts and investment that yield obscenely low returns to society, distort labor markets, reduce countries' overall productivity, impair international competitiveness, and easily fall prey to vested interests."[10] Western donors and international financial institutions came to appreciate a link between good governance and economic development.[11] This led them to conclude that global governance arrangements and outside actors needed to concern themselves with changing domestic governance practices and arrangements. This is in line with the overall concern with behind-the-border issues that Western powers pushed in the context of recasting sovereignty in terms of responsibility.

Third, and related, corruption emerged as a key concern on the global agenda, chiefly a result of pressure by organizations such as Transparency International. Corruption had been ignored until the 1990s. Until that time, the U.S. Foreign Corrupt Practices Act of 1977 had been the only law effectively criminalizing bribes abroad: in fact, bribes had been tax deductible in many European countries, which arguably promoted such behavior by home firms in global markets.[12] This started to change with the adoption by the OECD's thirty member states of the 1997 Convention on Combating Bribery of Foreign Public Officials, which was followed by the Inter-American Convention against Corruption (1996) and the UN Convention against Corruption (2004). The fact that James Wolfensohn helped to lift the taboo around discussions of corruption at international financial institutions also facilitated discussions of such matters in the energy arena.[13] Subsequent policy suggestions varied from the voluntary and faintly reformist to the radical call for tough regulation of financial flows, but everywhere business practices across the developing world (and in the energy sector in particular) were under scrutiny. Similar policy shifts happened with regard to human rights and sustainability, which also posed profound challenges to the practices of resource extraction in developing countries, practices that traditionally disregard human rights and environmental concerns.

Fourth, the behavior of transnational corporations in developing countries reemerged as a key concern in the globalization debate from the mid-1990s onward.[14] Many in the public see transnational corporations, and oil companies in particular, as economic and political heavyweights. The 200 largest corporations

10. Naím (2000), p. 99.
11. Gillies (forthcoming).
12. Eigen (2007).
13. Mallaby (2004).
14. Benner and Witte (2006).

account for a quarter of the world's gross domestic product. Many of them—especially oil companies—were seen as engaging in reckless behavior in developing countries, leading to calls for rules for global players, calls that multinational corporations themselves could not ignore. Particularly venal acts such as the execution of Nigerian activist Ken Saro-Wiwa in 1995 put the public spotlight on the dismal conditions in the Niger Delta and forced Royal Dutch/Shell to confront its own role and involvement. This made it increasingly clear that the traditional "the business of business is business" approach was no longer tenable for brand-sensitive Western-based multinational corporations.

Savvy norm entrepreneurs in civil society (in organizations such as Global Witness, Transparency International, Catholic Relief Services, and the Open Society Institute) and a number of progressive government officials (mainly in countries such as Norway and the United Kingdom) took advantage of these four trends and framed the debate on good resource governance around the norm of transparency.[15] Transparency emerged as the chief remedy for bad energy governance; two such initiatives were Publish What You Pay and Extractive Industries Transparency. The diagnosis was simple: "Opacity is the glue holding together the patterns of revenue extraction and distribution that characterize petro-states as well as the entire international petroleum sector. Companies do not publish what they pay to states, and states do not disclose what they earn and spend."[16] As a consequence, "huge amounts of money are virtually untraceable and not subject to any oversight." Transparency was the necessary and logical antidote.

A recent report by Transparency International sums up the core assumptions of transparency activists:

> Transparent resource governance is a vital ingredient to transform this resource curse into a blessing. To do this, companies and governments need to provide more and better quality information on the scale of revenues derived from the extractive industries and on how these revenues flow from producers to governments. If accompanied by greater civil society oversight, this improved revenue transparency can make decision-makers more accountable for their actions. With better information on natural resource wealth, citizens can pressure governments to use these revenues for social and infrastructure programs that can boost economic growth and reduce poverty. Transparent resource governance is therefore a shared responsibility.[17]

15. Gillies (forthcoming).
16. Karl (2007).
17. Transparency International (2008).

Another observer notes that the "most promising initiatives so far are those that seek to put in the hands of citizens more information about how much revenue their governments receive and how they spend it, so they can demand accountability."[18] Former U.K. prime minister Tony Blair explained why he regards transparency as a win-win for all parties:

> Increased transparency will also help to create the right climate for attracting foreign investment, and encourage an enterprise culture. Governments need to create this favorable environment, but companies have an interest in promoting transparency too. Transparency should help companies to reduce reputational risk, to address the concerns of shareholders and to help manage risks of long-term investments. And transparency is a positive contribution to development as it increases the likelihood that revenues will be used for poverty reduction.[19]

These arguments in regard to lack of transparency in financial transactions between resource-rich states and Western corporations fell on fertile ground. A receptive media and public opinion in the West quickly accepted that this particular aspect of North-South relations played a key role in causing the dismal development outcomes in resource-rich developing countries. That said, transparency around oil and gas extraction never gained the same urgency as the debate on diamonds fueling conflicts in places such as Sierra Leone and Angola. The campaign against "blood diamonds" captured the Western public's imagination and led to swift action in the Kimberley Process Certification Scheme. No major nongovernmental organization has even tried to launch a campaign on "blood oil" or "blood gas." Unlike with diamonds, the ultimate luxury goods, average Western citizens are implicated daily in the oil and gas business when filling up their cars or turning on the heat in their apartments.[20]

Still it is a remarkable development that the reformist transparency and good governance agenda that originated in small activist constituencies were elevated to the level of high politics in global energy governance. The recognition of the importance of transparency by the G-8 (which at least until recently fashioned itself as the world's most exclusive and powerful club) is proof of this. Equally important, belatedly policymakers in the United States, where the government was a bystander at best during the Bush presidency, have also translated the good

18. Marina Ottaway, "Tyranny's Full Tank," *New York Times*, March 31, 2005.
19. Blair (2003).
20. Ross (2008).

resource governance progressive agenda into the language of foreign policy realists. This includes reframing bad resource governance as a threat to U.S. security, economic, and foreign policy interests. U.S. Senator Richard G. Lugar, a Republican, for example noted in 2008 that the so-called resource curse "exacerbates global poverty which can be a seedbed for terrorism, it dulls the effect of our foreign assistance, it empowers autocrats and dictators, and it can crimp world petroleum supplies by breeding instability."[21]

While the rhetorical rise of the good resource governance agenda is remarkable, it is important to appreciate the conditions that enabled the rise of the reform agenda: a unique window of opportunity of unquestioned Western dominance in world affairs and energy markets, lasting from 1990 until roughly 2005, set the normative tone (if not the substance) of the post–cold war international system. The rise of China and India, the arguably diminished status of the West, and the rise of plurality of global power centers mean that this window for normative tone setting may have now closed. Before we explore how this has come to pass it is important to disaggregate claims of the wholesale and all-encompassing normative shift and note the holes in the subscription to the agenda even when it seemed to have traction.

First, even among the committed drivers of the agenda—the United Kingdom, Norway, and Germany—not all parts of the government signed on to promote it. In Germany, for example, it was mainly the development cooperation ministry pushing the agenda, while the economics ministry continued its disregard of good governance concerns. The United Kingdom remained uncooperative about stolen funds from oil-rich countries that found a haven in the City of London banks.[22]

Second, the progressive reform rhetoric, even at its height, always contained a strong realist element: it figured prominently in Western engagements with failed, weak, or new states but not, for instance, with Russia, Venezuela, or Saudi Arabia. It is astonishing that this discourse played next to no role in the last decade when dealing with the major oil and gas producers, several of which also exhibit the pathologies of corruption and environmental destruction. Needless to say, many of the traditional oil producers (OPEC and Russia) never showed any interest in the reform agenda.

Third, from the start the progressive agenda of putting the "good" at the heart of global energy governance had little traction with some of the most important new players in the energy game, namely the new importers in Asia

21. Lugar (2008).
22. Peel (2009).

such as China and India and their national oil companies.[23] Their understanding of energy remained firmly realpolitik and showed little patience with the reformist agenda.

Reform Drives: Their Shape and Record

The initial reluctance to embrace the reformist agenda applied to Western oil corporations as well. Despite varying degrees of commitment to reform, ranging from BP's and Statoil's seeming enthusiasm to ExxonMobil's and Chevron's reluctance, Western corporations engaged in reformist bids from an essentially defensive position. The reform agenda originated outside these companies and was very much against their decades' long practices.[24] Oil firms understood that some form of commitment to the new trend had to be made if a popular backlash in Western countries was to be avoided. On the other hand, these companies had not been that negatively affected by the business practices that characterized energy-rich states. They were fearful that the pursuit of reform (especially if it meant overriding domestic secrecy laws that protected oil contracts) might damage carefully cultivated relationships with incumbents or benefit less brand-conscious companies not facing the same pressures.

That being said, the fact that key Western players, with emphasis on the governments of G-7 states, adopted a commitment to transparency however defined would make this an unavoidable dimension of global governance discussions in the coming decade. This resulted in the rhetorical acceptance of transparency, and engagement with transparency initiatives, by actors that were not fully on board but could ill afford to opt out of the new reformist lexicon. In short, a concern that had barely registered outside small constituencies was now seemingly accepted by everyone in the West. Even the governments of energy-rich states that were blatantly uncommitted to the spirit of the reform effort felt that they should pay lip service to this reform drive.

23. Chen (2007). India's policy change toward Burma is particularly interesting. Before 1993 Indian national oil companies did not prospect Burmese natural gas due to India's normative opposition to the military junta. However, in 1993 the Indian government dramatically changed its policy by declaring Burmese political development to be a domestic matter that should be resolved internally. Thereafter Indian companies began natural gas exploration and production.

24. Soares de Oliveira (2007).

Transparency: Voluntary and Regulatory Approaches

Unsurprisingly, this new centrality of transparency gave birth to a number of high-profile multistakeholder initiatives. One of the earliest came from the private sector in the form of a discourse on corporate social responsibility (CSR). This appeared as an endeavor by companies to both deflect criticisms on the environmental and social impact of their activities and prevent the creation of putative transnational regulatory frameworks to tackle them. Many observers portray CSR—which today is an industry employing thousands and producing social audits and community relations advice—as primarily a public relations exercise.[25] The noteworthy innovation of CSR lies in the fact that companies for the first time admitted as their responsibility tasks and consequences that were formerly seen as beyond their purview.

Most high-profile companies have since adopted nonbinding good behavior codes. Home states have taken to the CSR concept with equal enthusiasm, as have international governmental organizations.[26] In particular, the UN has formed the Global Compact, a voluntary forum of more than 7,000 member companies. The Global Compact publicizes good performance in the hope of creating benchmarks for industry best practices.[27]

The key initiative in the transparency arena over the past decade is the EITI, a policy framework launched by Prime Minister Tony Blair in 2002 and subsequently developed by a series of conferences. EITI aims to improve the management of public revenues in resource-rich countries of the developing world through the voluntary disclosure by companies and states of payments resulting from the sale of both solid minerals and hydrocarbons.[28] According to its website, EITI membership is now composed of investors, civil society groups, extractive industries, implementing governments, and supporting governments. The EITI is currently directed by a board supported by an international secretariat based in Oslo. The initiative is financed by a multidonor trust fund run by the World Bank. As of 2008 there were twenty-three EITI candidate countries (about half of the world's natural resource exporters) at different levels of reform implementation: these are Azerbaijan, Côte d'Ivoire, Cameroon, Democratic Republic of

25. Blowfield and Frynas (2005); Christian Aid (2004).
26. For the British government's CSR activities, see www.berr.gov.uk/whatwedo/sectors/sustainability/corp-responsibility/page45192.html/ (February 2009).
27. For the activities of the Global Compact, see www.unglobalcompact.org (February 2009).
28. For more information on the initiative, see www.eitransparency.org (January 2009).

the Congo, Equatorial Guinea, Gabon, Ghana, Guinea, Kazakhstan, Kyrgyzstan, Liberia, Madagascar, Mali, Mauritania, Mongolia, Niger, Nigeria, Peru, Congo-Brazzaville, São Tomé and Príncipe, Sierra Leone, Timor-Leste, and Vietnam.

The other high-profile initiative, Publish What You Pay, was also launched in 2002. It was the culmination of a number of civil society activities, especially by Global Witness.[29] Global Witness had been active since the mid-1990s in investigating the links between conflict and the exploitation of natural resources. One of its reports on the Angolan civil war and the involvement of foreign business actors, published in 1999, triggered the formation of an NGO alliance. The alliance eventually included more than 300 organizations. The support of George Soros for the PWYP campaign would prove instrumental. While sharing the same normative agenda and goals as EITI, PWYP pushed for mandatory, as opposed to voluntary, disclosure of revenue payments by companies to the governments of resource-rich countries. Ideally this should be achieved by way of revenue disclosure laws in both host and home states. But the crucial pressure point is the home governments of stock markets: PWYP aims to have regulators such as the Securities and Exchange Commission force oil companies to divulge payments made to foreign governments.

PWYP has been an agenda setter, and some of its ideas have been picked up by important players, as shown by ongoing discussions in the U.S. Congress on the Extractive Industries Transparency Disclosure Act. Moreover, even if EITI provided those skeptical of a regulatory approach with a safer initiative, EITI's and PWYP's agendas share two basic assumptions. The first is that transparency creates a deterrence logic that will discourage decisionmakers of energy-rich states from stealing from the national coffers. The second is that, once provided with real information about revenues, the civil societies of resource-rich states will demand more accountable governance.[30]

This said, the trend over the past decade has been a consistent preference for voluntary over regulatory solutions. Companies make philanthropic commitments to affected communities or issue vaguely worded codes of conduct. Energy exporters sign on to schemes like the EITI, which are hard to enforce in the best of times. Norway's several capacity-building initiatives are a case in point. In this

29. For more information on the campaign, see www.pwyp.org (January 2009).
30. Cross-fertilization among the several groups is exemplified by the fact that Transparency International is one of the founders of PWYP; that Peter Eigen, TI founder, is the chairperson of the EITI board; and that Global Witness, with a record of collaborative work with EITI, is a key force in PWYP.

context, the experience of EITI deserves a detailed discussion, especially in the so-called pilot countries, Nigeria and Azerbaijan.

NIGERIA

Nigeria is one of the world's leading oil producers, but the resulting wealth has not served the country's development: despite more than US$400 billion in oil earnings since 1970, Nigeria's income per capita is still 25 percent lower than the African average, and some of the country's human indicators are lower than at independence in 1960.[31] The poor management of Nigeria's extractive industries, the almost unparalleled degree of oil sector corruption, and the Niger Delta oil-related conflict are the defining issues in Nigerian politics.[32]

Nigeria was not the obvious country to spearhead the EITI drive, but it did so in 2004 under the initiative of President Olusegun Obasanjo, known as a major supporter of Transparency International. Although some anticorruption measures were sketched during Obasanjo's first term in office (1999–2003), a concerted effort in this area was not undertaken until after his election for a second term in April 2003.[33] One of its high-profile programs is the Nigerian Extractive Industries Transparency Initiative (NEITI), described as "an attempt to throw light at the policies and practices of the Nigerian Extractive Industry."[34]

NEITI was launched in February 2004 with the goal of "following due process and achieving transparency in payments" made by foreign companies "to government and government linked entities and in the revenues received and reported by those governments and agencies."[35] The U.K.'s Department for International Development, the World Bank through its EITI trust fund, and the EITI international secretariat based in Oslo jointly supported the process. The tasks of NEITI include reconciling amounts of crude lifted with amounts paid; raising public awareness of NEITI; and publishing audits, reports, and statistics. The National Stakeholders Working Group (NSWG) has been described as a platform for the implementation of NEITI.[36] To address the great capacity deficiencies identified

---

31. Richard Murphy and Nicholas Shaxson, "African Graft Is a Global Responsibility," *Financial Times,* June 1, 2007; Peel (2009).

32. Watts (2008).

33. The first three years of the second Obasanjo administration saw a number of high-profile officials enacting reforms in macroeconomic management (including debt repayment), the banking sector, financial crimes prosecution, oil sector governance, and counterfeit drugs.

34. NEITI Secretariat (2005).

35. NEITI Secretariat (2005).

36. This NSWG was dissolved in 2007 and a new one appointed the following year. Its activities remain limited.

in government agencies responsible for oversight of the extractive industries, the NSWG set up a focal team to put together training programs, secondments of expertise, and support for "selected government agencies and civil society."[37]

The biggest achievement of NEITI was without doubt its audit of the five-year operational period (1999–2004), which unearthed several discrepancies and deficiencies in the physical and financial records of oil sector entities, including oil company payments to the Nigerian state.[38] This was unprecedented. However, Obasanjo's brief engagement with reform ended in 2006, as the president wasted much political capital seeking to change the constitution to allow himself a third term and allowing public spending to increase ahead of elections. Some skeptics argued that the reform language was being deployed, in the time-honored Nigerian way, to pursue the enemies of the president.[39] Despite the 2007 NEITI act, which enshrines the initiative in Nigerian law, this trend became undeniable, as presidential allies remained unscathed by law enforcement agencies and Obasanjo-related questionable behavior (for example, regarding oil rounds) emerged.

Most important, the major claim common to all of the transparency initiatives— that civil society would use the information made newly available to enact political change and reform in the direction of greater accountability—failed to materialize for NEITI. Unlike countries (such as Equatorial Guinea) whose public sphere is tightly controlled, lack of political space is not a factor in Nigeria. On the other hand, the fragmentation of civil society and its vulnerability to inducements or pressure from the elites, together with the technical complexity of audits that can only be deciphered by specialists, may provide an explanation.[40] As Nicholas Shaxson writes, "The changes that have happened have all depended on the political context in which they have been embedded."[41] NEITI was not so much driving reform as being enabled by an overarching reformist moment, which proved temporary. When that evaporated, so did the political priority

---

37. NEITI Secretariat (2005). Government representation was very significant (50 percent of the NSWG, or fourteen members). Other stakeholders represented in the NSWG included the media, indigenous and multinational companies, the organized private sector, state and regional Houses of Assembly, and the National Assembly (two members, one from the Senate and the other from the House of Representatives). Civil society organizations had only two representatives.

38. This paragraph owes considerably to an analysis provided by Nicholas Shaxson, associate fellow at Chatham House, who is currently writing a major report on NEITI implementation.

39. Michael Peel, "Britain and Nigeria's Half-Hearted War against Corruption," *Financial Times,* October 17, 2005.

40. Ricardo Soares de Oliveira, interviews with author, Abuja, March 2006. Additional interviews in Angola (January 2004) and Congo-Brazzaville (October 2005) point toward a lack of understanding and political inoperability of oil sector audits.

41. Shaxson (2008).

accorded to NEITI, and the record since 2006 is essentially that of paralysis. Meanwhile, the resource-linked problems besetting Nigeria have not obviously been mitigated by reformist zeal.

AZERBAIJAN

Azerbaijan, a family-run, authoritarian, petrostate in the Caucasus, was the second unlikely early implementer of EITI. After a decline in the late Soviet years, investor interest in the 1990s led to a major oil boom under the leadership of the former KGB strongman Heydar Aliyev and, since 2005, his son Ilham. Rising oil prices throughout the last five years further contributed to substantial GDP growth rates (34.5 percent in 2006 and 23.4 percent in 2007). Despite this wealth, large segments of Azerbaijan's population are poor (24 percent are below the poverty line). Hydrocarbons represent more than 90 percent of government revenues, and non-oil-sector economic activity, other than closely associated sectors such as construction, is negligible.

In November 2004 a memorandum of understanding was signed between the government, foreign and local oil companies, and local NGOs with a view to increasing transparency through the implementation of EITI. Azerbaijan has been successful in gaining company support, as all twenty-six oil and gas companies active in the country joined EITI (although NGOs complain that many corporations have not yet disclosed the data they committed to publishing). In February 2008 Azerbaijan's government proposed a UN General Assembly resolution in support of EITI. Five months later, Azerbaijan became the only country to publish the eight EITI reports and to launch validation, thus achieving EITI compliant country status.

Throughout this process, space for civil society increased, and reactions by normally critical voices have been positive. "This is a significant milestone and shows that the EITI standard is achievable," said Ingilab Ahmadov, director of the Public Finance Monitoring Centre in Azerbaijan. "We also welcome the establishment of a permanent Multi-Stakeholder Group in Azerbaijan, which we have sorely lacked in the past. This is a positive achievement that has been the direct result of the validation process, and we expect to see a stronger and more robust multi-stakeholder process take root over the next few months."[42] Azerbaijan's engagement with reform seems serious and sustained, but what does that mean in terms of concrete reforms?

42. Publish What You Pay International (2009).

The goal of President Aliyev's engagement with EITI is better portrayed as an attempt to shore up the status quo and win the regime a degree of external respectability, especially in the context of a closer relationship with the West.[43] Examples of this effort abound, such as the country's hosting of the Transparency International 2007 meeting. Yet throughout the period of EITI implementation, the political situation has remained problematic, with fraudulent elections, high-level corruption, the assassination of prominent journalists, and persecution and torture of political opponents.[44] According to a 2007 Council of Europe report, "The number of political prisoners is not as high as it was some years ago. That is of course a positive development, but we should not confuse such small positive steps with the very problem of political prisoners."[45]

This shows that meeting EITI expectations is not a particularly difficult balancing act for Azerbaijan, because EITI, even when properly implemented, does not pose a challenge to the president's grip on the country or to the oil sector's practice of business as usual. Many of the routes normally deployed to satisfy key internal constituencies (either distribution of contracts or management of revenues) are unaffected by the EITI brand of transparency. If reform did constitute a threat to vested interests and political control over Azerbaijan, it would not have been pursued in the first place. Of course, EITI advocates are the first to say that EITI is not an attempt at systemic change (in the sense of regime transformation, for instance). But since the problems that beset oil-rich but badly governed states are emphatically of a systemic nature, the example of Azerbaijan and its adherence to the letter (if not the spirit) of reform illustrates the circumscribed limits and dubious efficacy of even a successful EITI process. A typical example of this is the March 2009 referendum that changed the constitution to permit Aliyev an unlimited number of presidential terms. To single out a minor EITI technocratic success amid such a degree of regime consolidation is a singular act of myopia.

The published data in Azerbaijan (as in Nigeria) have been certified as valid and often provide an exceptional degree of detail on minute segments of the oil economy. However, these data, especially when made available in raw format, are virtually unreadable by nonexperts, including members of the press who are financially literate. Even when the data are deciphered, it is difficult to get an overall image of the sector from them or to derive politically relevant information that

43. Sergie Markedonov, "Azerbaijan: From Bad to Worse," *openDemocracy*, March 30, 2009.

44. Sabrina Tavernise, "With a Collective Shrug, Azerbaijan Votes for Its Leader," *New York Times*, October 15, 2008; Human Rights Watch (2004).

45. See http://assembly.coe.int/Main.asp?link=/Documents/Records/2007/E/0704161500E.htm.

can be easily interpreted by the general public. More important, the limits to political action in authoritarian states mean it is difficult to act on this information, even when clear malfeasance is identified, as illustrated by the experience of NGOs, journalists, and the opposition in Baku.

CORRECTING THE GAPS IN THE VOLUNTARY APPROACH: EITI++

As Graham Baxter, BP's first representative on the EITI board, pointed out in 2009, it is "easy to be critical about the slow rate of progress which has been achieved in the seven years since the initiative was launched. . . . As a result, the endorsed ambition that EITI should become 'mainstreamed' common practice, and thus cease to be necessary as a voluntary initiative, seems as far away today as it did when the vision was first established."[46] This slow progress of EITI has garnered it considerable criticism. Five issues have been brought forward.

First, the choice of multistakeholder group efforts tends to water down the reform thrust of EITI, as would-be targets for reform come to decidedly affect the timing and terms of the reform process.[47] A second criticism is that the technical complexity of EITI means that it is not always clear that a member is infringing its rules. This problem is worsened by the "neither consistent nor comprehensive" manner in which organizations nominally supporting EITI, such as the World Bank and the IMF, have gone about promoting transparency.[48] Third, even when it is clear that there is malpractice, the lack of sanctions render EITI toothless in the face of free riding.[49] Fourth, EITI's debatable premise that corruption is resented by the private sector and that transparency would motivate investors is not borne out by reality: mineral sector investors have never shied away from involvement in some of the world's most corrupt countries because of the geological imperative of going where resources exist. Finally, the idea that EITI would empower civil society has had unclear results: EITI has not prevented NGO

46. Graham Baxter, "The EITI Story So Far: A Personal Reflection" (www.eitransparency. org/node/692).
47. This said, the most common experience among major oil companies has been nonparticipation in EITI rather than lukewarm engagement aiming at the cooptation of critics. According to a Transparency International survey of forty-two oil firms, only seventeen had signed up. TI also found that disclosures by signatories were not higher than those by non-EITI members and, therefore, that an "EITI effect" had failed to spread. Transparency International (2008).
48. Bank Information Center and Global Witness (2008).
49. Despite rumors that countries such as Equatorial Guinea, the DRC, and Congo-Brazzaville might be ejected from EITI for not fulfilling basic membership criteria, this has not happened thus far. See for example Hugh Williamson, "Poor Governance Can Boot a Country out of the Industry," *Financial Times,* January 28, 2008.

activists in Congo-Brazzaville and Gabon, for instance, from being arrested, mistreated, or even killed, and incumbents have been able to tame the role of civil society either by not giving it a sufficient role in implementation or by colonizing civil society through the creation of fake, government-supported NGOs that then become pliable partners in corruption.

From 2006 onward a generally revamped effort and an activist EITI board have sought to address some of these criticisms. This has culminated in the World Bank's launching of EITI++, a new initiative designed to encompass not just payments but the whole value chain in the extraction of mineral resources.[50] The initiative is designed to provide technical assistance to resource-rich countries across all dimensions of the extractive industries. Its immediate focus, however, is on the granting of concessions and the negotiation of contracts notorious for corruption as well as "information asymmetries" between governments and foreign corporations. These contracts sometimes result in poor outcomes for resource-rich states. The two states that have sought EITI++ assistance, Guinea and Mauritania, both have had coups in the past year, and their medium-term politics remains unclear. EITI++ seems better tailored to address some of the most significant shortcomings of EITI and provide a more ambitious approach to the governance problems associated with resource wealth. This said, it remains unclear whether reform can ever be meaningful (least of all by a risk-averse agency like the World Bank Group) in instances when empowered domestic actors in resource-rich states are determined to pervert reform or severely circumscribe its impact.

Beyond the Transparency Agenda

While matters of transparency remained central to the reformist agenda, other initiatives also played an important role during the window of opportunity described earlier. Few advocates of the transparency agenda would claim that it was the silver bullet for underdevelopment in resource-rich countries, but others criticized their assumption about direct linkages between transparency and good governance. In many of the countries where resource wealth had not borne the expected fruits, the idea that the population, once armed with the knowledge that there is malfeasance at the top of government, would somehow change the status quo was unrealistic.[51] The additional initiatives were therefore premised on the understanding that other dimensions were equally important in explaining

---

50. "International: EITI ++ Targets Resource Management," *Oxford Analytica*, July 2, 2008.
51. Hilson and Maconachie (2009).

poor governance outcomes, most notably the manner in which revenues that did materialize in the central banks of energy-rich states ended up being managed.

Some of these initiatives were phrased in the language of technocratic innovation and macroeconomic reform that assumed the neutrality of the local state and the good faith of local decisionmakers. These efforts saw lack of capacity as a major reason for negative outcomes. This is the case with some of the World Bank's research and policy prescriptions, which focused on stabilization, future generations funds, the management of Dutch disease, and development commissions. In other instances, however, and even while preserving the language of partnership with energy-rich governments, prescriptions were more adversarial and assumed that the leeway of oil-rich governments needed to be curtailed. The argument was that, to bring about the desired developmental outcomes, important aspects of public policy, especially at the level of oil revenue management, should be supervised by the international community. Chad, one of the world's poorest, most unstable, and worst-governed states, was the setting for the first major instance of this latter approach.

THE CHAD-CAMEROON EXPERIMENT

The project was reminiscent of nineteenth-century attempts at controlling the public finances of bankrupted states such as Greece, Egypt, and the Ottoman Empire and was appropriately dubbed an instance of shared sovereignty by the political scientist Stephen Krasner.[52] Because Chad is landlocked, the only way to bring its oil onto the world market was the construction of a long pipeline connecting oil fields to Cameroon's Atlantic coast. After years of reluctance on account of the country's security situation, a consortium headed by ExxonMobil finally got the crucial support of the World Bank in 2000 for the building of a US$4.2 billion, 1,078-kilometer oil pipeline.

In exchange for the financing and political support for building the project, the Chadian government had to sign on to a number of apparently constraining agreements, especially in terms of directing revenues to social and economic infrastructure.[53] The Law of Petroleum Revenue Management (the so-called Law 001), adopted in 1999 as a precondition for World Bank involvement, included scrutinized offshore escrow accounts holding direct revenues, a Future Generations fund, and the earmarking of most direct revenues for priority sectors. Law 001 left

52. Krasner (2004).
53. World Bank (2000). For a briefing on the project, see Guyer (2002).

only 5 percent of revenues for the government to spend at its discretion.[54] The nine-member Revenue Oversight Committee (the Collège de Contrôle), with four civil society representatives, was created to oversee the use of the oil set-aside for priority sectors.[55] The International Advisory Group, a five-expert team appointed by the World Bank in February 2001, monitored the project through periodic trips to the region. In addition, the External Compliance Monitoring Group, under a contract with the International Finance Corporation, specifically monitored the consortium's compliance with the environment management plan.

The arrangement was premised on restraining the Chadian elite's free use of oil revenues.[56] Chad's president, Idriss Déby, was therefore not enthusiastic about the agreement, but in spite of countless mishaps along the way, including fraudulent elections in 2001 and the use of a signature bonus to buy weaponry, he played along with it while the pipeline was being built. Once it was up and running, Déby reneged on important sections of the agreement. Faced with a mounting insurgent challenge from the east (partly a Darfur conflict spillover but decidedly fueled by Déby's own oil-hungry clansmen), the president concocted a solution that to his mind would bring in the additional resources needed to shore up the regime and fight the rebels. Law 001 was to be modified and the pesky foreign intrusion done away with.

The rubber-stamp parliament obliged him in December 2005, despite vociferous opposition by Western donors and the World Bank. The modified law was a shadow of its predecessor.[57] The Future Generations Fund was scrapped and the US$36 million in it gobbled up; defense and administration were added to the priority sectors' list, whose share of revenues fell from 80 percent to 65 percent; and the national budget received 30 percent, as opposed to 5 percent, of revenues. The World Bank, under its new president, Paul Wolfowitz, reacted with rare outrage by freezing an estimated US$124 million in loans to Chad as well as all oil payments to the government.

---

54. The rest is earmarked as follows: 80 percent for social spending in priority areas (education, rural development, health, infrastructure, and environmental resources), 10 percent for the future generations fund, and 5 percent to the oil-producing region.

55. Gary and Reisch (2005).

56. Kojucharov (2007).

57. Chip Cummins, "Exxon Oil-Fund Model Unravels in Chad; Government Breaches Deal Requiring It to Spend Royalties on Development," *Wall Street Journal*, February 28, 2006; Lydia Polgreen, "Chad Backs out of Pledge to Use Oil Wealth to Reduce Poverty," *New York Times*, December 13, 2006.

The stalemate continued into April 2006, with President Déby threatening the consortium with a pipeline shutdown if it did not hand over an estimated US$100 million in oil revenues.[58] Chadian officials claimed to be making alternative oil deals with others, such as China.[59] By then there were indications that Western critics were ready to flinch. The ensuing compromise accepted most Chadian demands. The Future Generations Fund was eliminated and its US$36 million kept by the government. Chad revised its 2006 budget, and the World Bank recommenced its loans and released the oil revenues it held. But this April 2006 agreement was only valid until 2007, when the whole deal was again up for grabs, and subsequent developments pointed to continuing unpredictability: claiming the nonpayment of taxes, President Déby went after Petronas and Chevron with threats of eviction.[60] Finally, after two more years of acrimonious relations with the World Bank, the agreement that had been announced with great fanfare in 2000 was quietly dropped in 2008.[61] Throughout, the World Bank scheme or the post-2003 availability of oil revenues made no dent in Chad's poverty level and abysmal human indicators.

In retrospect, the project was doomed to fail. To start with, Chad was an unlikely location to pioneer such an ambitious scheme. The absence of a strong reformist constituency and the character of the Chadian elite precluded local ownership of the reforms. In the absence of this, the work of international bureaucrats alone could never achieve meaningful results. This applies to civil society as well. Despite the courageous work of a few individuals and the illusion of partial empowerment in the heyday of the project, Chadian civil society was too weak, divided, and vulnerable to government repression to be a transformative agent in Chadian politics.

OTHER INITIATIVES: DEVELOPING TEETH?

After close to a decade of attempts at tackling the governance implications of energy resources and five years pursuing variants of the transparency agenda, there

58. Chad's oil minister, Mahmat Hassan, warned that "either the World Bank unblocks the offshore account and the frozen revenues enter into that account, controlled by Chad, or the oil companies make direct payments." Daniel Flynn, "Chad Confident of World Bank Deal by End of April," Reuters, April 18, 2006. See also Stephanie Hancock, "Chad Threatens to Halt Oil Output," BBC News, April 20, 2006.

59. David White, "The 'Resource Curse' Anew: Why a Grand World Bank Oil Project Has Fast Run into the Sand," Financial Times, January 23, 2006.

60. "Chad Tells 2 Oil Firms to Pack Up," International Herald Tribune, August 27, 2006.

61. "Breaking the Bank: A Vaunted Development Project Goes Awry," The Economist, September 25, 2008.

are scarcely any overt challenges at all to the normative claims made in favor of abolishing the status quo ante. Below this apparent convergence of views—with stakeholders from all corners of the energy nexus rhetorically committed to some sort of improvement—there is a degree of fragmentation. By far the most important trend is for a quiet return to the tenets of old (which were never really abandoned), now justified by the rise of non-image-conscious Asian companies and the rise in oil prices from 2003 onward. On the other hand, the poor or insufficient results of reform lite, such as EITI, have led some unexpected constituencies to revisit hard regulation as a more appropriate form for tackling these matters.

Perhaps the most tangible recent initiative is that pursued in the U.S. Congress, where an Extractive Industries Transparency Disclosure Act (H.R. 6066) was introduced in July 2008.[62] The bill calls for the disclosure of payments by energy companies to foreign governments for the extraction of natural resources. This information is to be made publicly available. The bill uses the language of shareholder rights, stating that shareholders need to access this sort of information to determine the associated risks of investment in energy-rich countries. The process to achieve this, however, is straight out of the PWYP campaign, with Global Witness enthusiastically describing it as a "low cost but high impact" rule change.[63] The key regulator is to be the SEC, which if the bill ever becomes law will see section 13 of the Securities Exchange Act of 1934 amended by adding a new subsection:

> Each issuer required to file an annual report with the Commission shall disclose in such a report the total amounts, for each foreign country and for each category of payment for each foreign country, of any and all payments made, directly or indirectly, by the issuer or any of its subsidiaries, to an agency or instrumentality of a foreign government a) for natural resources in a foreign country; or b) in any connection with the extraction of natural resources from a foreign country.

H.R. 6066 did not become law during the 110th Congress (2006–08), but was reintroduced as the Energy Security through Transparency Act of 2009 on September 23, 2009, by a bipartisan coalition of prominent senators. Whether it will be adopted by Congress in the current session will be an important litmus

---

62. See www.house.gov/apps/list/press/financialsvcs_dem/frank_144_xml.pdf (December 2008).
63. See www.globalwitness.org/data/files/pages/myths_and_facts_sheet.pdf (February 2009).

test for how serious Congress takes the lessons of the global financial crisis and the weak record of nonmandatory approaches to regulation.

Another reform agenda that has recently gained ground is an anticorruption drive best exemplified by the research work and advocacy of the Tax Justice Network. Starting from the understanding that much of the work during the 1990s on these matters was important in pioneering anticorruption agendas, critics contend that the anticorruption orthodoxy is too fixed on country-specific realities (as exemplified by the Transparency International's *Corruption Perception Index*), thus missing the transnational nature of corruption and, most important, the end point for much of the looted revenues.[64] This is not simply a matter of probing the usual offshore tax havens, though these played a role in the international political economy of money laundering. Campaigners went further to prove that banks based in financial centers such as Paris, London, New York, and Zurich were deeply implicated in aiding political elites and multinational corporations to siphon off money toward lightly regulated Western jurisdictions.[65] Approaching the bad governance/natural resources nexus without asking these obvious questions was always going to lead to unsatisfactory and superficial reform efforts, yet these questions played only a peripheral role in efforts such as EITI.[66]

It is difficult to overstate the importance of capital flight from resource-rich states. One of the major advocates of reform of the international financial system, the former banker Raymond W. Baker, argues that the amounts of illicit money involved could be as high as US$1.5 trillion a year.[67] A significant part of this money stems from resource-rich states.

The loot-seeking elites that control parts of Africa illicitly send capital out of the region to the tune of US$20 [bn] to US$28 bn per year. Illicit money flows are hard to quantify, but this is the new estimate by Raymond Baker of the NGO Global Financial Integrity, the most careful and ingenious study to date. Capital flight of this magnitude is roughly equivalent to the entire aid inflow to the region, so closing it would generate a similar resource transfer to doubling aid.[68]

64. Shaxson (2007).
65. A high-profile case involved the previously reputable Riggs Bank and Equatorial Guinea's presidential family. See U.S. Senate Foreign Relations Committee (2008).
66. Baker, Christensen, and Shaxson (2008).
67. Baker (2005).
68. Paul Collier, "A Chance to Crack Down on Africa's Loot-Seeking Elites," *Guardian*, October 7, 2008.

Although initially perceived as destabilizing of both the business-as-usual process and the carefully domesticated "voluntary" reform process, this new anti-corruption agenda is gaining (for the time being, still limited) traction with some of the bodies it started by fiercely criticizing, such as the World Bank and Transparency International. The development economist Paul Collier subscribes to the agenda and points out that money "flows out of Africa into our banks, and into the offshore banks that depend for their existence upon being able to transact with our banks." He continues:

> US rules on banking transparency are even weaker than the European rules: vast sums looted from the public purse in Africa are being held in nominee accounts and moved around the world at greater speed than our cumbersome legal processes can track them down. Western legal systems are stacked, thanks to the hired hands of skilled lawyers, to protect the rights of the crooked over the rights of Africa's ordinary citizens.[69]

Outlook: Forward to the Past?

According to Leif Wenar, "Oil is big business; in fact, oil is the biggest business. Five of the ten largest corporations in the world are oil companies, and oil accounts for about half the value of all global commodity transactions: over one and a half trillion dollars a year."[70] Yet in most countries, the profits from oil exports are more likely to contribute to clientelism, corruption, human rights abuses, and conflict than to benefit the broad majority of citizens. This is the direct result of bad resource governance.

Over the past fifteen years the good and the bad have been established as normative terms (along with transparency) in progress toward better resource governance. This is no small feat for the activists and progressive government officials in both the developed and the developing world, who took advantage of an opening

---

69. Paul Collier, "A Chance to Crack Down on Africa's Loot-Seeking Elites," *Guardian*, October 7, 2008. Leif Wenar even goes further: "Because of a major flaw in global markets, consumers today send their money to tyrants and brutal rebels when they make their daily purchases. This article has suggested that this damaging flow of money can be stopped by enforcing property rules against the middlemen who channel consumer spending into resource-cursed countries: against the international resource corporations, and against the foreign governments that deal with the worst regimes. The citizens of affluent countries can abolish the disastrous 'might makes right' rule by using their own institutions to enforce the basic principles of legal trade." Wenar (2008).

70. Wenar (2008).

during a period of unquestioned Western dominance in global affairs. The mere fact that this norm managed to challenge the entrenched realpolitik approach, which dominated global energy governance for the past century, is a cause for celebration for all those who care about justice and development.

At the same time, the commitment to the progressive good governance agenda needs to go hand in hand with a realistic assessment of the success on the ground thus far. Here the picture is sobering: the good governance and transparency agenda has not affected the core rules of the game of global energy governance. Instead the agenda has remained only a niche concern, mostly at a superficial rhetorical level. This is due to a number of factors.

—Lack of interest on the part of producers and new consumers. The reformist agenda has not gained traction with pivotal producers (Russia and key OPEC members) as well as consumers now playing a prominent role in global energy markets (India and China). Their public reactions range from the noncommittal to the dismissive, and in no instance have these vital participants in the international economy of energy played a supportive, let alone a furthering, role.

—Lack of commitment on the part of established consumers. Even among governments (such as Germany) and businesses rhetorically committed to the agenda, the commitment to action is weak because powerful constituencies (often economics ministries) hold sway. The United States has thus far, especially during its period of unrivalled dominance, not been a forceful advocate of the reform agenda (due to influence of the business lobby with the Bush administration), although this might change with recent initiatives by Congress and the new administration.

—Lack of leverage of voluntary disclosure. Voluntary approaches such as the Extractive Industries Transparency Initiative underestimate the staying power of reform-resistant elites, who might sign up to the EITI agenda but do not change their clientelist and antidevelopment approach to the energy business—or to state governance more generally. These elites realize that Tony's Blair's promise of EITI as a win-win situation only holds as long as they prevent real change on the ground. EITI advocates also overestimate the power of civil society, however heroic individual efforts of activists in EITI member countries might be, to hold antidevelopment elites to account. No amount of Western capacity building can easily change the power equation that has the majority of capacity in the hands of powerful elites. As John Githongo, the leading Kenyan transparency campaigner, found out through bitter experience, "The [big] fish don't fry themselves."[71]

71. Celia Dugger, "Battle to Halt Graft Scourge in Africa Ebbs," *New York Times,* June 10, 2009.

—Lack of mainstreaming information into markets. Participants in global energy markets do not factor good governance and transparency concerns into their decisions. There is little to no evidence that investors punish companies with a bad governance record. Private oil companies' ability to raise capital rarely if ever is affected by their governance records. National oil companies have their independent access to capital anyway, as long as their governments remain creditworthy or have currency reserves. The shady world of international oil trading remains immune to reputational concerns. Likewise, private rating agencies do not factor transparency and good governance records into their rating decisions. Western secrecy laws continue to shield oil and gas profiteers. Confidentiality clauses in investment contracts perpetuate obfuscation and corruption. What is more, consumers at the pump do not have any ability or inclination to base their decisions on which gas to buy based on the development stance of the oil company.

Although a coalition of the United Kingdom, Norway, Germany, and other like-minded countries pushed the agenda of good governance in the global energy field during its window of opportunity from 1995 to 2005, the agenda did not succeed. Imagine what a powerful coalition led by the United States and propelled by an enlightened regulatory philosophy could have achieved during the period. Given its unrivalled power situation, it could have locked in regulatory reforms in a way that new consumers, their national oil companies, and the elites in oil-rich countries could not have easily undermined. Today it may be too late to achieve systemic change on the basis of a Western epicenter. The unique window of opportunity seems to have closed with the rise in global importance of countries outside the G-7.

Does this mean a move forward into the dark ages of realpolitik energy governance, rolling back even the modest amount of progress achieved? Not necessarily. Instead, Western countries and activists should increase their efforts to get rising powers into the good governance boat. In the case of China, for example, there are obvious linkages to the domestic Chinese agenda against corruption.[72]

---

72. Any efforts to establish linkages between the domestic Chinese and the international anticorruption agenda need to be mindful of the fact that the Chinese domestic agenda is driven purely by concerns about the harmful effects of corruption on growth. It is not embedded in a broader Western-style rule-of-law agenda. Anticorruption speed trials and public executions testify to this (and so does the fact that there is still significant support for "good" corruption that speeds up processes and thus contributes to higher GDP growth). We thank Björn Conrad for clarifying this point.

Proreform constituencies (mainly in the West) still have significant structuring power, such as controlling the nodes of the global financial system (the major stock exchanges).[73] Proponents of good resource governance need to set their aims higher in advocating regulatory answers. Voluntary approaches such as the EITI have provided a valuable service in terms of spreading the word about the need for better resource governance but have fallen short of changing the facts at the heart of the global energy system and on the ground in oil-rich countries. They need to be superseded by binding mechanisms that aim to anchor good governance in the core rules of the global energy game.

Reform-minded consumer countries need to work through their own legislatures and through intergovernmental forums to make reporting and disclosure mandatory. A recent U.S. Senate report proposes concrete steps to turn the G-8 rhetoric on good governance into action.[74] In addition, sanctions should target the most venal of the elites in oil-producing countries. Civil society organizations should launch a campaign to reveal the complicity and linkages of the financial sector and, by extension, of consumers. Now that the global financial system is in shambles and its underlying libertarian philosophy has been at least partly discredited, it should be possible to make a convincing case for abolishing banking secrecy laws. Moving forward on this path, reform-minded governments, corporations, and activists can at least prevent a return to the realpolitik of the past.

Still, good governance is likely to remain only a niche concern. Measures to change this rather dismal trajectory are on the global table although currently not in the cards of the most powerful players. At the very least, the powerful can no longer claim to not know the tragic outcomes of bad resource governance.

---

73. Thorsten Benner and Ricardo Soares de Oliveira, "Getting Tough with the Petroelites," *International Herald Tribune,* April 10, 2007. This plays to the technological and financial advantage that Western oil multinationals still hold; ultimately it is a self-interested agenda.

74. "The U.S., in conjunction with the other G-8 nations, should require that oil and mining companies listed on their stock exchanges publish country-by-country data on their royalty, tax and other relevant payments as part of routine financial reporting, and ask credit rating agencies and commercial banks to take explicit account of a country's transparency record. . . . The Securities and Exchange Commission and the Treasury Department should encourage the International Organization of Securities Commissions (IOSCO) to develop consistent requirements for disclosure of extractive payments by companies to governments so that all the major stock exchanges require the same information. They should also support an International Accounting Standard for disclosure of extractive payments to governments." U.S. Senate Foreign Relations Committee (2008).

References

Baker, Raymond W. 2005. *Capitalism's Achilles Heel: Dirty Money and How to Renew the Free-Market System.* London: Wiley and Sons.

Baker, Raymond W., John Christensen, and Nicholas Shaxson. 2008. "Catching Up with Corruption." *American Interest* 4, no. 1.

Bank Information Center and Global Witness. 2008. "Assessment of International Monetary Fund and World Bank Group: Extractive Industries Transparency Implementation." Washington.

Benner, Thorsten, and Jan Martin Witte. 2006. "Rules for Global Players? Governing Multinational Corporations in Developing Countries." *Internationale Politik,* global ed. (fall).

Blair, Tony. 2003. Speech. Conference on the Extractive Industries Transparency Initiative. London, June 17.

Blowfield, Michael, and Jedrzej George Frynas. 2005. "Setting New Agendas: Critical Perspectives on Corporate Social Responsibility in the Developing World." *International Affairs* 81, no. 3.

Chen, Matthew. 2007. *National Oil Companies and Corporate Citizenship: A Survey of Transnational Policy and Practice.* James A. Baker III Institute for Public Policy, Rice University.

Christian Aid. 2004. *Behind the Mask: The Real Face of Corporate Social Responsibility.* London.

Collier, Paul, and Anke Hoeffler. 2004. "Greed and Grievance in Civil War." *Oxford Economic Papers* 56, no. 4.

Eigen, Peter. 2007. "Fighting Corruption in a Global Economy: Transparency Initiatives in the Oil and Gas Industry." *Houston Journal of International Law* 29, no. 2.

G-8. 2007. *Growth and Responsibility in the World Economy.* Heiligendamm: G-8.

Gary, Ian, and Nikki Reisch. 2005. "Chad's Oil: Miracle or Mirage? Following the Money in Africa's Newest Petro-State." Washington: Catholic Relief Services and Bank Information Center.

Gillies, Alexandra. Forthcoming. "Reputational Concerns and the Emergence of Oil Sector Transparency as an International Norm." *International Studies Quarterly.*

Guyer, Jane. 2002. "Briefing: The Chad-Cameroon Petroleum and Pipeline Development Project." *African Affairs* 101, no. 402.

Hilson, Gavin, and Roy Maconachie. 2009. " 'Good Governance' and the Extractive Industries in Sub-Saharan Africa." *Mineral Processing and Extractive Metallurgy Review* 30, no. 1.

Human Rights Watch. 2004. *Crushing Dissent: Repression, Violence, and Azerbaijan's Elections.* New York.

Humphreys, Macartan, Jeffrey D. Sachs, and Joseph Stiglitz. 2007. "Introduction." In *Escaping the Resource Curse,* edited by M. Humphreys, J. D. Sachs, and J. Stiglitz. Columbia University Press.

Karl, Terry Lynn. 1997. *The Paradox of Plenty: Oil Booms and Petro-States.* University of California Press.

———. 2007. "Ensuring Fairness. The Case for a Transparent Fiscal Social Contract." In *Escaping the Resource Curse,* edited by M. Humphreys, J. D. Sachs, and J. Stiglitz. Columbia University Press.

Kojucharov, Nikola. 2007. "Poverty, Petroleum, and Policy Intervention: Lessons from the Chad-Cameroon Pipeline." *Review of African Political Economy* 34, no. 113.

Krasner, Stephen. 2004. "Sharing Sovereignty: New Institutions for Collapsed and Failing States." *International Security* 29, no. 2.

Lugar, Richard G. 2008. "Letter of Transmittal." In *The Petroleum and Poverty Paradox: Assessing U.S. and International Community Efforts to Fight the Resource Curse*. U.S. Senate Foreign Relations Committee. Government Printing Office.

Mallaby, Sebastian. 2004. *The World's Banker: A Story of Failed States, Financial Crises, and the Wealth and Poverty of Nations*. New York: Penguin.

Naím, Moisés. 2000. "Washington Consensus or Washington Confusion." *Foreign Policy* (Spring).

NEITI Secretariat. 2005. *Handbook on Transparency and Reform in the Oil, Gas, and Solid Minerals Sectors*. Abuja.

Peel, Michael. 2009. *A Swamp Full of Dollars: Pipelines and Paramilitaries at Nigeria's Oil Frontier*. London: I. B. Tauris.

Publish What You Pay International. 2009. "Doha 2009: Civil Society Protection a Priority; Other Measures Needed to Complement EITI Implementation." London (www.publish whatyoupay.org/en/resources/doha-2009-civil-society-protection-priority-other-measures-needed-complement-eiti-implemen).

Ross, Michael L. 2001. "Does Oil Hinder Democracy?" *World Politics* 53, no. 3.

———. 2008. "Blood Barrels." *Foreign Affairs* 83, no. 3.

Shaxson, Nicholas. 2007. *Poisoned Wells: The Dirty Politics of African Oil*. New York: Palgrave Macmillan.

———. 2008. "Oil, Corruption, and the Resource Curse." *International Affairs* 83, no. 6.

Soares de Oliveira, Ricardo. 2007. *Oil and the Politics in the Gulf of Guinea*. London: Hurst.

Transparency International. 2008. *Promoting Revenue Transparency: 2008 Report on Revenue Transparency of Oil and Gas Companies*. Berlin.

U.S. Senate Foreign Relations Committee. 2008. *The Petroleum and Poverty Paradox: Assessing U.S. and International Community Efforts to Fight the Resource Curse*. Government Printing Office.

Watts, Michael, ed. 2008. *Curse of the Black Gold: 50 Years of Oil in the Niger Delta*. New York: powerHouse Books.

Wenar, Leif. 2008. "Property Rights and the Resource Curse." *Philosophy and Public Affairs* 36, no. 1.

World Bank. 2000. *Chad-Cameroon: Petroleum Development and Pipeline Project*. Project Appraisal Document. Washington.

15

Building Global Rules for Sovereign Wealth Funds

Jamie Manzer and Jan Martin Witte

Institutions matter in the world of energy security. Institutions not only help make markets tick, they also act as standard setters, determinants of the rules of the game. Up until now, sovereign wealth funds (SWFs) have not been subject to international or multilateral rules, but rather their investment practices and data have been largely unscrutinized and regulated only at the national level.

On September 8, 2008, representatives of sovereign wealth funds, finance ministries, central banks, and the International Monetary Fund (IMF) convened in Santiago, Chile, after a six-month negotiation process to launch the so-called Santiago Principles, a set of twenty-four Generally Accepted Principles and Practices (GAPP) designed to provide guidance to SWFs regarding their management and investment strategies. Hamad al Suwaidi of the Abu Dhabi Investment Authority and cochair of the International Working Group (IWG) that developed the principles hailed the agreement as "an important step forward in clearing up any confusion with regard to the agenda of the sovereign wealth funds."[1]

The authors would like to thank Nicolas Véron (Bruegel Institute) and Thorsten Benner (Global Public Policy Institute) for very constructive comments on a draft of this chapter.

1. Comments made by Hamad al Suwaidi at press briefing, October 11, 2008, Washington (www.iwg-swf.org/tr/swftr0802.htm [December 2008]).

The launch of the Santiago Principles indeed represents an important milestone in the evolving debate on the role of SWFs in the world economy. These rules are designed to prescribe and even constrain the behavior of SWF investors. The rhetoric in broader energy security debates reflects why the political machinery of the OECD world necessitated these rules: age-old concerns about the motivations of state-owned energy companies and, now, state-owned investments drawn from oil wealth. Thus the call for multilateral rules for SWFs has emerged as one aspect of the global energy governance debate.

While SWFs are far from a new phenomenon, their rapid growth and a corresponding rise in their influence in recent years have attracted a lot of attention and have triggered much suspicion and criticism. A price boom in commodity markets, and specifically in oil and gas, has since the start of the decade triggered a new wave of petrodollar recycling. Since, as in the 1970s, oil and gas producers earn substantially more money selling their commodities than they can usefully invest in their own economies, they search for opportunities to invest their surplus abroad.[2] However, the new wave of petrodollar recycling differs from earlier ones. Rather than simply investing in highly secure U.S. government Treasury bills or other low-risk (and thus low-return) investments such as government bonds, many oil- and gas-producing nations increasingly use SWFs to put their wealth to productive use.[3] Much like private equity funds, these SWFs take direct stakes in companies. And indeed, although data are somewhat scarce, the evidence suggests that return on investment for SWFs is on average double that earned through traditional methods of petrodollar recycling.

The rise of the SWFs has also triggered concern and criticism. Critics focus in particular on two things. First, some warn about the potential impact that the failure of a large SWF may have on global financial stability. Second, and more significantly, critics highlight the political-economic implications of the rise of SWFs. Noting that SWFs are owned and controlled by governments, they argue that SWFs may use their financial power to pursue foreign (economic or political) policy objectives rather than just maximizing return on investments. Thus in recent years an increasing number of commentators and policymakers have called for a multilateral framework for SWFs, a framework designed to curb contagion as well as political abuse. The Santiago Principles are a first attempt.

---

2. On absorptive capacity of OPEC members, see Amuzegar (2001).

3. Some commentators also highlight the fact that much of the oil revenues earned during the oil crisis in the 1970s was not invested at all but squandered in white elephant investment projects or misappropriated by corrupt officials. As such, the drive toward investing and investing for higher returns should be commended. Griffith-Jones and Ocampo (2008).

Two aspects of the principles are noteworthy and are explored in this chapter. First, despite political pressure from governments in OECD countries (most notably, the United States, France, and Germany), the Santiago Principles are entirely voluntary (that is, there is no sanctioning mechanism attached to the principles to punish noncompliance), and they are weak on two of the issues that critics of SWFs highlight: transparency and accountability.[4] Second, the swiftness within which the Santiago Principles were drawn up and agreed upon is notable. From the setting up of the IWG to the concluding meeting in Santiago, the group took less than six months for negotiation, despite the complexity and contentiousness of the issues involved.

This chapter offers an analysis of the emergence of the Santiago Principles. We argue that the swiftness of the negotiating process, as well as the specific shape of the outcomes, is a result of two factors. First, in their substance the principles reflect to some extent the victory of reason over often unsubstantiated criticism of SWFs. In some ways, the multilateral process that led to the Santiago Principles may even represent a perfect compromise for policymakers from OECD nations and SWF owners. The first face significant pressure at home to push for tough regulation while knowing very well that such an outcome would both be unjustified by the facts and likely be counterproductive from an economic standpoint. The latter feel unjustly criticized yet realize that some movement on the regulatory front is necessary to avoid a continued witchhunt, which could result in worse outcomes.

Second, the principles also reflect the shift in the balance of power between investors (the SWFs) and receiving countries (in particular the United States and Europe) that took place during the negotiations leading up to the Santiago Principles, a shift that occurred as a consequence of the global financial crisis. In fact, from a broader perspective, the emergence of the SWFs as well as the process that resulted in the Santiago Principles can be interpreted as a manifestation of a structural shift in the global economy that is causing G-7 and G-8 countries to lose ever more rule-making capacity, underscoring the necessity of making multilateral governance processes more inclusive.

Scope and Relevance of Sovereign Wealth Funds

State-owned investment funds can be characterized as "large pools of capital controlled by a government and invested in private markets abroad."[5] According to

4. Truman (2008a).
5. Kimmitt (2008b), p. 35.

Table 15-1. *Sovereign Wealth Funds Fueled by Commodity Sales,*
Ten Countries, 2007

Country	Fund	Assets (US$ billion)	Inception year
United Arab Emirates	Abu Dhabi Investment Authority	875	1976
Norway	Government Pension Fund–Global	322	1990
Saudi Arabia	Various funds	300	n.a.
Kuwait	Kuwait Investment Authority	250	1953
Russia	Stabilization Fund of the Russian Federation[a]	127	2003
Libya	Reserve Fund	50	n.a.
Qatar	Qatar Investment Authority	40	2000
United States	Alaska Permanent Reserve Fund Corporation	40	1976
Brunei	Brunei Investment Agency	35	1983
Algeria	Reserve Fund	25	n.a.

Source: Adapted from Kern (2007).
a. Technically, the Stabilization Fund of the Russian Federation does not exist anymore. It was broken up recently into two parts—a Reserve Fund (investing abroad in low-yield securities, to be used when oil and gas incomes fall) and a National Welfare Fund (investing in riskier assets as well as in federal government expenditures).
n.a. Not available.

the IMF, SWFs can be split into at least five categories: stabilization funds (funds designed to protect the government budget and domestic economy against adverse effects of commodity price swings on international markets), savings funds (funds designed to preserve some current wealth for future generations), reserve investment corporations (funds established to increase the return on reserves), development funds (funds designed to stimulate domestic socioeconomic development), and contingent pension reserve funds (funds designed to provide for contingent unspecified pension liabilities of the government).[6]

Having more than doubled both in size and in total assets over the last decade, SWFs now manage assets in excess of US$3 trillion, making them increasingly visible in the economic and political sphere (table 15-1). The share of funds linked to commodities (such as the sale of oil and gas) accounts for close to 70 percent of existing SWFs. Not only have their assets rapidly increased, so too has the scale of investments: SWFs invested US$92 billion in the global economy in 2007, compared with US$3 billion in 2000.[7] Recent growth helps underscore why such optimistic projections have been mapped for SWFs for the coming years. In the

6. International Monetary Fund (2008), pp. 5ff.
7. Fisher and others (2008).

first quarter of 2008 alone, SWFs invested US$58 billion, or more than the US$50 billion total invested in 2000–05.[8]

By some calculations, the assets held by SWFs could more than triple in ten years.[9] However, with most change comes fear. OECD nations worry that the funds might overheat global markets or invest in sensitive sectors. So more than their absolute size, the more pressing question is, in comparison to what? Despite what the political debate suggests, compared to other investment vehicles, SWFs play a small role in the global financial system. Though state-owned funds currently outsize hedge funds by two to one, SWFs account for a mere 3 percent of equity and bond markets globally. Bank assets, pension funds, securities, and so forth still dominate the global market (figure 15-1). This is unlikely to change in the near future. Should recorded SWF assets more than double in five years, as projected by Deutsche Bank, Morgan Stanley, the International Monetary Fund, and others, SWFs would still account for less than 6 percent of all global financial assets.[10]

How much SWFs will grow is up for debate, particularly with commodity prices down since mid-2007 and global markets in turmoil. A number of projections map the potential growth trend of SWFs over the next fifteen years. The key conclusion is that growth in SWFs, even taking into account a significant global economic downturn as well as the drop in commodity (and particularly oil) prices since late 2007, is likely to be substantial in the years ahead. The IMF says SWFs may reach US$10 trillion by 2012; Morgan Stanley predicts US$12 trillion by 2015; what is sure is that SWFs will exceed global official currency reserves by the end of 2011.[11]

High oil and gas prices coupled with solid returns on investments have driven SWF growth and will continue to do so in the future. With the price per barrel of oil sustained at levels way above those experienced in the 1990s for the foreseeable future, major oil exporters will continue to see their funds swell.[12] In addition to high commodity prices, the diversity of SWF investment portfolios also stimulates growth. With long-term investment horizons and diversified portfolios, returns can average about 6 percent a year.[13] Thus most projections suggest that growth of SWFs

---

8. Fisher and others (2008).
9. Kern (2007).
10. Gieve (2008).
11. Beck and Fidora (2008).
12. While the price of oil came down by two-thirds in the latter part of 2008 to roughly US$45 a barrel (from an all-time high of close to US$150 a barrel during the summer of 2008), this still represents a significant price increase compared to levels during much of the 1980s and 1990s.
13. Kern (2007); see also Jen (2007).

Figure 15-1. *Investments in Global Equity and Bond Markets, 2006*

US$ trillion

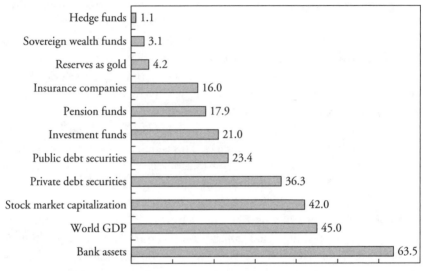

Source: Adapted from Kern (2007).

(in terms of financial volumes invested) is likely to stay solid, with overall volumes at least likely to double, and in some cases triple, over the next two to ten years.

One other notable fact is that, since Kuwait created the first SWF—the Kuwait Investment Authority—in 1953, the number of SWFs has increased rapidly (figure 15-2). To put the number of new funds into perspective, however, it is important to emphasize that five countries account for 75 percent of the total value of state-owned assets.[14] So sovereign wealth is heavily concentrated in a few hands.

Yet while investments of SWFs increased to record levels in 2008 and future growth seems likely, it should also be noted that SWFs have recently incurred record losses. Reports have come out specifying major blows dealt to SWFs taking stakes in ailing U.S. banks.[15] Investments by some SWFs dropped by 30–50 percent within six months' time between late 2007 and early 2008. This U.S. dollar depreciation cost SWFs billions of dollars; for example, Singapore's Temasek paid US$4.4 billion for stocks that were later valued at US$3.4 billion,

14. Morgan (2008).
15. Steven Johnson and Gertrude Chavez-Dreyfus, "Asia May Benefit as Sovereign Funds Shun U.S. Dollar," *Reuters*, July 18, 2008; Heather Connon, "Why Sovereign Wealth Funds Can't Get Enough of Banks," *Guardian*, June 22, 2008.

Figure 15-2. *Number of Sovereign Wealth Funds Launched, by Decade, 1950–2000*

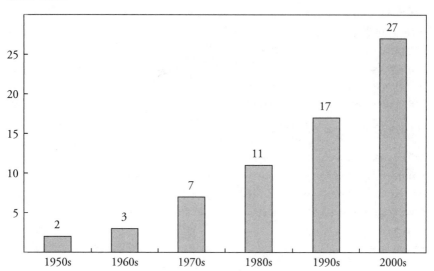

Source: Adapted from Gieve (2008).

and this was not their only loss of the year. In fact many stocks were trading at 50 percent of their original value. Norway's Government Pension Fund–Global posted the worst results in its history.[16] Thus it is likely that in the coming years SWFs will be weighing their heavy losses in the U.S. and European financial sectors when deciding where to invest their funds. It is also worth noting, though, that once the economic situation stabilizes many stocks will be hugely undervalued, such that there exist attractive buying opportunities. Presumably, cash-rich SWFs will be well placed to take advantage of those opportunities and will see solid returns once things start picking up.

The SWF Controversy: Political Pressures in the United States and Europe

Even though overly optimistic projections of SWF growth may have to be adapted in light of the global economic crisis in 2008 and 2009, there can be no doubt that SWFs are here to stay and are bound to increase in number as well as size.

16. Giovanni Legorano, "Norwegian Fund Reveals Results 'Worst in History,' " *Global Pensions*, November 25, 2008.

The rise of SWFs has not gone unnoticed. In recent years, sovereign funds have become the subject of continuous reporting in leading international newspapers. SWFs have also been the subject of numerous hearings on Capitol Hill, in the European Parliament, and in various other national parliaments. Criticism of SWFs has resulted in a flurry of legislative initiatives in the United States and Europe designed to regulate foreign government investment. Why exactly have SWFs attracted so much attention? What triggered the political momentum in the United States and Europe toward the emergence of the Santiago Principles?

The Case for SWF Regulation

In the case of SWFs, the already turbulent politics of foreign investment is compounded by the important fact that SWFs are not private but are government-owned and government-controlled investment vehicles. As pointed out by one observer, the rise of SWFs represents a dramatic increase in government owner-ship and control of international assets.[17] For many in the United States and Europe, that fact is cause for much alarm. In addition, the absence of regulatory rules regarding transparency and accountability means that SWFs' investment strategies and performance are shrouded in secrecy. As pointed out by Roland Beck and Michael Fidora, the seven least transparent SWFs account for almost half of all global SWF holdings.[18] As a consequence, SWFs have primarily been confronted with two sets of criticisms.

First, critics allege that SWFs might not invest simply for economic gain but also for political and strategic gain. For example, SWFs may invest on behalf of their government owners in strategic industries to facilitate a transfer of technol-ogy and knowledge to their home country. U.S. observers are particularly wary of SWF investment in industries relevant to national security, arguing that in a post-9/11 world the United States cannot afford to let foreign powers gain access to security-relevant technologies and information. Concern over foreign-government ownership extends to domestic assets as well. As the under secretary for inter-national affairs of the U.S. Treasury, David H. McCormick, pointed out in November 2007, "Treasury is also considering non-national-security issues related to potential distortions from a larger role of foreign governments in markets. For example, through inefficient allocation of capital, perceived unfair compe-tition with private firms, or the pursuit of broader strategic rather than strictly

17. Truman (2007).
18. Beck and Fidora (2008).

economic-return-oriented investments, sovereign wealth funds could potentially distort markets."[19]

Second, critics point out that SWFs, due to their growing size, could have systemic implications for the global financial system in case of failure. In their view, SWFs represent large, concentrated, and mostly nontransparent entities that, in case of trouble, could have unforeseen consequences for systemic stability. For example, the IMF writes that "actual or rumored transactions may affect relative valuations in particular sectors and result in herding behavior, adding to volatility. Similarly, if SWFs begin to pursue riskier investment strategies, particularly involving the use of leverage and margin requirements that may be called quickly, they may act so as to amplify rather than stabilize cycles."[20] In addition, SWFs may constitute a risk for global financial stability in case of portfolio reshuffling, specifically if SWFs move out of the US$ in an uncoordinated fashion.[21]

The evolving debate on the role and significance of SWFs is strongly influenced by the fact that six of the ten largest SWFs are owned and controlled by governments characterized as authoritarian by the *Economist*'s democracy index, further heightening concerns of skeptics over foreign government control of domestic assets.[22]

Yet much of the public debate on SWFs, particularly in Europe and the United States, appears to be driven not just by concerns over greater government control of private assets or the systemic implications of the rise of unregulated and, for the most part, nontransparent investment vehicles. The tone of the debate suggests that at least part of the concern over SWFs is structural global economic change. In a way, the emergence of SWFs is a symptom of a larger process currently reshaping the global economy. It appears that at least part of the discussion on SWFs in the United States and Europe is shaped by a sense of relative economic decline in the industrialized countries, with SWFs being symbols of the rise of emerging economies.[23] In many ways, the reaction to Chinese and Russian investors making

19. McCormick (2007).

20. International Monetary Fund (2008), p. 12.

21. For a review of the debate on the systemic implications of SWFs, see Beck and Fidora (2008); International Monetary Fund (2008); Mattoo and Subramanian (2008).

22. Kekic (2007).

23. Kavaljit Singh, "SWFs Mark Structural Shift in World Financial Order," *Economic Times*, November 11, 2008. For a related argument, see Malcolm Rifkind, "Europe and America in the Shadows as a New Era Dawns," *Daily Telegraph*, October 26, 2008.

high-profile investments in Europe and America is reminiscent of the reaction to the Japanese shopping spree in the United States during the 1980s.[24]

In any event, most of the perception of a potentially negative political or strategic impact of SWFs is not based on fact. While little is known about the investment strategies of most SWFs, there is little evidence of SWFs investing for other than economic gain. Instead, rather than buying controlling stakes, most SWFs remain minority holders (usually less than 5 percent of publicly traded shares).[25] So far not a single case of an SWF investment has been reported in which political rather than economic priorities were clearly the driving factor, and by some estimates, less than 5 percent of all SWF investments are allocated to acquiring controlling interests in strategic sectors in OECD markets.[26] If anything, the recent global financial crisis highlights the role SWFs can play as sources of liquidity for troubled American and European banks: without that infusion of capital, the banks would have failed earlier, and the eventual bailout by the U.S. government would have had to be on an even larger scale.[27] In fact, as indicated above, SWFs have incurred significant losses on their investments in U.S. financial institutions.[28]

Potent Political Reactions

Despite the lack of evidence of abuse by the SWFs or negative implications for the stability of the global financial system, the political response to the rise of SWFs, especially in the United States and Europe, paved the way for attempts at SWF regulation at both national and multilateral levels.

Ironically, the debate on the role and significance of SWFs was transformed into high politics in the United States as a result of a case that had nothing to do with a sovereign fund. In 2005 the state-owned Chinese company CNOOC Ltd. bid to buy out Unocal, a U.S.-based oil company. The Chinese bid struck a particularly sensitive nerve with politicians in the U.S. Congress because Chevron Corp., a

24. John Greenwald and others, "Sure, We'll Take Manhattan," *Time,* November 13, 2008.

25. Although about half of SWFs on occasion take majority stakes in companies, only 2 percent of those deals are in sensitive industries. Fisher and others (2008).

26. Drezner (2008).

27. Eckart Woertz, "GCC Needs the Dollar and the US Needs the Funding," *Newsweek,* May 29, 2008; Aaron Bernstein, "SWFs to the Rescue," *Directorship: Boardroom Intelligence,* April 1, 2008.

28. "Sovereign Wealth Funds Turning Cautious," Agence France-Presse, November 8, 2008; "Sovereign Wealth Funds to Lose 25% This Year: Morgan Stanley," Reuters, November 7, 2008 ("The outcome of all this is that sovereign wealth funds will be spending less on risky assets in advanced economies, and with emerging market economies also now in trouble, they will probably also be focusing more on helping to fund domestic operations"); Parmy Olson, "Sovereign Funds' $2 Trillion Setback," *Forbes,* July 11, 2008.

U.S.-based company, was the rival and consequently the losing bidder. Members of Congress as well as Chevron aggressively criticized the Chinese maneuver, arguing that CNOOC received Chinese government loans with reduced interest rates to finance its bid, contending that no other bidder would be able to compete under such conditions. Beyond concerns about competition, members of Congress urged President Bush to block the deal, claiming that it would "enable the Chinese government to influence or manipulate oil prices and supplies."[29]

One year later, a second deal further propelled the issue of foreign government ownership onto the political agenda, ultimately resulting in action by the U.S. Congress. In 2006 Dubai Ports World (DPW), a port management company, acquired the London-based Peninsular and Orient Stream Navigation Company. This deal, if approved, would have given DPW management responsibilities over six U.S. ports.

Neither the Committee on Foreign Investment in the United States (CFIUS), an interagency committee of the U.S. government that reviews the national security implications of proposed commercial transactions involving U.S. companies, nor President Bush raised concerns over the deal until a congressional press conference called attention to it. Senator Barack Obama commented: "Over four years after the worst terrorist attack in our history, not only are we failing to inspect 95% of the cargo that arrives at U.S. ports, but now we're allowing our port security to be outsourced to foreign governments. Clearly, more time should have been spent investigating this deal and consulting with homeland security experts and local officials." In addition, in a letter to President Bush, House member Sue Myrick (R-N.C.) wrote: "In regards to selling American ports to the United Arab Emirates, not just NO—but HELL no."[30] Eventually, the threat of unilateral regulation from Congress forced DPW to divest. A House of Representatives committee had already voted against the deal, and it appeared as though the Senate was to follow when DPW decided to pull out of the deal.

Overall, while the Bush administration remained generally supportive of SWF investments in the United States, the political tone changed over time, responding to the increasingly aggressive climate on Capitol Hill. While on the one hand praising the potential stabilizing role of SWFs in light of the emerging credit crisis, Robert Kimmitt (U.S. deputy treasury secretary) on the other hand argued in a widely noted *Foreign Affairs* article that both sides—the SWFs as well as receiving

---

29. Ronald Brownstein, "Fair Play at Issue in Unocal Bid," *Los Angeles Times,* July 20, 2005.

30. Quoted in Bernard Wysocki and others, "Port Debate Exposes Conflicts between Security Needs and Foreign Investment," *Wall Street Journal,* February 23, 2008.

countries—would need to sign on to "policy principles" to structure investments. One of the principles that SWFs should follow, according to Kimmitt, was to "invest commercially, not politically."[31] In the end, a strong stance by Congress and a heated public debate forced the Bush administration to adopt a more critical attitude toward SWFs.

The Unocal and DPW controversies, combined with the rising profile of SWFs investing in the U.S. economy, helped pave the way for legislative action by Congress. In the autumn of 2007 Congress expanded the CFIUS mandate through FINSA, the Foreign Investment and National Security Act of 2007, which added "homeland security" to the definition of "national security." The expansion effectively increased the number of industry sectors treated as "critical to national security," thus potentially opening further avenues for restricting SWF investment in the U.S. economy.[32] While the new legislation does not go much beyond previously existing rules, "the post-DPW political environment has led CFIUS to be much tougher and more regulatory. CFIUS has extended more reviews into a second phase and is imposing more conditions on transactions going through the process."[33] Perhaps more important, both the Unocal and the DPW episodes contributed to a chilly political climate in the United States for SWFs, creating a backlash from various funds.[34] As recently as May 2008 Democrats also called for a tougher application of the new rules.[35]

In Europe the rise of SWFs triggered a flurry of legislative and regulatory initiatives designed to curb the negative implications of sovereign investment in European corporate assets. In a way, Europe's "Unocal" was the Russia-Ukraine gas crisis at the end of 2005, which emphasized the growing dependence of European nations on Russian gas and prompted a debate on whether Gazprom, Russia's government controlled gas-producing giant, should be allowed to invest in Europe's gas distribution network. The Russia-Ukraine gas crisis and its shortfall on gas deliveries to Europe in the winter of 2005–06 triggered a heated debate about foreign government control of critical domestic assets and led to increasing calls in many EU member states for more regulation and oversight.

---

31. Kimmitt (2008b), p. 38.

32. For more background on FINSA, see "The Foreign Investment and National Security Act of 2007: Improved Transparency and Slower Deal Making," *Bracewell and Giuliani Washington Update*, October 24, 2007 (www.bracewellgiuliani.com/index).

33. Marchick and Slaughter (2008), p. 6.

34. A 2006 Pew poll found that more than 50 percent of Americans believe that foreign ownership of U.S. corporate assets is "bad for America." Barlas (2008). See also David Lascelles, "The Tables Have Turned on Developed Countries," *Business Day* (South Africa), August 4, 2008.

35. Barlas (2008).

France and Germany have been at the forefront of the debate and in taking legislative action. France has traditionally been one of the most activist nations in protecting domestic industries from foreign investment. What is notable is that French rules are not aimed just at foreign government investment (led by SWFs) but at foreign investment more generally. In keeping with a strong French tradition of interventionist industrial policy, a government decree issued in late 2005 requires foreigners who intend to invest in "strategic sectors" of the French economy to obtain prior authorization from the Ministry of Economy, Finance, and Employment.[36]

The rise of sovereign funds has also been cause for concern in Berlin. In August 2008, after a one-year deliberation process, the German government approved, and the Bundestag ratified, legislation that empowers the government to veto, for reasons of national security, any non-European investment in the German economy above 25 percent of any company's stock.[37] In drafting this law, the German chancellor, Angela Merkel, didn't follow some of the hawks in her own party, who wanted to see even more restrictive language in the new legislation. The government also emphasizes that the new law will be applied only "in very rare cases."[38] However, the somewhat wobbly language of the law provides German policymakers with considerable flexibility regarding its application, and the German government reserves the right to review a case for up to three months, a potential deal breaker for many commercial investments.

A more measured tone regarding investments by SWFs was struck in the United Kingdom, where the chancellor of the exchequer, Alistair Darling, stresses the fact that SWF investment is welcome and that further regulatory action would not seem warranted. Arguing that inward investment by SWFs is "not only necessary, but welcome," he emphasizes that the British government is "vehemently against" any moves that would foster protectionism.[39]

---

36. Marchick and Slaughter (2008), p. 11. However, it could also be argued that the real problem in France is not existing regulation but the government's attempts to defend national incumbents outside of any legislative or regulatory framework and the use of direct government equity stakes to prevent foreign takeovers. Nicholas Veron, Bruegel Institute, e-mail to authors.

37. Klaus Stratmann, "Federführung bei Staatsfonds entschieden," *Handelsblatt*, July 14, 2008.

38. BMWi (2008), p. 9.

39. Quoted in Sean O'Grady, "G-7 Compromises over Calls to Reform Sovereign Wealth Funds," *Independent*, October 20, 2007. It is also important to note, however, that Darling did strongly support the setting up of the IWG to develop a code of best practice, arguing, "We welcome inward investment from sovereign wealth funds, but it has to be a two-way street. They have to operate on a commercial basis and no other basis." "Chancellor Backs G-7 Move to Get Tough on Sovereign Wealth Funds," *Guardian*, October 20, 2007.

An influential Brussels think tank has also called for action at the EU level, arguing that new rules are needed to ensure a sufficiently open and liberal investment regime that attracts SWF investments (especially in the midst of a global financial crisis) while at the same time guaranteeing that security and other "legitimate concerns" are taken into account.[40] In striking a tone similar to that of the U.K. chancellor of the exchequer, European Commissioner Charlie McCreevy is careful to point out that the European Commission will not support any protectionist measures and, indeed, warns EU member states not to adopt sweeping legislation designed to keep SWFs out.[41]

Development of the Santiago Principles

The rise of SWFs has attracted significant public attention and has led to considerable legislative debate and, in some notable instances, legislative action in the United States and the European Union. Despite the lack of conclusive evidence regarding the potentially positive consequences of sovereign investment in their economies, American and European policymakers have been quick to design new (or to update existing) rules regulating foreign investment in their economies.

Multilateral Action: Toward a Voluntary Code

Throughout 2007 there was also a growing sense that unilateral rules designed to rein in SWFs would not be sufficient and that a multilateral framework would be required to meet the challenge presented by sovereign funds. The G-7 presidency was held that year by Germany, one of the countries most active regarding new legislation on foreign government investment. In consultation with the German G-7 presidency, the U.S. Treasury Department took the initiative and invited officials from major SWF owners to an "outreach dinner." The objective of the meeting was to explore interest by the SWFs in a multilateral process to define best practices for SWFs. The team from the U.S. Treasury viewed the IMF as the most appropriate platform for such a process. In their conception, defining best prac-

---

40. Roeller and Veron (2008), pp. 2, 8.

41. In a report published in February 2008 that outlines the EC's stance on SWFs and the various legislative proposals considered by member states, the EC comments: "All these suggestions run the risk of sending a misleading signal—that the EU is stepping back from its commitment to an open investment regime." Quoted in Carter Dougherty and Stephen Castle, "EU Warns against Overreaction on Sovereign Wealth Funds," *International Herald Tribune,* February 25, 2008. As a response, the EC proposed to develop a voluntary code of conduct for SWFs. Commentators note that this push for voluntary codes "may have prevented stronger regulation. By calling for a code of conduct the Commission has stumbled across a middle ground." Butkiewicz, Pettifer, and Young (2008).

tices for SWFs would not result in binding and enforceable rules but instead in a voluntary code of practice. This preference from the outset for a voluntary code was a result of at least two developments in the second half of 2007.

First, despite significant pressure at home, many governments saw virtue in promoting an open, multilateral, investment framework and were opposed to introducing rules that could inhibit the free flow of capital. That was in particular true for the United States. Despite its support for the strengthening of FINSA rules, the administration generally remained in favor of promoting rather than restricting investment, including by SWFs.[42] In addition, the European Commission, generally distrustful of steps taken by member countries to restrict foreign investment in response to the rise of SWFs, strongly supported the voluntary multilateral route.[43] From its perspective, pushing for a process to develop multilateral standards would serve the purpose of creating a level playing field internationally and avoiding a further fragmentation of investment frameworks across countries.

Second, and more significantly, the fallout from the credit crunch and the onset of the global financial crisis were already clear in late 2007 and had started to affect the political establishment on both sides of the Atlantic. Policymakers recognized that the public debate about SWFs was bound to shift in light of well-publicized financial investments by SWFs in ailing U.S. banks, investments generally considered bailouts. While major SWF investments in foreign companies drew negative attention from policymakers in recipient countries for years, once the full scale of the global financial crisis became apparent, the debate was fundamentally transformed. While jumpy lawmakers in Berlin, Paris, and Washington never fully gave up their suspicion of SWFs, they were far more afflicted by the threat of a major national and global recession—a more short-term and public concern—than by SWFs buying minority shares in a bank begging for funds.

August 2007 in particular was a rough month for governments, homeowners, investment institutions, and banks. Liquidity dried up for firms and securities markets. The problem spread throughout nonbank institutions, such as mortgage lenders and hedge funds. As fear of risk "increased, these institutions saw sources of credit vanish and struggled to meet existing financing commitments, to post additional collateral, and to cope with portfolio losses."[44] Ill prepared to jump headfirst into the bank rescue business, governments forced banks and financial

---

42. Kimmitt (2008a).
43. Rachel Ziemba, "Sovereign Wealth Funds: Tallying the Losses (Again)," *RGE Analysts EconoMonitor,* November 26, 2008.
44. Getter and others (2007), p. 2.

institutions to court other pools of liquidity, namely SWFs.[45] Financial institutions and even governments were grateful for these financial heavyweights, as their investments not only recapitalized the market but also kept lawmakers from having to make immediate decisions regarding nationalization and bailouts.

November 2007 saw a continuation of the investment hustle and bustle. Abu Dhabi's SWF announced on November 27 its intentions to invest billions in the distressed Citigroup, the largest U.S. bank. This investment clarified the necessity of accepting financing from SWFs.[46] By mid-December SWFs proved their willingness to continue taking risks when Morgan Stanley accepted a US$5 billion deal from China's CIC and the Swiss Bank UBS took US$11.5 billion from Singapore. Citigroup, along with Merrill Lynch, UBS, and Morgan Stanley, accepted more investments in January. The reason was the need for rapid recapitalization to "stabilize their shaky financial foundations. Already, foreign governments [had] invested about $US27 billion in Merrill, Citi, UBS and Morgan Stanley."[47] Following these high-profile investments, a series of articles and editorials citing investment statistics helped emphasize the economic motivations of SWFs.[48] Even Europe caught on, perhaps by necessity. By January 2008 the financial crisis was public knowledge and fear was spreading: in a time of crisis, sovereign funds were suddenly more welcome in Europe.[49]

Even though the political debate had shifted from getting tough on SWFs to developing a collaborative best practices code at the multilateral level, the SWFs viewed the invitation to the outreach dinner with considerable wariness. Indeed, most of them initially resisted the move toward the development of a best practices code. Many felt unfairly singled out and feared a witchhunt that would result in regulations that would put them at a competitive disadvantage compared to other investment funds (such as hedge funds). Some SWFs even pointed out the possibility of moving their investments into other markets should the push for regulation proceed. For example, the Kuwait Investment Authority, the oldest SWF, considered investing more funds in Japan and emerging markets.[50] Chinese offi-

---

45. Jack Ewing, "The New Financial Heavyweights," *Business Week,* November 11, 2007.

46. "Abu Dhabi Stake in Citigroup Highlights Growing Power of Sovereign Wealth Funds," *International Herald Tribune,* November 27, 2007.

47. "Citi and Merrill Seeking $14bn," *Australian,* January 11, 2008.

48. Mark Landler and Jula Werdigier, "Subprime Surprise: UBS Writes Down $10 Billion," *International Herald Tribune,* December 10, 2007.

49. Carter Dougherty, "In a Time of Crisis, Sovereign Funds Suddenly More Welcome in Europe," *International Herald Tribune,* January 16, 2007.

50. Steven Johnson and Gertrude Chavez-Dreyfus, "Asia May Benefit as Sovereign Funds Shun U.S. Dollar," Reuters, July 18, 2008.

cials, speaking on behalf of the China Investment Corporation, cited regulations as one reason to consider new markets for investment: "Fortunately there are more than 200 countries in the world. And fortunately there are many countries who are happy with us."[51]

At the same time, however, European and American markets remain by far the largest and most attractive investment destinations for SWFs. Some estimate that SWFs currently invest more than 75 percent of their assets in the OECD world.[52] Thus while SWFs may have some flexibility in reallocating investments to investment-friendly nations, they cannot afford a complete rupture of relations, at least not in the short or medium term.[53]

Thus despite initial opposition, representatives from eight major owners (China, South Korea, Kuwait, Norway, Russia, Saudi Arabia, Singapore, and the United Arab Emirates) agreed to attend the outreach dinner hosted by the U.S. treasury secretary Hank Paulson on October 19, 2007. The meeting was to initiate a process of developing consensus and collaboration on the next step forward for a multilateral process, that is, to define a code of best practices for SWFs. Considering the resistance by many SWFs to new rules, building consensus on how to move ahead proved to be a tricky process and required careful diplomatic maneuvering. Ultimately, however, both sides understood their mutual need. Even funds from China and Russia, which had been openly critical of codes of conduct in general (and which regularly criticized Western governments for pushing for them), shifted their language in favor of the multilateral process. Representatives from the United Arab Emirates and China agreed that improving the transparency of investment standards was important, even while voicing concerns about U.S. and EU protectionism.[54]

After the outreach meeting it remained unclear what the next steps would be. What would be regulated? Which SWFs would be targeted? Who would create the rules? And how would compliance be managed? Critics were convinced that codes of conduct were unnecessary. The Bush administration certainly recognized the risk of alienating SWFs, given the United States' own vulnerability resulting from the subprime mortgage crisis.[55] Meanwhile, the United States Congress and various EU parliaments continued to demand tough regulation.

51. Stephen Schwartzman, "Reject Sovereign Wealth Funds at Your Peril," *Financial Times,* June 19, 2008.

52. Eschweiler (2008).

53. Drezner (2008).

54. "G-7 Frets over International Money Issues; Investing of Sovereign Wealth Funds by Developing Countries Sparks Concern," *Daily Yomiuri,* October 23, 2007.

55. Steven R. Weisman, "Overseas Funds Resist Calls for a Code of Conduct," *New York Times,* February 9, 2008.

Eventually, participants at the G-7 finance ministers' meeting following the outreach dinner found compromise, facilitated in part by the U.K. government.[56] The United Kingdom's adamant defense of SWFs and open market investment helped bring G-7 protectionist stalwarts to the center, while the United States quietly approved. Perhaps more significantly, facing the weakening dollar, global economic cooling, and the credit crunch, France and Germany crept over to the moderate side.[57] In its meeting communiqué, G-7 ministers officially invited the IMF and the OECD to examine issues related to the rise of the SWFs and to assist in the development of suitable tools to address the challenges.[58] More specifically, the G-7 called upon the IMF to coordinate the development of a code of conduct for SWFs, covering issues such as corporate governance, risk management, transparency, and accountability.

Getting to Work: The International Working Group

The IMF quickly responded to the G-7's request. On October 20, 2007, the International Monetary and Financial Committee (IMFC) released a statement in which it called on the organization to start a dialogue with SWFs to identify best practices. Less than a month after the G-7 meeting in Washington, the IMF convened a roundtable discussion for sovereign asset and reserve managers.[59] The IMF board of directors also backed the creation of the International Working Group (IWG) for Sovereign Wealth Funds under the auspices of the IMF.[60]

On February 29, 2008, the IMF drafted and proposed a "Work Agenda on SWFs" for the IMF board. This document included a schedule of major meetings with members of the IWG. However, the document did not provide any information as to who would be asked to participate or how, specifically, they would proceed. The draft agenda was clear on a start date of April 2008 and a deadline of late August 2008 for the circulation of a draft set of principles to the IMF's board.[61]

56. "G-7 Compromises over Calls to Reform Sovereign Wealth Funds," *Independent*, October 20, 2007.
57. "G-7 Compromises over Calls to Reform Sovereign Wealth Funds," *Independent*, October 20, 2007.
58. U.S. Department of the Treasury (2007).
59. International Monetary Fund (2008).
60. Delamaide (2008).
61. International Monetary Fund (2008).

On March 20, 2008, exactly five months after the G-7 finance ministers' meeting, representatives from Abu Dhabi and Singapore SWFs signed a nonbinding commitment to

—Invest for solely commercial reasons
—Improve disclosure
—Support strong governance structures
—Compete fairly
—Comply with host-country rules.[62]

These five points served as a template for issues to be addressed by the IWG. However, SWFs maintained that they would not be willing to disclose the actual size of their funds. Further, some lawmakers wanted to see other issues addressed more specifically within these five points: foreign ownership, foreign shareholder voting rights, and any initiatives that would avoid the buildup of SWFs in the first place, such as currency manipulation. (Currency manipulation was a perpetual sticking point between the United States and China.)[63]

On April 30, 2008, the IWG was officially recognized by the IMF. Members included representatives from Australia, Azerbaijan, Bahrain, Botswana, Canada, Chile, China, Equatorial Guinea, Iran, Ireland, South Korea, Kuwait, Libya, Mexico, New Zealand, Norway, Qatar, Russia, Singapore, Timor-Leste, Trinidad and Tobago, the United Arab Emirates, and the United States. Oman, Saudi Arabia, Vietnam, the OECD, and the World Bank participated as permanent observers. The IMF was tasked to facilitate and coordinate the work of the IWG by providing a secretariat. At a two-day plenary in April 2008 the final meeting in Santiago was agreed upon and the targets for the working group and all subgroups were determined. Three meetings took place throughout 2008: in Washington in April, in Singapore in July, and in Santiago in September. Jaime Caruana, head of the IMF's Monetary and Capital Markets Department, acted as a cochair, along with Hamad al Suwaidi, director of the Abu Dhabi Investment Authority (ADIA). al Suwaidi proved a successful mediator and is also credited with helping finalize the aforementioned nonbinding agreement between the United States, ADIA, and Singapore in March 2008.

The IWG structure was not unique. The talks were modeled on the work of the United Kingdom's hedge fund working group set up to defuse criticism of

62. Delamaide (2008).
63. Stokes (2007).

hedge funds.[64] This group formulated voluntary standards of transparency and governance. The IWG announced that it was also planning to adopt existing and internationally accepted standards for cross-border investment.

The Principles: Result of a Multilateral Approach

Expectations going into the IWG were rather optimistic among lawmakers in OECD countries but rather realistic among other observers.[65] For example, Sherman Chan, an economist at Moody's in Australia, pragmatically noted the distinction between long-term transparency goals and short-term liquidity needs, suggesting that "the need for capital in the West is far greater than the urge for SWFs to invest their surplus funds. . . . Therefore, rescue efforts will not be affected, but other nonpressing investment talks will."[66]

Despite early consensus among policymakers and some SWFs that an IMF-backed code would be a likely starting point for achieving a solution, the GAPP end product did not come easily. In fact, most SWF representatives were outwardly against any guideline or regulation, whether voluntary or not. Some countries, especially Russia and China, went so far as to accuse the West of xenophobic discrimination.[67] As late as June 2008, three months before the Santiago Principles were completed, Russia's and China's SWF representatives expressed intense frustration at being targeted by what they called "political grandstanding" by OECD nations.[68]

Gao Xiqing, the president of China's Investment Corporation, made it clear that if China was not welcome to invest, it would simply direct its much needed capital elsewhere. Russia's finance minister, Alexei Kudrin, called codes of conduct a double standard, arguing that funds from developed economies did not receive the same level of discrimination faced by Russia and were certainly not questioned about their investment motivations.[69] Bader al-Saad, the managing director of the Kuwait Investment Authority, not only cited the singular economic focus of its investment strategy but also reminded reporters that worried financial

---

64. International Monetary Fund (2008).

65. This discussion is based on Delamaide (2008).

66. Kevin Lim, "Sovereign Wealth Funds Set Code of Ethics Goal," *International Herald Tribune,* July 8, 2008.

67. Steven R. Weisman, "Overseas Funds Resist Calls for a Code of Conduct," *New York Times,* February 9, 2008.

68. Stephen Schwartzman, "Reject Sovereign Wealth Funds at Your Peril," *Financial Times,* June 19, 2008.

69. William Watts, "World a Better Place Thanks to Sovereign Wealth Funds," *Marketwatch,* January 24, 2008.

institutions were encouraging their funds to invest overseas, not the other way around. Citigroup and Merrill Lynch made the initial contact with the KIA to discuss the possibility of major acquisitions. Meanwhile, Muhammad al-Jasser, a representative from the Saudi Arabian Monetary Agency, which was about to create a US$900 billion fund, summarized the general irritation of SWFs: "It's like the sovereign wealth funds are guilty until proven innocent."[70]

The tension leading up to Santiago wasn't simply between SWFs and OECD member states. Rather, funds like the Kuwait Investment Authority, Singapore's Temasek, and Canada's Pension Plan Investment Board were critical of newer funds from the Middle East, China, and Russia, because before they came on the scene the traditional, more mature funds had operated without incident or much public attention. Canada's fund complained that the regulatory net was "cast too broadly" and claimed that, rather than target risky newcomers, codes of conduct might actually punish SWFs that have been operating without problems for upward of fifty years. A representative from one of Singapore's SWFs, the Government of Singapore Investment Corp, demonstrated his distrust of the rookie funds when he questioned if newly developed disclosure benchmarks for sovereign wealth funds would "work" and actually "make the Chinese and others also be as open . . . as they themselves planned to be after some minor, internal institutional reforms."[71]

Nonetheless, after less than six months of negotiations, the IWG was able to agree on a best practices code for SWF behavior. The principles were published on October 11, 2008, in Santiago. Compared to the public debate on SWFs in 2006 and 2007, press coverage of the event was relatively modest.

While most details about the discussions within the IWG are not publicly known, the results of the process suggest that the strain on banks and financial institutions caused by the credit crunch created desperate circumstances for recipients and opportunities for investors. So while in February 2008 some pundits and SWFs were still speculating about the possibility of severe regulations, and the more defensive politicians continued to call for severe regulations, others recognized the likely prospect of a "relatively modest" set of standards.[72]

Put differently, in an intensifying global financial crisis, which emphasized the potentially crucial role of SWFs in stabilizing the U.S. banking system, the IWG

70. Ariana Eunjung Cha, "Foreign Wealth Funds Defend U.S. Investments," *Washington Post,* March 27, 2008.

71. "IMF Asks Singapore to Help Set SWF Benchmarks," Reuters, January 24, 2008.

72. Steven R. Weisman, "Overseas Funds Resist Calls for a Code of Conduct," *New York Times,* February 9, 2008; Pettifer (2008).

gave the system some breathing space. While a few months earlier public pressure on SWFs had been enormous, the credit meltdown now consumed the attention of policymakers and the general public. The focus of public discussion had moved toward more urgent things.

Noting that the purpose of the GAPP is "to provide a framework for generally accepted principles and practices that properly reflect appropriate governance and accountability arrangements as well as the conduct of investment practices by SWFs on a prudent and sound basis," the IWG outlines twenty-four principles seeking to accomplish four objectives: first, to foster SWF compliance with appropriate local regulatory requirements (including on public disclosure); second, to promote safe and sound corporate governance practices among SWFs; third, to establish rules to promote global financial stability; and fourth, to ensure that SWFs invest for commercial and not political objectives.[73] The twenty-four principles are divided into three areas: legal, institutional, and investment and risk management.

At first sight, the principles are comprehensive and do contain specific best practices that respond directly to concerns voiced by SWF critics. One prominent commentator says that "the GAPP is a solid piece of work that should help dispel some of the mystery and suspicion surrounding SWFs" and that the principles are "quite forthright in confronting the issue of political motivation by calling, in principle 19.1, for SWFs to declare publicly their use of non-economic considerations."[74] The GAPP also includes some aggressive wording on ethical standards for internal SWF management.

However, the principles also have notable weaknesses. First, they remain silent on two of the core issues that SWF critics originally fought to put on the agenda: transparency and accountability. Some principles do contain language regarding enhancing accountability structures and reporting, but this is limited to internal management and the transparency of funds to their owners. Another issue not covered is public disclosure of financial statements and of the size and composition of assets under management. On balance, while the Santiago Principles constitute useful progress toward defining globally accepted standards for best practices in many important areas, they fall short of being a comprehensive framework.

It seems fair to argue that the economic crisis proved to OECD countries just how much they really need SWF capital. As such, the crisis proved useful to SWFs

---

73. International Working Group of Sovereign Wealth Funds (2008), p. 4.
74. Truman (2008a).

in two ways: demonstrating the interdependence of SWFs and OECD economies and distracting policymakers from the political and frequently ideological battle about SWF investments. Ultimately, with policymakers out of the picture, cooler heads prevailed, and the dialogue regarding codes of conduct was limited primarily to economic advisers and SWF owners. In essence, the economic crisis created room for SWFs to finalize aspects of the Santiago Principles.

Conclusion

The launch of the Santiago Principles in the autumn of 2008 was hailed as an important step in building a rules-based multilateral framework for SWF investment. Both the SWFs and their main critics in the OECD called the new rules an important step forward.

And yet the new rules are entirely voluntary, do not contain specifics regarding transparency and accountability, and lack a coherent monitoring process.[75] That does not necessarily imply, however, that the voluntary rules agreed upon by the IWG will not have any impact or that these rules represent the final word on multilateral regulation regarding SWF investment. There are multiple examples from other policy arenas that suggest that voluntary codes of conduct can make a difference over time. For example, studies suggest that "naming and shaming" has been a very effective strategy for international voluntary codes for labor standards.[76]

However, other examples suggest the limits of voluntary codes. As discussed in chapter 14 of this volume, by Thorsten Benner and Ricardo de Soares Oliveira, the experience of the voluntary Extractive Industries Transparency Initiative (EITI) suggests that voluntary instruments have built-in structural limits and that their effectiveness depends on a variety of factors. Voluntary codes are market based, that is, based on incentives and information rather than mandatory rules and sanctions. Thus the eventual impact of the Santiago Principles will depend on how effective incentives and information can be employed. There exists an attentive audience that will monitor how consistently the principles are followed by the various SWFs. Thus public pressure, a key driver behind the success of voluntary standards in other areas, is likely to be fairly significant. However, peer pressure, another effective factor in voluntary standards, is likely to be rather low.

75. The IMF will not play a monitoring role under the GAPP. Alternatively, the IWG will work to create a standing group of SWFs primarily to maintain a dialogue between the funds and to address issues "of value to us and of value to recipient countries in particular." *Inside US-China Trade* (2008).
76. Witte (2008).

One thing seems fairly certain: the Santiago Principles are an important bench-mark, against which the performance of SWFs will be measured.[77] In addition, it is unlikely that these principles represent the final word on SWF regulation. Instead, there is some evidence that, once the current financial crisis has subsided, the issue of SWF regulation might return to the policy agenda of many OECD nations.

One extreme of OECD opinion is exemplified by French President Nicolas Sarkozy, who says, "I don't accept that certain sovereign wealth funds can buy anything here and our own capitalists can't buy anything in their countries. I demand reciprocity before we open Europe's barriers."[78] In his call for reciprocity in investment rules, Sarkozy has been supported by Italy, among others. Germany, representing the other point of view, is skeptical of this French proposal. Now the Russia-Ukraine gas crisis of early 2009 has returned the issue of foreign government ownership of critical infrastructure to the political agenda.[79] Just when the SWF issue will reemerge on political agendas depends partly on the effectiveness of the Santiago Principles.

One issue that both the owners of SWFs as well as OECD policymakers have to keep in mind is that a reliable and stable policy environment for SWF invest-ment is in the interest of all parties. The global financial crisis underlines the important but often overlooked fact that SWFs and recipient countries are highly interdependent. "The more the KIA invests in Europe," says Bader al-Saad, man-aging director of the Kuwait Investment Authority, "the greater our vested inter-est to ensure Europe's continued economic growth and stability, otherwise our investments would be adversely impacted."[80] Similarly, many policymakers in the OECD world recognize the stabilizing role SWFs can play in their economies. The recognition of this mutual interdependence should be the starting point and guiding factor for future discussions of multilateral SWF regulation.

Regardless of the eventual effectiveness of the Santiago Principles, the IWG process testifies to an underlying power shift in the broader global governance architecture. This is the first time in modern economic history that capital flows are reversing themselves. Rich Middle East states, flush with cash from commod-ity revenues, are investing on an unprecedented scale in the West. Under these

---

77. Rachel Ziemba, "Sovereign Wealth Funds: Tallying the Losses (Again)," *RGE Analysts EconoMonitor,* November 26, 2008.

78. "Sarkozy Attacks Wealth Funds on Eve of Mideast Trip," Reuters, January 12, 2008.

79. Jonathan Elkind and Edward Chow, "Don't Act Surprised," *International Herald Tribune,* January 7, 2009.

80. "Global Outlook: SWFs—Out of Proportion," *Financial Times,* August 1, 2008.

conditions, the ability of the G-7 to determine unilaterally the rules of the game in the global economy is severely undermined. Governance of the global economy increasingly requires bringing in new actors with the power and wherewithal to affect policy outcomes. Much as in the areas of consumer-consumer cooperation and consumer-producer cooperation, governance needs to be inclusive to be effective.

References

Amuzegar, Jahangir. 2001. *Managing the Oil Wealth: OPEC's Windfalls and Pitfalls.* London: I.B. Tauris.

Barlas, Stephen. 2008. "Democrats Want Tougher Reviews of Investments by Sovereign Wealth Funds." *Strategic Finance* (May).

Beck, Roland, and Michael Fidora. 2008. "The Impact of Sovereign Wealth Funds on Global Financial Markets." Occasional Paper. Frankfurt am Main: European Central Bank.

BMWi. 2008. "Investitionsfreiheit und Pruefung auslaendischer Investitionen—kein Widerspruch." *Schlaglichter der Wirtschaftspolitik* (March).

Butkiewicz, Lynann, Nicholas Pettifer, and Tom Young. 2008. "Sovereign Wealth Funds: Don't Overreact." *International Financial Law Review* (April 23).

Delamaide, Darrell. 2008. "The IMF Is Back." *Institutional Investor* (American ed.) (September).

Drezner, Daniel. 2008. *Sovereign Wealth Funds and the (in)Security of Global Finance.* Hearing. U.S. House of Representatives (www.house.gov/apps/list/hearing/financialsvcs_dem/9-10-08_drezner_house_testimony.pdf).

Eschweiler, Bernard. 2008. "A Bottom-Up Primer on Sovereign Wealth Funds." New York: JP Morgan Research.

Fisher, Drosten, and others. 2008. "Assessing the Risks: The Behaviors of Sovereign Wealth Funds in the Global Economy." Cambridge, Mass.: Monitor Group.

Getter, Darryl E., and others. 2007. "Financial Crisis? The Liquidity Crunch of August 2007." Congressional Research Service.

Gieve, John. 2008. "Sovereign Wealth Funds and Global Imbalances." Paper presented at Sovereign Wealth Fund Management Conference, March 14.

Griffith-Jones, Stephany, and Jose Antonio Ocampo. 2008. "Sovereign Wealth Funds: A Developing Country Perspective." UN World Investment Report.

International Monetary Fund. 2008. "Sovereign Wealth Funds: A Work Agenda." Washington.

International Working Group of Sovereign Wealth Funds. 2008. *Generally Accepted Principles and Practices ("Santiago Principles").* Washington: International Monetary Fund.

Jen, Stephen. 2007. "Currencies: How Big Could Sovereign Wealth Funds Be by 2015?" Frankfurt am Main: Morgan Stanley Global.

Kekic, Laza. 2007. "The Economist Intelligence Unit's Index of Democracy." *The World in 2007.* London: The Economist.

Kern, Steffen. 2007. "Sovereign Wealth Funds: State Investments on the Rise." Frankfurt am Main: Deutsche Bank Research.

Kimmitt, Robert. 2008a. "In Praise of Foreign Investment: Best Practices for Sovereign Wealth Funds." *International Economy* (Spring).

————. 2008b. "Public Footprints in Private Markets: Sovereign Wealth Funds and the World Economy." *Foreign Affairs* (January/February).

Marchick, David J., and Matthew J. Slaughter. 2008. "Global FDI Policy: Correcting a Protectionist Shift." Special Report 34. New York: Council on Foreign Relations, June.

Mattoo, Aaditya, and Arvind Subramanian. 2008. "Currency Undervaluation and Sovereign Wealth Funds: A New Role for the World Trade Organization." Working Paper WP-02. Washington: Peterson Institute.

McCormick, David H. 2007. Testimony before Senate Committee on Banking, Housing, and Urban Affairs, November 14.

Morgan, Bryn. 2008. "Economic Indicators." Research Paper. House of Commons Library Series. London.

Pettifer, Nicholas. 2008. "IMF Persists with Pointless Sovereign Wealth 'Code.' " *International Financial Law Review* (September).

Roeller, Lars-Hendrik, and Nicolas Veron. 2008. "Safe and Sound: An EU Approach to Sovereign Investment." Policy Brief 2008/8. Brussels: Bruegel Institute.

Stokes, Bruce. 2007. "Gold Sovereigns." *National Journal* 39, no. 35.

Truman, Edwin M. 2007. Testimony before Senate Committee on Banking, Housing, and Urban Affairs, November 14.

————. 2008a. "Making the World Safe for Sovereign Wealth Funds." *Economic Issues Watch* (www.petersoninstitute.org/realtime/?p=105).

————. 2008b. "Blueprint for Sovereign Wealth Fund Best Practices." IIE Policy Brief PB08-3 (www.petersoninstitute.org/publications/pb/pb08-3.pdf).

U.S. Department of the Treasury. 2007. *Statement of G-7 Finance Ministers and Central Bank Governors.* HP-625 (www.treasury.gov/press/releases/hp625.htm [January 2009]).

Witte, Jan Martin. 2008. "Realizing Core Labor Standards: The Potential and Limits of Voluntary Codes and Social Clauses." Bonn: BMZ.

16

Global Energy Governance: The Way Forward

Andreas Goldthau, Wade Hoxtell, and Jan Martin Witte

This book presents a new analytical perspective for examining contemporary public policy challenges in global energy. As emphasized in the introduction to this volume, much of the recent debate in the field is characterized by a fairly narrow focus on resource nationalism, access to energy, and corresponding geopolitical implications. This perspective, it is argued, is based on the myopic assumption that global energy politics is necessarily a zero-sum game, in which one country's energy security is another's lack thereof. We posit that this traditional focus on energy security is incomplete at best and quite frequently results in misleading policy conclusions.

Instead, the book's ambition is to widen the debate on global energy politics by focusing on the role of world energy markets and, more important, on the institutions that underpin and structure these markets. As all contributions to this volume emphasize, this focus on markets and institutions does not negate the relevance of politics in determining outcomes in global energy. Quite to the contrary: politics plays a crucial role. However, the focus on markets and institutions also highlights the ever increasing interdependence that characterizes global energy markets and points to the significance of the design of frameworks of exchange.

The chapters in this volume make two important contributions. First, they close an obvious gap in the current research discourse on energy security by introducing a governance-oriented perspective. Assessing the key drivers and levers that determine the behavior of actors in global energy relations (such as energy companies, governments, public and private financial organizations), the chapters offer a complementary perspective on prevalent state-centered analyses in current debates. Second, based on this governance-oriented perspective, the contributions to this book also offer policy recommendations on how to improve global energy governance, particularly in light of several fundamental challenges to international energy markets, including the rise of new energy consumers, the resurgence of state players in energy, and climate change. In this chapter we pull together the main results of the analyses contained in this book and summarize the main policy conclusions.

Widening the Perspective: From Energy Security to Global Energy Governance

Various contributions to this book emphasize that a singular focus on hard security in global energy alone entails the risk of generating misleading analyses and policy prescriptions. For example, at closer inspection, the popular concept of energy diplomacy provides a rather disingenuous perspective on the realities of today's energy markets. As Amy Myers Jaffe and Ronald Soligo show in chapter 6, an inherent principal-agent problem delimits the ability of governments in China, Russia, and elsewhere to manipulate their national oil companies (NOCs) in pursuing the country's national interest. All too often, the NOCs are the drivers rather than the tools of expansion strategies. This has significant implications for any policy recipes designed to counter the alleged resource nationalism of new global energy players.

Furthermore, empirical evidence also suggests that energy diplomacy may be much less effective and beneficial to those who pursue it than is widely assumed. In fact, as Andreas Goldthau shows in chapter 2, many of the deals that are being put together by NOCs may be problematic from a business point of view. Energy deals that come together as a result of foreign policy interventions by governments tend to feature high political risk and a low return on investment, thus resulting in higher energy prices for the country pursuing energy diplomacy. A case in point is China's engagement in Africa. In contrast to popular perceptions, the apparent Chinese "scramble for resources" may in the end mean that China is "taking one for the team" by producing African oil at higher cost and shoring up global supply while at the same time taking a significant international political beating for its reconnaissance efforts with corrupt, and in some cases violent, African regimes. China's problems in Africa were (and are likely to remain) compounded in an environment of a soft international oil market with lower price levels.

Moreover, this book emphasizes that widely held beliefs regarding the role of state-backed financing of oil (and gas) projects need to be reassessed. As Amy Myers Jaffe and Ronald Soligo underline, NOCs tend to finance their investments much less via favorable, state-backed financing schemes than is widely assumed. Instead, in their home countries they are confronted with demands for granting sizable subsidies for domestic energy consumption by households as well as by industry. As a consequence, the NOCs face strong financial limitations to expanding business and tackling demanding projects, which may put in question their ability to increase supply.

Finally, as Enno Harks emphasizes in chapter 12, the key problem in global oil is not the famously looming peak; rather, it is above-ground factors of oil production, such as investment levels and a low level of information on oil markets. Yet since these are often ignored, popular debates on energy security tend to portray a simplistic picture of lock-up efforts in resources. As a result, analyses and policy recommendations center on geopolitical solutions.

In all, the contributions to this book suggest that a narrow focus on energy security—conceptualized as a zero-sum game, in which nations compete for access to resources—is not sufficient for understanding the dynamics of global energy politics. Instead, it is crucial to understand the role that markets and institutions play in determining outcomes in global energy relations. Again, this does not deny the fact that contemporary global energy challenges are highly political. As Albert Bressand stresses in chapter 13, there exists the paradox of a truly global market coinciding with an ever more powerful role of governments in setting the long-term energy parameters. As a consequence, and as the various contributors to this volume emphasize, a perspective that takes markets and institutions seriously needs to include their underlying political-economic dynamics. However, this perspective does move the policy debate on contemporary energy challenges away from the traditional notion of energy security and toward a discussion of global energy governance: the complex web of codified rules and regulations that informs and incentivizes market players (energy companies, commercial banks, and so on) and that is managed, monitored, and enforced by the public sector (governments as well as international organizations).

Understanding the Role of Institutions in Global Energy Governance

Access to oil and gas will, despite mounting concerns over accelerating climate change and efforts to engineer a renewable energy revolution, remain a key policy objective for governments around the world. As Ralf Dickel stresses in chapter 5,

UN Resolution 1803 stipulates that it is indeed governments that are the owners of the resources on their territory (with a prominent exception being the United States), which by definition puts them in charge of defining the modes of resource access and extraction. Yet it is important to recognize that key aspects of energy ventures—finance, trade, and even risk management—are by definition first and foremost mediated through the market.

This does not imply that markets exist in a vacuum, like a God-given infrastructure that, through the invisible hand, self-creates and maintains itself. Instead it is important to point out that markets are created by policy and maintained by institutions. The specific shape of such institutions, formal as well as informal, determines the effectiveness of the provision of the good in question, be it energy supply at affordable prices, efficient allocation of capital, or security of investment.

For the purpose of this book, and following Douglass North, institutions are defined as the rules of the game according to which actors play. Consisting of formal rules (laws, regulations), informal constraints (norms, conventions), and often embracing enforcement mechanisms, institutions are crucial in setting incentives for market participants to compete on price and quality. Three functional categories of institutions in global energy are introduced in chapter 1. First, there are institutions designed to correct for market failures; second, there are institutions designed to lower transaction costs; and third, there are institutions designed to set rules and standards for market exchanges. While these categories do not represent a full-fledged typology of the institutions structuring interaction in global energy, they are useful heuristic devices for highlighting the types of incentive structures and the issues they are designed to address.

The analyses of institutions contained in this volume span the entire spectrum of the global energy arena: trade and investment rules (part 1), the structure of financial markets and how they affect oil and gas markets (part 2), and institutions governing short-term supply management and long-term energy cooperation (part 3). The book also includes analyses of emerging issues in global energy, such as the implications of petrodollars recycling through sovereign wealth funds and the emerging international rules on resource governance (part 4). If relevant and possible, analyses also take account of the global financial crisis, which started in 2008 and is likely to have a significant impact on global energy and its underlying institutions. In what follows, we summarize the key points that emerged from the analyses.

Institutions for Correcting Market Failures

A number of chapters in this volume reinforce the basic insight that energy markets, much like any other market, sometimes fail. Market failure can be a consequence of various factors. For example, the high capital intensity of the oil market, combined with the significant political risk that is often associated with upstream investments, has historically resulted in less than perfect market structures. The market dominance of the Seven Sisters until the late 1960s is one of the most striking examples. More recently, the consolidation of the European energy market has given rise to similar concerns over increasing industry concentration and potential implications.

Various chapters in this volume point to institutions designed to address market failures in global energy markets. For example, the International Energy Agency's (IEA) emergency response mechanisms, as pointed out by Wilfrid Kohl in chapter 10, address a potential market failure triggered by intentional or unintentional supply-side problems in the international oil market. The latter may occur as a consequence of the producers' inability to make up for sudden shortages, caused for instance by adverse incidents in major producing countries, such as domestic turmoil or a strike; by natural disasters, such as hurricanes; or by collective action of producing states within the realm of the Organization of the Petroleum Exporting Countries (OPEC).

The IEA's mechanisms to address market failure, most prominently the Coordinated Emergency Response Mechanism (CERM), face significant challenges ahead, most obviously caused by the rise of new consumers such as China and India and the resulting shift of the traditional consumer base for oil and gas. Yet in addition to necessary institutional reforms with regard to OECD membership and the allocation of voting shares in the organization, important additional issues need to be considered. These include the potential for free riding by new consumers and the impact of the ongoing financial crisis on the buildup of strategic petroleum reserves (SPRs) in new consumer countries. With regard to the latter, the financial crisis may actually trigger two alternative results. On the one hand, the new consumers may find it easier to build up SPRs due to lower crude prices (at least in part triggered by the global economic recession of 2008 and 2009). On the other hand, the recession will likely drain the public coffers of these countries and undermine their ability to develop their SPRs. It remains to be seen which effect will have a larger impact in the months and years ahead. With regard to the challenge of free riding by new consumers, no clear-cut solutions appear to be at hand.

In recent years, the specter of supply disruptions has been discussed in other institutional forums such as the European Union (EU) and even the G-8, which also includes producer countries (in particular Russia). Yet despite their desire and stated intention to deal with issues of market failure, these forums at present seem ill equipped to fulfill this objective. In addition, the role and value of forums such as the G-8 vis-à-vis the IEA remain unclear. The proliferation of forums and organizations dealing with energy issues may not help to address the underlying problem but instead create a patchwork of competing structures.

In gas markets, mechanisms designed to address short-term security of supply are emerging as well; yet, as highlighted by Dick de Jong, Coby van der Linde, and Tom Smeenk, in chapter 11, costs play a more prominent role and hence render buffer mechanisms such as those established for oil more complicated in the case of gas. Given uncertainty about the future of liquefied natural gas (LNG) and rapidly changing business models in international gas markets, these authors suggest that consumers diversify their energy mix and enhance regional cooperation on energy in order to reduce market risks. Furthermore, they emphasize that focusing on the creation of additional LNG capacity in the EU may come at the expense of a more secure and potentially cost-effective way of handling short-term supply crises, namely through the construction and utilization of more storage facilities. Producers, by contrast, could use the emerging Gas Exporting Countries Forum (GECF) as a risk management device. In addition, the authors suggest that producer and consumer companies integrate along the value chain, sharing risk in a market characterized by a high degree of uncertainty.

Finally, Hill Huntington and Christine Jojarth, in chapter 8, point to a different form of market failure in the case of alternative energy. Here markets fail to provide a sufficient amount of the good in question (renewable energy) even if demanded by consumers. This market failure is a consequence of investment obstacles created by tightening credit markets and, ironically, plummeting oil prices. These authors argue that incentives—that is, government policies—are required to internalize the negative spillover effects of fossil fuel dependence and the externalities associated with investments in research and development of alternative energy, ensuring its effective provision.

Institutions for Lowering Transaction Costs

Various chapters address the key role that institutions play in reducing transaction costs in global energy markets. For example, at present the global oil market is characterized by a lack of encompassing and reliable data, caused by certain countries' lacking the willingness (or the ability) to reveal information on production and consumption levels. This lack is exacerbated by the fact that emerging consumers such as China, which play an increasingly dominant role in the global oil market, also reveal no detailed information. In addition, while almost all producer countries in the Persian Gulf have kept their production levels notoriously opaque since the 1970s, domestic consumption in these states is on the rise and remains an equally unknown factor. In all, available information on these two crucial market factors for the world outside of the OECD at best reflects an educated guess; yet at the same time most of the demand and production growth will be in non-OECD countries, according to IEA projections. This lack of information creates enormous transaction costs, which, as Kohl points out, are partly addressed by the IEA's data-gathering exercises.

Yet, as Harks argues, the International Energy Forum (IEF) may offer a platform to address this thorny issue. In fact it is somewhat of a surprise that the IEF has only emerged in recent years, given the stakes both consumers and producers have in stable markets, low price volatility, and hence, reduced adjustment costs. As Dickel argues, enhancing transparency on the producers' side would not affect sovereign depletion decisions but would help to avoid bottlenecks and price volatility. At the same time, however, consuming countries would need to create transparency regarding their policies that affect future demand. According to Harks, the IEF's Joint Oil Data Initiative (JODI) has great potential to make oil markets more transparent and data more reliable, while the IEF itself could then be used for discussions on a price floor, on depletion paths, and on how to deal with the impact of the financial crisis on both consumption and investment levels. In this respect, the unprecedented price volatility in oil markets during 2008, which has been harmful for both consumers and producers alike, presents a unique window of opportunity for both sides to come together and discuss these issues in depth. Overall, however, Harks points out that the IEF should remain flexible and incomplete so as to allow for adaptation to current and future challenges.

Finally, supporting the idea of a price floor, Albert Bressand in chapter 13 points to an interesting alternative proposal initially put forward by Robert Mabro. Mabro argues that keeping oil prices within an agreed band would require the equivalent of controls over money supply at the disposal of central bankers. This would mean that consumer and producer countries would need to cooperate on commercial and strategic inventories as well as spare production capacities in order to keep prices at the desired levels. While this suggestion is certainly not common sense, elements of a de facto cooperation along these lines apparently already exist between the United States and Saudi Arabia.

Institutions for Setting Standards and Rules

Various chapters in this book analyze institutions designed to set standards and rules for market exchange in global energy markets. In contrast to institutions designed to lower transaction costs (for example, by sharing and disseminating market information), rules-setting institutions seek to create a level playing field for energy markets. That does not imply that standards and rules have to be binding. In fact many of the rules and standards that exist in global energy markets emanate from private sources and are nonbinding.

As Yulia Selivanova shows in chapter 3, the existing global frameworks governing trade and investment in energy are an institutional patchwork, with significant overlaps but also sizable gaps. Existing institutions setting rules in this context include the World Trade Organization (WTO), regional trade bodies both general in scope or specific to energy, such as the Energy Charter Treaty (ECT), and a myriad of bilateral trade and investment agreements that have an impact on energy. Selivanova also shows that the patchwork is not necessarily to the detriment of international regulation of energy trade and investment. Given the obvious absence of a Leviathan at the international level, and considering the difficult decision-making process in the WTO as well as the fact that the interests of its member states strongly diverge, she considers energy-specific forums such as the ECT potentially more effective providers of rules and standards specific to energy trade.

Will Blyth's contribution (chapter 7), by contrast, underlines the challenge of potentially conflicting structures of emerging carbon markets at the national and regional level. In their attempt to find suitable systems for the regulation of greenhouse gas emissions, policymakers have not just invested in the development of global rules (especially through the UNFCCC process) but, partly because of the slowness of these global negotiations and the significant potential for failure, have also launched national and regional regulatory structures to facilitate the emergence of carbon markets. These different systems are not fully compatible. While Blyth argues that this bottom-up approach is necessary to begin moving forward with national and regional systems (a process much more politically feasible and thus easier to quickly enact than a global scheme), he stresses that progress needs to be made in parallel at the global level to develop standards alongside which these national and regional systems can evolve harmoniously. Otherwise, the eventual linkage of these different carbon markets into a functioning global system will become a difficult task indeed.

Simonetta Zarrilli, in chapter 4, points to a similar problem for the case of biofuels. Biofuels, while at the front and center of major consuming nations in their efforts to find substitutes for fossil fuels, are not simple. Although they constitute a promising market, they also raise concerns related to food security, rising agricultural commodities prices, and environmental preservation. In addition, their provision is hampered by a lack of general market structures. Certifying biofuels on the basis of their sustainability, Zarrilli argues, may encourage more sustainable production worldwide. In addition, reduced and binding tariffs on biofuels, along with more precise customs classification, could improve market potential. Yet as the recently failed Doha trade talks reveal, general standards for such a crucial and emerging market are hard to achieve, leaving the biofuels industry subject to bilateral or regional negotiations, which do not necessarily yield globally optimal solutions.

Setting binding standards is also difficult in the case of an emerging theme in global energy politics, that is, resource governance. In their contribution to this volume, Thorsten Benner and Ricardo Soares de Oliveira (chapter 14) show that, thus far, the international resource governance regime is characterized by rather weak, nonbinding rules that therefore do not provide an effective, rules-based framework. They also show that, in contrast to the attention that consumer governments, especially in Europe, have attached to the issue in recent years, very little effort has been made to integrate rules for resource governance into mainstream international instruments regulating energy trade and investment. It appears that consumers and producers alike engage in a strategy of institutional forum shopping, where issues such as resource governance are delegated to rather soft institutional settings with little or no prospect of devising either binding rules or sanctioning mechanisms that could foster compliance.

Finally, in chapter 15, Jamie Manzer and Jan Martin Witte shed light on the political-economic dynamics underlying the setting of global rules for the investment of Sovereign Wealth Funds (SWFs). SWFs are government-owned investment vehicles that have seen tremendous growth during the past decade, primarily as a result of the energy price boom. Many OECD countries have voiced concerns over the rising prominence of these funds, fearing that they will pursue political-strategic rather than economic objectives. In this regard, the launch of the Santiago Principles in 2008, a framework providing rules for SWFs' investment behavior, is widely considered a success and a major step toward further regulation of these funds. Yet as Manzer and Witte show, the rules are entirely voluntary, do not include details regarding transparency and accountability, and lack a coherent monitoring process. As explained in the chapter, the emergence of this rather weak set of multilateral rules reflects the shift in the balance of power between investors (the SWFs) and receiving countries throughout late 2007 and 2008. As a result of the global financial crisis, calls for stricter regulation of SWFs were muted in recognition of the fact that SWF investments played a significant role in addressing the financial crisis. The SWFs in turn recognized the fortuitousness of the moment and pushed for a fast conclusion of the International Working Group's process.

All in all, and not surprisingly, institutions designed to set rules and standards tend to be the most conflictual and also appear to be the most incomplete and ineffective in terms of compliance management. The redistributive implications of changes in the rules of the game in global energy markets ensure that any significant changes will encounter considerable opposition. By contrast, institutions designed to lower transaction costs appear less conflictual, as they are focused on promoting joint gains among participating parties. The 2008 oil price roller-coaster, for example, induced enhanced producer-consumer dialogue under the auspices of the IEF in order to investigate both the causes and the effects of this unhealthy market development. One of the tangible results is an agreement among producers and consumers to set up a high-level group of experts to develop proposals for strengthening the institutional architecture of the IEF, presumably to help avoid such occurrences in the future.

Institutions in Energy: An Agenda for Future Research

This book is only a first cut at the much-neglected research on the role of institutions in global energy and covers only a subset of existing institutions. The categories put forward here are useful as heuristic devices but need to be further refined. The research agenda is vast, but a few issues stand out that require attention.

UNDERSTANDING THE HISTORICAL CONTEXT OF ENERGY INSTITUTIONS

Interestingly, many energy institutions were formed in response to a particular crisis: the IEA, OPEC, and most recently, the International Renewable Energy Agency (IRENA), along with various carbon trading schemes. Future research should focus in more detail on the political-economic dynamics underlying the emergence of new rules and institutions in the energy domain. Lessons can undoubtedly be learned from the recent major price shocks and their possible effects on the emergence of institutions. Lessons can also be learned from other public policy fields.

UNDERSTANDING THE DYNAMICS OF INSTITUTIONAL REFORM

As highlighted in all chapters in this volume, institutions governing global energy cannot remain static but constantly need to adapt to a changing global environment. Hence, future research needs to address the following important questions:

—Under what conditions do energy institutions adapt?
—How does the internal institutional logic determine reform paths?
—What tools are provided by concepts such as new institutional economics?
—How potent is new institutional economics in addressing and explaining institutional change in global energy?
—Where are the prescriptive limits, especially regarding transnational policy networks, advocacy coalitions, and all the fuzzy and messy issues in the agora of global governance?

UNDERSTANDING THE IMPLICATIONS OF INSTITUTIONAL PATCHWORKS

The global energy governance arena is, much like other policy domains, characterized by a patchwork of overlapping and sometimes competing rules and institutions. As shown in some chapters in this book, this patchwork can have negative implications for the efficiency and effectiveness of global energy governance. Future research could determine where and how the different institutional forums tie together, how they compete, and what implications this has for the effectiveness and efficiency of global energy governance.

UNDERSTANDING THE IMPLICATIONS OF INSTITUTIONAL REFORM FOR THE GLOBAL DEVELOPMENT AGENDA

Most energy-related goals of the global development agenda, such as fostering sustainable energy use, lowering energy intensity, and translating resource wealth into economic growth, require an assessment of the existing rules of the game. While the importance of resource governance and the potential economic benefits of the biofuels industry for developing countries are addressed in this book, a more encompassing approach is needed to fully understand the needs of developing countries regarding rules for trade, investment, and regulation in global energy. For example, what incentives are needed to foster knowledge and technology sharing so as to assist developing countries with low-carbon energy resources? Do initiatives such as the World Bank's Clean Energy Investment Framework offer a promising route, as Bressand suggests in chapter 13? And what global public policy agenda follows from that?

The Way Forward: Implications for Public Policy

The contributions to this book do not just provide a new analytical perspective on global energy politics. In addition, and building on the strong focus on rules and institutions, they also highlight areas that require urgent policy attention in order to strengthen the existing system of global energy governance.

Increasing Information and Transparency

Various chapters point to the fact that market-making institutional arrangements (providing for a greater degree of information, notably through data collection and exchange) must be fostered. Here, expanding the IEA's data-generating efforts becomes essential. However, existing institutions of producer-consumer cooperation must also be strengthened.

The IEF, in Riyadh, is the only meaningful forum for mutual exchange between producers and consumers on energy market developments and policies. Strengthening the institutionalized dialogue within the IEF will provide the capital-intensive upstream sector with planning security on future energy mixes in consuming nations and the latter with a clearer picture of depletion strategies and supply trends in major producing regions. Moreover, the IEF helps countries with a more mercantilist approach to energy security to move toward a more market-open approach. In this respect, it is important to reconcile the differences in methodology (and therefore projections) of the IEA's and OPEC's data-gathering mechanisms to help eliminate mistrust and incompatible projections. As illustrated by recent movements in the price of oil, the costs of volatility are painful for producers and consumers alike and should provide a new impetus for cooperation.

Furthermore, Western countries and activists should increase their efforts to get rising powers into the good governance boat. While voluntary approaches such as the Extractive Industries Transparency Initiative (EITI) have helped promote the need for better resource governance, they have failed to make significant changes on the ground in oil-rich countries. To be effective, these approaches must be superseded by binding mechanisms that anchor good governance in the core rules of global energy.

Bringing in the New Consumers

The existing mechanisms of emergency supply management require substantial adjustments, both to deal with new consumers and to account for potential market failure. Hence Western nations should search for ways to acquaint the newcomers with the IEA's key mechanisms. While some suggest IEA membership for the new consumers, this could prove problematic on a number of fronts. For example, these countries cannot easily satisfy the requirements of the International Energy Program (IEP) regarding oil stocks, data transparency, and commitment to a coordinated response mechanism. Others suggest the establishment of associate member status (see for example Wilfrid Kohl, chapter 10), a status that would allow these consumers into the IEP and CERM while the requirements were being met. Regardless of which avenue is pursued, it is necessary to determine the willingness of these countries to participate in these mechanisms. While the IEA has engaged new consumers such as China and India for quite some time, the IEA should continue its engagement and promote their participation, either through eventual full membership or a more flexible associate member approach.

The outlines of an emergency supply management system for the emerging global gas market are yet to be hammered out, a challenge that policymakers will inevitably have to address, depending on the speed with which markets integrate as a result of the rise of LNG. As de Jong, van der Linde, and Smeenk point out, the development of a global market for natural gas (along with other trends in the natural gas business) may decrease the energy security of consumers rather than increase it.

Setting Incentives for Trade and Investment

As highlighted in various contributions to this volume, institutions providing incentives for investment need to be reconsidered. In fact supply-side bottlenecks in oil and gas are less a question of resource availability (the infamous looming peak) than a question of investments in the right places and at a sufficient pace. As many authors point out, government policies are key in overcoming adverse market incentives and in ensuring sufficient investments in the right projects. This holds true for fossil fuels as well as for renewables. A lack of investment needs to be understood as a market failure, which requires joint action to be addressed.

As for trade in energy commodities, the existing international legal framework needs to be overhauled or adjusted, as trade agreements in the framework of the WTO (and GATT) were designed primarily to grant market access, not to address export restrictions and investment protection, which are most crucial for dealing with deficits in oil and gas upstream capacities. While a solution would be to push for the establishment of WTO rules to govern access and fair competition within the energy sector, such a move appears rather hypothetical given the recent failure of the Doha round. Yet it would be worth trying to convince producer nations that an institutional environment favoring an effective allocation of capital and investment is more likely to generate stable and reliable revenues than a situation in which price hikes result from inelastic supply and overstretched oil and gas infrastructure.

The recent return to "low" prices for global energy may alter the time horizons of the political leadership in exporting nations and make cooperative solutions possible. In addition, specialized frameworks targeting energy specifically may offer solutions. A case in point is the ECT, which, as proposed by Yulia Selivanova, could take over the function that the WTO is unable to fulfill. Due to the increasing reliance on internationally traded energy, a multilateral legal framework would provide the most effective way of achieving security of supply and demand and the necessary investment, predictability, and transparency.

Addressing Climate Change

The problem of climate change requires a shift of the rules of the game in global energy markets, specifically with regard to the regulatory framework for alternative energy sources. As the contributions of Huntington and Jojarth, Zarrilli, and Blyth show, synergies must be found between any international climate change mitigation framework and existing (or new) multilateral trade frameworks. It may indeed be necessary to build a new subset of rules specifically for international trading of renewable energy products, perhaps the most pressing of which are global rules for biofuels.

As the global biofuels market grows, it will be essential to avoid a patchwork of rules and individual sustainability or certification schemes through the establishment of commonly accepted standards, a process in which all stakeholders, including developing countries, should be involved. On the developmental side, the largely rural developing countries could profit from a boom in biofuels by serving (and perhaps more important, participating in) growing world markets while at the same time reducing dependency on increasingly expensive fossil fuel imports. Furthermore, fostering international classification can lead to a commercialization of environmentally sustainable and cost competitive bioenergy technologies.

As noted, the development of rules for carbon markets will face a multitude of challenges. Although global negotiations in the context of the UNFCCC process, even with an open-minded U.S. administration, are likely to be slow, various national and regional carbon markets are emerging. These rules, while trying to accomplish the same thing, are not entirely compatible. In fact, as Will Blyth argues, without some standardization of carbon market rules at the international level, this patchwork of national and regional carbon markets may at some point become a significant hurdle for effective global action on climate change.

The Financial Crisis and Its Implications

As several authors in this book note, the current financial crisis is likely to affect global energy considerably along a number of fronts. Due to the downturn in economic activity, the demand outlook has become highly uncertain. The resulting lower prices have a negative effect on producers' revenues, which may lead them to siphon even more money off the profits of their NOCs to sustain domestic programs begun during period of higher prices. This will most likely hinder crucially needed upstream investments. Hence chances are that the recent price hike, followed by a relative low-price phase, will end up in another high-price phase further down the road.

In a decade's time the combination of delayed projects, a cap on corporate research and development, and a lack of credit may translate into a supply crunch. In addition, not only the volume but also the timing of investment decisions, both in oil and in gas, may be affected. Major gas producers such as Gazprom have already announced cuts in spending in upstream and field development. In turn, lower prices for fossil fuels may also undermine the economic incentives to invest in renewables. This could once again shift the consumers' focus away from the use of alternatives, a pattern observed in the aftermath of the 1970s' oil price shocks. As Joe Stanislaw points out in chapter 9, with world leaders absorbed by economic survival, the challenge of reworking the world's approach to global energy governance may no longer be a top priority.

It remains to be seen what sectors the current economic stimulus packages will target and what effect they will have on energy. In all, while an in-depth examination of the impact of the ongoing financial and economic crisis is not possible at this stage, two policy implications can be drawn.

First, the financial crisis underlines the need for effective multilateral investment frameworks that can contribute to security of supply. As noted above, the financial crisis is likely to exacerbate the investment gap that already exists in many producing countries. Facilitating international investment will be essential to develop new energy resources. Progress in this highly politicized area depends to a large extent on a strengthening of the producer-consumer dialogue in the context of the IEF. Such dialogue is important to share data and to enhance transparency in energy markets. Perhaps even more important, dialogue will build trust. To achieve those objectives, the IEF will have to be strengthened. This provides additional urgency to the creation of a high-level expert group to make proposals for strengthening the institutional architecture of IEF, as suggested by Harks. In light of increased oil price volatility—a fact that has negative implications for both consumers and producers—there may be a new political will to make progress on that front.

Second, the financial crisis is likely to have a significant impact on the climate change agenda. Most important, there will be less money for fostering the growth of renewable energies. As Huntington and Jojarth point out, the challenge for governments will be to find ways to shoulder the costs of emissions caps while also running big budget deficits. In addition, it is likely that the economic downturn will generate political pressure to slow down a switch from oil and gas into more expensive renewable energy sources.

In all, the current economic crisis calls for meaningful and encompassing policies that include all stakeholders and that target the adverse incentives provided by faltering energy prices. And, as Stanislaw pointedly argues in his chapter, a crisis is a terrible thing to waste. Now, governments are able to spend unprecedented amounts of money and have a unique window of opportunity to tackle the twin challenges of energy security and climate change.

Outlook

In conclusion, and counter to popular perceptions, the energy world of the future is unlikely be a world of producers versus consumers, or of old consumers versus new ones. The main reason for this is that all actors in the energy domain have shared interests. Most fundamentally, consumers' quest for supply security is matched by producers' quest for demand security. And while the new consumers' interest lies in overcoming the disadvantages of being latecomers in the global market, the old consumers' interest is to accommodate them at least possible cost—that is, in a conflict-free manner. In a nutshell, as stressed by Bressand, consumers should make the effort and look at the world energy scene through the eyes of producers, and vice versa. Hence public discussions centering on who wins and who loses focus on the wrong question. Instead, and following an argument raised by Joseph Stanislaw in an earlier piece, they should address how we can best balance competition and cooperation in a changing energy world, accommodating the interests of producers and consumers in ways most effective and efficient.[1]

In fact, it is not only Western import dependencies of up to 100 percent of consumption that are at stake in a price shock but also oil revenues accounting for approximately 50 percent of Venezuela's, 90 percent of Saudi Arabia's, and almost 100 percent of Kuwait's government income. Hence rather than pointing to geopolitical options, the answer to these challenges is that functioning markets play a key role and, if properly managed and structured through appropriate rules and institutions, can satisfy the needs of all players. Avoiding zero-sum games requires adapting the rules of the game in global energy markets along all three fronts sketched above: building and extending markets, addressing market failures, and setting standards.

Existing institutions need to be overhauled and made ready for the energy realities of the twenty-first century. Such an institutional overhaul must capitalize on the cooperative potential among consumers as well as between producers and consumers, to ensure that market forces can work even in the face of enhanced state control over reserves, strong state players in the industry, and a tight supply-demand balance. In that, make no mistake: reforming the rules of the game for global energy governance is a thoroughly political exercise and will require major efforts by all involved players.

---

1. Joseph A. Stanislaw, "Energy Competition or Cooperation: Shifting the Paradigm," *Economic Perspectives* 9 (May 2004), pp. 17–20.

Contributors

THORSTEN BENNER
Global Public Policy Institute, Berlin

WILLIAM BLYTH
*Chatham House, Royal Institute for
International Affairs, London*

ALBERT BRESSAND
*School of International and Public
Affairs, Columbia University*

DICK DE JONG
*Clingendael International Energy
Programme*

RALF DICKEL
Energy Charter Secretariat

ANDREAS GOLDTHAU
*Central European University, Budapest,
and Global Public Policy Institute,
Berlin*

ENNO HARKS
*Global Public Policy Institute,
Berlin*

WADE HOXTELL
*Global Public Policy Institute,
Berlin*

HILLARD HUNTINGTON
*Energy Modeling Forum,
Stanford University*

CHRISTINE JOJARTH
*Center on Democracy, Development,
and the Rule of Law, Stanford
University*

FREDERIC KALINKE
*Department of Politics and
International Relations, Oxford
University (MPhil candidate)*

WILFRID L. KOHL
*School of Advanced International
Studies, Johns Hopkins University*

JAMIE MANZER
*Global Public Policy Institute,
Berlin*

AMY MYERS JAFFE
*James A. Baker Institute for Public
Policy, Rice University*

YULIA SELIVANOVA
Energy Charter Secretariat

TOM SMEENK
*Clingendael International Energy
Programme*

RICARDO SOARES DE OLIVEIRA
*Department of Politics and
International Relations,
Oxford University*

RONALD SOLIGO
Rice University

JOSEPH A. STANISLAW
*Deloitte LLP and The JAStanislaw
Group, LLC*

COBY VAN DER LINDE
*Clingendael International Energy
Programme*

JAN MARTIN WITTE
Global Public Policy Institute, Berlin

SIMONETTA ZARRILLI
*Division on International Trade and
Commodities, United Nations
Conference on Trade and
Development*

Index

Aasgard field development, 120
Abdullah (Crown Prince of Saudi Arabia), 257
Abu Dhabi National Oil Company, 107
Abyssinia invasion by Italy, 27
ACP Group (African, Caribbean, and Pacific countries), 81, 82
Afghanistan: as ECT member, 62; Soviet invasion of, 113
Africa: China's energy diplomacy in, 28, 34–35, 36–38, 43–44; exploration and development investment, 109, 111; Gazprom expansion in, 31, 33. *See also specific countries*
African, Caribbean, and Pacific countries (ACP Group), 81, 82
Agreement on ASEAN Energy Cooperation, 66–67
Agreement on Basic Telecommunication Services, 55
Agreement on Technical Barriers to Trade (TBT Agreement), 91
Agriculture: biofuels classified as, 78; and mandatory biofuel use policies, 79, 87; and renewable energy, 15; sustainable practices, 89
Ahmadov, Ingilab, 300
Aid-for-oil approach, 34–35
Algeria: FDI in, 116; Gazprom expansion in, 33; LNG production, 225, 229, 233, 243; NOC fuel subsidies, 115; service contracts in, 117
Aliyev, Heydar, 300

Aliyev, Ilham, 300
Alternative energy, 161–81; and climate change, 170–77; economics of, 165–68; and energy security, 168–70; future investments, 172–79; investment drivers, 17, 162–72, 183; politics of, 168–72; research and development policies, 177–79; technology investments, 163–65
American Depositary Shares, 121
Andean Trade Preferences Pact, 84
Anglo-Iranian Oil Company, 3
Angola: and energy diplomacy, 36; FDI in, 116; governance and transparency in, 293; nationalization of resources in, 124
Anhydrous ethanol. *See* Ethanol
Antidumping duties, 82
APEC (Asia-Pacific Economic Cooperation), 13
Arbitration under ECT, 65
Arctic National Wildlife Refuge, 169
Argentina and WTO negotiations, 95
Armenia: and biofuels import tariffs, 81; and energy diplomacy, 35
Arms sales, 35–36
Asbestos case (GATT), 92
ASEAN (Association of Southeast Asian Nations), 66–67
Asia: China's FDI in, 37; LNG market, 224–25, 228–30, 241. *See also specific countries*

Asia-Pacific Economic Cooperation (APEC), 13
Asia-Pacific region: LNG trading basin, 5–6,
228–30; natural gas market exchanges, 40
Association of Southeast Asian Nations (ASEAN),
66–67
Atlantic LNG trading basin, 228–30, 231
Auction markets for carbon allowances, 149
Australia: biofuels import tariffs, 80, 83; carbon mar-
kets in, 155; concession agreements in, 117; as
ECT member, 62; ethanol production, 76; FDI
in, 116; and IEA, 216; in International Working
Group, 333; LNG production, 229
Austria and renewable energy targets, 175
Azerbaijan: and biofuels import tariffs, 81; and EITI,
296; FDI in, 117; in International Working
Group, 333; Russia's energy diplomacy in, 38;
transparency reforms, 300–02

Baker, Raymond W., 308
Baker Institute, 109, 119, 127
Baku–Tblisi–Ceyhan pipeline, 27
Bali Action Plan, 135
Baxter, Graham, 302
Beck, Roland, 322
Belarus: and energy diplomacy, 35; and Gazprom,
33; Russia's energy diplomacy in, 38
Belgium and biofuels certification system, 90
Beltransgaz, 38
Benner, Thorsten, 19, 287, 337, 349
Berle, Adolph, 124–25
Bilateral agreements: and biofuels import tariffs, 84;
energy markets, 14; and market systems, 40; and
NOCs, 130; trade and investment framework,
51, 66–68
Biodiesel: as chemical product, 78; EU imports of
feedstocks for, 82; production process, 75–76,
93–94; tax credit, 80. See also Biofuels
Biodiversity, 86–87, 89, 90, 91
Biofuel Directive (EU), 175
Biofuels, 73–98; certification, 89–93; and commodities pricing, 83–85; defined, 74–76; and emissions
reduction, 85–86; environmental concerns,
86–87; existing policy framework, 87–96; and
food security, 83–85; governance of, 15; import
tariffs, 80–83; mandated market usage, 79, 175;
mutually supportive policies, 87–89; production
and international trade, 76–78; production incentives, 78–83; second-generation technologies,
93–94; subsidies, 79–80, 174; tax rebates, 79–80;
technology-driven investment in, 163; trade
regimes, 81–83b, 84b; and WTO, 14–15, 94–96
Biregional forums, 13
Blair, Tony, 202, 293, 296, 310
Blood diamonds, 293
Blue Stream pipeline project, 33
Blyth, William, 16–17, 133, 187, 188, 190, 348,
353, 354

Boards of directors, 128
Bolivia: and biofuels import tariffs, 81, 84; and
energy diplomacy, 270; nationalization of
resources in, 124; self-investment, 112
Border taxes, 59–60, 152
BP. See British Petroleum
Brazil: biodiesel production, 77; biofuel production,
74; biofuels certification system, 90; biofuels
import tariffs, 81; cooperative networks, 209,
215, 217; energy diplomacy, 270; ethanol pro-
duction, 76, 77, 163; FDI in, 116; feedstock vs.
food production, 85; and G-8, 202, 203; and
international capital markets, 119; NOC operations in, 108, 114; and WTO negotiations, 95
Bressand, Albert, 19, 269, 343, 347
Bribes, 291
British Petroleum (BP), 90, 123, 269–70, 295
Burma, IOC activity restricted in, 30
Bush, George W., 144, 201, 277, 325
Buy-back service contracts, 118

CAC gas pipeline system, 35
CAFTA (Central America Free Trade Agreement), 84
Cambridge Energy Research Associates (CERA), 10
Cameroon: and EITI, 296; governance reforms in,
20, 304–06
Canada: biofuels certification system, 90; biofuels
import tariffs, 83; ethanol production and
exports, 76, 77; FDI in, 116; feedstock vs. food
production, 85; free trade agreement with Chile,
67; and G-8, 202, 203; and IEA, 216; in International Working Group, 333; LNG exports,
223; NOCs in, 124
Capacity building, 297–98
Cap-and-trade, 133, 139, 174. See also Carbon
markets
Capital costs, 10, 111
Carbon capture and storage (CCS), 141, 212, 214
Carbon markets, 133–59; and alternative energy
investments, 173–74, 177–79; and climate
change challenges, 135–42; existing frameworks
for, 142–51; future of, 151–55, 189–90; international, 145–47; regional, 147–51; role of, 16–17
Carbon taxes, 58–59, 275–76
Cargill, 85
Caribbean Basin Initiative, 77, 84
Caribbean countries: ethanol exports, 77; trade and
investment agreements, 67. See also specific
countries
Caruana, Jaime, 333
Caspian region: exploration and development invest-
ment, 111; Gazprom expansion in, 31; natural gas
supply contracts, 40–41; oil reserves, 27; Russia's
energy diplomacy in, 28. See also specific countries
Catholic Relief Services, 292
CCS. See Carbon capture and storage
CDM. See Clean Development Mechanism

CEIF (Clean Energy Investment Framework), 204, 283
Center for Energy Economics (University of Texas), 128
Central America: ethanol exports, 77; free trade agreements, 84. *See also specific countries*
Central Asia: and energy diplomacy, 35; and gas transit routes, 270; Gazprom expansion in, 33; LNG production, 233, 245; Russia's energy diplomacy in, 38. *See also specific countries*
Central Europe: Gazprom expansion in, 31, 33; LNG imports, 225; natural gas market in, 40; Russia's energy diplomacy in, 38. *See also specific countries*
CERA (Cambridge Energy Research Associates), 10
CERM. *See* Coordinated Emergency Response Mechanism
Certification of biofuels, 89–93, 97
CFIUS (Committee on Foreign Investment in the United States), 325, 326
Chad, governance reforms in, 20, 304–06
Chan, Sherman, 334
Chandler, Alfred, 123
Chavez, Hugo, 114, 270
Chemical products and biofuels, 78, 87
Chevron, 295, 306, 324–25
Chicago Climate Exchange, 150–51
Chile: free trade agreements, 67; in International Working Group, 333; nationalization of resources in, 124
China: and carbon markets, 145; and climate negotiations, 153; coal reserves, 169; as consumer nations, 205–08; and cooperative networks, 195, 215, 217, 270; emergency reserves, 205–06, 218; energy diplomacy, 13–14, 25, 28–30, 34–35, 37–38, 39, 43–44; ethanol production, 76, 77; gas demand in, 28; and G-8, 202, 203; GHG emissions by, 212; governance reform in, 20; Green New Deal packages in, 187; and IEA, 190, 217–19, 249, 272, 277, 352; and IEF, 257; and international capital markets, 119; in International Working Group, 333; and Kyoto Protocol, 175; LNG market in, 224, 228, 232, 235; and natural gas demand, 42; NOC revenues in, 114; oil demand in, 10–11, 14, 16, 28, 205; oil import data, 250; Russia's energy diplomacy with, 42–43; and Santiago Principles, 334; and sovereign wealth funds, 330, 331
China–Africa Development Fund, 34
China Investment Corporation (CIC), 330, 331
China National Offshore Oil Corporation (CNOOC), 30, 128, 324–25
China National Petroleum Corporation (CNPC), 30, 36, 107, 123, 269–70
China's Power Sector Reforms in 2006 (IEA), 207
Chu, Stephen, 186
CIAB (Coal Industry Advisory Board), 207, 208

CIC (China Investment Corporation), 330, 331
CIS. *See* Commonwealth of Independent States
Citigroup, 330, 335
Clean Coal Centre, 207, 209
Clean coal technologies, 213–14
Clean Development Mechanism (CDM), 145–46, 147, 154, 282
Clean energy, 60–61
Clean Energy Investment Framework (CEIF), 204, 283
Clean Technology Fund, 204
Climate change: and alternative energy, 170–77; and biofuels, 86–87; and border taxes, 59–60; carbon pricing theory and limitations, 138–39; and carbon taxes, 58–59; and clean energy technologies, 60–61; and consumer nations, 200–02, 211–16; EU policy on, 200; global energy market role of, 12, 16–17; and investment decisions, 140–42; regulatory framework for, 61; science and economics of, 136–38; and short-term supply risk management, 18; trade and investment impact of, 50; and WTO rules, 69
Clinton, Hillary, 187
CNOOC. *See* China National Offshore Oil Corporation
CNPC. *See* China National Petroleum Corporation
Coal: China's demand for, 205, 207; globalization of, 101; IEA role in, 213–14; India's demand for, 205, 208; reserves, 169; South Africa's demand for, 209; technology replacement, 213
Coal Industry Advisory Board (CIAB), 207, 208
Coal in the Energy Supply of India (CIAB), 208
Coal-to-liquids synthetic fuels, 209
Collier, Paul, 309
Colombia: biofuel production, 74; and biofuels import tariffs, 81, 84; ethanol production, 76; service contracts in, 117
Committee on Energy Research and Technology (IEA), 215
Committee on Environment and Natural Resources of the National People's Congress (China), 207
Committee on Foreign Investment in the United States (CFIUS), 325, 326
Committee on Trade and Environment Special Session (WTO), 95
Commodities: biofuels classification codes, 78; biofuels impact on pricing of, 83–85; and mandatory biofuel use policies, 79; markets for, 251–52; natural gas markets, 40–41; prices and self-investment, 112; and sovereign wealth funds, 316; speculative market activity, 79, 99–100
Commodities Future Trading Commission, 100
Common Market, 121
Commonwealth of Independent States (CIS): natural gas supply contracts in, 40; pipelines in, 33
Communist Party (China), 29
Competition: and monopoly enterprises, 56–57, 128–29; for natural gas supply, 42

Concession agreements, 117
Congo-Brazzaville and EITI, 297, 302–03
Conservation Fund, 191
Consumer nations: and climate change, 200–02, 211–16; cooperative organizations, 196–204, 214–16; and ECT, 8–9; emerging economies as, 209–11; energy security measures of, 169; EU role, 199–200; G-8 summit process, 202–03; IEA role, 196–98; LNG risk management, 241–42; natural gas supply contracts, 40–41; and NOCs, 130; producer cooperation with, 19, 269–84; recommendations for, 216–19; rise of new, 9–12, 204–11; World Bank as cooperative organization for, 203–04. *See also specific countries*
Contingent pension reserve funds, 318
Convention on Combating Bribery of Foreign Public Officials (OECD), 291
Cooperative frameworks: consumer nations, 196–204, 214–16; international governance approach, 278–83; market approach, 277–83; policy arenas for, 270–76; and sovereign objectives, 274–76, 283; trade and investment agreements, 52, 66–68
Coordinated Emergency Response Mechanism (CERM), 7, 197–98, 345
Corn, 86
Corporate governance, 125–28
Corporate income taxes, 111
Corporate social responsibility (CSR), 296
Corruption, 291
Corruption Perception Index (Transparency International), 308
Costa Rica: and biofuels import tariffs, 81; ethanol dehydration plants in, 84
Cost of capital, 111
Côte d'Ivoire and EITI, 296
Cotonou Agreement, 81, 82
Council for Trade in Services (WTO), 95
Countervailing duties, 82
Crop choice and rotation, 89
Cross-price elasticity of demand, 92
CSR (corporate social responsibility), 296

Darling, Alistair, 327
Data consistency for oil market recommendations, 264
DDA (Doha Development Agenda), 94–96
Déby, Idriss, 305–6
Deforestation, 146–47, 154
Dehydrated ethanol. *See* Ethanol
De Jong, Dick, 18, 221, 269, 270, 274, 275, 346, 352
Demand: for coal, 207; government influence on, 102–03; LNG, 222–23; and mandatory biofuel use policies, 79; transparency in reporting of, 104. *See also specific countries*

Democratic Republic of the Congo: and biofuels import tariffs, 81; and EITI, 296–97
Denmark, wind power in, 163
Department for International Development (UK), 298
Depletion: national policy on, 102; oil market recommendations, 261–62; and trade and investment agreements, 70
D'Estaing, Valery Giscard, 202
Deutsche Bank, 319
Developing China's Natural Gas Markets 2002 (IEA), 207
Developing countries: and biofuels certification, 93; biofuels impact on, 74, 88; and climate negotiations, 143; and global energy negotiations, 188; and governance, 289–95; oil reserves in, 108
Development assistance, 34–35, 36
Development cost risk exposure, 118
Development funds, 318
DeWenter, Kathryn, 127, 128
Dickel, Ralf, 15, 99, 343, 347
Direct land use change, 86
Directorate of Global Energy Dialogue (IEA), 208, 217
Dirreccion General de los Yacimientos Petroliferos Fiscales, 108
Discrimination risks, 64
Doerr, John, 166
Doha Development Agenda (DDA), 94–96
Downs, Erica, 36
Downstream water quality, 86–87
Drilling technology costs, 10
Dual pricing, 53
Dubai and sovereign wealth funds, 20
Dubai Ports World (DPW), 325, 326
Dutch disease, 289, 304
Duty-free market access, 82

Eastern Europe: and carbon markets, 149; Gazprom expansion in, 31, 33; Russia's energy diplomacy in, 38. *See also specific countries*
EBA (Everything But Arms) initiative, 81, 82
EC. *See* European Commission
Economic growth: and alternative energy, 162, 165–68; biofuels impact on, 73, 75; and energy growth, 102, 290–91; and NOCs, 124
Economic Partnership Agreement (ACP–EU), 82
Economic rent, 111
Economic sanctions, 27
Economies of scale, 165
Economist democracy index, 323
Economy, Finance, and Employment Ministry (France), 327
ECT. *See* Energy Charter Treaty
Ecuador: and biofuels import tariffs, 81, 84; and energy diplomacy, 270

Education financed with NOC revenues, 116
Efficiency: and alternative energy, 165, 169; of capi-
    tal allocations, 16; and carbon markets, 276; in
    China, 207; ECT on, 62, 65–67; Gleneagles
    Action Plan on, 212–13, 219; IEA on, 197, 203,
    219; in India, 208–09; investment in, 185–87,
    191; state-backed project financing, 114–15,
    128–29
Egypt: and biofuels import tariffs, 81; LNG
    production, 229
EITI. See Extractive Industries Transparency
    Initiative
EITI++, 303
Electrabel, 90
Electricity: alternative energy sources, 170; in Brazil,
    209; and carbon pricing, 140–41, 179; market
    dynamics, 167–68; in South Africa, 209–10;
    technology-driven investments in, 163–64
Electricity in India (IEA), 208
Eller, Stacy, 109, 114
El Salvador: and biofuels import tariffs, 81; ethanol
    dehydration plants in, 84
Embargoes, 3, 5, 27
Emergency stocks: China, 205–06, 218; and IEA,
    197; India, 205–06, 218, 250; strategic petroleum
    reserves, 7–8, 345
Emerging economies, 209–11. See also Developing
    countries
Emissions reduction: and biofuels, 85–86; in China,
    205; in India, 205
Employment-to-assets ratio, 127
Energy Bill of 2007 (U.S.), 87
Energy Charter Treaty (ECT), 61–66; dispute resolu-
    tion, 65; energy market governance by, 189; and
    energy trade, 348, 353; and gas transit routes,
    270; investment issues, 64; and NOCs, 130; as
    plurilateral trade and investment agreement, 51;
    role of, 8–9, 13, 14, 65–66, 100; rules, 62–63;
    on sovereignty over national wealth and
    resources, 102; transit issues, 63; and WTO
    framework, 70
Energy Department (U.S.), 30, 186–87
Energy diplomacy, 25–47; and access, 36–39;
    defined, 27–28; impact of, 36–43; and inter-
    national governance, 43–44; intervention modes
    and forms, 34–36; market structures vs., 39–43;
    state efforts to secure supply, 28–30; state inter-
    ventions to secure reserves and markets, 31–34
Energy efficiency. See Efficiency
Energy Independence and Security Act of 2007
    (U.S.), 175
Energy security and alternative energy, 168–70
Energy Security through Transparency Act of 2009
    (U.S.), 307
Energy Technology Perspectives (IEA) on alternative
    energy, 212, 219

Environmental goods, 95–96
Environmental issues: and biofuels, 86–87; border
    taxes, 59–60; carbon taxes, 58–59; clean energy,
    60–61; regulatory framework, 61. See also
    Climate change; Greenhouse gases
Equatorial Guinea: and EITI, 297; in International
    Working Group, 333; LNG production, 229
Equity interest ownership, 111, 119
Equity oil, 39
Eskom, 210
Ethanol: as agricultural product, 78; excise tax credit,
    80; import tariffs on, 80–83; industry perform-
    ance, 167; production process, 75, 84; U.S.
    imports of, 84. See also Biofuels
EU Emissions Trading Scheme (EU-ETS), 142, 145,
    147–51, 153–54, 189, 199
EU Energy Taxation Directive, 174
EU–Gulf Cooperation Council, 13
Eurasia: and ECT, 270; exploration and development
    investment, 109; natural gas market in, 5–6, 40
Euratom Treaty, 199
Euro-Mediterranean Agreement, 81
European Climate Exchange, 173
European Coal and Steel Community, 199
European Commission (EC): and biofuels certifica-
    tion system, 90; on emission reduction targets,
    153; environmental taxes, 59; role of, 199
European Court of Justice, 199
European Economic Area, 122
European Economic Community, 199
European Energy Charter (1991), 62
European Union (EU): and biofuels policy, 74, 80,
    81–83, 87–88; carbon tariffs, 176; and climate
    change negotiations, 136, 152–53; as cooperative
    organization, 199–200; as ECT member, 51;
    energy policy in, 188, 248; energy prices in, 1;
    ethanol production in, 76; feedstock vs. food
    production, 85; and G-8, 202; LNG market in,
    6, 11, 225, 228, 232, 233–40; LNG risk man-
    agement, 242–44; natural gas demand in, 41; oil
    demand in, 16; renewable energy targets, 175;
    and short-term supply risk management, 18,
    242–44, 272; and sovereign wealth funds,
    321–28; and WTO negotiations, 96. See also
    headings starting "EU"
EU–Russian Dialogue, 13
Everything But Arms (EBA) initiative, 81, 82
ExIm Bank (China), 36
Exploration financing, 110–23; and China's energy
    diplomacy, 38; and ECT, 64; foreign direct
    investment, 117–18; initial public offering,
    118–23; international capital markets, 118–23;
    lack of, 10; NOCs vs. private investments in,
    16; and Russia's energy diplomacy, 39;
    self-investment, 111–17
Export barriers, 53

Exporters. *See* Producer nations
Expropriation risks, 64
External Compliance Monitoring Group, 305
Extractive Industries Review, 290
Extractive Industries Transparency Disclosure Act (proposed), 297, 307
Extractive Industries Transparency Initiative (EITI): in Azerbaijan, 300–02; as bad governance remedy, 292; EITI++, 303; enforcement, 306–09; and G-8, 288; implementation of, 19–20, 296–97; in Nigeria, 298–300; policy implications, 352; recommendations for, 310; voluntary approach gaps, 302–03
ExxonMobil, 231, 295, 304

FAO (Food and Agriculture Organization), 85
Farming. *See* Agriculture
Federal budget outlays financed with NOC revenues, 114
Feed-in tariffs for alternative energy research, 168, 174, 275
Feedstocks: and biofuel production, 74, 78, 85; EU imports of, 82; production subsidies, 79
Fertilizer use, 86–87
Fidora, Michael, 322
Financial aid, 36
Financial reporting, 125
Finland and renewable energy targets, 175
FINSA (Foreign Investment and National Security Act of 2007), 326, 329
First-generation biofuels, 85, 93
Fixed infrastructure. *See* Infrastructure
Flexible LNG, 238–42, 244–45
Flexifuel engines and vehicles, 96
Food and Agriculture Organization (FAO), 85
Food security, 74, 83–85, 88, 90, 91
Foreign Corrupt Practices Act of 1977 (U.S.), 291
Foreign direct investment (FDI), 36–37, 116–18. *See also* Sovereign wealth funds
Foreign Investment and National Security Act of 2007 (FINSA), 326, 329
Foreign market access, 53
Foreign policy: and energy diplomacy, 28, 33; and governance, 294
Former Soviet republics: and ECT, 51, 61–62; oil reserves in, 254–55. *See also specific countries*
Foss, Michelle, 128
Framework for Energy Technology Cooperation, 206
France: and G-8, 202; and sovereign wealth funds, 317, 327
Freedom of transit, 56, 63
Free rider problem, 68, 250
Fuel subsidies, 114–16, 167
Funds transfers and ECT, 64
Future Generations Fund, 304–05, 306
Futures contracts, 4, 79, 99–100, 251–52

G-7, 202, 295
G-8: climate change negotiations, 135, 144, 157; and consumer nation cooperation, 202–03, 216–17; and energy market governance, 190; and IEA, 198, 213; and short-term supply risk management, 18; and technology investments, 279; and transparency, 19, 288, 293
G-20, 190
G-77, 188
Gabon and EITI, 297, 302–03
Gaffney, Cline and Associates, 279
Gao Xiqing, 334
GAPP. *See* Generally Accepted Principles and Practices
Gas. *See* Liquefied natural gas (LNG); Natural gas
Gas Exporting Countries Forum (GECF), 102, 227–28, 272, 346
Gasohol. *See* Ethanol
GATS (General Agreement on Trade in Services), 54–55
GATT. *See* General Agreement on Tariffs and Trade
Gazprom: and Azerbaijan, 39; and energy diplomacy, 28; and EU supply security, 272; expansion strategy of, 31–34; and international capital markets, 122; natural gas production, 210, 237; production capacity of, 110; ranking of, 107
General Agreement on Tariffs and Trade (GATT): and biofuels certification, 92; and climate change, 57; and energy trade, 50, 52–53, 66, 68, 70, 248, 353; environmental taxes, 59; freedom of transit, 56, 63; infrastructure investments, 54–55
General Agreement on Trade in Services (GATS), 54–55
Generalized System of Preferences (GSP), 81
Generally Accepted Principles and Practices (GAPP), 315, 334, 336
Georgia and biofuels import tariffs, 81
Geothermal energy, 171
Germany: and biofuels certification system, 90; and CERM-coordinated stock releases, 198; energy diplomacy by, 27; ethanol imports, 77; and G-8, 202; and governance, 294, 311; and IEF, 267; renewable energy in, 174; and sovereign wealth funds, 317, 327
Ghana and EITI, 297
Githongo, John, 310
Gleneagles Action Plan, 144, 202, 207, 209, 211–12
Global Compact, 296
Global Financial Integrity, 308
Global Witness, 292, 297, 307
Glycerin, 76
Goldthau, Andreas, 1, 14, 20, 25, 271, 277, 280, 341, 342
Gordon, Richard, 121
Gore, Al, 174, 183

Governance, 287–314; and biofuels import tariffs, 81; and China's energy diplomacy, 34; corporate, 125–28; EITI reforms, 303–09; for energy trade, 134; and FDI, 117; future outlook for, 309–13; future research needs, 350–51; good/bad nexus in global energy markets, 289–95; reforms, 295–309; of short-term supply risk management, 18; state-backed project financing, 128–29; transparency reforms, 296–303; and WTO framework, 94–96
Government control of energy resources, 226–27. *See also* National oil companies
Government of Singapore Investment Corporation, 335
Government Pension Fund (Norway), 321
Go Zero program, 191
Grants for alternative energy research, 168, 187
Great Britain. *See* United Kingdom
Greater Nile Petroleum Operating Company, 37
Greenhouse gases (GHG): and biofuel production, 75, 85–86; and biofuels certification, 89–91; China's emissions, 205; and energy policy, 103–04; governance structures for, 101; and IEA, 212–16; India's emissions, 205; UNFCCC and Kyoto Protocol targets for, 201. *See also* Carbon markets
Green New Deal, 185–87
Green subsidies, 60
GSP (Generalized System of Preferences), 81
Guatemala and biofuels import tariffs, 81
Guinea and EITI, 297, 303

Harks, Enno, 19, 247, 275, 278, 279, 281, 343, 347
Hartley, Peter, 109, 114, 125
Health care financed with NOC revenues, 116
Honduras and biofuels import tariffs, 81
Hospital construction, 34
Houser, Trevor, 30
Hoxtell, Wade, 20, 341
Hu Jintao, 36
Human rights, 81, 298–300
Huntington, Hillard, 17, 161, 184, 346, 353, 355
Hydroelectric power, 170, 209

IAS (International Accounting Standards), 280
IEA. *See* International Energy Agency
IEF. *See* International Energy Forum
IEP (International Energy Program), 7, 196
IMF. *See* International Monetary Fund
IMFC (International Monetary and Financial Committee), 332
Importers. *See* Consumer nations
Import tariffs, 53, 80–83, 88
Incentives: biofuels production, 78–83; price, 35; tax rebates and credits, 79–80, 168. *See also* Subsidies
Income redistribution, 114

Independent corporate boards of directors, 128
India: biofuel production, 74; as consumer nation, 205–06, 208–09; and cooperative networks, 195, 215, 217, 270; emergency reserves in, 205–06, 218, 250; ethanol production, 76; and G-8, 202, 203; GHG emissions, 212; and governance reform, 20; and IEA, 190, 217–19, 249, 272, 277, 352; and IEF, 257; and international capital markets, 119; LNG market in, 224, 228, 235; NOCs in, 108; oil demand in, 10, 205; and WTO negotiations, 95
Indian Strategic Petroleum Reserves Limited, 206
Indirect land use change, 86
Indonesia: biofuel production, 74; EU imports of feedstocks from, 82; FDI in, 117; fuel subsidies in, 115; LNG production, 224, 229; NOC revenues in, 114
Infrastructure: biofuel subsidies for, 79; and energy diplomacy, 34, 37; and FDI, 117; oil market recommendations, 264–65; and supply security, 265; transit, 49. *See also* Pipelines
Initial Contingency Response Plan, 197
Initial public offerings (IPOs), 116–18, 130, 166
Institutions: future research needs, 350; markets governed by, 6–9
Intellectual property rights, 94, 177–78
Inter-American Convention against Corruption (OECD), 291
Intergovernmental Panel on Climate Change (IPCC): climate change assessment report, 183, 201; GHG emissions targets, 101, 170; recommendations for, 282; role of, 217
International Accounting Standards (IAS), 280
International Advisory Group (World Bank), 305
International capital markets: exploration financing, 117–18; and NOCs, 16, 129, 130
International carbon markets, 145–47
International climate negotiations, 136, 142–44, 152–53, 157
International Energy Agency (IEA): on carbon markets and electricity prices, 140–41; on carbon pricing, 142; and China, 28, 29, 205, 206–08, 277, 352; and climate change, 211–16; as cooperative network, 195, 196–98; creation of, 4, 7, 101; emergency response mechanism, 7, 197–98, 345; energy market governance by, 189–90; and energy policy, 248, 249; on exploration and development investments, 10, 16; and G-8, 203; and India, 205, 208–09, 277, 352; on investment delays, 266; on LNG supply and demand, 6, 242–43; on oil production plateau, 255; on oil reserves in developing countries, 108; on renewable energy, 170; and short-term supply risk management, 18, 272
International Energy Forum (IEF): as cooperative organization, 256–60, 269; on investment delays, 266; and market transparency, 259–60;

recent meetings and milestones, 257–59; role of, 8, 100, 190
International Energy Program (IEP), 7, 196
International Finance Corporation, 305
International governance: and energy diplomacy, 43–44; and producer-consumer cooperation, 278–83
International Monetary and Financial Committee (IMFC), 332
International Monetary Fund (IMF): and EITI, 302; and privatization of state-owned firms, 129; and sovereign wealth funds, 315, 319, 328–29, 332–34
International oil companies (IOCs): and cooperative organizations, 269, 273; and energy diplomacy, 30; and governance reforms, 295; internal trading systems of, 3–5; and production-sharing agreements, 118; reserves controlled by, 107; and service contracts, 280
International Renewable Energy Agency (IRENA), 189–90, 350
International Trade Organization, 52
International Working Group (IWG) for Sovereign Wealth Funds, 332–34
Investment: agricultural, 88; in alternative energy, 162–79; biofuel technologies, 163; carbon markets influence on, 133–59; climate change impact on, 140–42; and energy diplomacy, 43–44; lack of, 9–12; LNG development, 226; and mandatory biofuel use policies, 79; in oil exploration and development, 108–09; oil market recommendations, 260–63; risk management, 273–74, 279–82
Investor myopia, 126
Investor-state arbitration, 65
IOCs. See International oil companies
IPCC. See Intergovernmental Panel on Climate Change
IPOs. See Initial public offerings
Iran: buy-back service contracts in, 118; China's energy diplomacy in, 38; economic dependence on oil industry, 116; and energy diplomacy, 35–36; FDI in, 117; fuel subsidies in, 115–16; in International Working Group, 333; IOC activity restricted in, 30; LNG market in, 235; nationalization of oil reserves in, 108; NOC revenues in, 114; and oil export embargo, 3
Iraq: economic dependence on oil industry, 116; exploration and development investment, 109; and IOCs, 273; nationalization of oil reserves in, 108; and spare capacity, 253, 254
Ireland in International Working Group, 333
IRENA (International Renewable Energy Agency), 189–90, 350
Israel–U.S. Free Trade Agreement, 84
Italy: Abyssinia invasion by, 27; and G-8, 202; LNG imports, 225

IWG (International Working Group) for Sovereign Wealth Funds, 332–34

Jamaica, ethanol dehydration plants in, 84
Japan: biofuels policy in, 74, 80; and carbon markets, 145; and CERM-coordinated stock releases, 198; as ECT member, 51, 62; energy diplomacy by, 13–14, 25, 27, 36; ethanol imports, 77; and G-8, 202; Green New Deal packages in, 187; and IEA, 216, 218; LNG market in, 228; NOCs in, 108; and sovereign wealth funds, 330; supply security role of government in, 11
Japan National Oil Corporation, 36
Al-Jasser, Muhammad, 335
Jatropha oil, 78
Jensen, C. M., 125
Joint Oil Data Initiative (JODI): and IEF, 259–60; and India, 208; and natural gas data, 266; and transparency, 19, 263–64, 279, 347
Jojarth, Christine, 17, 161, 184, 346, 353, 355
Jordan as ECT member, 62

Kalinke, Frederic, 287
Karl, Terry Lynn, 113, 126
Kazakhstan: China's energy diplomacy in, 38; as ECT member, 62; and EITI, 297; and energy diplomacy, 35; FDI in, 116–17; Russia's energy diplomacy in, 38; self-investment, 112
Keidanren Voluntary Action Plan, 145
Khosla Ventures, 166
Kimberley Process Certification Scheme, 293
Kimmitt, Robert, 325–26
Kleiner Perkins Caufield and Byers, 166
Kohl, Wilfrid L., 18, 195, 272, 273, 279, 282, 345
Korea. See South Korea
Krasner, Stephen, 304
Kudrin, Alexei, 334
Kuwait: China's energy diplomacy in, 38; and IEF, 267; in International Working Group, 333; and IOCs, 273; self-investment, 112; and sovereign wealth funds, 331; and spare capacity, 253
Kuwait Investment Authority, 320, 330, 334–35
Kuwait Petroleum Corporation, 107
Kyoto Protocol: and carbon markets, 134, 151, 155; and Clean Development Mechanism, 145; equity considerations, 143; GHG targets, 201; and renewable energy, 172, 175; and trade and investment agreements, 57
Kyrgyzstan: as ECT member, 62; and EITI, 297

Labor: and biofuels import tariffs, 81; cost of, 10; intensity, 127; WTO standards, 93
Labour Party (Norway), 120–21
Land conversion, 86, 87, 91
Landlocked states, 57, 111
Large Combustion Plant Directive (EU), 148

Latin America: China's FDI in, 37; exploration and development investment, 109, 111; nationalization of resources in, 124; self-investment, 112. *See also specific countries*
Latvia and renewable energy targets, 175
Law of Petroleum Revenue Management (Chad), 304
League of Nations, 27
Lease bonuses, 111
Leverage, 127
Liberia and EITI, 297
Libya: and energy diplomacy, 36; in International Working Group, 333
Lignocellulosic biomass, 85, 93–94, 163
Liquefied natural gas (LNG), 221–45; Asian markets, 224–25, 241; business models, 229–33; data collection on, 264; European markets, 225, 233–40, 242–44; and GECF, 227–28; and global gas markets, 6, 18–19, 101; government control of industry, 226–27; market expansion, 228–29; regional markets, 223–25, 232–33; risk management, 227–28, 240–44; supply and demand for, 222–23; U.S. market, 223–24, 241–42
Liquid transportation fuels. *See* Biofuels
Lisbon Treaty, 199, 272
London ICE, 252
Long-term bilateral contracts: LNG, 40, 223, 225, 231, 237, 245; natural gas market, 5–6; oil market, 3
Long-term investment risk management, 273–74, 279–82
Lugar, Richard G., 294
Lukoil, 107

Mabro, Robert, 281, 282, 347
Madagascar and EITI, 297
Maize, 86
Major Economies Meeting on Energy Security and Climate Change, 135, 143–44, 157, 188, 201
Malaria prevention centers, 34
Malatesta, Paul, 127, 128
Malaysia: biofuel production, 74; EU imports of palm oil from, 82; FDI in, 117; LNG production, 224, 229
Mali and EITI, 297
Managerial capitalism, 123–24
Mandated biofuels use, 79, 87–88, 275
Manufacturing plants (biodiesel), 79, 86
Manzer, Jamie, 20, 315, 349
Marcel, Valerie, 109
Marketing costs, 88
Markets: access to, 53, 95–96; and energy diplomacy, 31–34, 39–43; importance of, 3–6; institutions governing, 6–9; and producer-consumer cooperation, 277–83. *See also specific energy markets*
Marrakech Accords, 135, 145

Mauritania and EITI, 297, 303
McCormick, David H., 322
McCreevy, Charlie, 328
McKibbin, Warwick, 152
Means, Gardiner, 124–25
Meckling, W. H., 125
Medlock, Kenneth, 109, 114, 125
Medvedev, Dmitry, 32
Merkel, Angela, 203, 327
Merrill Lynch, 330, 335
Methyl esters, 75–76. *See also* Biodiesel
Mexico: and cooperative networks, 210, 215, 217; economic dependence on oil industry, 116; exploration and development investment, 110; free trade agreement with Chile, 67; fuel subsidies in, 116; and G-8, 202, 203; and IEF, 267; and international capital markets, 118; in International Working Group, 333; and IOCs, 273; NAFTA reservations by, 66; NOC operations in, 108, 281; self-investment by, 112
MFN (most-favored-nation) tariffs, 80–83, 84
Middle East: exploration and development investment, 109; LNG production and reserves, 226, 233, 234, 245; resource development in, 16; self-investment, 112; and sovereign wealth funds, 338–39. *See also specific countries*
Military cooperation and assistance, 35–36
Mitchell, John, 109
Moldova, Russia's energy diplomacy in, 38
MoldovaGaz, 38
Mongolia: and biofuels import tariffs, 81; as ECT member, 62; and EITI, 297
Mongstad oil refinery, 120
Monopoly enterprises: and governance, 128–29; and trade and investment framework, 56–57
Morgan Stanley, 319, 330
Morse, Ed, 278, 281
Most-favored-nation (MFN) tariffs, 80–83, 84
MTBE additive, 75
Multilateral trade systems, 50, 53, 100, 130
Myers Jaffe, Amy, 16, 107, 342, 343
Myrick, Sue, 325

Nabucco pipeline project, 236
NAFTA. *See* North American Free Trade Agreement
Naftohaz Ukrainy, 33
National Bureau of Statistics (China), 206
National debt financed with NOC revenues, 113–14
National Development and Reform Commission (NDRC, China), 205, 207
National Iranian Oil Company (NIOC), 107, 110, 114, 115
Nationalization of resources, 64, 108
National oil companies (NOCs): in China, 30, 205–06; and cooperative organizations, 269, 273; and energy diplomacy, 28; expansion of, 14; IEA impact on, 4, 249; limitations of, 342;

reserves controlled by, 107; role of, 11, 15–16; and state-backed finance, 16; trade and investment by, 50

National Oil Reserve Office (China), 205

National sovereignty. *See* Sovereignty

National Stakeholders Working Group (NSWG), 298

Natural gas: and energy diplomacy, 43–44; and EU–ETS, 200; and globalization, 101; market for, 5–6; regional commodity markets for, 40–41. *See also* Liquefied natural gas (LNG)

NDRC (National Development and Reform Commission, China), 205, 207

NEET. *See* Networks of Expertise in Energy Technologies

Negotiating Group on Non-Agriculture Market Access (WTO), 95

NEITI (Nigerian Extractive Industries Transparency Initiative), 298–300

Netherlands: and biofuels certification system, 90; ethanol imports, 77; wind power in, 163

Networks of Expertise in Energy Technologies (NEET), 207, 215, 279

New International Economic Order (NIEO), 271–72

Nicaragua and biofuels import tariffs, 81

NIEO (New International Economic Order), 271–72

Nigeria: China's arms sales to, 35; and EITI, 297; and energy diplomacy, 37; FDI in, 116; LNG production, 225, 229; nationalization of resources in, 124; NOC revenues in, 114; self-investment, 112; transparency reforms, 298–300

Nigerian Extractive Industries Transparency Initiative (NEITI), 298–300

Nigerian National Petroleum Corporation, 107

NIOC. *See* National Iranian Oil Company

NOCs. *See* National oil companies

Nonactionable subsidies, 60

Nondiscriminatory rules on exploration and development, 64

Nonedible feedstocks, 85

Nonfinancial development assistance, 34

Nordhaus, William, 136

Nord Stream pipeline project, 33

North, Douglass, 7, 284, 344

North Africa, Gazprom expansion in, 31, 33. *See also specific countries*

North America: biodiesel production, 77; China's FDI in, 37; natural gas market in, 5–6, 40. *See also* Canada; United States

North American Free Trade Agreement (NAFTA): and biofuels import tariffs, 84; energy trade and investment, 51, 66; and NOCs, 130; role of, 13; and WTO framework, 70

Norway: capacity-building initiatives, 297–98; FDI in, 116; and governance, 294, 311; and

international capital markets, 119–22; in International Working Group, 333; LNG production, 225, 233; and sovereign wealth funds, 321, 331

NSWG (National Stakeholders Working Group), 298

Nuclear energy, 169, 215

Nuclear Energy Agency (OECD), 215

NYMEX, 252

OAO Gazprom. *See* Gazprom

Obama, Barack: and carbon markets, 189; energy and environment priorities, 184, 185–86, 190; on energy security, 168; on port security, 325

Obasanjo, Olusegun, 298, 299

OECD countries: anti-corruption reforms, 291; and carbon markets, 189, 200; and climate negotiations, 142; emergency oil sharing mechanisms, 4; and energy diplomacy, 36; FDI in, 116; and IEA, 196, 218, 248, 345; LNG demand in, 6; nuclear energy governance, 215; oil consumption trends, 262; oil reserves in, 108; short-term supply risk management by, 18; and sovereign wealth funds, 317, 324, 336–37, 338; wind power in, 164

Office of Energy Efficiency and Renewable Energy (U.S.), 187

Oil-indexed prices, 225

Oil Industry Development Board (India), 206

Oil market: and energy diplomacy, 43–44; globalization of, 101; and IEF, 256–60; information levels for, 249–50, 263–64; infrastructure, 264–65; overview, 3–5; price volatility, 250–52, 260–61; production plateau, 254–55; recommendations, 260–65; risk management, 247–67; spare capacity, 252–54, 262–63; supply security, 252–54, 264–65. *See also* State-backed financing

Oil Market Report (IEA), 198

Oil shale recovery, 169

Oil Supply Group (EU), 200

Oil Titans (Marcel & Mitchell), 109

Open Society Institute, 292

Organization of Petroleum Exporting Countries (OPEC): creation of, 101; and depletion policy, 102; energy market governance by, 189; and liberalization of oil market, 5; as renewable energy competitor, 167; and spare capacity, 253, 262–63

Outreach Five, 203

Oxford Energy, 281

Pachauri, Rajendra K., 282

Pakistan: and biofuels import tariffs, 81, 82; as ECT member, 62; LNG market in, 235

Palm oil, 82, 86

Panama and biofuels import tariffs, 81

Pan-Central Asia pipeline, 38

Paraguay and biofuels import tariffs, 81
Partial privatization, 129
Paulson, Hank, 331
PDVSA (Petróleos de Venezuela, S.A.), 107, 110
Peak oil, 17, 254
PEMEX, 107, 108, 110, 116, 210
Peninsular and Orient Stream Navigation Company, 325
Pension Plan Investment Board (Canada), 335
Pérez Alfonso, Juan Pablo, 289
Persian Gulf exploration and development, 109. *See also specific countries*
Peru: and biofuels import tariffs, 81, 84; and EITI, 297
Pesticides, 86
Petrobras, 107, 209, 270
Petro Caribe, 67, 114
Petrofluorocarbons, 149
Petróleos de Venezuela, S.A. (PDVSA), 107, 110
Petroleum and Natural Gas Ministry (India), 208
Petroleum Intelligence Weekly on oil company rankings, 107
Petronas, 107, 123, 306
Philippines, biofuel production in, 74
Photovoltaic power. *See* Solar power
Pipelines: and China's energy diplomacy, 38; and Gazprom, 33; natural gas, 225, 242–44, 272; and Russia's energy diplomacy, 35; and transit regulation, 61. *See also specific pipelines*
Plurilateral trade organizations, 51
Policy framework: biofuels, 87–96; for carbon markets, 142–51; trade and investment, 99–104
Political economy: of alternative energy investment, 162, 168–72; of international climate negotiations, 142–44; of sovereign wealth funds, 324–28
Pollitt, Michael, 128
Portugal and renewable energy targets, 175
Potential for Gas-Fired Power Supply in India (IEA), 208
Poverty reduction, 91, 290
Price incentives, 35
Pricing, dual, 53
Principal-agent paradigm, 125, 342
Private sector: economic rent extraction from, 111; exploration and development investment, 109; and FDI, 117; in India, 208; upstream investments by, 16
Privatization, 108, 119–20, 129
Producer nations: consumer cooperation with, 19, 269–84; and ECT, 8–9; emerging economies as, 209–11; LNG risk management, 227–28, 240–41; natural gas, 40–41, 237–38
Production incentives, 78–83
Production-sharing agreements, 117, 118
Production tax credit, 80
Progressive governance agenda, 294–95

Property rights, 89
Public Finance Monitoring Centre, 300
Publish What You Pay (PWYP) initiative, 292, 297
Putin, Vladimir, 35

Qatar: in International Working Group, 333; LNG production, 228, 229, 231, 240
Q-Cells (company), 167
Quota-free market access, 82

Rapeseed oil production, 82
Refineries: ethanol, 79, 84; GHG emissions from, 86; investment in, 120
Regasification terminal capacity, 242
Regional carbon markets, 142, 147–51
Regional Greenhouse Gas Initiative, 150
Regional trade: agreements, 50, 51; and biofuels import tariffs, 84; energy markets, 14; LNG, 223–25, 232–33. *See also specific regions and countries*
Regulatory framework: electricity industry, 168; environment and climate change issues, 61; LNG, 237; risk management for, 141; for sovereign wealth funds, 322–24
Renewable energy: IEA role in, 214; subsidies, 58; trade and investment in, 50, 183; WTO regulations on, 14–15
Renewable Energy Working Party (IEA), 207
"Request and offer" method, 95
Research and development: alternative energy technologies, 163–65, 177–79; carbon markets influence on, 156; clean energy subsidies for, 60; and climate change, 139; IEA role in, 214–15; international cooperative networks for, 214–16
Reserve investment corporations, 318
Reserves: in developing countries, 108; dwindling of, 9–12; emergency, 7, 197–98, 345; energy diplomacy to secure, 31–34; IEA system for, 7–8; and market systems, 39–40; natural gas, 222
Resource development: and alternative energy, 169; and China's energy diplomacy, 38; and ECT, 64; future research needs, 351; investments, 10, 16; LNG, 226; natural gas, 222–23; and Russia's energy diplomacy, 39; and sovereign objectives, 274–75
Resource nationalism, 50
Return on equity, 127
Revenue Oversight Committee (Chad), 305
Risk management: and carbon pricing, 141; development cost exposure, 118; and FDI, 117; and IEA, 7; LNG markets, 227–28, 240–44; long-term investments, 273–74, 279–82; oil market, 247–67; short-term supply, 17–19, 271–72, 278–79, 346
Risk premiums, 253–54
Romer, Paul, 185

Rosendahl, Knut, 139
Rosneft (company), 42, 122–23, 129
Roundtable on Sustainable Biofuels, 90, 91
Royal Dutch/Shell, 90, 292
Royalties, 111
Russia: China's energy diplomacy with, 42–43; and
    cooperative networks, 210–11; and ECT, 9, 270;
    energy diplomacy by, 14, 25, 27, 31–34, 35–36,
    38–39; EU dependence on natural gas imports
    from, 200; exploration and development invest-
    ment, 109; foreign gas assets of, 14; and G-8,
    202, 203; and governance, 294; and IEF, 257;
    and international capital markets, 119; in Inter-
    national Working Group, 333; LNG production,
    225, 233, 234–35, 243; and natural gas markets,
    40–41; reserves in, 31, 32; resource development
    in, 16, 274–75; and Santiago Principles, 334;
    self-investment, 112; and sovereign wealth
    funds, 20, 331

Saad, al-, Bader, 334, 338
Santiago Principles, 315–17, 328–37
Sarbanes-Oxley Act, 277
Sarkozy, Nicolas, 338
Saro-Wiwa, Ken, 292
Saudi Arabia: energy diplomacy by, 114; export
    routes from, 265; and governance, 294; and
    IEF, 258, 267; International Working Group
    observer status of, 333; and IOCs, 273; and
    market transparency, 44; nationalization of oil
    reserves in, 108; NOC revenues in, 113; and oil
    market liberalization, 4; oil production and
    export data, 250; resource development in, 274;
    self-investment, 112; and sovereign wealth funds,
    331; U.S. cooperation with, 282, 347
Saudi Aramco, 107, 114, 128
Savings funds, 318
Science and Technology Ministry (China), 206
SCM (Subsidies and Countervailing Measures)
    Agreement, 59, 60
Scotland, wind power in, 163
Second-generation biofuels, 75, 85, 93–94, 97
Securities and Exchange Commission (U.S.), 127,
    280, 297
Securities Exchange Act of 1934 (U.S.), 307
Security Council (UN), 34, 37
Self-investment in exploration financing, 112–16
Selivanova, Yulia, 14, 49, 348, 353
Service contracts, 117–18, 273, 280
Shanghai Cooperation Organization, 39
Shaxson, Nicholas, 299
Shell Corporation, 90
Shenhua (company), 207
Shleifer, Andrei, 126
Short-term supply risks: and IEA, 7; and LNG, 18;
    management of, 17–19; producer-consumer
    cooperation on, 271–72, 278–79

Sierra Leone: and EITI, 297; governance and trans-
    parency in, 293
Simmons, Matthew, 273
Singapore: in International Working Group, 333;
    and sovereign wealth funds, 320, 330, 331,
    333, 335
Sinopec, 30, 36
Smart grid investment program, 186
Smeenk, Tom, 18, 221, 269, 270, 274, 275,
    346, 352
Soares de Oliveira, Ricardo, 19, 287, 337, 349
SOCAL (company), 38
Social welfare programs, 110, 116
Soil erosion, 87, 89
Solar power, 164–65, 167, 170
Soligo, Ronald, 16, 107, 342, 343
Sonatrach, 107
Soros, George, 123, 297
South Africa: biofuels policy in, 74, 81, 82; and
    cooperative networks, 209, 215, 217; and G-8,
    202, 203
South America: LNG market in, 228; NOCs in,
    108; resource development in, 16. See also
    specific countries
Southeast Asia: biodiesel production, 77; LNG
    production, 224. See also specific countries
South Korea: in International Working Group,
    333; LNG market in, 228, 235; and sovereign
    wealth funds, 331
South Stream pipeline project, 33, 236
Sovereignty: ECT confirmation of, 62, 64; and
    EU–ETS, 199–200; and producer-consumer
    cooperation, 274–76, 283; and trade and
    investment agreements, 100
Sovereign wealth funds (SWFs), 315–40; Inter-
    national Working Group for, 332–34; political
    pressures on, 321–28; regulation of, 322–24;
    role of, 20; and Santiago Principles, 328–37;
    scope and relevance of, 317–21
Soviet Union: Afghanistan invasion by, 114; energy
    diplomacy by, 27. See also Former Soviet
    republics
Spain: LNG market in, 243; renewable energy in, 174
Spare capacity, 252–54, 258, 262–63
Speculative market activity: and mandatory biofuel
    use policies, 79; and oil prices, 99–100
"Splash and dash," 83
Spot markets, 4, 6, 225, 232
Sri Lanka and biofuels import tariffs, 81
Stabilization funds, 318
Stanislaw, Joseph A., 17, 183, 354, 355, 356
State-backed financing, 107–32; exploration financ-
    ing, 110–23; governance, efficiency, and trans-
    parency, 128–29; and NOCs, 16; theory vs.
    practice, 123–28
State-controlled firms. See National oil companies
State Department (U.S.), 187

State Economic and Trade Commission (China), 207
State-to-state arbitration, 65
State trading enterprises, 54–55
Statoil, 119–22, 128, 295
Stenvoll, Thomas, 119
Stern Review: on carbon pricing, 139; on GHG emission levels, 136, 137
Strategic Climate Fund, 204
Strategic Energy Technology Plan (EU), 200
Strategic Framework for Development and Climate Change (World Bank), 204
Strategic petroleum reserves (SPR), 7–8, 345
Sub-Saharan Africa, access to energy resources in, 283. *See also specific countries*
Subsidies: agricultural, 15; alternative energy research, 168, 275; biofuels, 79–80, 84, 174; clean energy, 60; and energy diplomacy, 35; fuel, 114–16, 167; renewable energy, 58
Subsidies and Countervailing Measures (SCM) Agreement, 59, 60
Sudan: China's energy diplomacy in, 34, 37, 38; IOC activity restricted in, 30
Suez Canal crisis (1956), 3
Sugar cane ethanol, 75, 86, 93, 163
Suntech Power, 167
Superfund case, 59
Supply: energy diplomacy to secure, 28–30; government influence on, 101–02; LNG, 222–23, 233–36; and mandatory biofuel use policies, 79; risk management of, 271–72, 278–79; security, 264–65; transparency in reporting of, 104. *See also specific countries*
Sustainable development, 81, 93, 97
Suwaidi, al, Hamad, 315, 333
Swaziland and biofuels import tariffs, 81
Sweden and renewable energy targets, 175
SWFs. *See* Sovereign wealth funds
Switzerland and biofuels policy, 83, 90
Synthetic fuels, 209

Tajikistan as ECT member, 62
Tanaka, Nobuo, 196, 207, 217
Tax Justice Network, 308
Tax rebates and credits: alternative energy research, 168; biofuels, 79–80
TBT Agreement (Agreement on Technical Barriers to Trade), 91
Technology: alternative energy, 162, 163–65; transfer issues, 94, 104, 178
Temasek (company), 320, 335
TEN (Trans-European Network) programs, 272
Thailand, ethanol production in, 76
Thermal power. *See* Solar power
Tidal energy, 171
Tight gas recovery, 169
Timor-Leste: and EITI, 297; in International Working Group, 333

Trade and investment agreements, 49–72; bilateral agreements, 66–68; biofuels, 76–78, 81–83, 84; challenges for, 53–68; energy transit issues, 55–57; environment and climate change issues, 57–61; existing framework, 51–53; fixed infrastructure issues, 54–55; policy perspective, 99–104; recommendations for, 68–70. *See also specific agreements*
Trans-European Network (TEN) programs, 272
Transit: of biofuels, 85–86, 87; trade and investment agreements, 49, 55–57. *See also* Pipelines
Transit countries: and ECT, 8–9, 63; trade and investment agreements, 55–57
Transnational corporations, 291–92. *See also* International oil companies (IOCs)
Transneft (company), 42
Transparency: EITI reforms for, 296–303; and energy diplomacy, 43–44, 292–95; in exploration and development rules, 64; IEA requirements for, 219; in NOC operations, 128; in oil investment plans, 261; oil market recommendations for, 263–64; role of, 19–20; in state-backed project financing, 128–29; in supply and demand data, 104
Transparency International, 291, 292, 298, 308
Treasury Department (U.S.), 328
Trinidad and Tobago: ethanol dehydration plants in, 84; in International Working Group, 333
Turkmenistan: as ECT member, 62; and energy diplomacy, 35, 38; LNG market in, 235; oil reserves, 279
Twilight in the Desert (Simmons), 273

UBS, 330
UCCI (Upstream Capital Costs Index), 10
Ukraine: and biofuels import tariffs, 81; and energy diplomacy, 35; and Gazprom, 33; natural gas supply interruptions, 210, 211, 216, 326; Russia's energy diplomacy in, 38–39
UN Convention against Corruption, 291
UN Framework Convention on Climate Change (UNFCCC): and carbon markets, 134, 135, 143, 144; GHG targets, 101, 103, 151, 157, 201; and renewable energy, 172; role of, 217
United Arab Emirates: FDI in, 117; in International Working Group, 333; and sovereign wealth funds, 330, 331, 333
United Kingdom (UK): and biofuels certification system, 90; concession agreements in, 117; Department of International Development, 298; and energy diplomacy, 36; FDI in, 116; and G-8, 202; and governance, 294, 311; Green New Deal packages in, 187; and IEF, 267; LNG imports, 225, 240; and sovereign wealth funds, 327, 332; wind power in, 163
United Nations: and China's energy diplomacy, 35, 37; and energy policy, 248; on sovereignty over national wealth and resources, 101–02

United States: biodiesel production, 77, 82–83; biofuels policy in, 74, 80, 84, 87–88, 90, 175; and
carbon markets, 135, 150–51; and carbon tariffs,
176; and CERM-coordinated stock releases, 197,
198; and climate negotiations, 142–43, 144,
153; coal reserves, 169; concession agreements
in, 117; energy diplomacy by, 25, 27; energy
policy in, 1, 185–87; environmental taxes, 59;
ethanol imports and production, 76, 77; feedstock vs. food production, 85; and G-8, 202;
GHG emissions reduction, 201; and governance,
312; and IEA, 216, 217–18; in International
Working Group, 333; LNG market in, 223–24,
228–30, 232, 245; natural gas market in, 5; oil
demand in, 16, 183; renewable energy targets,
174–75; Saudi Arabia cooperation with, 282,
347; short-term supply risk management,
241–42; and sovereign wealth funds, 317,
321–28, 329; subsidies and tax credits, 80, 84,
174; supply security measures, 169, 241–42;
and transparency, 293–94; wind power in, 163;
and WTO negotiations, 96
University of Texas–Center for Energy Economics,
128
Unocal, 324, 326
Upstream Capital Costs Index (UCCI), 10
Upstream investments. *See* Exploration financing;
Resource development
U.S.–Central America Free Trade Agreement
(U.S.–CAFTA), 84
U.S.–Israel Free Trade Agreement, 84
Uzbekistan: as ECT member, 62; and Russia's energy
diplomacy, 38

Van der Linde, Coby, 18, 221, 269, 270, 274, 275,
346, 352
Venezuela: and biofuels import tariffs, 81; and energy
diplomacy, 36, 114, 270; FDI in, 117; and governance, 294; NOC revenues in, 113–14; self-
investment, 112; service contracts in, 117; social
programs financed with oil revenues, 110, and
spare capacity, 253, 254; trade and investment
agreements, 67
Venture capital firms, 166, 183
Verasun (company), 167
Vietnam: and EITI, 297; International Working
Group observer status of, 333

Wainberg, Miranda, 128
War risks and ECT, 64
Water resources and biofuels production, 86–87

Waxman-Markey energy bill (proposed), 151, 154,
186
Weitzman, Martin, 138
Wenar, Leif, 309
West Africa exploration and development, 111.
See also specific countries
Western Europe: biodiesel production, 77; and ECT,
61; energy security measures by, 169; natural gas
market in, 40. *See also specific countries*
Western oil companies. *See* International oil companies
Wilcoxen, Peter, 152
WilderHill clean energy index, 166
Wind energy, 163–64, 170
Windfall gain, 111
Witte, Jan Martin, 1, 20, 271, 277, 280, 315, 341, 349
Wolf, Christian, 128
Wolfensohn, James, 291
Wolfowitz, Paul, 305
Woods, Ngaire, 34
World Bank: on carbon markets, 146; as consumer
nation cooperative organization, 203–04; and
EITI, 302, 303; extractive industries review by,
290; and G-8, 203; International Working
Group observer status of, 333; privatization,
129; and technology investments, 279;
transparency initiatives of, 298, 305
World Coal Institute, 208
World Energy Outlook (IEA): on alternative energy,
212; on cap-and-trade impact, 133; on China's
emergency reserves, 207; on India's oil reserves,
206, 209; oil demand forecasts in, 204; transparency of data in, 198, 264
World Oil Outlook (OPEC) data consistency, 264
World Trade Organization (WTO): and biofuels, 91,
94–96; border taxes, 59; and carbon taxes, 59,
176; and climate change, 57–58; as cooperative
organization, 271; dispute resolution under, 65;
and ECT, 63, 65–66; and energy trade, 50, 53,
68–69, 248, 278, 348, 353; and infrastructure
investments, 54–55; and investment policy, 64;
and monopoly enterprises, 56–57; and NOCs,
130; on renewable energy, 14–15; role of, 8, 13,
14, 100
World Wildlife Fund, 90, 136

Yarrow, George, 127
Yukos, 32

Zarrilli, Simonetta, 15, 73, 348, 353
Zimbabwe: and biofuels import tariffs, 81; China
energy diplomacy in, 34, 38